THE PERSON AND MINISTRY
OF THE HOLY SPIRIT

A Wesleyan Perspective

THE PERSON AND MINISTRY
OF THE HOLY SPIRIT
A Wesleyan Perspective

Charles Webb Carter

BAKER BOOK HOUSE

Grand Rapids, Michigan

Library of Congress Catalog Card Number: 74-75959
ISBN: 0-8010-2359-9
Copyright, 1974, by Baker Book House Company

PHOTOLITHOPRINTED BY CUSHING - MALLOY, INC.
ANN ARBOR, MICHIGAN, UNITED STATES OF AMERICA
1974

It is with grateful appreciation and affection
that the author dedicates this book
to his beloved companion, Elizabeth Carter,
who faithfully typed the manuscript,
and
to his students at China Evangelical Seminary
during his years of challenging association
and instruction

THE CHRISTIAN HOLINESS ASSOCIATION
OFFICIAL ENDORSEMENT STATEMENT

The Christian Holiness Association has defined and proclaimed the Wesleyan interpretation of Scripture since 1867. Dr. Charles W. Carter's book, *THE PERSON AND MINISTRY OF THE HOLY SPIRIT: A WESLEYAN PERSPECTIVE,* is considered by us to be a scholarly and exhaustive exposition within the Wesleyan interpretation of the Holy Spirit as presented in the Scriptures. It is for this reason that we give our full endorsement. The Christian Holiness Association is hopeful that this significant book will have an extensive acceptance.

Thomas H. Hermiz
Executive Director

Preface

The title of this book is intended to be definitive of its content, namely, *The Person and Ministry of the Holy Spirit.* The subtitle, *A Wesleyan Perspective,* is further definitive in that it locates, though it does not limit, the work within the Wesleyan theological tradition. Both the title and the subtitle of the book were considered and agreed upon by the author and the publishers jointly. The title is further definitive in that it indicates this work to be a study of the *person* and *activities* of the Holy Spirit, and *not a doctrine* of the Holy Spirit *per se.* It may be seriously questioned whether the Bible sets forth any doctrine of the Holy Spirit *per se,* though such a doctrine may be deduced from the Bible. Nor is this book intended as a *systematic theology* of the Holy Spirit, though quite inescapably it does reflect certain theological *implications.* Rather, the present work attempts to understand and trace, from a Biblical perspective, the *divine person* and *activity* of the Holy Spirit from His participation in the creation of the universe, and particularly man, throughout the Biblical history of redemption to the final call of man to salvation in Christ, as is recorded in the closing words of the Bible in Revelation 22:17.

It is the author's conviction that the main emphasis upon the Holy Spirit in the Bible concerns His activities as the divine executive of the Godhead. Thus the present study is *dynamic* rather than propositional *per se*. This is commensurate with the sub-title, *A Wesleyan Perspective*. It is a well-known fact that John Wesley was a *dynamic* rather than a systematic theologian. He was practical rather than speculative. Wesley was interested primarily in the application of divine truth to the spiritual, moral, and social needs of men. Thus he brought dynamic truth to bear upon these needs and consequently became God's instrument in the precipitation of one of the greatest human and history-changing revivals known to the Christian era. Nor was the eighteenth-century revival under Wesley's dynamic preaching limited to the transformation of England and the British Isles. Rather it spread to North America, where it inundated most of the continent with the Methodist revival emphasis and teaching, and it became a major contributing force to the eighteenth- and nineteenth-century missionary movement that carried the gospel of Jesus Christ to practically every part of the inhabited globe.

The foregoing characterization of the person and activity of the Holy Spirit as dynamic, rather than systematic, is commensurate with Christ's own statement concerning the mission of the Spirit. Christ said, " . . . He will guide you into all truth; for He will not speak on His own initiative [or, "of himself," *KJV*; "on his own authority," *RSV*], but whatever He hears, He will speak; and He will disclose to you what is to come. *He shall glorify Me; for He shall take of Mine, and shall disclose it to you*" (John 16:13, 14). Nowhere from His initial activity in creation to His last invitation to men in Revelation is the Spirit recorded in the Bible as either representing Himself or calling attention to Himself. He is everywhere and always the representative of the Godhead to men on earth, and the revealer of the great divine plan and provision of redemption for man and the universe which center in Jesus Christ, from the fall of man to the last call to man. The Spirit's function is to focus all interest and attention upon Jesus Christ as the Messiah-Savior of mankind and to show that in Christ the revelation of God centers. In this sense He is the liaison authority between Jesus Christ and men. Without Him there can be no personal knowledge of God nor access to God in Christ. He is the final bridge that spans the otherwise impassable gulf between God and man. It is in this perspective that the Spirit is treated in the present work.

The author's interest in the Holy Spirit springs from several different sources. First, during many years of missionary service in Africa, and later in the Island World, South America, Mexico, and the Orient, he has had opportunity to witness the unusual manifestations and activities of the Holy Spirit on the mission fields. These have included many powerful and far-reaching spiritual awakenings and revivals among pagans and Christians. Further, he has engaged in extensive revival and evangelistic efforts throughout the United States, Canada, and various other countries in which he has witnessed the unusual manifestations of the Holy Spirit in His redemptive activities. Second, in colleges and theological schools, both in America and abroad, the author has taught the Book of Acts for many years with major emphasis upon the Holy Spirit. Third, he collaborated with Ralph Earle in the production of a major commentary on the Book of Acts which was published by the Zondervan Publishing House of Grand Rapids, Michigan, in 1959, under the title "The Acts of the Apostles," *The Evangelical Commentary*. This work met with very favorable and wide acceptance which called forth highly commendatory reviews from abroad by such noted scholars as F. F. Bruce of Manchester University and William Barclay of Glasgow University, as well as many like reviews in America and elsewhere. This work was republished in a slightly revised form by the Zondervan Publishing House in January 1973 under the title *The Acts of the Apostles*. Third, in 1952 the writer was privileged to deliver the annual Lienard Lectures at the Nazarene Theological Seminary in Kansas City, Missouri, on the subject of "The Meaning of Pentecost." These lectures were subsequently published in *The Preacher's Magazine*. In 1971 and 1972 a work on *The Holy Spirit in the Early Church* was completed and translated into Chinese for publication in Taiwan.

In the summer of 1972 the author was invited by Cornelius Zylstra, editor of the Baker Book House in Grand Rapids, Michigan, to prepare for publication a full-scale Biblical work on *The Person and Ministry of the Holy Spirit, A Wesleyan Perspective*, for publication by that company. The present work is in response to that invitation. The research and writing of this work has been carried out, for the most part, during full-time engagement as Professor of Theology and Ethics at China Evangelical Seminary in Taipei, Taiwan, and part-time Professor at the Oriental Missionary Society, Central Taiwan Theological College at Taichung, Taiwan.

In keeping with the designated subtitle of the book, *A Wesleyan Perspective*, the resource material for this work has been drawn in considerable measure from Wesleyan sources, both earlier and later works. Much use has been made of Adam Clarke, the greatest of the early Wesleyan commentators, and the writings of Wesley himself. However, several non-Wesleyan sources have been used whose writings have harmonized in general with the Wesleyan interpretation and have served to enrich that interpretation. Special mention is hereby made of, and gratitude expressed for, the insights of William Barclay's perceptive and helpful little book, *The Promise of the Spirit* (London: The Epworth Press, 1960). Likewise, special acknowledgment is rendered to the work of Walter Thomas Conner, *The Work of the Holy Spirit: A Treatment of the Biblical Doctrine of the Divine Spirit* (Nashville: Broadman Press, 1949). The latter work has been especially useful in relation to the Spirit in the Old Testament, and its influence will be reflected to some extent in the present work. However, the author's interpretations and conclusions are entirely his own, and for these *he only* is responsible.

Certain other special acknowledgments are due. Only late in the preparation of this work did the writer discover the existence of a rare and little known three-volume work of over 2600 pages by John Wesley, entitled *Explanatory Notes Upon the Old Testament,* published by William Prine in Wine-Street, Bristol, England, in 1765, but never reprinted as far as knowledge goes. It is understood that not more than three sets of this work are known to be extant in America. One complete set of the three-volume work is housed in the Asbury Theological Seminary Library at Wilmore, Kentucky. Through the kindness of William M. Arnett, Professor of Theology at Asbury Theological Seminary, and Miss Susan Shultz, Librarian at that institution, the author was furnished several xeroxed copies of select notes from this work from which he drew upon Wesley's comments on certain Old Testament passages concerning the Spirit. Due documentary credit is given where these appear. A very revealing, scholarly article upon this rare work of Wesley, written by Dr. Arnett, has been published in the 1973 issue of *The Wesleyan Theological Journal,* available at Asbury Theological Seminary.

Further grateful acknowledgment is hereby rendered to William M. Greathouse, President of Nazarene Theological Sminary, and W. T. Purkiser, Editor of the *Herald of Holiness,* for permission to quote from a most splendid definitive article by Dr. Greathouse entitled "Who is the Holy Spirit?" (May 21, 1972, issue *Herald of Holiness,* W. T. Purkiser, ed., Kansas City, Missouri: Nazarene Publishing House). Grateful acknowledgment is also rendered to William B.

Eerdmans, President of the Eerdmans Publishing Company of Grand Rapids, Michigan, for permission to draw upon certain materials written by the author and other contributors of the *Wesleyan Bible Commentary,* Chas. W. Carter, General Editor (Grand Rapids: Wm. B. Eerdmans Publishing Company, 1964-69), as also for permission to quote from various other works published by the Eerdmans Company. Likewise grateful appreciation is expressed to the Zondervan Publishing House of Grand Rapids, and to the Baker Book House for permission to quote from their publications in the present work. These and all other quoted or cited materials in this book are duly acknowledged in the footnote documentations.

Throughout this work the Bible version used, except where otherwise indicated, has been the *New American Standard Bible* (La Habra, California: ©The Lockman Foundation 1960, 1962, 1963, 1968, 1971). For permission to use the text of the *New American Standard Bible,* gratitude is expressed to the Lockman Foundation. Further, it is with the written permission of the Lockman Foundation that the author has in various instances underscored for italics, and thus emphasis, certain portions of the text of Scripture from the *New American Standard Bible* without the laborious necessity of following each such underscore with the notation "italics added," a practice which when occurring frequently may become somewhat awkward and even confusing. Similiarly this practice has been followed in relation to certain other works quoted in this book.

Special appreciation is further expressed to Cornelius Zylstra, Baker Book House editor, for the invitation to write this work for publication by the Baker Book House of Grand Rapids, Michigan. Mr. Zylstra and his associates have been most helpful in offering suggestions for valuable revisions and improvements of the manuscript and in lending encouragement to the author during the production of the work.

For his special interest in and careful reading of the manuscript during a busy schedule of seminary teaching, the author is deeply indebted to Richard S. Taylor of Nazarene Theological Seminary of Kansas City, Missouri. Dr. Taylor has offered many helpful suggestions for the improvement of the work, and has afforded the author much encouragement in his efforts to complete the book for publication. For his evaluation of the author's treatment of the subject of *The Person and Ministry of the Holy Spirit, A Wesleyan Perspective,* sincere appreciation is hereby expressed.

Early in the production of this work special interest was expressed by Dale O. Emery, past Executive Director of The Christian Holiness Association, and Thomas H. Hermiz, current Executive Director of that organization. Realizing that the author was treating a subject of major interest to the Christian Holiness Association (formerly known as The National Holiness Association), these men suggested the possible official endorsement of the work by the Executive Committee of that body. Accordingly copies of the manuscript were furnished the members of the Executive Committee and were read by them. At the annual meeting of the Executive Committee held in Indianapolis, Indiana, in October 1973, this body gave its official endorsement of the work as representing the interpretation of the person and ministry of the Holy Spirit, as understood and taught by the Christian Holiness Association, by a "full and unanimous" vote of approval. Thus to Dr. Emery, Mr. Hermiz, and the Executive Committee of the CHA, the author wishes to express his most sincere appreciation and gratitude.

No one person has contributed more to the production of this book in devoted labor and encouragement offered the author than has Elizabeth Carter, wife of the author. Throughout many long hours, often working late into the night, during weary days, weeks, and months she labored at the typewriter putting the manuscript in shape for publication. For her uncompensated labor of love the author expresses his most sincere gratitude.

Chas. W. Carter
China Evangelical Seminary
Shihlin, Taipei, Taiwan, Jan. 11, 1974

Contents

Preface 7

1 The Holy Spirit in the Judeo-Christian Religion 15
2 The Person and Ministry of the Spirit
    from Creation Through the Prophets 37
3 The Person and Ministry of the Spirit
    from the Prophets to the New Testament 63
4 The Holy Spirit in the Synoptic Gospels 89
5 The Holy Spirit in the Gospel According to John 115
6 The Hebrew-Jewish Pentecost in Relation to the
    Effusion of the Holy Spirit in Acts 2 145
7 The Baptism with the Spirit in the Pentecostal
    Experience 157
8 The Spirit's Gift of Communication to the Church 191
9 The Effects of the Spirit's Effusion upon the
    Multitudes at Pentecost 221
10 The Holy Spirit in the Expansion of the Church 247
11 Graces and Gifts of the Spirit in Paul's Epistles 261

12 The Fruit and Guarantee of the Spirit in Paul's
  Epistles 291
13 The Holy Spirit in the General Epistles and the
  Revelation 307

  Bibliography 337
  Index 351

Chapter 1

The Holy Spirit
in the
Judeo-Christian Religion

I. THE CONTEMPORARY EMPHASIS UPON THE HOLY SPIRIT

In the history of Christian thought two tendencies have prevailed in relation to the person and work of the Holy Spirit. The one has been either to neglect or ignore entirely the Holy Spirit in the redemptive scheme, and the other to disproportionately magnify the revelation concerning the Spirit. On the first tendency Samuel Chadwick, in his well-known work *The Way to Pentecost* remarks,

> The Apostles' Creed contains ten articles on the person and work of Christ, and only one on the Holy Spirit [though the Spirit is mentioned twice]. The proportion of ten to one about represents the interest in the doctrine of the Spirit in the history of Christian thought. No doctrine of the Christian faith has been so neglected. Sermons and hymns are significantly barren on this subject.[1]

However significant the foregoing observation may have been in Chadwick's day, it is noteworthy that recent times have witnessed a renewed emphasis upon the Spirit's person and ministry. A review of the major creeds of Christendom reveals that the Holy Spirit has not

---

1. (Berne, Indiana: Light and Hope Publications, 1957), p. 5.

been wholly neglected by the church. He is mentioned twice in the Nicene Creed, four times in the Athanasian Creed, eleven times in the Augsburg Confession, seven times in the Articles of Religion of the Protestant Episcopal Church, twelve times in the Westminster Shorter Catechism, eighteen times in the Confession of the Friends or Quakers, seven times in the New Hampshire Baptist Confession, eighteen times in the Batak Protestant Church Confession (of Indonesia), and once only in the Statement of Faith of the United Church of Christ, for a total of eighty-two times in the aforementioned creeds. In the eighteenth-century Wesleyan-Arminian revival in England and in the nineteenth- and early twentieth-century Wesleyan-Arminian revivals in America, a large place was given to the Spirit.

From the 1920s to the end of World War II there existed a noticeable neglect of interest in and emphasis upon the Holy Spirit in both theological writings and pulpit proclamations. At least three factors seem to have contributed to this neglect. First, this was the era in which the emphasis upon science and the scientific method reached its zenith and passed over into the death-dealing period of scientism, or practically a worship of the scientific method, mistaking it as an end in itself rather than a method or a means to a higher end or purpose. Second, concurrent with the foregoing, was the climax of an era of materialism in which God and everything beyond the reach of man's material grasp was denied, forgotten, or neglected. In the third place, it was during this time that the destructive higher criticism of the Bible bore its fullest harvest in an attitude of religious skepticism. Thus, in the light of these, and perhaps other contributing factors, there was little place in religion or the thought of man generally for any consideration of the supernatural, not to mention the Holy Spirit *per se.*

Two important factors helped to pave the way for a radical change in the climate of more recent thought. The first was the development and final explosion of two atomic bombs to end the war with Japan in 1945, which revealed the reduction of matter to invisible, though powerful, energy. No longer could man view matter as a solid, stable, or permanent substance. The reduction of matter to energy broke the backbone of philosophical materialism. This opened once more the way to consideration of spiritual entities. The second factor was of a religious and theological nature. The influence of the theology of Karl Barth and other neo-orthodox thinkers, in reaction against the deadening effects of German higher criticism and liberalism, turned the tide of theological thinking into more serious and spiritual channels. It is not argued that either of the foregoing factors was *directly* related to the revival of interest in spiritual entities and the Holy Spirit in particular. However, if the pagan king Cyrus could be called by God "My Shepherd" and "His anointed" (Isa. 44:28; 45:1), for the return of Israel from captivity, it is not incredible that the foregoing factors may have been used of God to prepare the way for a return to a new emphasis upon the Spirit and spiritual values. Nor is it supposed that these factors stand alone in their influence upon this change in the climate of religious thought during the past few decades. Many other factors may well have combined to produce the obvious effects.

However the foregoing may be considered, it is undeniable that the past few decades have witnessed one of the most marked emphases upon the Holy Spirit in religious circles since the first Christian century. This marked new emphasis upon the Spirit in the Christian religion demands a serious and careful restudy of the Scriptures in relation to the person and work of the Holy Spirit in the divine redemptive plan.

II. THE ETYMOLOGY AND MEANING OF *SPIRIT* AND *HOLY SPIRIT* IN THE BIBLE

Our English word *spirit* is translated from the Hebrew word *ruach*, which may mean "breath," "wind," or "spirit." In fact, Girdlestone says that "With the exception of Job 26:4 and Proverbs 20:27, where *neshamah* . . . , 'a breathing being,' is used, the word *spirit* always represents the Hebrew *ruach*. . . ."[2] Girdlestone further notes that *ruach*, as with its Greek equivalents *pneuma* and *anemos*, Latin *spiritus*, English *ghost*, and like words in other languages, originally signified "wind" or "breath," and that *ruach* is the only word rendered "wind" in the Old Testament. Then Girdlestone adds: "Thus, as blood represents the animal life, so does *wind* the spiritual element in life."[3]

Ruach is usually translated *pneuma* ("breath" or "wind") in the Septuagint. In Genesis 2:7 we read of "the breath [*ruach*] of life." According to Job 27:3, he lives as long as the breath (*ruach*) of God is in his nostrils. The psalmist says of mortal man that when "his spirit [*ruach*] departs, he returns to the earth" (146:4). Breath and

---

2. Robert Baker Girdlestone, *Synonyms of the Old Testament* (Grand Rapids: Wm. B. Eerdmans Publishing Company, 1897, rep., 2nd ed.), p. 22.
    3. *Ibid.*

wind (*ruach*) are remarkably identified in their function in relation to life-giving in Ezekiel's vision of dry bones (37). Here, as sometimes elsewhere in the Old Testament, it is difficult to distinguish between the physical and the super-physical breath, as they are both God's gifts to man.

However, Girdlestone sees the Hebrew word *nephesh* (Greek, *psuchē*) as the equivalent of our English word *soul,* or the source of animation to the body, or simply life.[4] There are, however, certain passages in which the word *person* seems a more fitting rendering of *nephesh.* Another authority makes the distinction between *ruach* and *nephesh* sharper when he states that *nephesh* (originally "breath") refers predominantly to the emotional life, and that it is a strong personal or reflexive pronoun which is equivalent to *person.* However, this authority states that *ruach* (originally "wind") indicates especially *supernatural* influences acting upon man from without.[5] In the Greek Old Testament (the Septuagint), *nephesh* is rendered *psuchē* ("soul"), while *ruach* is rendered *pneuma* ("spirit").[6] In the New Testament *pneuma* usually refers to supernatural influences (see exceptions in Romans 1:9; 8:16; II Corinthians 7:1).

Thus, generally it appears that in the Old Testament *nephesh* usually refers to soul, or person, while *ruach* usually refers to the supernatural Spirit of God.

III. THE PERSONALITY OF THE HOLY SPIRIT

A. The Personality of the Holy Spirit—
Implicit in the Old Testament, but *Explicit* in the New Testament

Any adequate understanding of the nature of the Holy Spirit, but especially His personality, must be derived from the New Testament. It is in the New Testament that the truth found in bud form in the Old Testament comes to full flower. As observed by Augustine long ago, the Old Testament is the New Testament infolded; the New Testament is the Old Testament unfolded. All that we know about the Holy Spirit, and probably all that we ever shall know, is *implicit* in the teachings concerning Him in the Old Testament. It remains for those teachings to be made *explicit* in the New Testament, where the

---

4. *Ibid.*
5. Alexander Souter, *A Pocket Lexicon to the Greek New Testament* (Oxford: Clarendon Press, 1966 rep.), pp. 206, 207.
6. *Ibid.*

great drama of redemption is unfolded in all its clarity and significance. It is the reflected light of the New Testament upon the
sometimes dim, half-hidden, though nonetheless real, truths of the
Old Testament, that illumines and clarifies those truths.

The foregoing is well exemplified, concerning the Holy Spirit in
the Old Testament teaching, by Peter's explanatory sermon on the
Day of Pentecost. It is obvious that the multitudes present on that
occasion, though they were Jews in religion with extensive knowledge of the Old Testament Scriptures, did not understand the teachings of those Scriptures concerning the Holy Spirit. When this mighty
manifestation of the Spirit occurred, Luke records concerning the
multitudes present that " . . . they continued in amazement and
perplexity, saying to one another, 'What does this mean?' " (Acts
2:12). Had the promise of the Spirit been clear to them from their
knowledge of the Old Testament there would have been no occasion
for their question, "What does this mean?" It required the Spirit-
illumined and inspired explanation of the apostle Peter to make clear
to them what was taught in their Old Testament Scriptures concerning the Holy Spirit. Peter, as spokesman for the other apostles,
denied, with good evidence, the mistaken notion of some that the
disciples were intoxicated (Acts 2:13). Having canceled out this false
charge with the contrastive conjunction "but," he proceeded to give
them the true meaning of the manifestation from their own Scriptures. Said Peter:

> *But* this is what was spoken of through the prophet Joel: "And it
> shall be in the last days," God says, "that I will pour forth of My
> Spirit upon all mankind; and your sons and your daughters shall
> prophesy, and your young men shall see visions, and your old men
> shall dream dreams; Even upon My bond-slaves, both men and
> women, I will in those days pour forth of My Spirit and they shall
> prophesy . . . . And it shall be, that every one who calls on the name
> of the Lord shall be saved" (Acts 2:16-18, 21).

When the Old Testament teaching concerning the Holy Spirit was
illumined and related to its New Testament fulfillment in God's plan
of redemption by Peter, those Jewish multitudes "were pierced in
the heart [or smitten in conscience], and said to Peter and the rest of
the apostles, 'Brethren, what shall we do?' " (Acts 2:37). This
response gave Peter his opportunity to call them to genuine repentance and saving faith in Jesus Christ with the result that "there were
added [to the believers in Christ] that day about three thousand
souls [i.e., *persons*]" (Acts 2:41). Had these Jews understood their
Old Testament teachings concerning the Holy Spirit, there would

have been no call for their question or Peter's explanation. Likewise the teaching concerning the Holy Spirit throughout the Old Testament can be correctly understood only under the floodlight of the New Testament fulfillment of the Old Testament promises.

However, the foregoing is not peculiar to the Spirit in the Old Testament. The same principle holds true concerning the divine plan of redemption, the Trinity, the messianic promises, and the future life. That there are dim shadows and sometimes momentary clear images of these great truths in the Old Testament can be denied only by the most skeptical Bible scholars.

Thus while the personality of the Holy Spirit does come to the surface here and there in the Old Testament, His personality is made most explicit in the New Testament. One reason the Holy Spirit is not as clearly understood in the Old Testament as in the New is suggested in the statement of John in his Gospel: "the Spirit was not yet *given,* because Jesus was not yet glorified" (7:39). These words of John have been a stumbling block to many interpreters, even with some of the Wesleyan theological persuasion. Judgments based upon this passage, combined with Paul's words in Romans 8:9, "But if anyone does not have the Spirit of Christ, he does not belong to Him," have concluded that Christ's disciples were not actually Christians until they experienced the effusion of the Holy Spirit on the day of Pentecost. Others have mistakenly designated the Pentecostal experience as the *birthday* of the Christian church, whereas *dedication* or *inauguration* of the Christian church would be a more accurate designation. The denial of genuine Christian experience to the disciples and believers in Christ before the Day of Pentecost can never be reconciled with Christ's own claims for them in such discourses as we find in John 10 and 17.

What then is meant by the apparently strange words of John, "the Spirit was not yet *given,* because Jesus was not yet glorified"? The meaning, when considered in the light of all the teaching concerning the Spirit in the Old and New Testaments, is that up to the time Christ spoke these words the Spirit had not been given in the fullest sense as He would be at Pentecost, and that this fullest manifestation of the Spirit must await Christ's glorification upon His return to the Father in the ascension (see John 17:5). Thus the Spirit given at Pentecost in the New Testament sense is the result of the finished redemptive work of Christ. Wesley's remarks on these words of John that "the Holy Ghost was not yet given" are significant. "That is, those fruits of the Spirit were not yet given, even to true believers, in that full measure."[7]

R. H. Strachan interestingly notes that "the rabbinical teaching was that the Holy Spirit had departed from Israel when the last of the prophets, Zechariah and Malachi, died. They looked for a fresh outpouring in the Messianic age."[8]

Leon Morris[9] thinks that the explanation for Christ's infrequent reference to the Spirit in the Synoptic Gospels may be due to the fact that the word *Spirit* had been debased by ecstatics claiming to be spirit-possessed, and thus it was necessary that a better and fuller concept of the Spirit be exemplified in Jesus' ministry and life before the idea of the Spirit could be taught effectively. Also he thinks that since the way to Pentecost was via Calvary and the resurrection, and the disciples understood so imperfectly these experiences, it would be fruitless to give them fuller instruction concerning the Spirit—until a later time. However, he concludes that these are little more than conjectures.

The very reason Jesus speaks sparingly of the Spirit in the Synoptic Gospels may very well account also for the absence of extensive emphasis upon the baptism with the Holy Spirit in relation to sanctification of believers in the writings of John Wesley. Wesley had his problems with super-enthusiasts and even with fanatics in his day also. Nor was Luther exempt from the same problems in the period of the Reformation. Both leaders attempted to steer a middle course between blighting legalistic-formalism and wild fanaticism, while at the same time keeping a dynamic emphasis upon vital spiritual religion.

In reference to John 7:39, "the spirit was not yet given, because Jesus was not yet glorified," William Barclay[10] is quite correct when he notes that to take these words in a literal sense would pose an insoluble problem for the doctrine of the trinity. However, since John has already spoken of the descent of the Spirit upon Jesus when He was baptized by John in the Jordan such a literal sense cannot be applied to these words. Likewise, Christ taught Nicodemus the necessity of the Spirit in the new birth. Rather he means that

7. John Wesley, *Explanatory Notes Upon the New Testament* (London: Epworth Press, rep. 1954), p. 335.

8. *The Fourth Gospel,* 3rd ed. (London: SCM Press, Ltd., rep. 1960), p. 203.

9. *Spirit of the Living God* (London: Intervarsity Fellowship, 1960), p. 31.

10. *The Promise of the Spirit* (London: Epworth Press, 1960), p. 32.

after Christ's glorification and ascension the Spirit will be out-poured upon the believers in all His plenitude and power. The Pentecostal effusion of the Spirit must await Jesus' return to His glory.

B. Evidences of the Personality
of the Holy Spirit in Scripture

Now, however, it may be asked, What are the evidences for the personality of the Holy Spirit found implicit in the Old Testament and made explicit in the New Testament? In an attempt to deal with that question we shall observe first the New Testament record and later examine Old Testament records in another context.

1. The Scriptures Ascribe Personal Characteristics to the Holy Spirit

Contrary to the disposition of many, even Christians, to think often of the Holy Spirit as an impersonal influence or energy emanating from God—an *it* instead of a *person* represented as *He* or *Him*—the New Testament clearly represents the Holy Spirit as *personal*. The essential notes of a person—that is, those characteristics without which personhood would be unthinkable and impossible— include spiritual essence, intelligence or rationality, volition, emotions, and moral responsibility. Obviously there are varying degrees of development, from the potential to the actual, of these characteristics in different individuals.

The first of these essential notes of personhood may simply be designated "spiritual essence." Above all, a person is distinguished from all other orders of creation by essential spirituality. The integrity of personality is dependent on man's unique spirituality. This is everywhere assumed in the Hebrew-Christian Scriptures. In the second instance the Spirit is characterized in the Scriptures by intellect or intelligent activity. His intelligence is clearly presupposed by Paul when he says of the Spirit, "He who searches the hearts *knows* what the *mind of the Spirit is,* because He intercedes for the saints according to the *will* of God" (Rom. 8:27). Again in I Corinthians 2:10-13 Paul credits the Holy Spirit with rationality when he says,

> The Spirit searches all things, even the depths of God. . . . the *thoughts* of God no one knows except the Spirit of God. . . . we have received . . . the Spirit who is from God, that we might know the things freely given to us by God . . . not in words taught by human wisdom, but in *those taught by the Spirit.* . . .

Further, the mind or intelligence of the Spirit is clearly evident when Paul and his party were "forbidden by the Holy Spirit to speak the word in Asia" (Acts 16:6) on Paul's second missionary journey.

When Luke informs us in Acts 2:4 that the disciples at Pentecost were "all filled with the Holy Spirit and began to speak with other tongues, *as the Spirit gave them utterance* [or, *ability to speak out*]*," he clearly implies both the intelligence and the volition of the Holy Spirit. In a similar vein Paul informs the Corinthians that the Spirit's intelligence and volition are manifested as *He distributes* the spiritual gifts "*to each one* individually just *as He wills*" (I Cor. 12:11b; see also Acts 13:4; 15:28; 21:11; I Cor. 2:13; Heb. 2:4; 9:8; 10:15; II Peter 1:21).

Paul implies the emotional nature of the Spirit's personhood when he admonishes the Ephesian Christians that they should not "*grieve the Holy Spirit of God, by whom* [they] *are sealed for the day of redemption*" (4:30); and again when he admonishes the Thessalonians: "Do not quench the Spirit" (I Thess. 5:19).

The emotional nature and moral responsibility of the Spirit are suggested in the apostles' letter sent out from the Jerusalem Conference in which they wrote: "For it seemed good to the Holy Spirit and to us to lay upon you no greater burden than these essentials" (Acts 15:28). The Spirit's emotional nature is evident in Paul's words in Romans 5:5: "the love of God has been poured out within our hearts through the Holy Spirit who was given to us." Again, Paul writes to the Colossian Christians concerning their "*love* in the Spirit" (Col. 1:8b).

Perhaps nowhere is the personality of the Spirit made more evident than in Christ's solemn warning against blaspheming the Holy Spirit with the dire consequences (Matt. 12:31-32; Mark 3:29; Luke 12:10).

But in a positive vein Christ treats the Spirit as a person in His farewell discourses in John 14-16. Here He is designated the *paraklētos* (John 14:16, 26; 15:26; 16:7). While a fuller treatment of this subject will be considered later, it is sufficient to note here that the personality of the Spirit is clearly indicated. The title *parakletos* given the Spirit by Jesus characterizes Him, among other things, as a *counselor,* a *witness,* or an *advocate,* all of which definitely mark out His personality. Further, His moral character is indicated when Jesus calls Him "the Spirit of truth . . . " (John 14:17). Likewise Jesus makes clear the rationality of the Spirit when He states that "He will *teach* you all things, and *bring to your remembrance* all that I said to you" (John 14:26). In John 15:26 Jesus says that "the Spirit of truth, who proceeds from the Father, He will *bear witness* of Me." Again, Jesus indicates the personality of the Spirit when He states that "when He comes, [He] will *convict* the world concerning sin, and righteousness, and judgment" (John 16:8). *Convict* is a forensic term which implies a rational and just exercise of the mind. In John 16:13-14 He is designated "the Spirit of truth . . . [who] will guide you into all truth; for He will not speak on His own initiative, but whatever He hears, He will speak; and He will disclose to you what is to come . . . He shall take of Mine, and shall disclose it to you."

Edwin C. Palmer correctly points out that we can clearly see that "the Spirit is a person by placing Him in juxtaposition with other persons."[11] We readily ascribe personality to God the Father and the Son; but Jesus commissions His disciples to baptize believers "in the name of the Father and the Son and the Holy Spirit" (Matt. 28:19; see also II Cor. 13:14). James, moderator of the First General Church Council at Jerusalem, likewise indicates the personality of the Spirit by placing Him in juxtaposition with the apostles, having the same judgment with them when he says: "For it seemed good *to the Holy Spirit and to us* to lay upon you no greater burden than these essentials" (Acts 15:28).

2. *Scripture Ascribes Divine Attributes to the Holy Spirit*

Scripture clearly indicates the divinity of the Spirit by assigning to Him divine attributes, as well as personality. His omnipotence, or all-powerfulness, is indicated in His creative activities (Gen. 1:2; Ps. 104:30); in Jesus' supernatural conception (Luke 1:35); and in the regeneration of sinners (John 3:5-6). His omnipresence is clearly implied by the psalmist when he asks, "Where can I go from Thy Spirit? Or where can I flee from Thy presence?" (Ps. 139:7; see also verses 8-18). His eternal coexistence with the Father and the Son (John 1:1-2, 14) is indicated in Hebrews 9:14, where He is called "the eternal Spirit" (an allowable rendering of this passage).

The Spirit's personality as distinct from the Father and the Son, though of the same essence in the Godhead, is emphasized at Christ's baptism where all three members of the divine Trinity appear in their *personal* distinctiveness. So important is this fact considered in the New Testament—the *Father* in heaven, sending the *Spirit* in the form

---

11. *The Holy Spirit*, rev. ed. (Philadelphia: Presbyterian and Reformed Publishing Company, 1971), p. 12.

of a dove upon the *Son* on earth at His baptism—that all four of the Gospel narrators considered it necessary to record the event in almost identical terms. This is done with but few other events in the New Testament. Jesus' statement likewise bears out the distinctiveness of the Spirit's personality from that of the Father and the Son when He says:

> And I will ask the father, and He will give you another *Helper* [*paraklētos*], that He may abide with you forever; *that is* the Spirit of truth, whom the world cannot receive, because it does not behold Him or know Him, *but* you know Him because He abides with you, and shall be in you (John 14:16-17).

Peter bears out the same truth when he states in his Pentecostal day sermon:

> This Jesus God raised up again, to which we are all witnesses. Therefore having been exalted to the right hand of God, and having received from the Father the promise of the Holy Spirit, He has poured forth this which you both see and hear (Acts 2:32-33).

Certainly the foregoing Scriptural evidence (and much more could be produced) should convince any honest believer in the Bible of the personality of the divine Holy Spirit.

The personality of the Holy Spirit in the Old Testament, while not as obvious or explicit as in the New Testament, is nevertheless *implicit* and even emerges into clear perspective in several instances. However, this aspect of the Spirit may be best investigated and understood in relation to the general treatment of the Spirit in the Old Testament, and will be dealt with accordingly in that connection. But before any adequate understanding of the Holy Spirit in the Old Testament can be gained, it is necessary to consider the Spirit in relation to the Holy Trinity.

IV. THE HOLY SPIRIT IN RELATION TO THE DIVINE TRINITY

The word *trinity* is not found in either the Old or New Testaments. Like other developed New Testament doctrines, such as the Incarnation, Atonement, and Resurrection, the doctrine of the Trinity is found, for the most part, implicitly in the Old Testament, whereas it becomes explicit in the New Testament.

A. The Doctrine of the Trinity in History

Actually the doctrine of the Trinity seems not to have found its place in the theology of the Christian church until about the fourth

century, though Tertullian is reported to have used it in the latter
part of the second century. R. A. Finlayson states that the doctrine
of the Trinity "is, however, the distinctive and all comprehensive
doctrine of the Christian faith and [in the words of Lowry] 'gathers
up into the seam of a single grand generalization with respect to the
being and activity of God all the major aspects of Christian
truth,' "[12]

In the Wesleyan theological tradition the Trinity has probably not
been more adequately defined than in the words of S. J. Gamertsfelder.

> By the term Trinity, as a doctrine of the Christian faith, we mean
> that the one Divine Essence exists in a union of co-equal persons
> related as the Father, the Son of the Father by eternal generation,
> and the Holy spirit eternally proceeding from the Father and the
> Son. The fundamental truths affirmed in the doctrine are, there is
> one essence and three persons in the Godhead.[13]

This definition accords well with both the teachings of the Scripture and the *Nicene Creed,* which was the formal statement made on
the subject by the Fathers of the Christian church at the Council of
Nicaea in A.D. 325, and which has stood the test of the ages as the
orthodox view of Christianity to the present time. This creed reads in
part, as pertains to the Trinity, as follows:

> I believe in one God the Father Almighty; Maker of heaven and
> earth, and all things visible and invisible. And in one Lord Jesus
> Christ, the only-begotten Son of God, begotten of the Father before
> all worlds [God of God], Light of Light, very God of very God,
> begotten, not made, being of one substance [essence] with the
> Father; . . . and was incarnate by the Holy Ghost of the Virgin Mary,
> and was made man. . . . And [I believe] in the Holy Ghost, the Lord
> and Giver of Life; who proceedeth from the Father [and the Son];
> who with the the Father and the Son together is worshiped and
> glorified; who spoke by the Prophets.[14]

Gamertsfelder asserts that "the fundamental truths affirmed in the
doctrine are, there is one essence and three persons in the Godhead"[15] This same authority states that during Christian history

---

12. "Trinity," *The New Bible Dictionary,* ed. J. D. Douglass (Grand Rapids:
Wm. B. Eerdmans Publishing Company, 1962), p. 1298.
    13. *Systematic Theology* (Harrisburg, Pa.: Evangelical Publishing House,
1921, rep. 1952), p. 210.
    14. Phillip Schaff, *The Creeds of Christendom* (New York: Harper and
Brothers, 1879), II, 45.
    15. *Op. cit.,* p. 210.

the main question concerning the Father has been concerned with the unity of the essence. The chief question as to the Son has been . . . the question of His divinity; and the chief question of the Spirit is the question of His personality.[16]

Gamertsfelder says, further, that

the doctrine of the Trinity is based on the truths of Divine revelation. Neither theism nor reason can furnish sufficient data out of which to construct the Christian doctrine of the Trinity. We readily admit that a certain degree of mystery attaches to the doctrine, and that it is not open to full explication in human thought. . . . However the Trinity in the Godhead is a precious doctrine of the Christian Religion and is firmly rooted in the Sacred Scriptures.[17]

That the doctrine of the Trinity is incapable of complete human comprehension is logical and understandable. That man's finite mind, or human limitations, can never fully comprehend the infinity or limitlessness of divinity is obvious. To comprehend God fully would necessitate that man himself possess the limitless wisdom of God, in which unthinkable event he would no longer be man, but God.

Bishop William Ragsdale Cannon notes that the latter part of the seventeenth century witnessed the Trinitarian controversy in English theology when Burnet and Tillotson tended to make of the three persons of the Godhead *only* three manifestations of one God. Cannon says that Wesley evaded the controversy entirely and simply affirmed the Catholic position of Nicaea and Chalcedon. Wesley, Cannon notes, drew upon the Bible for his doctrine of God, and gave little notice to metaphysics and philosophy. His position with regard to the Godhead was practical rather than speculative. His sermon on the Trinity was based upon I John 5:7. In this sermon Wesley does not consider it wise to attempt an explication of the Trinity, as such may lead to confusion rather than clarification. Nor does he think that anyone should be burned at the stake for blasphemy if he does not use the word *trinity*. Cannon says that Wesley's position is that "on the basis of the divine testimony alone, he believes the fact of the Trinity, but it is foolish to reject what God has revealed merely because we do not comprehend what He has not revealed [LV, sec. 15]. The significant thing in this revelation is that Jesus Christ is God, the Holy Spirit is God, and the Father is God." Cannon notes further that with Wesley "What matters is not an explanation of this but that all men honor the Son, the Holy Spirit, and the Father as

---

16. *Ibid.*, pp. 210, 211.
17. *Ibid.*, p. 210.

One God" [*Sermon* LV, sec. 17].[18] However, Cannon regards Wesley as consistent in his position on the Trinity when he says that his "doctrine of God is not alien to the other principles of his theology; all rest on religious insights alone . . . [*Works*, IX, 467]."[19]

John Wesley's own words are clear and unequivocal concerning his position on the divine Trinity when he states:

> Nothing therefore is more absurd than the objections of unbelievers against the Christian mysteries, as unintelligible; since Christianity requires our assent to nothing, but what is plain and intelligible in every proposition. Let every man first have a full conviction of the truth of each proposition in the gospel, as far only as it is plain and intelligible, and let him believe as far as he understands. Let him firmly believe, there is but one God, the object of any divine worship whatsoever; and think and speak of him under the plain scriptural distinction of the Father, Son, and Holy Ghost, leaving the incomprehensible nature of that union and distinction to the great author of our faith Himself.[20]

Let it be noted at once that the Trinity is not presented in a formulated doctrine in either the Old or New Testaments. Rather it appears in fragmentary allusions (cf. Heb. 1:1-2). It is left to us to go beyond the content of Scripture to give a rational organization and meaning to the Old Testament implications and evidence. To the extent that we glean the evidence for the doctrine of the Trinity from the Old Testament it is revealed therein and not discovered by human reason.

It is instructive to note that the Judeo-Christian religion *only,* of all the religions of mankind through the ages, has attained a true trinitarian doctrine. Indeed a pseudo-trinitarian doctrine appears in Mahayana Buddhism, though not in the original Hinayana Buddhism, but even that is most likely borrowed from Christianity during the early contacts of these two religions in Northern China. The Judeo-Christian religion is unique in its ability to give us the truth concerning God and man.

The *I-Thou* concept, clarified and popularized by Martin Buber, is helpful in understanding the importance of the Trinity to the very reality of God Himself. It is a well-known and accepted fact of epistomology that all knowledge is dependent upon the *subject-*

---

18. *The Theology of John Wesley* (New York-Nashville: Abingdon Press, 1946), p. 205.

19. *Ibid.,* pp. 160, 161.

20. *A Compendium of Natural Philosophy* (II, 447-79).

object relationship. Neither a subject nor an object could possibly stand alone. This principle is well exemplified by the simple sentence in grammar. Neither the subject nor the object has any meaning in the absence of the other. It is likewise in the divine Trinity, as opposed to the Unitarian concept where one divine person stands alone in the Godhead and has no means of self-identification. The Trinitarian concept, on the other hand, provides an *I-Thou* (or *subject-object*) personal relationship of the members of the Trinity, and thus the personal self-identification of each member, while retaining the essential unity of the Godhead. George W. Forell supports this position. He thinks that it is the I-Thou relationship, which, as Martin Buber sees it, constitutes the basis of all relationships, human as well as the God-man relationship. Forell holds that this is a reflection of the image of the primary I-Thou relationship in the being of the Godhead. "The doctrine of the Trinity," Forell says, "testifies to the eternal encounter in the one living God, Father, Son, and Holy Spirit."[21] It is worthy of note that the Unitarian church has not been included in the World Council of Churches. Sabellianism, which asserted that there is one God, and that the Father, Son, and Spirit are but three modes in which the one God appears, was rejected as heterodoxy early in the history of Christianity.

On the other hand, the doctrine of the Trinity protects Christianity against the error of *tri-theism*. The church fathers who formulated the doctrine of the Trinity saw in it the means of preventing error in the faith and of preserving all the confessions of the Christian faith about God. These confessions appear much more prominently in the adoration and worship of God in the church than in logical arguments or attempted Scriptural agreements. While many of the hymns of the church reflect faith in the Trinity, none is more popular and often used than the so-called "doxology." In this hymn the Trinity is the central concept. "Praise God from whom all blessings flow, Praise Him, all creatures here below. Praise Him above, ye heavenly hosts; Praise Father, Son and Holy Ghost."

Likewise Horatius Bonar well expresses this disposition to give worship and adoration to the triune God in the lines of his famous hymn:

---

21. *The Protestant Faith* (Englewood Cliffs, N.J.: Prentice-Hall, Inc., 1960), p. 202.

> Glory be to God the Father!
> Glory be to God the Son!
> Glory be to God the Spirit!
> God eternal, Three in One![22]

The same disposition characterized the early Methodists and is conspicuously prominent in the hymns of the Wesleys, as is noted by Roy S. Nicholson. One alone of Wesley's hymns will suffice to exemplify his belief in and emphasis upon the triune God in which he guarantees the realization of full salvation through the involvement of the Trinity in that gracious work.

> Come, Father, Son and Holy Ghost,
>   And seal me Thine abode;
> Let all I am in Thee be lost;
>   Let all I am be lost in God.
> Plunged in the Godhead's deepest sea,
>   And lost in Thine immensity.
> Come, Holy Ghost, all-quickening fire,
>   My consecrated heart inspire,
> Since I am born of God.
>   Let earth no more my heart divide,
> With Christ may I be crucified,
>   And to Thyself aspire.
> On Thee, O God, my soul is stayed . . .
>   Thy loving Spirit, Christ, alone
> Can lead me forth and make me free.
>   Now let Thy Spirit bring me in . . .
> The land of perfect holiness.
>   My God! I know, I feel Thee mine . . .
> And all renewed I am.
>   Jesus, Thine all-victorious love
> Shed in my heart abroad,
>   Come, Holy Ghost, for Thee I call,
> Spirit of burning come.[23]

While the doctrine of the Trinity is not discoverable by human reason, it is nevertheless supported by human reason. As previously noted in the *I-Thou* self-identification of the persons within the Trinity, reason sets the doctrine of the Trinity in opposition to the abstract monadic notion of divinity, such as that of the seventeenth-century philosopher Spinoza. Further, the doctrine of the Trinity is a safeguard of Christian teaching against all forms of pantheism and extreme mystical notions, such as are found in Hinduism and in the

---

22. *Service Book and Hymnal of the Lutheran Church of America*, No. 139.
23. "The Holiness Emphasis in the Wesleys' Hymns," *The Wesleyan Theological Journal*, Vol. 5-No. 1 (Concord, Mich.: Published by the Wesleyan Theological Society, 1970), pp. 49-61.

so-called liberal theology of the late nineteenth and early twentieth centuries, especially as represented by such works as Albert Schweitzer's *The Mysticism of the Apostle Paul.* With Forell we agree that

> Protestant Christians believe in the Holy Trinity because the one God, the God of Abraham and Isaac and Jacob, as the Old Testament likes to call Him, has revealed Himself in the Scriptures as Father, Son, and Holy Spirit.[24]

B. Intimations of the Divine Trinity in the Old Testament

The first Old Testament intimation of the divine Trinity appears in the opening words of the Bible: "In the beginning God [Heb. *Elohim*] created the heavens and the earth" (Gen. 1:1). The Hebrew word *Elohim*, used here for God, is plural in form. This divine plurality in no way sanctions polytheism. However, the question at stake is, Does it indicate the divine Trinity of Father, Son, and Holy Spirit? Certain scholars, including Calvin and some of the Roman Catholics, have preferred to consider *Elohim* as a *plural of majesty*, indicating the greatness, the infinity and the incomprehensibleness of deity.[25] That this concept of majesty may be recognized in the plural form of *Elohim* may be freely granted. However, such admission need not cancel out the possible divine intent of suggesting plurality within the unity of the Godhead. Writing in the Wesleyan theological tradition, Adam Clarke strongly supports the Trinitarian significance of the plural form of *Elohim* used for God in Genesis 1:1.

> The original word *Elohim*, God, is certainly the plural form of *El.* or *Eloah,* and has long been supposed, by the most eminently learned and pious men, to imply a plurality of persons in the divine nature. As this plainly appears in so many of the sacred writings to be confined to three persons [thus not an indefinite plurality as in pagan polytheism], here the doctrine of the Trinity has formed a part of the creed of all those who have been deemed sound in the faith, from the earliest ages of Christianity. The verb *bara,* "he creates," being joined in the singular number with the plural noun, has been considered as pointing out the unity of the divine persons in this work of Creation. In the ever-blessed Trinity, from the infinite and indivisible unit of the persons, there can be but one will, one purpose, and one infinite and uncontrollable energy.[26] (Comment on Gen. 1:1)

---

24. *Op. cit.,* p. 201.
25. Girdlestone, *op. cit.,* p. 22.
26. *Commentary on the Holy Bible,* One-volume edition, Abridged by Ralph Earle from the original six-volume work (Grand Rapids: Baker Book House, 1967), p. 16.

On the question of *Elohim* in Genesis 1:1, Wesley remarks:

> The plural name of God in *Hebrew*, which speaks of him as many,
> tho' he be but one, was to the *Gentiles* perhaps a *savour of death
> unto death*, hardening them in their idolatry; but it is to us a *savour
> of life unto life*, confirming our faith in the doctrine of the Trinity,
> which, tho' but darkly *intimated* in the Old Testament, is clearly
> *revealed* in the New.[27]

Elohim is the general Hebrew name used for God in the Old
Testament. It sometimes appears with the definite article and sometimes without it. Girdlestone notes that *Elohim* occurs no less than
2555 times in the Old Testament, and that in 2310 instances of this
number it signifies the "living and true God [cf. I Thess. 1:9], and
that it is used in a lower sense in 245 instances."[28] Girdlestone states
further, concerning the plurality of persons in the Godhead in
relation to the name *Elohim*, that "it is certainly marvelously consistent with this doctrine and must remove a great stumbling-block out
of the path of those who feel difficulties with regard to the acknowledgment of the Trinity in Unity."[29] Again in Genesis 1:26 the
Trinitarian significance of *Elohim* is strengthened by its association
with the plural pronouns *us* and *our* used for divinity. "Then God
[*Elohim*] said, 'Let *us* make man in *our* image, according to *our*
likeness,' " Girdlestone states with telling force that

> as long as the passage above quoted [Gen. 1:26] stands on the first
> page of the Bible, the believer in the Trinity has a right to turn to it
> as a proof that plurality in the Godhead is a very different thing
> from Polytheism, and as an indication that the frequent assertions of
> the Divine Unity are not inconsistent with the belief that the Father
> is God, the Son is God, and the Holy Ghost is God.[30]

However, the doctrine of the Trinity is not confined to certain
isolated passages in the Old Testament. It is rather interwoven in the
entire structure of the Old Testament revelation. There appears to be
a trinitarian suggestion in Genesis 1:2-3 where the *Spirit* and *Word* of
God become the creators of order and light. "The Spirit of God was
moving [or "hovering"] over the face of the waters," thus bringing
order out of chaos, and God's Word (personalized) brought forth
light as He *said*, "Let there be light" (cf. John 1:1-5). Finlayson
expresses it as follows:

27. John Wesley, *Explanatory Notes Upon the Old Testament* (Bristol:
Printed by William Prine in Wine-Street, 1765), I, 2.
28. Girdlestone, *op. cit.*, p. 19.
29. *Ibid.*, p. 22.
30. *Ibid.*

There is revealed thus a threefold centre of activity. God as Creator throughout the universe, expressed His thought in a Word, and made His Spirit its animating principle, thus indicating that the universe was not to have a separate existence apart from God or opposed to Him.[31]

Finlayson further notes that at a later stage both God's creative activity and His government are associated with the divine Word *personified* as Wisdom (Prov. 8:22ff; Job 28:23-27), and with the Spirit in His activity of imparting blessings, physical strength, courage, culture, and government (Exod. 31:3; Num. 11:25; Judg. 3:10).[32]

Again, in the unfolding of the redemptive plan the Trinity is suggested when the *Angel of Jehovah* (the Angel of the Covenant— Heb., *malak yahweh*) is entrusted with the divine revelation. Certainly not every reference in the Old Testament to the Angel of Jehovah implies a divine being, but in certain instances such a being is made clear (see Gen. 16:7; 24:7; 48:16). It is important to note that the title Jehovah is consistently used in the Old Testament with the expression, "the angel of the Lord [*ASV*, Jehovah]." Wesley and Clarke both regard these special appearances of "the angel of Jehovah" as theophanies, or visible manifestations of the second number of the divine Trinity.

On the appearance of "the angel of the Lord" in Judges 13:3, Clarke remarks that he is "generally supposed to have been the same that appeared to Moses, Joshua, Gideon, etc., and no other than the Second Person of the ever-blessed Trinity."[33] Further, Clarke notes on the appearance of "the angel of the Lord" to Hagar, as recorded in Genesis 16:7-13, that "the person mentioned here was greater than any created being. . . . "[34] Clarke's reasons for this judgment are based on the following evidence. The angel's promise to Hagar required divine authority and power; what he foretold to her only God could know; she regards and addresses him as God; the author of Genesis designates the angel *Jehovah;* the angel (*malak-Jehovah*) is the same as is called "the redeeming Angel," or "the Angel the Redeemer" in Genesis 48:16, "the Angel of God's presence" in Isaiah 63:9, "and the Messenger of the Covenant" in Malachi 3:1. Again in Genesis 18:3 Abraham first addresses one of the angels who

31. *Op. cit.,* p. 1298.
32. *Ibid.*
33. *Op. cit.,* p. 279.
34. *Ibid.,* p. 39.

appeared to him as *Adonai,* not Jehovah, because, Clarke thinks, he
did not know as yet the quality of his guests. However, one of the
three angels is later called *Jehovah* (Gen. 18:13), a name never
ascribed to a created being. Therefore, the Angel of the covenant,
Jesus Christ is obviously meant.[35]

One of the most remarkable appearances of the "Angel of the
Lord" is found in Zechariah 3. Clarke[36] regards this theophany as
the Messiah Himself. Not only is this angel spoken of as Jehovah
Himself but He is also represented as saying to Satan the Adversary
of Israel, "The Land rebuke you" (Zech. 3:2). In Genesis 31:11, 13
"the angel of the Lord" addresses Jacob by saying of Himself, "I am
the God of Bethel."

The Spirit of God also enters into the plan of God in revelation
and redemption and becomes the Messiah's special enablement for
His redemptive work (Isa. 11:2; 32:15; 42:1; 61:1; Joel 2:28; Ezek.
36:26, 27). Finlayson sees in the threefold Aaronic blessing a prototype of the apostolic Trinitarian blessing in the New Testament
(Num. 6:24-26).[37]

Clarke remarks on Genesis 15:1, where it is said that "the word of
the Lord came to Abram": "this is the first place where God is
represented as revealing himself by His Word. Some learned men
suppose that the *debar Yehovah,* translated here *word of the Lord,*
means the same with the *logos tou theou* of St. John, chapter
1:1."[38] If the observation is correct in identifying *"the word of the
Lord"* with the second person of the Trinity, then it would appear
that this identification with the Father may have been in Christ's
mind when He said to the Jews who opposed His claims: "My
Father is working until now, and I Myself am working." Apparently
those Jews caught the implications of His identity with the Father,
for they sought to kill Him for blasphemy (John 5:17, 18).

A number of Scripture passages in the Old Testament which refer
to *Jehovah* (*ASV*) are recognized in the New Testament as fulfilled in
Jesus Christ Himself. Among these are Joel 2:32, which is applied to
Christ by Paul in Romans 10:13 (cf. Acts 2:21). John quotes the
words of Jehovah from Isaiah 6:9-10, and then identifies them with
Christ's own glory (John 12:36-41). Isaiah speaks of the preparation
of the way of *Jehovah* (Isa. 40:3), and John the Baptist identifies

---

35. *Ibid.,* p. 42.
36. *Ibid.,* p. 752.
37. *Op. cit.,* p. 1298.
38. *Op. cit.,* p. 37.

this prophecy with his mission to prepare the way for the Messiah, Jesus Christ (Matt. 3:3). Malachi's prophecy (3:1) involving the Lord (*Jehovah*) is identified in the Gospels with Christ the Messiah (Matt. 11:10-14; Mark 1:2; Luke 7:27). Paul (Rom. 9:33) and Peter (I Peter 2:6-8) both identify Christ as a stone of stumbling and a rock of offense with the same title given to Jehovah in Isaiah 8:13, 14.

There are, of course, many other intimations, but those pointed up are sufficient to clearly indicate the evidence for the Trinity in the Old Testament.

Chapter 2

The Person and Ministry
of the Spirit from Creation
Through the Prophets

I. THE PERSON AND MINISTRY OF THE HOLY SPIRIT
IN RELATION TO CREATION

A. The Priority of the Spirit's Presence in the Cosmos

The priority of the *first person* of the divine Trinity, God the Father, both in appearance and creative activity at the outset of the Judeo-Christian Scripture (Gen. 1:1) is perfectly consistent with all that is or ever has been known by man about God. This is true in every area of human thought, including the scientific, philosophical, theological, or any other area. The mind of man has never been capable of penetrating beyond God as the personal "First Cause" of all essence and existence in the universe. Nor is there any present prospect that the reach of the human mind will ever exceed that limit.

It may be safely restated in plain language that *God is first of all or He is not at all!* That the latter position (*atheism*) is totally untenable the history of human thought and experience amply demonstrates. That the first proposition is valid and true is both epistomologically and experientially inescapable, notwithstanding the futile atheistic and nihilistic attempted reasoning of such world renowned thinkers as Friedrich Wilhelm Nietzsche (1844-1900), Bertrand Arthur Russell (1872-1971), or Jean-Paul Sartre (1905-).

God's initial creative act may rightly be designated "the beginning" by reason of the fact that human thought and existence itself is bounded by time. Since *time* is best measured by the revolutions of the heavenly bodies, there could have been *no time* or measurement of duration before the creation of the heavens and the earth, as stated in Genesis 1:1—*eternity only* subsisted and existed. Consequently the words of Genesis 1:1, "in the beginning," refer to God's first creative act rather than to God's existence, since God Himself transcends time and has always existed (cf. Rev. 10:6). In opposition to the various "precreation theories," Clarke notes that

> the rabbis, who are legitimate judges in a case of verbal criticism on their own language, are unanimous in asserting that the word *bara* [Heb., "create"] expresses the commencement of the existence of a thing. The supposition that God formed all things out of a preexisting, eternal nature is certainly absurd, for if there had been an eternal nature besides an eternal God, there must have been two self-existing independent, and eternal beings, which is a most palpable contradiction.[1]

Thus, God's first recorded act was the creation of the substance (the *prima materia,* or first elements) out of which the heavens and the earth were given form and meaning by the *third person of the Trinity, the Spirit of the Living God* (Gen. 1:2). Prior to the activity of the Spirit, as recorded by the author of Genesis, these *first elements* (the *prima materia*) created by God were "formless and void" (Heb., *tohu* and bohu = confusion and disorder—chaos), or "a waste and emptiness" enshrouded in utter darkness (Gen. 1:2).

B. The Priority of the Spirit's Creative Activity in the Cosmos

It is at this juncture that the Spirit is seen to move into His creative activity: "The Spirit of God was moving over the face of the waters" (Gen. 1:2 *RSV*). Here the Spirit (*ruach,* "breath, wind, or Spirit of God") is meant, for obviously the Spirit is represented (cf. John 3:8, Acts 2:2-4) in a threefold function in relation to creation. First, His personality and divinity is suggested by the author of Genesis when He is placed in juxtaposition with God—"the Spirit of

---

1. *Op. cit.,* p. 16.

God." Second, His infinite divine energy and power are indicated by His control over the chaotic elements out of which the cosmos was being formed. Third, His life-giving and formative function is suggested by the Hebrew expression which may be translated "moving over" (*RSV* and *NASB*), "moved upon" (*KJV*), or "was *brooding over.*"[2] The last expression seems the most fitting to bring out the true meaning of the Spirit's first activity in creation. Clarke notes that the words "brooding over" "express that tremulous motion made by the hen while either hatching her eggs or fostering her young. It here probably signifies the communicating of a vital or prolific principle to the water."[3]

Wesley says:

> The Spirit of God was the *first Mover*; He *moved upon the face of the waters—*He *moved* upon the face of the deep, as *the hen gathereth her chicken[s] under her wings,* and hovers over them, to warm and cherish them. [Matt. xxiii. 37] as the eagle stirs up her nest, and *fluttereth* over her young ('tis the same word that is here used) [Deut. xxxii. 11].[4]

This initial threefold function of the Spirit in the creation of the natural universe becomes a foreshadowing of His subsequent work in the great redemptive plan throughout the history of fallen, sinful man. Sin wrought disorder, confusion, chaos, and darkness in the spiritual and moral realms. The work of the Spirit has ever been to manifest the reality of the personal God and apply His divine power, life, and light to man's chaotic and meaningless state caused by sin, thus restoring spiritual life and order to man's otherwise hopeless condition.

When God spoke light into the darkness it is reasonably assumed that it was the Spirit who disseminated that light throughout the benighted chaos. Clarke points up that the Hebrew word here translated "light" might equally signify "fire" (cf. Isa. 31:9; Ezek. 5:2; Heb. 12:29). Thus considered it may be reasonable to suppose that the diffused divine heat-producing light was imparted to this inert primal substance by the activity of the Spirit that "brooded" over the chaotic mass, somewhat analogous to the hen's impartation of life-producing warmth to the eggs over which she broods and tremulously arranges and rearranges until they issue forth a new generation of chicks.

---

2. *Ibid.*
3. *Ibid.*
4. John Wesley, Explanatory Notes Upon the Old Testament (original), I, 3.

The author of the Genesis account does not stand alone in assigning to the Spirit this creative activity. Job likewise asserts that "by His [God's] breath [*ruach* "spirit"] the heavens are cleared [lit., "made beautiful, or orderly"]" (26:13). The *RSV* renders this passage: "By his *wind* the heavens were made fair."

Many theories have been advanced to account for the origin of the universe and man, all the way from crass "naturalistic evolution" through the more refined but little more satisfactory theories of "theistic evolution" to the contemporary "Big Bang" theory. However, none of these theories has promised to approximate the simple Biblical account of the personal divine creative act in which the Spirit played the executive role in bringing cosmic order out of the primal chaos. Thus, the work of the Spirit in original creation is both analogous to and suggestive of His function in producing in man by means of the redemptive process wholeness, completeness, perfection of being, or what Christ, Paul, and other New Testament writers and the eighteenth-century Wesleys designated *Christian Holiness* (see Matt. 5:48; I Thess. 5:23-24; Heb. 12:22-23). Wholeness or perfection of an organism consists in the purity, health, and orderly arrangement of all the parts of the living organism. Needless to say, the Wesleyan view of Christian perfection is a *perfection of love* and *not absolute perfection* as some have mistakenly supposed.

C. The Priority of the Spirit in Man's Creation

But the Spirit's creative work is not limited to the natural order of the universe. He is also represented as the agent of man's creation in Genesis 2:7, where it is said that "God formed man of the dust of the ground, and *breathed* into his nostrils *the breath of life;* and man became a living being [soul, or person]." The Hebrew verb here translated "breathed" is closely related to the noun *ruach,* or spirit, which represents the work of the Holy Spirit in man's creation. Job likewise identified the breath (*ruach*) of God with the divine Spirit (Job 27:3). And even Elihu, one of Job's pagan contestants, recognized man's creation to be by the Spirit of God, and his life to be sustained by the breath (*ruach* = spirit) of the Almighty (*Shaddai*)— (Job 32:8; 33:4). Thus the life of man is recognized here and elsewhere in the Old Testament as God's gift imparted to man by the Spirit of the living God.

Throughout the Old Testament the Spirit is recognized as God's own presence or power revealed to and present with man (Ps.

139:7-8). God is always present or omnipresent in His Spirit. The Spirit is God immanent in the world to express His power and execute His plans and purposes in creation and in the history of mankind. The presence and activity of the Spirit in this world is the assurance against a wholly transcendent God. The deistic doctrine of the late seventeenth and eighteenth centuries, with its concept of a wholly transcendent God, had no place or use for the divine Spirit. Though transcendent indeed, yet He is brought into the realm of creation and into personal relation with man by the person and activity of the Spirit. This activity of the Spirit is not to be equated with the mediatorial work of Christ in the New Testament, but it is to be understood as the principal means of divine revelation to man in the Old Testament.

II. THE PERSON AND MINISTRY OF THE HOLY SPIRIT IN RELATION TO RE-CREATION

A. The Spirit as the Revealer of the Redemptive Plan

Though *implicit* in the Old Testament, rather than *explicit* as in the New Testament, the Holy Spirit is essential to an understanding of the Old Testament record. To neglect or omit the person and function of the Holy Spirit from any serious study of the Old Testament is to render it meaningless. He is present in every movement of God from the first creative act to the coming of the Redeemer-Messiah, though His presence may be ever so unobtrusive, or even often hidden. What Christ said of the function of the Spirit in relation to His own person and ministry may be applied with equal meaning to the person and ministry of the Spirit in the Old Testament:

> But when He, the Spirit of truth, comes, He will guide you into all truth; *He will not speak on His own initiative,* but whatever He hears, He will speak; and *He will disclose to you what is to come. He shall glorify Me; for He shall take of Mine, and shall disclose it to you.* All things that the Father has are Mine; therefore I said, that *He takes of Mine, and will disclose it to you*" (John 16:13-15).

In the Old Testament the Spirit is the revealer of God's redemptive plan to be consummated in the future Messiah-Redeemer. In the New Testament the Holy Spirit is the revealer of the Redeemer in His accomplished work of redemption. The first points forward to the cross; the second points back to the cross. This is especially significant in the light of the fact that it is the Spirit Himself who is the inspirer and author of both the Old and the New Testaments. The apostle Peter makes this explicit when he says: "no prophecy was ever made by an act of human will, but *men moved by the Holy Spirit* spoke from God" (II Peter 1:21).

Writing to Timothy, his son in the gospel, Paul reminds him that under the instruction of his Jewish mother and grandmother he had from childhood "known the sacred writings [the Old Testament] which are able to give you *the wisdom that leads to salvation* through faith that is in Christ" (II Tim. 3:15). Thus Paul recognizes Old Testament Scripture as leading to Christ and having its fulfillment in Christ (cf. Gal. 3:24-29; 4:1-7). But again, writing to Timothy he states that "All Scripture is inspired by God [or possibly, "Every Scripture inspired by God"] is profitable for teaching, for reproof, for correction, for training in righteousness" (II Tim. 3:16). Here Paul uses the Greek word *Theópneutos,* which translates into our English word as "inspired." While this Greek word *Theópneutos* means "inspired by God," or "due to the inspiration of God," it is compounded of the two Greek words *Theós* = "God," and *pneuma* = "breath," or "spirit." Thus, the intention here is that God inspired or breathed by the Spirit the sacred Scriptures of the Old and New Testaments.

Since an authentic record of God's acts in the history of man's redemption from the Fall was necessary, it was the function of the Spirit to inspire and direct the accurate recording of those events.

B. The Spirit as the Executor of the Redemptive Plan

However, the Spirit is represented in Scripture as more than an inspirer and director of the divine record. He is also represented as the executor of the divine plan of redemption for man's salvation from the Fall and his restoration to the favor of God, of which the inspired Scriptures are the record. As in the New Testament He takes the things of Christ and makes them known to man, so in the Old Testament He takes the things of the Father and makes them known to men. It is His chief function in the Old Testament to represent God and His redemptive plan and provisions to alienated and lost men. This is the Spirit's work of re-creation in the Old Testament; the re-creation of what was destroyed of the original creation through man's Fall. Obviously, while God's redemptive plan is concerned primarily with man's salvation, it nevertheless extends to the whole creation affected by the Fall (cf. Rom. 8:19-23).

If the primal substance created before the Spirit's cosmic brooding was chaotic, in the sense of being an empty wasteland ("formless and void"), man's disobedience and consequent Fall plunged it into a deeper and more meaningless chaos, spiritually and morally. This was possible by reason of the fact that the primal substance was without intelligence, moral freedom, or responsibility, whereas there entered into the Fall an evil intelligence and design that defied God and His righteous purposes. The apostle Paul saw more vividly and described more graphically man's departure from God and his consequent descent into the maelstrom of evil and self-destruction than any other person throughout the ages, even than Dante or Milton. This depiction is recorded in his letter to the Romans 1:18-32 (cf. Jer. 17:9).

Man's otherwise hopeless state, following his Fall, is ameliorated by the future hope of a promised Messiah-Savior. This is to be a restoration to a golden age, a time when God's Spirit will be poured out without measure upon redeemed man. The Spirit will rest upon the Messiah Himself (Isa. 11:2; 61:1-3; Luke 4:17-19; Matt. 3:16; Mark 1:10; John 1:32). This is to be a time of restoration; a time of re-creation of man (II Cor. 5:17). God's Spirit will be poured out upon man redeemed by the Messiah (Isa. 44:3; Ezek. 39:29). It is Joel's prophecy that Peter seizes upon to identify and explain the effusion of the Spirit at Pentecost (Joel 2:28-32; cf. Acts 2:16-21). This is to be the age of the Spirit. The new age and renewed man will be made possible through the Spirit. William Barclay notes that men's planning may change the world while leaving it very much as it was before; but *only* by the power and activity of the Spirit can the world be recreated to conform to the plan and purpose of God and the sincere desires of men.[5]

Important as was the function of the Spirit in the original creation of the natural world when He brooded over the primal elements and brought a cosmos out of the chaos (Gen. 1:2), and when He breathed into man the breath of life making of him a living person (Gen. 2:7), there remained for Him an even more important work. That was to be the re-creation and restoration of man from the wreckage sustained in the Fall. This re-creative work of the Spirit in man's salvation was to be realized through His conviction of man, His wooing him back to God from sin, and His regeneration of the repentant, believing sinner, plus his sanctification and ultimate glorification. Indeed, the realization of this great re-creative work looks

---

5. *Op. cit.*, p. 20.

to the New Testament era for its fuller realization. However, from the Fall of man to the end of the age it is the work of the Spirit to bring to pass this redemptive plan and purpose. He is not absent from any part of it.

C. The Spirit as the Restorer of the Divine Image in Man

When man lost the moral image of God in the Fall (though not the natural or political image, marred as they were), the Spirit began to strive with man with a view to restoring that image in him. As early in the inspired record as Genesis 6:3 this becomes evident, when God warns that wicked generation before the flood, "My Spirit shall not strive with man forever." Just as the Spirit imparted to man in his original creation the moral image of God's righteousness and holiness, so in His re-creative work He seeks to restore to man that image. In the first instance the Spirit created man perfect in holiness. In the second, or re-creative act, the Spirit's work is to restore man to God in personal righteousness and holiness (Matt. 5:48; Heb. 12:22-24). As in the first creative act the Spirit gave to the inert, chaotic, primal material life, form and perfection, so in His re-creative work he moves upon man in his chaotic, spiritually inanimate condition, imparting to him a new life in Christ—restoring him to the righteousness and holiness that he enjoyed before the Fall (John 3:5-8; cf. II Cor. 5:17).

This is not another creation, as though man was nonexistent as a result of the Fall, a position held by Karl Barth in his earlier thought. Rather, in contrast to creation from an inanimate primal substance as in the first instance, the Spirit's re-creative function in the life of sinful, alienated man is that of restoration, renewal, regeneration, and sanctification. As He animated man in the beginning by breathing into his nostrils the breath of life, so He reanimates man in redemption by breathing into him a new life (John 20:22; Acts 2:1-4; cf. Ezek. 37:1-10).

The work of the Spirit is both physical and spiritual, both creative and re-creative in the Old Testament, as well as the New, in nature as well as in man.

The re-creative work of the Spirit is both personal and racial, both individual and social. He does work in and on the entire race of mankind, first through direct personal and providential means. However, in due time He functioned mainly in salvation history through the especially chosen people Israel, a people divinely chosen through salvation to the service of God to make known to the nations the special revelation of God. Further attention to this aspect of the Spirit's function will be considered in a later context.

D. The Spirit's Re-Creative Function Exemplified in Man

Perhaps the prime example of the Spirit's re-creative work on the personal and individual level is that of David's restoration from his fall, consequent upon his act of adultery with Bathsheba and the planned murder of her husband Uriah, to cover his first sin. In his penitential prayer, as recorded in Psalm 51, he cries out in the agony of his soul for restoration to God's favor: "Do not cast me away from Thy presence, and do not take Thy Holy Spirit from me" (v. 11). David is well aware that his only hope of restoration is through the operation of the Holy Spirit. If He should be withdrawn, all hope would be lost, and it is this that he most fears. What he prays for most desperately is expressed in verse 10: "*Create* in me a clean heart, O God, and *renew* a steadfast [or upright] spirit within me." The *creation* of a *clean heart* and *renewal of an upright spirit* within the penitent is the work of the Spirit. Without the Spirit this could never be accomplished. This is the re-creative work of the Spirit. Verse 17 indicates the accomplished re-creative work of the Spirit in David.

God promised Saul, through His prophet Samuel, on the occasion of his anointing to become King of Israel saying: "The Spirit of the Lord will come upon you *mightily,* and *you shall . . . be changed into another man*" (I Sam. 10:6). Chaos characterized Saul's life only when he later rejected God's Spirit.

But in an even greater measure is the Spirit active in the re-creation of the race. As noted in another context, God's warning to the evil generation before the flood; "My Spirit shall not *strive* with [or, "rule in"] man forever, because he also is flesh [or, "in his going astray he is flesh"] (Gen. 6:3), is a clear indication of the Spirit's efforts to bring alienated and wayward humanity back to the living relationship with God enjoyed before the Fall.

On this function of the Spirit Wesley says:

> The Spirit then strove by *Noah's* preaching, I Peter iii.19, and by inward checks, but 'twas in vain with the most of men, therefore saith God, he shall *not always strive, for that he also is flesh*—incurably corrupt and selfish, so that 'tis labour lost to strive with him. *He also,* that is, all, one as well as another; they are all sunk into the mire of flesh. *Yet his days shall be an hundred and*

twenty years—So long will I defer the judgment they deserve, and give them space to prevent it by their repentance and reformation. Justice said, cut them down; but mercy is interceded, *Lord, let them alone this year also;* and so far mercy prevailed, that a reprieve was obtained for six score years.[6]

Isaiah's inspired prophecy looks to the Spirit for His re-creative work in the future, notwithstanding the destruction and devastation wrought by man's sin and disobedience. The prophet describes in vivid word pictures this re-creative work of the Spirit as follows:

Because the palace has been abandoned, the populated city forsaken. Hill and watch-tower have become caves forever, a delight for wild donkeys, a pasture for flocks; *until the Spirit is poured out upon us from on high* [cf. Acts 2:2-4], and the wilderness becomes a fertile field and the fertile field is considered as a forest. Then justice will dwell in the wilderness, and righteousness will abide in the fertile field. And the work of righteousness will be peace, and the service of righteousness, quietness and confidence forever. Then my people will live in a peaceful habitation, and in secure dwellings and in undisturbed resting places (32:14-18).

As the Spirit brought order into the primal chaos, so He will eventually restore order to the chaotic condition caused by the disruptive effects of man's sin and disobedience. It was man's sinful rejection of God's will that brought about the confusion of languages and consequent separation and scattering of the nations at the tower of Babel. But it was God's Spirit that regathered and united the nations in His mighty effusion at Pentecost. It was to this end that the Spirit's re-creative activities functioned among men and nations throughout the history of the Old Testament.

III. THE SPIRIT OF GOD AND OTHER SPIRITS
IN THE OLD TESTAMENT

An examination of the word *spirit* in a Bible concordance reveals the presence and activities of *spirits* other than God's Spirit in the Old Testament. Those other spirits are sometimes represented as very powerful, but God's Spirit is represented as All-powerful.

A. The Spirit of God in Contrast with the Spirits of Materialistic Militarism in the Old Testament

The prophet Isaiah rebukes Israel for her disposition to rely upon Egypt's military strength for protection and security instead of

6. *Op. cit.* (original), I, 29, 30.

trusting in the spirit of God (Isa. 31:1-3). He warns Israel that "the Egyptians are men, and not God [*él*] and their horses are flesh [*bsar*] and *not spirit* [*ruach*] ." Though the military powers of Egypt are visible and mighty, the invisible power of God's Spirit is almighty, and the former is destined to fall before the latter. If Israel aligns herself with Egypt she will fall with Egypt before the stroke of God.

It may sound like impractical idealism in our day of militarism to recommend reliance upon the power of God's invisible Spirit for security rather than upon the visible machines of war. However, no matter how powerful any nation may become militaristically, every nation that trusts in its military strength is destined to fall to a greater military power eventually.

Many nations have caused the world to stand in fear and jeopardy, but time has proved each one in turn to be vulnerable to some greater power.

Alexander the Great could conquer what he thought to be the world of his day, if the tradition is reliable, but before he could place his seal upon his prize he died and his kingdom fell into four parts. Napoleon built the world's greatest military machines of his day, but he met his Waterloo and spent the rest of his life pining away in exile on the small island of St. Helena in the south Atlantic. Mussolini arose in the first quarter of the twentieth century and promised to revive the ancient Roman Empire and extend his Fascist dominion to the farthest reaches of the globe. But within approximately twenty years (1922-1943) he was defeated by the Allied forces, rejected and killed by his own followers, and his dream-empire fell into ruins.

Hitler followed Mussolini's Fascist fiasco with his wild dream of a Nazi world domination, but within the brief span of approximately a dozen years (1933-1945) his dream was shattered under the mighty stroke of the Allies' military power and Hitler himself, defeated and disillusioned, died from a self-inflicted bullet in his brain. Joseph Stalin and Khrushchev both had their daydreams of world conquest, were finally rejected by their own followers, and then passed into oblivion. And so will others who are of *another spirit* that rejects and seeks to displace the Spirit of God in His own universe.

John saw clearly the presence and function of other spirits in the world that reject and oppose the Spirit of God, and advised the followers of Christ to beware of them thus:

> Beloved, do not believe every spirit, but test the spirits to see whether they are from God; because many false prophets have gone out into the world.

> By this you know the Spirit of God: every spirit that confesses
> that Jesus Christ has come in the flesh is from God;
> and every spirit that does not confess Jesus is not from God; and
> this is the *spirit* of the antichrist, of which you have heard that it is
> coming, and now it is already in the world.
> You are from God, little children, and have overcome them;
> because greater is He who is in you than he who is in the world.
> They are from the world; therefore they speak *as* from the world,
> and the world listens to them (I John 4:1-5).

B. The Spirit of God in Contrast with the Spirits of Mighty Men in the Old Testament

The prophet Zechariah contrasts in vivid and forceful language the Spirit of God with the weakness of man motivated by another spirit. Zechariah reports the angel from Jehovah who spoke with him as bearing a message to Zerubbabel, who was governor of Judea under King Cyrus' appointment at the return of the Jews from seventy years of captivity, as follows: "Not by might nor by power, but by My Spirit, says the Lord of Hosts. What are you, O great mountain? Before Zerubbabel *you will become* a plain; and he will bring forth the top stone with shouts of 'Grace, grace to it' " (4:6-7). Clarke's comment on these words of God to Zerubbabel is noteworthy.

> This prince was in a trying situation, and he needed special encour-
> agement from God; and here it is: *Not by might* (of your own), *nor
> by power* (authority from others) [Cyrus' command to halt the
> building of the temple by reason of the opposition and misrepresen-
> tations of the envious pagan neighbours], *but by my Spirit*—the
> providence, authority, power, and energy of the Most High. In this
> way shall My temple be built; in this way shall My Church be raised
> and preserved. *O great mountain.* The hindrances which were thrown
> in the way, the regal prohibition to discontinue the building of the
> Temple. *Before Zerubbabel . . . a plain.* The sovereign power of God
> shall remove them. March on, Zerubbabel; all shall be made plain
> and smooth before you. *He shall bring forth the headstone.* As he
> has laid the foundation stone, so shall he put on the headstone; as he
> has begun the building, so shall he finish it.[7]

There are no powers of envious and evil men that can thwart the plans and purposes of God when His servants are under the control and power of the Spirit.

C. The Spirit of God in Contrast with the Evil Spirits of Satan and His Cohorts in the Old Testament

The evil spirit of the Adversary, Satan, sought by every conceivable means to destroy the faith of God's servant Job, but in the end

---

7. *Op. cit.,* p. 752.

of the struggle God brought Job out the victor over all of Satan's
infernal devices. Probably the secret of this evil spiritual force
emerges from its misty background most distinctly in the dream-
vision of Eliphaz, recited to Job with a view to breaking down his
faith in God, who in the prologue had pronounced him "a blameless
and upright man, fearing God and turning away from evil" (1:8b).
Under the influence of the Adversary, Eliphaz relates his spooky
dream-vision in a most awe-inspiring manner.

> Now a word was brought to me stealthily [or secretly], and my ear
> received a whisper of it. Amid disquieting thoughts from the visions
> of the night, when deep sleep falls on men, Dread came upon me,
> and trembling, and made all my bones shake. Then a spirit passed by
> my face; the hair of my flesh bristled up. It stood still, but I could
> not discern its appearance. A form was before my eyes; there was
> silence, then I heard a voice: "Can mankind be just before God? Can
> a man be pure before his Maker? He puts no trust even in His
> servants and against His angels He charges error" (4:12-18)

The personality and cunning wits of Satan and his accomplices
have never been set in bolder relief than in C. S. Lewis's world-
famous allegory, *Screwtape Letters*.

The apostle Paul likewise takes note of the presence in the world
of the prince of the power of the air, "the spirit that is now working
in the sons of disobedience" (Eph. 2:2b), the chief of the spirits that
stand in opposition to the person and work of God's Spirit.

D. The Spirit of God in Contrast with Those Having "Familiar Spirits" in the Old Testament

There were in the Old Testament, as there are today, men and
women, but particularly women, who were characterized by "familiar spirits." They appear in a number of instances in the Old Testament record.

The term "familiar spirit" in the Old Testament is used generally
to indicate the spirit of a dead person who is consulted by professed
spiritualist mediums who claim the ability to summon that departed
spirit back for consultation (Deut. 18:11). The very term "familiar"
derives from the Latin word *familiaris,* which indicates one's family.
Consequently such a "familiar [or family] spirit" was supposed to be
ready to serve the living as needed.

"Familiar spirits" were regarded as possessing secret knowledge of
the future which they could reveal to the inquiring living (I Sam.
28:7). God forbade the Israelites under pain of execution to consult
"familiar spirits" (Lev. 19:31; Isa. 8:19). To do so was regarded as

apostasy deserving of death (Lev. 20:6). Very early in his reign King Saul destroyed all the mediums in his realm except one. Apparently he spared the Witch of Endor for possible future reference, which was but another evidence of his incomplete obedience to the commands of God. When he became apostate and was rejected of God, Saul himself went to this woman with the "familiar spirit" just before his death, in desperate hope of a message from the departed prophet Samuel, but instead his despair was only deepened (I Sam. 28:3-25; I Chron. 10:13). (See other reference to "familiar spirits" in Lev. 20:27; II Chron. 33:6; Isa. 8:19; 19:3; I Sam. 28:3-9; II Kings 21:6; 23:24.)

Perhaps the most notorious, and saddest, contemporary example of apostasy from the Christian faith that led to the consultation of the spirits of the departed through a spiritualist medium is that of the world-famed Bishop James Pike, who finally lost his life in a fall from a cliff near Qumran in Israel in August 1969. It is one of the saddest commentaries upon the degeneracy of American and English society that there has recurred a widespread recrudescence of this brand of spiritism in recent decades. The author was amazed recently when told by a spiritualist medium that the pastor of one of the largest churches in a city of one hundred thousand people came to him regularly to consult the spirits of the departed. Such a practice is one of the clearest marks of awful religious apostasy known to God or man. It is a most insidious species of idolatry. Little wonder that the punishment was so severe against the practice in Old Testament times.

IV. THE SPIRIT OF GOD IN RELATION TO SPECIAL HUMAN ACHIEVEMENTS OF CERTAIN MEN IN THE OLD TESTAMENT

A. The Spirit's Gifts of Artistry and Craftmanship

There are certain instances in the Old Testament where the Spirit is represented as bestowing supernatural gifts upon selected individuals in the natural realms which made of them skillful artisans. In such instances these are not human attainments *per se,* but rather the results of supernatural gifts from God's Spirit bestowed upon them with divine purpose in relation to the redemptive plan. While these Spirit-inspired gifts are individually given, they are not for the personal benefit or aggrandizement of the recipient. Rather the divine purpose is theocentric—that is, for the control, direction, and function of Israel as God's chosen instrument to bring salvation to the world.

A notable example of such a supernatural gift in the natural realm is that of Bezalel and his associates in the service of God for the construction of the tabernacle and its appointments. The Book of Exodus gives a graphic picture of the divine choice of Bezalel and his associates and God's gifts for their special service which reads as follows:

> Now the Lord spoke to Moses, saying,
> 'See, I have called by name Bezalel, the son of Uri, the son of Hur, of the Tribe of Judah. And I have filled him with the Spirit of God in wisdom, in understanding, in knowledge, and in all *kinds of* craftsmanship, to make artistic designs for work in gold, in silver, and in bronze, and in the cutting of stones for settings, and in the carving of wood, that he may work in all *kinds of* craftsmanship. And behold, I Myself, have appointed with him Oholiab, the son of Ahisamach, of the tribe of Dan; and in the hearts of all who are skillful I have put skill, that they may make all that I have commanded you: the tent of meeting, and the ark of testimony, and the mercy seat upon it, and all the furniture of the tent, the table also and its utensils, and the pure *gold* lamp stand with all its utensils, and the altar of incense, the altar of burnt offering also with all its utensils, and the laver and its stand, the woven garments as well, and the holy garments for Aaron the priest, and the garments of his sons, *with which* to carry on their priesthood; the anointing oil also, and the fragrant incense for the holy place, they are to make *them* according to all that I have commanded you (31:1-11).

It is especially noteworthy that God says: "*I have called by name Bezalel. . . . And I have filled him with the Spirit of God in wisdom, in understanding, in knowledge, and in all kinds of craftsmanship.*" Primary among the Spirit's gifts to Bezalel is *wisdom*. Wisdom (*chokma*) was very highly esteemed among the Hebrews, as also among many of the ancient extra-Israelitish peoples. The inclusion in the Old Testament canon of the Books of Esther, Job, Proverbs, and Ecclesiastes is eloquent testimony to the value placed upon such wisdom literature by the Jews. Wisdom, as the word is used in relation to Bezalel's gifts, evidently suggests the ability to judge what was wise or best to be done in a given circumstance, or what might be termed good practical judgment.

Clarke sees the word *understanding* (*tebunah*) as meaning "to separate, distinguish, discern"; or it may suggest "the capacity to comprehend the different parts of a work, how to connect, arrange, in order to make a complete well-balanced and ordered whole."[8]

---

8. *Ibid.*, p. 143.

Perhaps the idea is best understood as architectural and construction ability to design and bring to completion a substantial and well-ordered piece of work in accordance with God's plan (cf. Exod. 25:40; Heb. 8:5). *Knowledge (daath)* Clarke thinks, denotes "particular acquaintance with a person or a thing; practical experimental knowledge."[9] *All kinds of craftmanship,* or "cunning works" *(machashaboth)* suggests "works of invention or genius in the goldsmith and silversmith line."[10]

It may be, however, that Bezalel and his associates were divinely chosen for their natural abilities and aptitudes which were illumined, quickened, and developed under the power and wisdom of God's Spirit bestowed upon them, rather than gifts of skill *per se* bestowed upon them by the Spirit. Such would seem to be the meaning of Exodus 31:6: "in the hearts of all who are skillful I have put skill [margin, wisdom], that they may make all that I have commanded you." Such would seem to be in harmony with God's manner of selecting and working through His servants.

Perhaps if the truth were known all the great artists and architects of the ages who have produced the classics of the Judeo-Christian culture owe more to the gifts of God's Spirit than may be realized. Perhaps such artistic classics as those of Leonardo daVinci, Handel, Bach, and many others owe more to the Spirit of God than to the natural geniuses of the artists.

B. The Spirit's Gifts of Superhuman Physical Powers

These superhuman powers may in a certain sense be regarded as the Spirit's special use of men's natural endowments. But in another sense the Bible recognizes even man's natural endowments as God's gifts to men. When God inspired the newly formed body of man with the breath *(ruach,* spirit) of life and he became a living soul, or person (Gen. 2:7), this was God's gift of life to man with all his natural powers, at least in potential. And even the development of those potentialities in man was, and is, in a certain real sense the gift of God to man.

The Spirit's brooding over the natural chaos brought out of those primal elements a living, Spirit-sustained organism that we call the cosmos, or universe, which affords the necessary conditions for even

---

9. *Ibid.*
10. *Ibid.*

the so-called natural life of man. Should God withdraw His sustaining Spirit from this universe it would revert automatically to an uninhabitable chaos—formless and meaningless.

Job seems to identify his very temporal life with the Spirit of God when he says, "For as long as life is in me, and the breath [*ruach*, Spirit] of God is in my nostrils" (27:3). Even the young Elihu, however irrelevant his tirade against Job may be otherwise, agrees with Job in his essential understanding that man's very rational life is from God (32:8; 33:4). Paul's view would seem to harmonize essentially with this Old Testament position when he looks upon all of man's abilities, even to sexual continence, as a special gift from God (I Cor. 7:7-9; cf. 9:5; 12:4, 11; Rom 12:6a). Even the words of Christ in this relationship demand serious consideration (see Matt. 19:4-12, but especially 11, 12). Thus we may reasonably inquire, Does man possess anything of value that is not a gift from God? Paul did not seem to think so.

Several Old Testament characters, especially in the Book of Judges, furnish notable examples of the foregoing position. Among these none, perhaps, stand out more vividly than Samson. Certainly the moral character and conduct of Samson sometimes falls far short of the Judeo-Christian ethical standard. Nevertheless we read of Samson that when he was confronted with the attack of a vicious young lion, "The Spirit (*ASV*) of the Lord *came* [lit. "rushed"] *upon him mightily,* so that he tore him as one tears a kid [young goat] though he had nothing in his hand . . . " (Judg. 14:6a).

Clarke remarks on this incident that "his strength does not appear to be his own, nor to be at his command. His might was, by the will of God, attached to his hair and to his being a Nazarite."[11]

Earlier in Judges we are informed that from childhood "the Lord blessed him. And the Spirit of the Lord began to stir him . . . " (13:24b-25a).

Clarke comments that the blessing of the Lord upon Samson "Gave evident proof that the child was under the peculiar protection of the Most High, causing him to increase daily in stature and extra-ordinary strength." Further, Clarke notes, "He felt the degrading bondage of his countrymen, and a strong desire to accomplish something for their deliverance. These feelings and motions he had from the Divine Spirit. Thus God began, from Samson's infancy, to qualify him for the work to which he had called him."[12]

---

11. *Ibid.,* p. 280.
12. *Ibid.*

On another occasion when Samson was betrayed by his Philistine wife, who told the secret of his riddle to her countrymen, we are informed that "Then *the Spirit of the Lord came* [lit. "rushed"] *upon him mightily and* . . . he killed thirty of their men and gave the spoils to their fellows" (Judg. 14:19). On yet another occasion when he was bound and delivered to his enemies for execution, we are informed that *"the Spirit of the Lord came* [lit. "rushed"] *upon him mightily* so that the ropes that were on his arms [possibly his arms and his legs] were as flax that is burned with fire, and his bonds dropped from his hands. And he found the fresh jawbone of a donkey, so he reached out and took it and killed a thousand men with it" (Judg. 15:12-15).

Though it is not so stated, it might be logically inferred that it was by a special empowerment of God's Spirit that Samson was enabled to remove and carry away on his shoulders at midnight the heavy city gate, with the pillars and bars, notwithstanding his questionable conduct in the city during the earlier hours of the night (Judg. 16:1-3). Likewise it would seem to be a legitimate inference that it was by the special power of God's Spirit that Samson was able to bring down the house of the Philistines with the destruction of their lives as his last mighty act (Judg. 16:23-31).

By way of contrast, it is noteworthy that when Samson was left to himself without the aid of God's Spirit he was helpless in the hands of his enemies, the Philistines. Thus when betrayed by Delilah and shorn of his locks, which were the divine symbol of his God-given strength, he fell as easy prey to his enemies. Clarke remarks wittily of Samson's love for and marriage to Delilah of the Philistines: "however strong his love was for her, she seems to have had none for him. He always matched improperly, and he was cursed in all his matches . . . . What a consummate fool was this strong man! After trifling with her, and lying thrice, he at last commits to her his fatal secret, and thus becomes a traitor to himself and to his God."[13]

The glaring inconsistencies in Samson's life may be best understood in the light of Clarke's reconciliation of the matter.

> His [Samson's] jurisdiction seems to have been very limited and have extended no farther than over those parts of the tribe of Dan contiguous to the land of the Philistines . . . . Many suppose that he and Eli were contemporaries, Samson being rather an executor of the divine upon the enemies of his people than an administrator of the civil and religious laws of the Hebrews. Allowing Eli and Samson

---

13. *Ibid.,* p. 282.

to have been contemporaries, this latter might have been entirely committed to the care of Eli.[14]

Another example of the bestowal of the Spirit upon an individual for the deliverance of God's people from the threats of their enemies is that of Jephthah. When challenged by the king of the sons of Ammon, Jephthah took the initiative against the enemy, and we read that *"the Spirit of the Lord came upon Jephthah* so that he passed through Gilead and Manasseh, then he passed through Mizpah of Gilead, and from Mizpah of Gilead he went on to the sons of Ammon" (Judg. 11:29). Though Jephthah possessed unusual military talent, he was an outcast from his own family. The narrator sets him in bold relief by saying: "Now Jephthah the Gileadite was a valiant warrior [or, "mighty man of valor"], but he was the son of a harlot" (Judg. 11:1a). It was this unfortunate circumstance of his life that placed him in disfavor with his family and people. However, it was his special enduement with the Spirit of God that brought him to the generalship of their army and victory over their enemy.

Certainly one of the most notable examples of deliverance wrought for Israel from intended destruction at the hands of their enemies was that of Gideon. When "the Spirit of the Lord came upon Gideon" (Judg. 6:34a) he was endowed with such military wisdom and courage as enabled him with three hundred select soldiers to completely defeat and rout the vast armies of "the Midianites and Amalekites and the sons of the east assembled" against Israel with the purpose of destroying them (Judg. 6:33).

The operation of God's Spirit in the natural realm is particularly characteristic of the Old Testament. While such is present in the New Testament it plays a minor role for the most part at least. One notable exception is seen in Paul's letter to the Romans where all creation seems to anticipate sharing in the redemptive-restoration to be accomplished by the Spirit (Rom. 8:19-23).

V. THE SPIRIT IN RELATION TO THE OLD TESTAMENT PROPHETS

The Old Testament prophets were men of the Spirit. They had no official political position in Israel such as characterized the priests. They were directly called of God, and their personal characteristics and the power of the Spirit upon their lives and ministry determined

---

14. *Ibid.,* p. 283.

their status and the extent of their influence. They spoke under the divine direction and inspiration of the Spirit. The initiative and sovereignty of God characterized their mission and message. Their objective was to bring individual men, but especially leaders, and the nations into alignment with God's will and purpose for Israel and the human race.

A. Characteristics of Old Testament Prophetic Ministry

The Old Testament prophetic ministry displays four chief characteristics.

First, as contrasted with the priests, whose office was hereditary, the prophets were directly chosen from among the people without regard to tribe, occupation, or social status, and called by God to do their work. Such was the experience of Samuel (I Sam. 3:1-14), Elijah (I Kings 17:1-6), Isaiah (1:1; 6:1-13), Jeremiah (1:1-10), Amos (7:14-15), and others whose records are found in the Old Testament. Their personal lives bore a direct relation to their messages.

Second, while the priests represented the people before God, the prophets represented God to the people. It might be somewhat of an over-simplification to say that the priests prayed to God for the people while the prophets spoke for God to the people. There was, as a matter of fact, often an overlapping of the functions of the two classes. But in general the priest faced the altar of God in the interest of the people, while the prophet faced the people with God's concern and message for them. Herein lies one of the chief differences between the Roman Catholic priesthood and the Protestant ministry. It is significant that Christ fulfilled both functions, plus the kingly office.

Third, the function of the priest was more or less perfunctory. Prophets spoke out of burning hearts the Spirit-inspired messages of God needed for the times and occasions. They bore "the burden of the Lord." While in a certain sense the "burden of the Lord" referred to the Spirit's message laid upon the prophet's heart, in another very real sense it represented the prophets' soul-suffering under the often unpleasant and condemnatory messages they were commissioned to deliver, sometimes even at the peril of their lives.

A fourth distinctive feature of the prophet's function was the unpleasant task of opposing and denouncing the false prophets who spoke in their own names, or whose messages were based upon their subjective experiences purported to be from God. This is vividly portrayed in the prophecy of Ezekiel thus:

> Then the word of the Lord came to me saying, "Son of man, prophesy against the prophets of Israel who prophesy, and say to those who prophesy from their own inspiration, 'Listen to the word of the Lord! Thus says the Lord God, "Woe to the foolish prophets who are following their own spirit and have seen nothing . . . . They see falsehood [lit., vanity] and lying divination who are saying, 'The Lord declares,' when the Lord has not sent them; yet they hope for the fulfillment of their word." . . . Therefore thus says the Lord God, "because you have spoken falsehood [lit., vanity] and seen a lie, therefore behold, I am against you," declares the Lord God' " (13:1-4, 6, 8).

On Ezekiel's scathing denunciatory words against these false prophets in 13:5, "You have not gone into the breaches, nor did you build the wall around the house of Israel to stand in the battle on the day of the Lord," Clarke says, "Far from opposing sinners, you are bringing down the wrath of God upon the place, you prevent their repentance by your flattering promises and false predictions."[15]

B. Ethical Qualities of Old Testament Prophetic Ministry

The ethical quality of the prophetic ministry in the Old Testament seems to have improved with the later prophets over some of the earlier ones. This becomes evident when the great and exalted ethical ideals of such prophets as Isaiah, Jeremiah, Ezekiel, Daniel, and certain others among the so-called minor prophets are compared with such sometimes irresponsible men as Saul (I Sam. 10:1-13) and Balaam (Num. 22:4-35; 23:1-30; 24:1-25; 31:8, 16). The sad ends of both of these men testify to the defectiveness of their characters. However, such irresponsible prophets are not limited to the earlier Old Testament times. Paul also had them to deal with in the early Christian church at Corinth with their subjective ecstatic experiences of glossolalia (I Cor. 12; 14).

Under the special inspiration of God's Spirit upon the later Old Testament prophets, religion rose to the highest spiritual and ethical level known to the world before the advent of Christ and Christianity. The special enduement of the Spirit of God was the true prophet's credentials. Isaiah and Jeremiah each make direct reference to the Spirit of God more than twenty times in their great prophecies. While the enduement of God's Spirit for the prophetic ministry seems to have been permanent with many of the great Old Testament prophets, with certain others used of God it was evidently temporary. This is evident in the case of Saul and certain others (see Num.

15. *Ibid.*, p. 668.

11:25-29). Nor was the enduement of God's Spirit for a prophetic function always related to the life and character of the prophet, as witness the lives of Saul and Balaam.

C. Transfer of the Spirit in the Old Testament Prophetic Ministry

Another interesting characteristic of the enduement of the Spirit in relation to prophecy in the Old Testament is the transfer of the Spirit from one prophet to another. Such was the case with Elijah and Elisha (II Kings 2:15), with Samuel and David (I Sam. 16:13-14), and with Moses and certain chosen men of Israel (Num. 11:17, 25, 26, 29).

Sometimes the prophets underwent a period of special training, formally or otherwise, before being endued with the Spirit for their ministry, as in the case of Samuel under Eli (I Sam. 2:18-19, 26; 3:1-21), and the sons of prophets under Elijah (II Kings 2:1-18). In other instances they seem to have been called directly from their previous occupations and endued with God's Spirit for their mission without any formal preparation, as in the case of Amos (1:1; 7:14-15).

D. Twofold Purpose of Old Testament Prophets

These Old Testament Spirit-called and inducted prophets served a twofold function. They were primarily preachers with messages of rebuke, warning, correction, and direction from Jehovah for the people of their country and day, as also often for the surrounding pagan nations. This required great courage on their part as they frequently met with opposition and persecution from the political and even religious leaders. Their credentials were for the most part their Spirit-inspired utterances, frequently introduced with the words "Thus saith the Lord." Their counterparts have been the God-sent evangelists of most every succeeding age.

However, the Old Testament prophets were also *foretellers,* or men with messages concerning future events not yet realized. Those messages sometimes warned of coming judgment and destruction, they were usually tempered with promises and bright rays of hope, on condition of repentance and return to the ways of God. Because the elements of optimism outweighed the note of pessimism in their message they were, for the most part at least, idealists—though realistic idealists. Jeremiah is perhaps the least optimistic among the

Old Testament prophets. It is interesting, and somewhat puzzling, that *Strong's Exhaustive Concordance of the Bible* does not list one direct reference to the Spirit of God in the entire prophecy of Jeremiah, while more than twenty are listed in each of Isaiah and Ezekiel.

These Old Testament prophets were often called *seers*. It appears that they were more than simply revealers of the omniscient mind of God concerning future events. Apparently when under the influence of the Spirit's inspiration they were often transported mentally into the future, as time is known to man, and thus shared temporarily in the transcendent, *timeless* knowledge of God (see II Kings 17:13; II Chron. 33:18-19; Isa. 29:10; 30:10; Mic. 3:7).

A special characteristic of Ezekiel's prophecy, though variously expressed, is that the Spirit transported him in space and time during his prophetic visions. Thus we read: "the Spirit lifted me up" (3:12); "the Spirit lifted me up and took me away" (3:14); "the Spirit lifted me up between earth and heaven" (8:3); "the Spirit lifted me up and brought me to the east gate of the Lord's house" (11:1); "the Spirit lifted me up and brought me in a vision by the Spirit of God to the exiles in Chaldea" (11:24); "He [God] brought me out by the Spirit of the Lord and set me down in the middle of the valley" (37:1); and "the Spirit lifted me up and brought me into the inner court" (43:5). Except for the revelation given to John on Patmos, the records of such experiences are relatively rare in the New Testament. Indeed Paul speaks of having been "caught up to the third heaven . . . into Paradise, and heard inexpressible words, which a man is not permitted to speak" (II Cor 12:2, 4). But such a record is exceptional.

It should be emphasized that the messages of the Old Testament prophets, while designed primarily for the historical situations of their own people and day, were *nonetheless timeless in their significance*. They presented the great moral and spiritual principles on which God deals with men, a fact which gave their messages permanent significance for all times and all people.

VI. THE SPIRIT OF GOD *UPON* AND *IN* MEN IN THE OLD TESTAMENT

While there are occasional exceptions to the general rule, a characteristic expression relative to the Spirit in the Old Testament is that *He "came mightily* [or "rushed"] *upon"* a selected servant of God for a special mission. In the New Testament such an expression is seldom used. Rather, the Spirit in the New Testament is represented, for the most part at least, as indwelling men and thus empowering and working from within the hearts and lives of men. Indeed, at the first Christian Pentecost at Jerusalem the effusion of the Spirit is represented under the symbol of "a noise like a violent, rushing wind, [which] filled the house where they were sitting" (Acts 2:2). However, the Acts record does not leave the matter there. Rather it continues "And they [the 120 disciples] were *all filled with the Holy Spirit*" (v. 4).

That there are exceptions to this general rule, both in the Old Testament and the New is obvious. However, for the most part the Old Testament believers looked forward to the time of which the prophets spoke when God would write His laws upon hearts of flesh by His Spirit, rather than on tablets of stone (cf. Jer. 31:32-33; II Cor. 3:3; Heb. 8:10; 10:16).

As already noted, men upon whom God placed His Spirit for the accomplishment of certain redemptive acts were not always men of right hearts or approved ethical conduct. Such, however, cannot be said of New Testament believers indwelt by the Spirit of God. They were men of clean hearts and pure motives who walked blamelessly, though not faultlessly, before God.

Strong's Exhaustive Concordance lists approximately one hundred direct references to the Spirit of God in the entire Old Testament. Approximately seventy-five, or about three-fourths, of the total references to the Spirit in the Old Testament describe Him as influencing men externally, and in some cases at least, using them instrumentally. On the other hand only approximately one-fourth of the references to the Spirit in the Old Testament represent Him as in some manner inhabiting man internally, though not necessarily permanently.

The chief significance of the difference between the Spirit's external influence upon men and His indwelling presence in the Old Testament is ethical. This ethical significance is twofold. It is understandable that God may sovereignly influence and even use a person instrumentally without the conscious consent of the individual's will. Such appears to have been the case with King Cyrus, who is called My Servant by God. Cyrus certainly was not the servant of God in the sense of the commitment of his life to God. He was, however, in the instrumental sense that he provided for the return of the Jews from captivity. In the second place God's Spirit is *the Holy Spirit of God*. Since the Spirit is entirely holy His personal presence necessarily and automatically purifies, or sanctifies, the place of His dwelling. Thus for men to be indwelt by God's Holy Spirit means that they are inwardly purified by His presence.

It is this sanctifying efficacy of the Spirit's personal presence that accounts for the spiritual form of worship in the Old Testament, as contrasted with the more prevalent legalistic and ritualistic type of Old Testament worship. This Old Testament spiritual worship is much more prevalent in the Psalms and the Prophets than in other Old Testament books. This fact accounts for the greater devotional value of these books than other Old Testament literature.

Chapter 3

The Person and Ministry
of the Spirit from the Prophets
to the New Testament

I. THE SPIRIT IN THE OLD TESTAMENT IN RELATION
TO THE COMING OF THE MESSIAH

A. The Prophetic Ministry in Relation to the
Hope of the Messiah-Savior

There are many evidences in the Old Testament of a divinely promised future Messiah-Savior, all the way from the first hint given in Genesis 3:15 to the last book of the Old Testament. However, it is in the Psalms and the writings of the prophets that this great promised hope becomes most evident—sometimes even quite explicit. It is in this Old Testament literature that we discover some of the richest spiritual insights into the nature of that future hope. It is here that the person and work of the Holy Spirit becomes most evident in the Old Testament.

From the sixth century onward to the coming of Christ the whole ancient world seems pregnant with the expectant hope of a coming Messiah-Redeemer. A variety of factors contributed to this awakened hope. To even mention them would be beyond the purpose of the present work. It must suffice to note only a few of the ancient evidences of this hope. Huffman calls attention to the following. Zoroaster, the reputed founder of the Zoroastrian religion, known in India as the Parsis, who probably lived from about 660-583 B.C., is reported to have said: "God will never be known unless he reveals himself in human form." Socrates (c. 470-399 B.C.) is said to have exclaimed "Oh, that someone would arise, man or God, to show us God." Plato (c. 427-347 B.C.) is reported to have said: "Unless a God-man comes to us, and reveals to us the Supreme Being, there is no hope." The pagan Roman philosopher-statesman Seneca (c. 7 B.C.-A.D. 65) queried: "Where shall he be found for whom we have been looking so many centuries?" Many others could be added to the list. Angus refers to these messianic expectations as "Voices crying in the wilderness of paganism."[1]

It is noteworthy that the captivities and exiles of the ten northern tribes of Israel (c. 722 B.C.), and Judah to the south (c. 586 B.C.) approximate the rise of Greek philosophy (Thales, b. 625 B.C.) and the births of several of the ancient world's great religious founders. This was also the era of several of Israel's greatest prophets. Jimmu Tenno, the reputed first divine emperor of Japan, and in that sense founder of the Japanese Shinto religion, is supposed to have been born in 660 B.C. Lao-tze, the founder of the Chinese Taoist religion, was born in 604 B.C. Mahavira, the founder of the Jain religion in India, was born in 599 B.C. And Gautama Buddha, the father of the great Oriental religion of Buddhism, was born in 560 B.C.

Thus there appears to have been a somewhat general religious awakening in the ancient world of the seventh and sixth centuries B.C. Can it be that the scattering of the exiled Jews among the pagan nations of this era served to spark this philosophico-religious renaissance? Can it be that the Spirit of God present in the midst of these Jews inspiring the hope of a messianic deliverer was responsible for the awakening in the minds of many pagans of a similar hope of salvation, however perverted the expression of that hope may have become? May the apostle Paul have had something of this in mind when he wrote in his Galatian letter: "When the fulness of time came, God sent forth His Son, born of a woman, born under the Law, in order that He might redeem those who were under the Law, that we might receive the adoption of sons" (4:4-5)? Be this as it

---

1. Jasper A. Huffman, *The Unique Person of Christ* (Winona Lake, Ind.: Standard Press, 1955), pp. 117-125.

may, the Spirit's inspiration of the messianic expectation in the prophets is clearly evident.

B. The Anointing with Oil as a Symbol of Enduement with the Spirit

Besides its medicinal use in Bible times, anointing the head with oil symbolized divine blessing (Ps. 23:5-6), and divine blessing was administered by the Spirit of God. Thus "the anointed of the Lord" was one upon whom the Spirit of God rested. The prophets' credentials from God for their mission and message consisted in the fact that their heads were anointed with oil, symbolizing their enduement with the Spirit of God. Furthermore, this anointing signified their qualification for service by Jehovah. The prophet Isaiah foresees the future Messiah as one anointed with the Spirit for His redemptive mission, and speaking for Him he says: "The Spirit of the Lord . . . has anointed me to bring good tidings to the afflicted" (61:1a). Jesus quotes this very prophecy and applies it to Himself in the synagogue at Nazareth (Luke 4:18). The apostolic church referred to Christ as "Thy holy Servant Jesus, whom Thou didst anoint" (Acts 4:27; cf. 10:38). Likewise Paul recognizes anointing as signifying the Holy Spirit when he writes to the Corinthians, "Now He who establishes us with you in Christ and anointed us is God" (II Cor. 1:21).

The relationship of anointing with oil to the bestowal of the Spirit was made clear when Samuel anointed David king. "Then Samuel took the horn of oil and anointed him in the midst of his brothers; and the Spirit of the Lord came mightily upon David from that day forward" (I Sam. 16:13). The transferability of the Spirit from one individual to another is also exemplified at David's anointing, for it is said that *"the Spirit* of the Lord *departed from Saul"* (v. 14). It is further instructive to note that with the departure of God's Spirit from Saul, an evil spirit came upon him (I Sam. 16:14, 23). Since most Bible versions, including the *NASB* and the *RSV*, say "an *evil spirit from the Lord*," which poses a serious problem of interpretation, Clarke's comments on these words are highly significant. He states:

> The word *evil* is not in the common Hebrew text, but it is in the Vulgate, Septuagint, Targum, Syriac, and Arabic. The Septuagint leaves out "of God," and has "the evil spirit." The Targum says, "The evil spirit from before the Lord"; and the Arabic has it, "The evil spirit by the permission of God"; this is at least the sense.[2]

---

2. *Op cit.*, p. 309.

Charles R. Wilson says on this incident that "while David developed in those virtues nurtured by the Spirit, Saul deteriorated to a state bordering on insanity."[3] And another says: "All antiquity was at one in ascribing . . . mind-sickness . . . to evil spirits . . . since Yahweh was supreme in the realm of Spirits, the evil spirit could only come from Him and by His permission."[4] The most likely resolution of this problem is that Saul's sad condition was both the result of a deep melancholy and harassment by a diabolical spirit which were permitted by God, since His protective Spirit was removed from Saul, though they were not sent upon Saul by God. It is hardly evident that Saul was demon possessed, though he was at times sadly demon oppressed.

C. Special References to Spirit-Inspired Prophecies of the Messiah-Savior's Advent

It goes without argument that certain Old Testament passages concerning the future Messiah-Savior are less clear than others. However, to deny the presence of such references in the Old Testament is tantamount to denying the divine inspiration of both the Old Testament that predicts His advent, and the New Testament that recognizes these predictions as having their fulfillment in Christ, including Christ's own testimony (Luke 4:18-21), as well as those of the apostles.

While such passages as I Samuel 2:10 and Psalms 2:2 may lack *clear* evidence of messianic prediction, there are many others in which the Spirit's inspiration leaves no reasonable doubt. Where Isaiah prophesies concerning the "stem of Jesse," upon whom "the Spirit of the Lord will rest" (11:1-10), Paul applies this very prophecy to Christ (Rom. 15:8-13).

In Isaiah 40-66 is found the figure of the *Servant of the Lord* who is to be anointed with the Spirit for His special redemptive mission.

In Isaiah 42:1 the prophet, speaking for the Lord, calls the Messiah "my Servant," "my chosen one," and designates Him *the one upon whom "I have put my Spirit,"* and declares that "He will bring forth justice to the nations [or, "Gentiles"]." From the figure of Cyrus, who was to be God's secular servant for the restoration of

---

3. *The Wesleyan Bible Commentary*, Vol. I, Part 2 (Grand Rapids: Wm. B. Eerdmans Publishing Company, 1967), p. 166.

4. A. R. S. Kennedy, "The Book of Samuel," *The New Century Bible* (London: Coxton, n.d.), p. 119.

the Jews to their land from seventy years of captivity, the prophet proceeds in unveiled language to describe His spiritual servant, the Messiah, who will accomplish the far greater deliverance of Jew and Gentile alike from their captivity to sin and Satan. Clarke remarks of this prophecy that "Matthew has applied it directly to Christ (Matt. 12:16-21), nor can it with any justice or propriety be applied to any other person or character whatsoever."[5]

There occurs in Isaiah 48:16 a messianic reference which has caused no little difficulty of interpretation. It reads: "And now the Lord God has sent Me, and His Spirit." Clarke's resolution of the apparent ambiguity of these words is probably the best available explanation. He sees it as meaning "the Father, who hath sent both Christ and the Holy Spirit."[6] Any careful reading of the New Testament makes it clear that both Christ and the Holy Spirit were sent to this world of men on their redemptive mission—Christ to provide salvation and the Spirit to administer to needy men the saving provisions of Christ.

Isaiah 59:21 appears to be an address by God through the prophet to the Messiah. Thus understood, the words, "My Spirit which is upon you, and My words which I have put in your mouth, shall not depart from your mouth," would seem to mean the Father's assurance that because the Spirit of God rests upon the Messiah His mission will be successfully accomplished.

It is probable that the prophet's primary allusion in Isaiah 61:1 is to himself as the herald of Israel's deliverance from their Babylonian captivity. However, the application does not rest there, for in Luke 4:18 Jesus applies this very prophecy to His own messianic mission. The Spirit rested upon Him because He was anointed for this special redemptive mission. No part of Christ's mission can be separated from the presence and power of the Spirit. The special anointing and descent of the Spirit upon Christ for His redemptive mission occurred at the Jordan River when He was baptized by John (Matt. 3:16-17; Mark 1:10; John 1:32).

II. THE SPIRIT IN MAN'S PERSONAL AND FUNCTIONAL RELATIONSHIP TO GOD IN THE OLD TESTAMENT

For the most part the Old Testament prophets were simply private citizens before they were called of God to their prophetic ministry.

---

5. *Op. cit.*, p. 595.
6. *Ibid.*, p. 600.

Whatever his relationship to God before his call to the prophetic office, as a prophet he bore a direct concern and responsibility for the moral and spiritual welfare of those under his ministry. Through their relationship to God and His will for their lives, whether as private citizens, public servants, rulers, or nations, the prophet sought to bring men into alignment with God's will and purposes. However, for the effectiveness of such a mission the prophet was under obligation to both God and society for his own personal relationship to God and the rectitude of his life.

In the background of their thinking, and the messages they bore, was always the twofold relationship of the commandments of God—man's responsibility to God as set forth in the first four commandments of the Decalogue, and his responsibility to society as set forth in the last six commandments of the Decalogue. As a man God dealt with the prophet on an individual basis. As a servant of God he was dealt with as a representative of those to whom he was sent to minister. However, in either event he was dealt with by God's Spirit as an individual in his relationship with and responsibility to God.

No better example of the foregoing is found in the Old Testament than that of Isaiah, especially as given in the sixth chapter of his prophecy. While the Spirit is not directly mentioned in this account, it is reasonable to assume that He is God's representative in dealing with the prophet during a decadent and dangerous period of the nation's history. The king who had reigned so long, and for a time so well, fell under the curse of God with leprosy during the later years of his life, and the kingdom consequently suffered serious decline. Political, moral, and religious corruption was destroying the nation from within, and powerful militaristic forces were threatening it from without. The young prophet took upon his heart a deep concern for the situation. As he bore this concern before God the divine response revealed to him, first, his personal need. Thus having seen God in His thrice-holy character, Isaiah is made to cry out, "Woe is me, for I am ruined! Because I am a man of unclean lips" (v. 5a).

However, Isaiah's confession extends to the interest of the kingdom of which he was a part, and to which he bears a personal and prophetic responsibility: "I live among a people of unclean lips" (v. 5b). The secret of his vision of the personal and social conditions is given in his own words as follows: "For my eyes have seen the King, the Lord of Hosts" (v. 5c). The spiritual illumination that wrung this confession from his lips also brought the divine remedy for his confessed condition. A live coal from the altar of sacrifice in the heavenly temple, which prefigured the Messiah's redemptive sacrifice, touched his lips and he was pronounced clean. It was then that he received and accepted his divine commission to bring to the nation of unclean lips the cleansing message of God's righteousness. His was a depth of inner spiritual experience that closely approximated the New Testament Christian experience under the Spirit's searching.

Beyond the prophet as a person, the Spirit of God is especially concerned with the prophet's message and his responsibility to deliver that message to the people for whom it is designed. The Spirit gave to Balaam his message concerning Israel's future greatness (Num. 24:2). But the Spirit was equally concerned for the effective delivery of that message. Therefore, when Balaam hesitated and wavered, even a donkey was supernaturally used to persuade the prophet to accept his responsibility. David, though not a prophet in the regular sense of the term, nevertheless recognized himself as a spokesman for God under the inspiration of the Spirit. In the closing experiences of his life he reflects upon his past and sees himself as

> the man who was raised on high . . . the anointed of the God of Jacob, and the sweet psalmist of Israel, [he declares] *the Spirit of the Lord spoke by me*, and His word was on my tongue (II Sam. 23:1b-2).

The Spirit's message was sometimes comforting and reassuring, as in the case of Isaiah (Isa. 61:1ff.). On the other hand, it was sometimes filled with condemnation, warnings, and impending judgment, as with Micah who says, "I am filled with power—with the Spirit of the Lord—and with justice and courage to make known to Jacob his rebellious act, even to Israel his sin" (Mic. 3:8). As Barclay observes, the Spirit's message is not a monotone proclamation but it is always expressed in the accents which speak to men. It is not an orthodox irrelevancy, but it is "a tract for the times"; and if men fail to heed that divine prophetic voice of the Spirit they do so at their own peril.[7]

Zechariah declares that "great wrath came from the Lord of hosts" because the people refused to "hear the law and the words which the Lord of hosts had sent by his Spirit through the former prophets" (7:12).

The Spirit of God moved men like Amasai to reassure David in a time of jeopardy (I Chron. 12:1-18); He came upon Azariah to call

---

7. *Op. cit.*, p. 16.

the people back to God during a time of apostasy (II Chron. 15:1-7); He moved Jahaziel to deliver a message of hope and reassurance when the Moabites and the Ammonites were a threat to Jehoshaphat and his people (II Chron. 20:1-17). These were men of courage to deliver the message of God because they were men moved upon by the Spirit of God. God always has a message for the needs of the times if He can but find a man who will deliver it in the wisdom and power of the Spirit.

In the Old Testament the prophet of God was a man of the Spirit, both in his life and his message. The Spirit gave the Old Testament prophets the courage and power to deliver God's message, whether it was bitter or sweet, condemnatory or commendatory.

Thus the Spirit is present throughout the world and the affairs of men in the Old Testament. God dwells by His Spirit among the people, even when they may be least aware of His presence (Isa. 59:21; 63:11-14; Hag. 2:4-5).

III. THE SPIRIT IN RELATION TO PERSONAL RELIGIOUS EXPERIENCE IN THE OLD TESTAMENT

The Psalms afford one of the richer Old Testament sources for the relationship of the Spirit to the subject of personal religious experience.

A. The Inescapableness of the Spirit's Presence

The Spirit and the presence of God are regarded as synonymous in the Psalms, as in certain other Old Testament representations. In fact in Psalm 139:7 they are presented in a familiar Hebrew parallelism thus: "Where can I go from Thy Spirit; Or where can I flee from Thy presence?" The psalmist's query here, as in certain other instances, seems to anticipate the New Testament experience of the Holy Spirit at and following Pentecost as representing the omnipresence of God in His universe, but especially in His personal confrontation of man. This is a rhetorical question which assumes a negative reply. God's presence is inescapable, the psalmist means to say. One is reminded of Francis Thompson's famous poem, *The Hound of Heaven,* from which we quote in part at this juncture.

> I fled Him, down the nights and down the days;
> I fled Him, down the arches of the years;

I fled Him, down the labyrinthine ways
  Of my own mind; and in the mist of tears
I hid from Him, and under running laughter.
    Up vistaed hopes I sped;
    And shot, precipitated,
Adown Titanic glooms of chasmèd fears,
  From those strong Feet that followed, followed after.
    But with unhurrying chase,
    And unperturbèd pace,
  Deliberate speed, majestic instancy,
    They beat—and a Voice beat
    More instant than the Feet—
"All things betray thee, who betrayest Me."

    I pleaded, outlaw-wise,
By many a hearted casement, curtained red,
  Trellised with intertwining charities;
(For, though I knew His love Who followèd,
    Yet was I sore adread
Lest, having Him, I must have naught beside).
But, if one little casement parted wide,
  The gust of His approach would clash it to.
  Fear wist not to evade, as Love wist to pursue.
Across the margent of the world I fled,
  And troubled the gold gateways of the stars,
  Smiting for shelter on their clangèd bars;
    Fretted to dulcet jars
And silvern chatter the pale ports o' the moon.
I said to Dawn: Be sudden—to Eve: Be soon;
  With thy young skiey blossoms heap me over
  From this tremendous Lover—[8]

In life or death, on earth, in heaven, or Sheol (the *nether world*), man is always and everywhere confronted with God's Spirit. It is as impossible to escape God's presence in His Spirit as to escape one's self.

But the presence of God's Spirit also means the knowledge and illumination given by His Spirit. To the Corinthian church Paul wrote, quoting in part from Isaiah 64:4 and 65:17:

> But just as it is written, Things which eye has not seen and ear has not heard, and which have not entered the heart of man, all that God has prepared for those who love Him. For to us God revealed them though the Spirit; for the Spirit searches all things, even the depths of God .... the thoughts of God no one knows except the Spirit of God (I Cor. 2:9-11).

The same Spirit who searches knows and reveals to man the nature of his deepest thoughts, often hidden from his own consciousness,

8. Geddes MacGregor, *Readings in Religious Philosophy* (Boston: Houghton Mifflin Company, 1962), pp. 26, 27.

judges and tries man. The Spirit who knows man's deepest consciousness, and even his unfathomable subconsçiousness, reveals to man his
own true self.

The function of the Spirit, from whom the psalmist cannot escape
in Psalm 139:7, is implored in verses 23 and 24. Here, captured by
the Spirit, he pleads: "Search me, O God, and know my heart; Try
me and know my anxious thoughts; and see if there be any hurtful
[lit., "way of pain"] way in me. And lead me in the everlasting
way."

Concerning Spirit (*ruach*) in verse 7, Clarke wisely observes:
"Surely *ruach* in this sense must be taken personally; it certainly
cannot mean either breath or wind [in the natural sense]. To render
it so would make the passage ridiculous."[9] It is interesting that the
expression *"from Thy Presence"* might be rendered *"from Thy
faces."* Clarke asks:

> Why do we meet with this word so frequently in the plural number
> when applied to God? and why have we His *Spirit* and His *appear-
> ances,* or *"faces"* both here? A trinitarian would at once say, "The
> plurality of the persons in the Godhead is intended, and who can
> prove that he is mistaken?"[10]

B. The Illumination of the Spirit's Presence

Nowhere in the Psalms, or elsewhere in the Old Testament in fact,
is intense religious experience so vividly portrayed as in Psalm 51.
Interpreters have generally regarded this penitential psalm as the
experience of King David, who had been rudely awakened from his
backslidden and hypocritical condition by the pungent parable of the
prophet Nathan.

We come to the very heart of this penitential prayer in verse 11,
where he pleads, "Do not cast me away from Thy presence [or
"faces"], and *do not take Thy Holy Spirit from me.*" In his now
awakened state of sin consciousness David well realizes that his only
hope of restoration to God's favor is through the aid of the Holy
Spirit. Should He be withdrawn, all hope of salvation would disappear. It is not to be understood that the Spirit now indwells David's
heart, if indeed such was ever the case with him. Rather, in a manner
somewhat analogous to the Spirit's brooding over the primal chaos at
creation, the Spirit hovered about this fallen but penitent sinner,
aiding him in his quest for spiritual restoration to God's grace.

---

9. *Op. cit.*, p. 532.
10. *Ibid.*

1. The Spirit's Presence Produces True Personal Repentance

First, the intensely personal nature of this Spirit-aided penitential prayer is seen in the frequent use of the personal pronouns *I, me,* and *my,* in his confession of sin. Combined, these three personal pronouns are used no less than thirty-three times in this prayer. Second, the psalmist's confession is a specific identification of the nature of his malady. Awakened and illumined by the Spirit, he sees and owns the heinousness of his offense: "*I know my transgression.*" No subtle psychological evasions or projections characterize this confession. When the Spirit reveals sin the honest penitent owns it as *his transgression.*

In the third instance the penitent acknowledges the haunting presence of guilt that has plagued him continuously: "*My sin is ever before me.*" From the commission to the confession of his transgression he had experienced no respite from the guilty consciousness that he had done something which was not his right to do—he had overstepped the legal boundaries and trespassed on another's rights. *The Hound of Heaven*—the pursuing Spirit, had allowed him no rest until he gave up his futile flight from justice.

2. The Spirit's Presence Makes Man Conscious of Personal Moral Responsibility Before a Righteous God

The psalmist's confession under the Spirit's illumination involves his sense of personal moral responsibility before God: "Against Thee, Thee only, I have sinned, and done what is evil in Thy sight" (v. 4a). All sin is primarily against God. Technically, a *tort* is an offense against an individual, a *crime* is an offense against society, while a *sin* is an offense against God. It is a serious defect of the Chinese language that it has no word to express sin as a moral evil against God. Therefore the very unsatisfactory term for crime has to be accommodated to evangelical preaching in China. This deficiency in the language is due to the absence of any clear concept of a personal, righteous God in the religious philosophy of this great people. The two religious philosophies which have most influenced the Chinese thought and language are Confucianism and Buddhism, both of which were basically atheistic in their founders' teachings, though both tended to deify their founders after their deaths.

It is the function of the *Holy Spirit* to reveal to the heart of sinful man *the holiness of God.* It is the contrast between God's holiness and man's unholiness that produces the awful consciousness of the sinfulness of sin and the consequent confession of sin which acknowledges the justice of divine judgment upon man. In His promise of the Spirit in John 16:8 Jesus clearly delineated His threefold mission in relation to unconverted men: "And He, when *He* comes, *will convict* the world concerning *sin,* and *righteousness,* and *judgment.*" The sin is man's offense, the righteousness is God's character, and the judgment of God is the consequence of the disparity between man's sin and God's righteousness. Without a revelation of God's personal holiness through the mediation of God's Holy Spirit, man cannot know the true nature of sin *per se.*

It is interesting that there occurs here one of only three instances in the Old Testament where God's Spirit is given the title *Holy Spirit* (see also Isa. 63:10, 11). Thus this psalmist's religious insights more nearly approximate the New Testament revelation than perhaps any other Old Testament writer.

On the problem that arises out of the penitent's confession, "Against Thee, Thee only, I have sinned," Clarke's insight is helpful.

> David being a king [*sovereign*], was not liable to be called to account by any of his subjects; nor was there any authority in the land by which he could be judged and punished. In this respect, God alone was greater than the king; and to Him alone, as King, he was responsible.[11]

Until sinful man sees his image reflected in the pure holiness of God there can be no true knowledge of sin and consequently no real confession of sin.

3. The Spirit's Presence Reveals the Inherited Depravity of Man's Nature

The Spirit gives to this penitent a yet deeper revelation of the true nature of his moral malady, in response to which he exclaims: "Behold, I was brought forth in iniquity, and in sin my mother conceived me" (v. 5). With Clarke we agree that

> a genuine penitent will hold nothing of his state; he sees and bewails not only the acts of sin which he has committed, but the disposition that led to those acts. He deplores, not only the transgression, but the carnal mind, which is enmity against God.[12]

This confession conveys no suggestion whatsoever of any relationship between evil and sex *per se.* It is simply the penitent's insight under the Spirit's illumination of the awful fact of inherited deprav-

---

11. *Ibid.,* p. 488.
12. *Ibid.*

ity. He now realizes that his transgression results from the fact that he came into this world with a warped moral nature that was out of alignment with the righteousness of God, though for the allowance of its expression in transgression he was fully responsible before God.

C. The Penitent's Spirit-Motivated Petition to God

Having truly confessed his sin and repented of it, the penitent now implores God for restoration to His favor.

1. *The Spirit Moves the Penitent to Plead for Divine Mercy*

The psalmist's insights into the nature of God, and man's hope of salvation, can, as an Old Testament character, come from no other source than the illumination of God's Spirit. As a king and an executor of justice among his people David knew well the meaning of justice. And as a truly awakened and convicted sinner before the Judge of all men, he knew the hopelessness of his condition before the bar of divine justice. In the light of Plato's definition of justice as "having and doing what is one's own" he deserved nothing short of everlasting exclusion from God's presence. Wisely does he bypass the lower court of justice and makes his appeal directly to the higher court of God's mercy, characterized by grace, lovingkindness, and compassion (v. 1). This prayer anticipates by several centuries Paul's New Testament enlightened explanation of the Holy Spirit's function in relation to man's limited knowledge and ability in prayer (see Rom. 8:26-27).

2. *The Spirit Moves the Penitent to Plead for the Complete Effacement of His Sin (v. 9)*

He does not ask for an amelioration of his condition. He pleads for the removal of the guilt of his transgression: "Blot out all my iniquities." "Hide Thy face from my sins." His request is to the effect that God will use the divine ink remover on the court record of his sin and crime. No New Year's resolution; no turning over a new page in his life's record will suffice. He wants the record to stand as though he had never sinned against God. In effect he prays for justification by divine grace. And such God promised, even in Old Testament times. If Psalm 103, as well as 51, was written by David, it is most likely that the latter psalm expresses his gratitude to God for the answer to this prayer for the complete effacement of his sin. The similarities of theological insights are remarkably parallel, or even identical, as he exults in God's graciousness.

> He has not dealt with us according to our sins, Nor rewarded us according to our iniquities. For high as the heavens are above the earth, So great is His lovingkindness toward those who fear Him. As far as the east is from the west, So far has He removed our transgressions from us. Just as a father has compassion on *his* children, So the Lord has compassion on those who fear Him. For He Himself knows our frame; He is mindful that we are *but* dust (Ps. 103:10-14).

3. The Spirit Moves the Penitent to Plead for Soul Cleansing (v. 7)

Having anticipated God's answer to his petition for forgiveness, the penitent views, under the searchlight of the Spirit's presence, the deeper depth of his moral malady, the depravity of his nature, and cries out: "Purify [or, Mayest Thou wash] me with hyssop, and I shall be clean; wash me, and I shall be whiter than snow." Clarke thinks that the penitent is alluding to the Levitical provision for the cleansing of a leper (Lev. 14:1ff.). At the depth of man's nature there is a moral malady for which there is no human cure.

All the great thinkers of the ages, from Plato to the present, have in one way or another recognized and admitted this disease for which humanity knows no remedy. Jeremiah expressed it most eloquently, though most awfully, when having turned the x ray of God's truth upon the sinful human heart and read the picture it produced he exclaimed: "The heart is deceitful above all things, and desperately wicked: who can know it?" (17:9 *KJV*). And yet again this prophet asked: "Can the Ethiopian change his skin or the leopard his spots? Then you also can do good who are accustomed to do evil" (13:23). The penitent's plea is for God to reach deep into his soul and cleanse the nature in which the sin thrives, to purify the culture in which the bacteria of sin grows and multiplies.

The penitent recognizes the impossibility of simply repairing the condition that God has forgiven. Under the Spirit's illumination he gazes into the deep, dark, dismal, polluted, inner recesses of his spiritual nature and in reaction to what he sees cries out: "Create in [lit., "for"] me a clean heart, O God, and renew a steadfast [or, "an upright"] spirit within me" (v. 10). Thus this penitent recognizes that salvation embraces the necessity and the provision of a divine fiat, the creation of a new heart (cf. II Cor. 5:17). A new heart will produce a right spirit.

It is one of those rare Old Testament insights that enabled the psalmist to anticipate the sanctifying provisions of Calvary many centuries before the author of the letter to the Hebrews wrote, "Jesus . . . that He might sanctify the people through His own blood, suffered outside the gate" (13:12), or before the apostle John wrote, "the blood of Jesus His Son cleanses us from all sin" (I John 1:7).

4. *The Spirit Moves the Penitent to Plead for Soul Preservation (v. 11)*

When this penitent prays, "Do not cast me away from Thy presence ["faces"], and do not take Thy Holy Spirit from me," are we to understand that he has not lost his relationship with God, that he is still the redeemed child of God, though out of grace with God? To thus conclude would do violence to the context of this whole psalm and make these words of petition both meaningless and ridiculous. Does he mean that God's Spirit still indwells him? This too would be a wholly irrational interpretation in the light of the context. What then do the words of this petition mean? The most reasonable and Scripturally consistent meaning seems to be that in God's mercy the Spirit hovers over him, aiding him to repent and regain his saving faith in the grace of God. This was what Wesley understood as prevenient grace.

There is an interesting account given in John 11 which by way of comparison may throw helpful light on these words of the psalmist. There Jesus came to Bethany and the home of Mary, Martha, and Lazarus, their brother. When He arrived He was informed by Martha that her brother Lazarus was already dead and buried. Plaintively she chided Jesus with the words, "Lord, if you had been here, my brother would not have died" (v. 32); or in other words she meant, "If you had come when first sent for, you could have saved his life." When Jesus visited Lazarus' tomb and ordered that the stone door be removed, Martha objected on the grounds that he had been dead four days and by then the decaying body would emit a stench. However, Jesus disregarded her warning and restored her brother to life.

Now there was a common superstition extant, which seems to have been shared by Martha and other Jews, to the effect that until the fourth day the spirit of the deceased hovered about the dead body in hopes of reentry and restoration of the life, but that by the fourth day the odor from the decomposing body had become so offensive that the deceased person's spirit gave up all hope of the restoration of the body and left, never to return. Evidently Jesus was acquainted with this superstition and purposely waited until the fourth day when all human hope was gone to arrive and perform the miracle of resurrection, thus demonstrating the power of God over the assumed impossible circumstance.

So, likewise it would seem that the penitent's great fear was that his moral condition had degenerated to the point that the offended and grieved Spirit of God might leave him forever in his hopeless, backslidden state.

5. The Spirit Moves the Penitent to Plead for the Restoration of Joy (v. 12)

Memories can be very moving in the experience of man. They have sometimes moved men to despair, insanity, and even suicide. On the other hand, they may be highly beneficial. The psalmist's petition to God for restoration of the joy of God's salvation suggests clearly that he has known and experienced something of value that has gone out of his life—something for the restoration of which he desperately longs. This "sweet singer of Israel" has experienced the joy of salvation which now lingers as a haunting memory. In his musical renditions the inspiration of heaven has lifted him to ecstasies of joy and spiritual insights, and to impart those joys and blessings to others, which were breathed upon him from heaven. He has been instrumental under the inspiration of the Spirit in awakening spiritual desires, of inspiring ideals that lifted the morale of the kingdom. For long he has not known the joy that once animated his life. But now, awakened by the Spirit's power, he reflects upon that which he once enjoyed. Like Peter, who remembered the Lord's words and wept bitterly, David remembers what once was precious to him, and longs for its restoration. Once before in verse 8 he has prayed, "make me to hear joy and gladness, let the bones which Thou hast broken rejoice."

David well realizes that joy is an essential ingredient of religious worship and life. He sees the relationship between the "joy of salvation" and "a willing spirit" that sustains the believer in his worship and service of God. Another inspired writer shared this same insight and exclaimed, "the joy of the Lord is your strength" (Neh. 8:10b).

Nicholson says that

> one distinguishing mark of an early Methodist congregation was its singing. . . . Much has been said about the Methodist Revival being

marked by great preaching, but it was also marked by great singing. Luccock and Hutchinson suggest that the singing voice "carried farthest," and that "scores of the communities which never heard any of the outstanding preachers" did hear the characteristic message of the evangelical revival [of the 18th century] by the singing of the hymns of the Wesleys and their friends. That message was declared "in such a form that it could not be easily forgotten. "Charles Wesley . . . [introduced] into Methodist worship a new concept of sacred music." It was his songs which gave the Methodist Movement "fire and warmth" and caused one to call the Methodists "a nest of singing birds."[13]

Little wonder that David could say that when "the joy of . . . salvation" is restored, *"Then* I will teach transgressors Thy ways, and sinners will be converted to Thee" (v. 13). Worship that does not result in evangelism is meaningless. A joyful worship is a contagious worship.

6. *The Spirit Moves the Penitent to the Renewal of His Covenant with God (v. 15)*

A renewed covenant of gratitude is expressed in the prayer: "O Lord, open my lips, that my mouth may declare Thy praise." Paul sets forth ingratitude to God as the first step in religious and moral apostasy which eventually leads to degeneracy and atheism.

For [says the apostle] even though they knew God, they did not honor him as God, or give thanks; but they became futile in their speculations, and their foolish heart was darkened. . . . And just as they did not see fit to acknowledge God any longer, God gave them over to a depraved mind, to do those things which are not proper (Rom. 1:21, 28).

The psalmist seems to gather up, in anticipation, God's reply to all of his earnest pleas, and then give his sincere word of promise to praise God. He seems to say to God, "If you will blot out my transgressions, cleanse my heart, renew within me a steadfast spirit, then I will declare Thy praise." If the early Methodists were known for their joyful singing, they were equally well known for their "class meetings" and "praise services." There is spiritual power in hearts and voices of worshipful praise, both of those who speak the praise and they who hear their praises. The spirit of praise seals the worshipful soul's covenant with God.

13. *Op. cit.*, pp. 49-61.

7. The Spirit Moves the Penitent to Service for God (v. 13)

David promises his life in service to God that others may be brought to know Him. "Then I will teach transgressors Thy ways, and sinners will be converted to Thee." He promises to be a religious instructor, a director, an evangelist, a messenger of God to lead his fellowmen into a saving relationship with God. A religious revival among God's people that does not eventuate in evangelistic outreach to lost men is spurious. Salvation work for God is as truly worship as is prayer or praise.

8. The Spirit Moves the Penitent to Confidence in God's Response (v. 17)

The psalmist has made his confession—a personal, open, frank, full confession. He has acknowledged the depth of the depravity of his heart. He has sued for forgiveness, cleansing, and restoration. He has made his promise of gratitude in witness, thanksgiving in song, and service for God. He is now prepared to believe. His faith, inspired by the Spirit, begins to lay hold upon God's promises. He exclaims in confidence, "A broken and a contrite heart, O God, Thou wilt not despise."

This whole psalm moves out of Old Testament law into the realm of New Testament grace centuries before Christ's sacrifice on the cross or the effusion of the Holy Spirit at Pentecost. It probably represents Spirit-inspired, intense personal religion in all of its varied aspects more fully than any other Old Testament example.

In summary, the psalmist's experience here parallels the New Testament experience of the Spirit's work in man's life.

(1) He reveals God's presence to man (Acts 2:1-4).

(2) He produces conviction for sin (John 16:8; Acts 2:37a).

(3) He produces repentance for sin (Acts 2:38).

(4) He effects heart purity (Acts 15:8-9; Rom. 15:16).

(5) He produces the joy of the Lord (I Thess. 1:6).

(6) He aids the petitioner in his prayer (Rom. 8:26-27).

(7) He produces spiritual fruit or motivates to evangelism (Gal. 5:22-23).

IV. THE OLD TESTAMENT PROMISE OF THE FUTURE AGE OF THE SPIRIT

While the promise of the future age of the Spirit comes to light in several instances in the Old Testament, nowhere is it more explicit and full than in Joel's prophecy. This prophecy is quoted by Peter on the Day of Pentecost as the explanation of the mighty effusion of the Spirit on that occasion. Joel's prophecy-promise reads as follows:

> And it will come about after this that *I will pour out of My Spirit on all mankind;* and your sons and your daughters will prophesy, your old men will dream dreams, your young men will see visions. Even on the male and female servants I will pour out My Spirit in those days. . . . And it will come about that whoever calls on the name of the Lord will be delivered (2:28-32a).

A. In the Future Age the Spirit's Effusion Was to Be Universal

In the effusion of the Spirit at the first Christian Pentecost at Jerusalem the Holy Spirit was released upon the world of mankind universally in a very personal and special sense. Two considerations confront the Bible interpreter concerning this effusion of the Spirit. First, from that time to the end of the age every man is confronted with the Spirit of God in his life. By His Spirit God made His presence personally omnipresent throughout the world of mankind to each succeeding generation. If man yields his life to God in his encounter with the Spirit he will find salvation. If he resists the Spirit in that encounter he will stand condemned in his heart by the Spirit. But there will be no possibility of escaping His presence. Second, when the Spirit was released upon the world at Pentecost this was for all time. In a technical sense there has been and can be but one Christian Pentecost. There have been many subsequent special visitations of the Spirit, and many subsequent fillings with the Spirit. However, at the Jerusalem Pentecost God poured out His Spirit without measure or restraint. Thus we need not pray for another Pentecost. We need only to pray that God will assist us to so condition ourselves in relation to Him and His will as will enable us to experience the benefits of the Spirit who is already present with us in our world.

In this age of the Spirit no one will be denied His presence and blessings if he will open his life to Him. Old and young men, sons and daughters, servants and master will alike have the equal benefits of the Spirit. In Old Testament times only certain select individuals were Spirit endued, or in special instances indwelt by His presence. At and following Pentecost the Spirit is God's personal provision for every man. On Joel's prophecy, concerning the outpouring of the Spirit upon all flesh, which occurred at Pentecost, Clarke remarks that the latter days always refer to the days of the Messiah; and thus this prophecy is to be interpreted. We have the testimony of St. Peter, Acts 11:17, that this prophecy relates to that mighty effusion of the Holy Spirit which took place after [lit., "on"] the Day of Pentecost.[14]

Again Clarke notes on Joel's words,

> *Your sons and your daughters shall prophesy.* Shall "preach," exhort, pray, and instruct so as to benefit the Church. The gifts of teaching and instructing men shall not be restricted to any one class or order of people. . . . He [God] left the line of Aaron and took His apostles indiscriminately from any tribe. He passed by the regular order of the priesthood, and the public schools of the most celebrated doctors and took His evangelists from among fishermen, tentmakers, and even the Roman taxgatherers and He, lastly, passed by the Jewish tribes, and took the Gentile converts, and made them preachers of righteousness to the inhabitants of the whole earth.[15]

On Joel's words at this juncture Wesley remarks:

> *I will pour*—In extraordinary gifts on the first preachers of the gospel, and in various graces on all believers. *Upon all flesh*—Before these gifts were confined to one particular nation; but now they shall be enlarged to all nations, and all that believe. *Shall prophesy*— This was in part fulfilled according to the letter in the first days of the gospel; but the promise means farther, by pouring out of the Spirit on your sons and your daughters, they shall have as full a knowledge of the mysteries of God's law, as prophets before time had. *Shall dream dreams*—This also was literally fulfilled in the apostles' days. But it may mean farther, the knowledge of God and his will shall abound among all ranks, sexes and ages in the Messiah's days, and not only equal, but surpass all that formerly was by prophecy, dreams, or visions. *My Spirit*—Of adoption and sanctification.[16]

It is noteworthy that Wesley's own movement followed this pattern prophesied by Joel and which was fulfilled with the effusion of the Spirit at Pentecost. Wesley's eighteenth-century revival in England, which extended to America, was characterized by small "classes" of believers ministered to by lay men and women, in many instances. Lay preachers, pastors, and evangelists were an essential element in the Wesleyan movement from its beginning, and such characterized the extension of this mighty movement into and throughout America. Most of the noted Methodist circuit riding preachers in America who did most to spread the gospel over the lands were men who lacked the culture and formality of the great

---

14. *Op. cit.*, p. 721.
15. *Ibid.*
16. *Op. cit.* (original), III, 2499-2500.

schools. Such were men like Francis Asbury and Peter Cartright, and many others.

B. In the Future Age the Spirit Was to Be the Believer's Internal Experience

Though there were certain individuals in the Old Testament who experienced the Spirit's indwelling presence in their lives, this experience was the rare exception. In many instances, as previously noted, *the Spirit came mightily upon* certain individuals for the performance of special redemptive acts in the interest of God's people. However, with the Spirit's effusion at Pentecost all believers were *"filled with the Holy Spirit"* (Acts 2:4). Paul later wrote to the Corinthian Christians saying, "Do you know that you are a temple [lit., "sanctuary"] of God, and that the Spirit dwells in you? If any man destroys the temple of God, God will destroy him, for the temple of God is holy, and that is what you are" (I Cor. 3:16-17). Again Paul says: "Do you know that your body is a temple of the Holy Spirit who is in you, whom you have from God, and that you are not your own?" (I Cor. 6:19; cf. Acts 7:46-49; Eph. 2:21-22).

It was by the Spirit that God indwelt man at his creation. Man's rebellion and consequent Fall evicted the Spirit from his inner life. From that sad experience until the Spirit's effusion on the Day of Pentecost it was God's purpose and plan to regain His rightful earthly dwelling place in the soul of redeemed and cleansed man. That great purpose and plan was finally consummated with the advent of the Holy Spirit on the Day of Pentecost, when the believers "were all filled with the Holy Spirit" (Acts 2:4). The prophets foresaw and predicted it, a few special individuals in the Old Testament experienced it as a pledge of what was to come, but all the believers on the Day of Pentecost and until the end of the age became the heirs of this great divine provision.

C. In the Future Age the Spirit Was to Establish a New Covenant with Man

No Old Testament prophet saw more clearly nor described more vividly the new covenant God was to establish with man through His Spirit in the future age than did Jeremiah. He declares:

> "Behold, days are coming," declares the Lord, "when I will make a
> new covenant with the house of Israel and with the house of Judah,

not like the covenant which I made with their fathers in the day I took them by the hand to bring them out of the land of Egypt, My covenant which they broke, although I was a husband to them," declares the Lord. "But this is the covenant which I will make with the house of Israel after those days," declares the Lord, "I will put My law within them, and on their heart I will write it; and I will be their God, and they shall be My people. And they shall not teach again, each man his neighbor and each man his brother, saying, 'Know the Lord,' for they shall all know Me, from the least of them to the greatest of them," declares the Lord, "for I will forgive their iniquity, and their sin I will remember no more" (31:31-34).

Under the Sinai Covenant, God's laws for the moral government of man were written on tablets of stone. At Pentecost a new version of the ancient Mosaic Law was to be written on the heart of man by the person of the Holy Spirit. The apostle John saw the identity and the distinctions of these divine laws for man and wrote:

Beloved, *I am not writing a new commandment to you, but an old commandment* which you have had from the beginning; the old commandment is the word which you have heard. On the other hand, *I am writing a new commandment to you,* which is true in Him and in you, because the darkness is passing away and the true light is already shining (I John 2:7-8).

The first covenant was etched on stone by the finger of God. The new covenant was etched on tablets of flesh, the hearts of men, by the Holy Spirit. Under the old, man had only a partial, limited knowledge of God's will. Under the covenant of the Spirit, he was to have a full knowledge of God's will because he would be indwelt by the omniscient Spirit of God. Thus each would know God and His will directly, and the teaching of His will by external methods would no longer be necessary for the Spirit-possessed believer. A knowledge of God's will would then be a matter of spiritual experience. Jehovah would then be their God and those with this inner personal knowledge of God would be His people. "And they shall be my people and I will be their God," says the prophet (Jer. 24:7), an expression many times repeated. Then Jeremiah continues: "And I will give them one heart and one way, that they may fear Me always, for their own good, and for the good of their children after them" (32:39).

Whereas in the Old Testament the visitation of the Spirit upon a man was temporary and even transferable from one to another, under the future new covenant His presence is to be a permanent, abiding experience of the believer. Says the prophet: "And I will make an everlasting covenant with them that I will not turn away from them, to do them good; and I will put the fear of Me in their hearts so that they will not turn away from Me" (32:40).

Ezekiel expresses a closely similar idea in his prophecy of the future age of the Spirit when he says:

> "And I will make a covenant of peace with them; it will be an everlasting covenant with them. And I will place them and multiply them, and will set My sanctuary in their midst forever. My dwelling place also will be with them; and I will be their God, and they will be My people. And the nations will know that I am the Lord who sanctifies Israel, when My sanctuary is in their midst forever" (37:26-28).

Ezekiel becomes even more specific in his depiction of the future age of the Spirit when he says:

> "And I shall give them one heart, and shall put a new spirit within them. And I shall take the heart of stone out of their flesh and give them a heart of flesh, that they may walk in My statutes and keep My ordinances, and do them. Then they will be My people, and I shall be their God" (11:19-20; cf. Luke 22:20; I Cor. 11:25; II Cor. 3:6; Heb. 7:22; 8:6, 8-13; 9:15; 12:24).

On Ezekiel 36:25, 26, Wesley has the following interesting comment:

> *Sprinkle*—This signifies both the blood of Christ sprinkled upon their conscience, to take away their guilt, as the water of purification was sprinkled, to take away their ceremonial uncleanness, and the grace of the Spirit sprinkled on the soul, to purify it from all corrupt inclinations and dispositions. *A new heart*—A new frame of soul, a mind changed, from sinful to holy, from carnal to spiritual. A heart in which the law of God is written, Jer. xxxi. 33. A sanctified heart, in which the almighty grace of God is victorious, and turns it from all sin to God. *A new Spirit*—A new, holy frame in the spirit of man; which is given to him, not wrought by his own power.[17]

On the expression *My Spirit* (v. 27) Wesley remarks:

> The holy Spirit of God, which is given to, and dwelleth in all true believers. *And cause you*—Sweetly, powerfully, yet without compulsion, for our spirits, framed by God's Spirit to a disposition suitable to his holiness, readily concurs. *Ye shall keep*—Be willing and able to keep the judgments, and to walk in the statutes of God, which is, to live in all holiness.[18]

The foregoing prophecies set in contrast the legal and the spiritual types of religion. They are indeed but two aspects of the same divine revelation—two sides of the same religious coin. However, in the Old Testament the side of the coin bearing the image of the law is turned toward the people. In the New Testament, the age of the Spirit, the side of the coin bearing the image of the heavenly dove representing

---

17. *Ibid.*, III, 2385.
18. *Ibid.*

the Holy Spirit, is turned toward the people. Indeed there were those exceptional, spiritually perceptive individuals who knew well that the dove was on the other side of that religious coin, and some even turned the coin to behold the pure image of the heavenly dove. He was always and everywhere present, but only a few were aware of His presence and work.

On the other hand, in the new era of the Spirit the religious coin was to have the image of the dove turned toward them. They, too, well knew that the tablets of the commandments were etched permanently on the other side of the religious coin, but it was the heavenly dove within them who would enable them to walk in those commandments before God blamelessly. Indeed there would be those in the era of the Spirit who would refuse to look on the side of the coin bearing the image of the dove, preferring to continue to gaze on the cold hard tablets of stone. They would be the legalists, and it was upon these legalists that Christ pronounced the greater condemnation in His day.

Clarke sums up this twofold nature of the Judeo-Christian religion in his comments on Paul's words in II Corinthians 3:6 thus:

> We are ministers of the new covenant; of this new dispensation of truth, light, and life, by Christ Jesus; a system which not only proves itself to have come from God, but necessarily implies that God himself by His own Spirit is a continual Agent in it, ever bringing its mighty purposes to pass. *Not of the letter, but of the spirit.* The apostle does not mean here, as some have imagined, that he states himself to be a minister of the New Testament, in opposition to the Old, and that it is the Old Testament that kills and the New that gives life; but that the New Testament gives the proper meaning of the Old, for the old covenant had its *letter* and its *spirit*, its "literal" and its "spiritual" meaning. The law was founded on the very supposition of the gospel; and all its sacrifices, types, and ceremonies refer to the gospel. The Jews rested in the *letter*, which not only afforded no means of life, but killed, by condemning every transgressor to death. They did not look at the *spirit*, did not endeavor to find out the spiritual meaning; and therefore they rejected Christ, who was "the end of the law" for justification, and so for redemption from death to everyone that believes. Every institution has its *letter* as well as its *spirit*, as every word must refer to something of which it is the sign or significator. The gospel has both its *letter* and its *spirit*; and multitudes of professing Christians, by resting in the letter, receive not the life which it is calculated to impart. Water, in baptism, is the *letter* that points out the purification of the soul; they who rest in this letter are without this purification; and dying in that state, they die eternally. Bread and wine in the sacrament of the Lord's Supper are the *letter*; the atoning efficacy of the death of Jesus and the grace communicated by this to the soul of a believer are the *spirit*. Multitudes rest in this *letter*, simply receiving these

symbols without reference to the atonement or to their guilt, and thus lose the benefit of the atonement and the salvation of their souls.[19]

In commenting on Jeremiah's prophecy concerning the future age of the Spirit, Clarke says further:

> [Christ] having ascended on high, shall have obtained the gift of the Holy Spirit to purify the heart, then God's *law* shall by it be put *in their inward parts,* and written on their hearts so that all within and all without shall be holiness to the Lord. Then God will be truly *their* God, received and acknowledged as their portion, and the sole object of their devotion; and they shall be His people, filled with holiness, and made partakers of the divine nature, so that they will perfectly love Him and worthily magnify His name.[20]

We conclude our study of the Spirit of God in the Old Testament by observing with St. Augustine that "The Old is in the New revealed and the New is in the Old concealed."

---

19. *Op. cit.,* p. 1133.
20. *Ibid.,* p. 639.

Chapter 4

The Holy Spirit
in the
Synoptic Gospels

There are not a large number of references to the Spirit of God in the Synoptic Gospels. However, these references are exceedingly important and demand our careful consideration. But before pursuing a study of the Spirit in the Gospels we must consider the teaching concerning the Spirit in the Old Testament as that teaching relates to the Spirit's preparation for the advent of the Redeemer.

I. THE HOLY SPIRIT IN THE PREPARATION FOR REDEMPTION THROUGH THE MESSIAH, CHRIST JESUS

All the works of the Holy Spirit from creation to the culmination of redemption are subservient to and focused upon Christ. When predicting the coming of the Spirit at Pentecost Jesus said: "He shall not speak on His own initiative, but whatever he hears, He will speak. . . . He shall glorify me: for he shall take of mine, and shall disclose it to you" (John 16:13,14).

It is noteworthy that following the universal diffusion and function of the Spirit in creation the broad diffusion is followed by a course of contraction in the divine redemptive plan which progres-

89

sively focuses upon and culminates in the Messiah who is the Christ, the Savior of mankind through His cross and resurrection. Then, as we shall note presently, at Pentecost as the Spirit was outpoured on and through the church, He became the universal diffuser of the new life, provided in Christ's death and resurrection, to all mankind. This function of the Spirit is graphically expressed by Harry R. Boer as follows:

> The movement of the Spirit in the discharge of His redemptive function pursued a course consisting of a process of contraction followed by a process of expansion, culminating in His indwelling of the universal church as the manifestation of the new humanity. . . . The central point of the movement is Christ. *To* Him all the work of the Spirit tends, *from* Him the Spirit and His work flow to effect the regeneration of men and of the cosmos. The movement is from the many to the One and from the One to the many.[1]

Johannes Blauw has set forth this principle in a most telling manner. Speaking of the mission of the Servant-of-the Lord in Isaiah's prophecy (Isa. 42:1, 49:1, 53:11), he remarks:

> The task of showing that Jehovah alone is God, which the other prophecies (notably Jeremiah and Ezekiel) affirm to be a task for all Israel, is here ascribed to the Servant. Through all the Old Testament historical and prophetic books we find a "progressive reduction" from the many to the few, from the nation to the remnant, from the remnant to the one Servant.[2]

In the light of the foregoing considerations it becomes evident that the Holy Spirit, in His person and preparatory work, was the "earnest," or advance pledge, of the inheritance yet to be realized in Christ. Thus the pre-Christian believers became partakers of the messianic blessing of salvation through anticipatory faith in Christ inspired in their hearts by the Holy Spirit. Before Christ men looked forward, by the aid of the types and shadows, to the cross for salvation (Heb. 1:1-2a; 10:1). Since Christ they have looked back to the cross for salvation. The former was anticipatory faith, the latter reflective faith. Both are saving faith.

Immediately after the Fall the soteric function of the Spirit went out to all mankind without regard to divisions in the human family. However, the concentration upon the *One* (the Savior), from concern with the universal, soon comes into view. While there is more than a

---

1. *Pentecost and Missions* (Grand Rapids: Wm. B. Eerdmans Publishing Company, 1961), p. 67.
2. "A Survey of the Biblical Theology of Missions," *The Missionary Nature of the Church* (New York: McGraw-Hill Book Company, Inc., 1962), p. 48.

hint of Christ as the *One* (the Savior) in Genesis 3:15, the broadening
movement becomes quite clear as the line of promised redemption
passes from Adam and Eve, in whom the whole human race was
represented, through the righteous line of Seth on to Noah, the
prototype of the future deliverer, and from thence to Abraham, the
father of God's specially chosen people, to make known the redemptive plan.

The convergence continues to narrow when Israel, as a nation, is
supplanted in large measure in the redemptive plan by the remnant
of Israel, and from the remnant to the prophets, and thence to John
the Baptist as the single representative of the remnant, and the
forerunner and the announcer of the Messiah, the Savior, on to the
personal appearance of the one and only Savior Jesus Christ in whom
the plan of redemption found its completion and fulfillment. The
redemptive function of the Spirit is evidenced at the outset by God's
pronouncement prior to the Flood: "My Spirit shall not strive with
man forever" (Gen. 6:3). This implies that He strove to restrain men
from wickedness and return them to God. The superintending activity of the Holy Spirit in the selection and direction of Abraham from
idolatrous Ur of Chaldees to become the father and founder of the
chosen people, Israel, is consistent with His general activities in the
Old Testament and the plan and purpose of God in redemption.
However, whereas the activities of the Spirit are implicit in the
foregoing divine directives, His function in the selection and inspiration of the prophets becomes explicit.

As we have noted in Chapter 3, it was in the Old Testament
prophets and the Psalms particularly that the Spirit of God became
most clearly manifest in His person and work. Through the prophets,
endued with God's Spirit, His will for Israel and His plan of redemption for all mankind comes into clearer focus than at any other point
in the Old Testament. Their mission was to call Israel back from
apostasy and bondage through sincere repentance and the acceptance
of God's will. In the midst of their humanly hopeless situation the
prophets promised them deliverance and restoration through the
hope of the Messiah-Savior. While the utterances of the prophets who
presented this hope had a primary historical application to the
conditions and needs of Israel then, they also had futuristic over-
tones of an eschatological nature for both Israel and all the nations
of mankind. In other words, the deliverance from sin and the offer of
salvation to Israel by the prophets was not limited to Israel, but was
God's provision through the future Messiah for all men, Jew and

Gentile alike, in the new age to be inaugurated by the Spirit at Pentecost. No one in the Bible saw this redemptive accomplishment more clearly or expressed it more explicitly than the apostle Paul when he wrote to his Gentile converts saying:

> *Remember* that you were at that time separate from Christ, excluded from the commonwealth of Israel, and strangers to the covenants of promise, having no hope and without God in the world. But now in Christ Jesus you who formerly were far off have been brought near by the blood of Christ. For He Himself is our peace, who made both *groups into* one, and broke down the barrier of the dividing wall, by abolishing in His flesh the enmity, *which is* the Law of commandments *contained* in ordinances, that in Himself He might make the two into one new man, *thus* establishing peace, and might reconcile them both in one body to God through the cross, by it having put to death the enmity. And He came and preached peace to you who were far away, and peace to those who were near; for through Him we both have our access in one Spirit to the Father. So then you are no longer strangers and aliens, but you are fellow-citizens with the saints, and are of God's household (Eph. 2:12-19).

The Spirit's function in relation to the Old Testament prophets comes to clearer focus, perhaps, in the words of Isaiah than at any other point in the Old Testament where he says: "The Spirit of the Lord God is upon me; because the Lord has anointed me to bring good news . . . " (61:1a; see also the balance of this chapter). This utterance of Isaiah, later to be appropriated by Christ to Himself (Luke 4:18), may be taken as representative of the Spirit's function in relation to all the prophets who foretold the Messiah's mission.

As noted in Chapter 2, the Spirit descended, on numerous occasions, upon certain men in the Old Testament for the accomplishment of specific redemptive acts. However, there are a number of instances in which the Spirit's presence is diffused among a larger number (Num. 11:25-26, 29), and sometimes throughout the congregation (Isa. 32:15; 44:3; Ezek. 39:29; Joel 2:28-29; Hag. 2:5), though some references are more promissory than present realizations with Israel. These intimations of the broader diffusion of the Spirit's presence among the Israelites may very well indicate three things: first, the Spirit's superintendency of the Israelites' religious and moral life in the Old Testament times; second, the providential guidance of the affairs of men and history to the ultimate culmination in the Messiah-Redeemer; and third, intimations of the future age of the Spirit when He would be poured out upon all mankind without limitation or national or personal discrimination (Joel 2:28-29).

Concerning the second of the three foregoing intimations,

Johannes Blauw has ably analyzed the function of Israel as the chosen servants of God to make His divine revelation known to the nations of Old Testament times. This, Blauw ably argues, on the basis of the Scriptural teachings involved in *universalism,* in the sense of God's concern and provision for all men, but not specific missionary activity in the sense of Israel's *going out* with the message to the nations. Israel was chosen and used by God to reflect God's revelation to the nations *that they might be drawn to God* through Israel, but they were *not specifically sent out* to the nations. This may be illustrated by a bright light placed outside the house on a warm summer night. The light is stationary, though it sends its beams afar. The insects are drawn to the light, though it is not carried among them. This, Blauw calls God's *centripetal* method in the Old Testament. The *centrifugal* method of disseminating the gospel awaited the atoning work of Christ and the effusion of the Spirit at Pentecost in the New Testament era.

Indeed the Old Testament record evidences only occasional instances of the indwelling presence of the Spirit in individuals, such as are found at and following His effusion at Pentecost. Such intimations may be found in Ezekiel 2:2; 3:24; 11:19; 36:27; 37:14; and Micah 3:8. However, His general superintending and occasional special empowering presence can be clearly traced from Creation to the Incarnation. As the contraction continues, there emerges from the unfaithful Israelitish nation a representative righteous remnant, and from the remnant a righteous family, from the righteous family the transitional representative, John the Baptist, and from John the Messiah-Savior Himself.

Thus, there seems to be a very real sense in which the contraction narrows to a single, and in certain respect unique, representative of both the former and the future functions of the Spirit in redemption as the transitional personage of John the Baptist appears on the scene to introduce the Messiah-Savior in whom all redemption focuses: "Behold, the Lamb of God, who takes away the sin of the world!" (John 1:29). Luke records of the birth of John that "he will be filled with the Holy Spirit, while yet in his mother's womb" (1:15), and his father was filled with the Spirit as he prophesied (1:7). Further John prophesied that Christ would be filled with the Spirit. Thus it was in John the Baptist that the Spirit brought His full light to focus upon the Christ.

As previously noted, there are but few references to the Holy Spirit in the first three Gospels, though these are not without their vital importance to an understanding of the Spirit in relation to the redemptive plan. These teachings may be thought of in relation to two general considerations. First, there are the events involving the Holy Spirit in relation to the birth and ministry of John the Baptist. Second, there are the events involving the Holy Spirit in relation to the incarnation, virgin birth, and ministry of Jesus Christ.

II. THE HOLY SPIRIT IN RELATION TO THE BIRTH AND MINISTRY OF JOHN THE BAPTIST

A. The Spirit in Relation to John's Birth

It is in Luke's Gospel that we meet the first reference, in chronological order, to the Holy Spirit in the Synoptic Gospels. Here an angel announces to Zacharias that his wife Elizabeth is to bear a son who is to be named John, and that *"he will be filled with the Holy Spirit, while yet in his mother's womb"* (Luke 1:15). Clarke remarks that he "shall be divinely designated to this particular office, and qualified for it, from his *mother's womb*—from the instant of his birth."[3] This special enduement with the Spirit is especially significant in consideration of the particular mission assigned to John Baptist. It fell to him to prepare the way for Christ, to baptize Him, and introduce Him as the Savior of the world. Furthermore, it was his mission to call Israel, in particular, to repentance and return to faith in God's promise of the coming Messiah, that Christ might be recognized and received by them at His advent. That John's mission was not entirely successful is not surprising. The apostle says: "He [Christ] came to His own [domain], and those who were His own [His own people—the Jewish nation] did not receive Him" (John 1:11). The prophets before John had met the same disappointment (Acts 7:51-52).

Further, because John was a Spirit-filled, righteous man he could suffer, without envy, jealousy, or resentment, the shift of his own popularity with the masses to Jesus whom he had introduced as the Messiah. Even when his own disciples sought to incite him to a negative reaction against the one to whom his disciples were defecting, John could see this as within the will and plan of God. Thus, he honored Christ when he was losing his own preeminence to Him. This comes to full focus in John's words: *"He must increase, but I*

---

3. *Op. cit.*, p. 835.

must decrease." John is able to assign this whole transitional affair from himself to Christ to the Spirit by saying: "He [Christ] whom God has sent speaks the words of God; for *He gives the Spirit without measure"* (John 3:24-36, but especially vv. 30, 34).

Finally, it was his mission to lay down his life as a martyr for the sake of Christ and the righteousness which Christ came to establish (Matt. 14:1-12). It is little wonder that Christ testified of John that there had "not arisen anyone greater than John the Baptist" (Matt. 11:11). Since man was created to be indwelt by God's Spirit, and thus the Spirit is essential to his true manhood, *no one can become truly great without the Spirit of God.* The same expression was used of Christ when the angel announced to Mary that she would bear a son whose name would be Jesus: *"He will be great . . . "* (Luke 1:32). That John Baptist was inwardly purified from his inherited sinful nature from the time he was "filled with the Holy Spirit" is logical from the fact that the Spirit's holy presence pervaded his inmost person, and from the consequent fruit of the Spirit that accompanied his life. Such instances of the ethical significance of the Spirit's presence and work in the lives of exceptional individuals before the Pentecostal effusion of the Spirit appear to be earnests of that forthcoming divine provision for all believers by way of anticipation, rather than being the norm.

On the occasion of Mary's visit to Elizabeth in Nazareth she (Elizabeth) was filled with the Holy Spirit and thus inspired she pronounced her blessings upon Mary, who was to be the mother of the long-promised Messiah (Luke 1:41-45).

On the occasion of John's circumcision (according to Jewish custom, on the eighth day) Elizabeth's neighbors proposed naming him Zacharias, after his father. However, Elizabeth, speaking from divine conviction, objected and announced that his name would be John (Luke 1:60). With this Zacharias immediately concurred by writing his name *John* on a tablet, at which time Zacharias himself was filled with the Holy Spirit and delivered a remarkable prophecy concerning the advent and mission of the Messiah, and the important part that his son John would play in preparing the way for the Messiah-Savior (Luke 1:67-79). Zacharias' prophecy includes both what God has done in the past and all of what he will do in the future to save mankind. This marks the transition from the function of the Spirit in relation to Israel and the promise of the coming Messiah in the Old Testament, and His relation to the Redeemer in the New Testament. The same Spirit who manifested Himself variously in the Old Testament now speaks in relation to the Redeemer in the new era of grace.

B. The Holy Spirit in the Ministry of John the Baptist

One of the most significant prophetic utterances concerning the Holy Spirit in the entire New Testament, or perhaps the entire Bible, was made by John the Baptist in his transitional mission between the old and the new eras. At the height of his successful ministry, when he was preaching the baptism of repentance and multitudes were thronging him, the people began to question whether he himself was the Messiah. John replied:

> "As for me, I baptize you in water for repentance, but He who is coming after me is mightier than I, and I am not even fit to remove His sandals; *He Himself will baptize you with the Holy Spirit and fire.* And His winnowing fork is in His hand, and He will thoroughly clean His threshing floor; and He will gather His wheat into the barn, but He will burn up the chaff with unquenchable fire" (Matt. 3:11-12; cf. Mark 1:7; Luke 3:16-17).

The significance of this prophecy concerning the work of the Holy Spirit cannot be overlooked nor overemphasized. Wesley's remarks on this passage give it a definite spiritual significance, and they seem readily to accord with the general New Testament teachings concerning the person and work of the Spirit. Wesley says on Matthew 3:10 concerning the ax:

> There is no room for such idle repentance [as evidently characterized many of John's audience]. Speedy execution is determined against all that do not repent. The comparison seems to be taken from a woodman that has laid down his axe, to put off his coat, and then immediately goes to work to cut down the tree. This refers to "the wrath to come" in the seventh verse. *Is hewn down*—instantly, without further delay.[4]

Then on John's word is verse 11, "He Himself will baptize you with the Holy Spirit and fire," Wesley says:

> He shall fill you with the Holy Ghost, inflaming your hearts with that fire of love which many waters cannot quench and this was done, even with a visible appearance as of fire, on the day of Pentecost.[5]

Wesley understands the fan in the winnower's hand as "the word of the gospel." The threshing floor he sees as "His Church, which is

---

4. *Op. cit.* (original), pp. 23, 24.
5. *Ibid.*, p. 24.

now covered with a mixture of wheat and chaff," and the wheat which will be gathered into His barn consists of "those who are truly good in heaven."[6] The chaff evidently consists of the unrepentant who will suffer the eternal loss of their souls (cf. Ps. 1:4-6; Matt. 13:30).

John's prediction that Christ's baptism will be with the "Holy Spirit and fire" indicates both the *personality* and the *nature* of the Spirit, and sets Christ's baptism in clear distinction from his own. John's baptism was with water, thus typifying cleaning from outward sin; Jesus' baptism was to be with the Holy Spirit and fire, thus accomplishing an inner purification of their natures. The effusion of the Spirit on the Day of Pentecost was characterized by *"tongues as of fire* distributing themselves, and they rested on each of them" (Acts 2:3). Fire is, throughout the Scriptures, a symbol of purity and thus a symbol of God's attribute of holiness. The author of the Epistle to the Hebrews declares: "Our God is a consuming fire" (12:29). Thus, we are amply warranted in concluding that the baptism "with the Holy Spirit and fire," of which John prophesied, was that which realized its fulfillment on the Day of Pentecost when the Spirit was manifest under the symbol of "tongues as of fire" purifying the hearts of the believers in preparation for their being "filled with the Holy Spirit" (Acts 2:3-4).

III. THE HOLY SPIRIT IN RELATION TO THE INCARNATION, BIRTH, AND MINISTRY OF JESUS CHRIST

The redemptive function of the Holy Spirit comes to focus in the Incarnation of Jesus Christ the Messiah—the world's Savior. But the Incarnation must be understood as representing the totality of Christ's redemptive work—His birth, His life and teaching, His death, and His resurrection and ascension. It is here that we see the specific function of the Spirit made explicit in the divine conception of the world's Savior in the person of Jesus Christ—the God-man. The divinely chosen virgin, Mary, was miraculously moved upon by the Spirit in such a manner that the conception of the Christ, who was to become the Savior of the world, took place without the concurrence of a human father. Matthew twice states this explicitly thus: *"She [Mary] was found with child by the Holy Spirit"* (1:18b); and again, "an angel of the Lord appeared unto him [Joseph] in a dream,

6. *Ibid.*

saying, Joseph, thou son of David, fear not to take unto thee Mary thy wife: for *that which is conceived in her is of the Holy Spirit,* and she will bear a son; and you shall call His name Jesus" (1:20, 21). Thus it was the Holy Spirit who effected all Creation, and then when the Fall had occurred, it was He who through the long process of history directed lost man back to God through a continuously converging process of selection until the whole plan of redemption focused upon and culminated in the world's Savior Jesus Christ through the Spirit-wrought miracle of the Incarnation.

A. The Angel's Announcement of the Incarnation and Birth of Christ

This announcement came first to Mary, who was divinely chosen to be the mother of the *God-man.* Luke informs us that "the angel Gabriel was sent from God to a city in Galilee, called Nazareth, to a virgin engaged to a man whose name was Joseph of the descendants of David; and the virgin's name was Mary" (1:26, 27). Mary's puzzlement over this announcement, in consideration of the fact that she was neither actually married to Joseph nor had had sexual relations with any other man, was allayed by the angel's announcement to her that "the Holy Spirit will come upon you and the power of the Most High will overshadow you; and for that reason the holy offspring shall be called the Son of God" (1:35). However adequate the explanation of this unique occurrence may have been in allaying the anxiety of Mary, it still remained for Joseph, to whom she was engaged, to receive a satisfactory explanation to save him embarrassment before both the Jewish law and the opinions of his fellow Jews.

Betrothal was, in the Jewish custom of that day, comparable to what we know as engagement, but it bore much stronger significance than engagement in Western custom. From the moment of engagement onward the agreement was as binding as a legalized and solemnized marriage in Western society, though the marriage relation was not consummated until the girl was taken to her husband's house sometime later. Any infidelity to this relationship on the part of the woman during the period of engagement was treated under the law with the same severity as if infidelity should occur after marriage *per se.* Upon the discovery of Mary's pregnancy, Joseph could have submitted Mary to the demands of the law that she be executed by stoning under conviction for adultery (John 8:3-5). However, Joseph's compassionate consideration for Mary moved him to a less severe decision. Thus to save embarrassment for Mary and for himself he decided to give her a private (or, secret) divorcement (Matt. 1:18-19). However, Joseph was reassured of Mary's fidelity to her betrothal to him by the message of an angel which came in his dream and announced: "Joseph, son of David, do not be afraid to take Mary as your wife; for that which has been conceived in her is of the Holy Spirit" (Matt. 1:20-21).

Following the angel's reassuring message to Joseph, Matthew explains:

> Now all this took place that what was spoken by the Lord through the prophet might be fulfilled, saying, "Behold, the virgin shall be with child, and shall bear a Son, and they shall call His name Immanuel"; which translated means, "God with us." And Joseph arose from his sleep, and did as the angel of the Lord commanded him, and took *her* as his wife; and kept her a virgin until she gave birth to a Son; and he called His name Jesus (1:22-25).

Thus, in all of the circumstances preceding and surrounding the birth of the Messiah, the Holy Spirit was the active agent of God. There is no other way of understanding or explaining the Incarnation of God in humanity than to accept it as a miracle wrought by the Holy Spirit. The Incarnation is a mystery incapable of complete human understanding for two reasons. First, it is a miraculous act of God, and since God is infinite and man is finite, God's special revelations can never be fully comprehended by limited man. In the second place the Incarnation is *unique*—nothing like it has ever occurred in human history. Since man's knowledge is in large degree dependent upon comparisons or contrasts with what he already knows, there is nothing with which to compare the Incarnation. *It stands alone as a special act of God in human history.* Like all the great truths of divine revelation to man, the Incarnation, wrought by the Holy Spirit, is an item of Christian faith. Orthodox Christianity has always accepted it as such and included it as an essential item in its theology. In fact there is not a more important doctrine of the Christian religion than the Incarnation. With the acceptance or rejection of this truth the Christian religion stands or falls. It is the very heart of the Christian faith—the life-giving principle.

B. The Spirit's Revelation to Simeon Concerning the Ministry of Jesus Christ

However, the work of the Spirit is not limited to the Incarnation, important as that is. The Spirit wrought a recognition of Christ's divine Sonship in the direction of the priest Simeon's dedicatory blessing upon Him in the temple on the occasion of His presentation to God (Luke 2:25-26).

Simeon well represents the experience of sincere religious men of the Jewish faith in his day in relation to the work of the Holy Spirit. He was a man upon whom the Spirit rested (Luke 2:25), as was the case with most Old Testament examples. As Barclay observes, the Spirit revealed to him the truth that he should see the Lord's Anointed before his death (Luke 2:26), directed him to the place of that revelation in the temple where the infant Jesus had been taken (Luke 2:27), and enabled him to recognize the truth of that revelation when he witnessed it. Barclay sees in Simeon's experience a complete summary of the Jew's belief in the Holy Spirit. The Spirit reveals the truth to men and helps them to recognize and understand that truth. Likewise the Spirit functions in His relation to believing men today.[7]

Barclay is very correct when he notes further that it is the Spirit's function to make known God's truth to men, to arraign them before that revealed truth, and to enable them to recognize it as God's truth when seen.[8] Without the Spirit's aid men can neither discover nor recognize the truth of God when revealed. This is the reason the Bible is a dead and meaningless book to the man devoid of God's Spirit. In the absence of its divine author the Bible is a closed book, for many an enigma in fact.

C. The Holy Spirit in Relation to the Baptism of Jesus Christ

At His baptism by John in the Jordan River, Matthew records that

> after being baptized, Jesus went up immediately from the water; and behold, the heavens were opened, and He saw the Spirit of God descending as a dove, and coming upon Him; and behold, a voice out of the heavens saying, "This is My beloved Son, in whom I am well-pleased" (Matt. 3:16-17; cf. Mark 1:9-11, Luke 3:21-22).

Since by reason of the Incarnation of God in humanity, thus redeeming the sinful human nature in Christ's own divine-human person, the question naturally arises concerning the necessity of Christ's baptism by John. Even John himself could not understand this necessity. However, Jesus' own words afford the most adequate answer to that question, as He replied: "Permit it at this time; for in

---

7. *Op. cit.*, pp. 21, 22.
8. *Ibid.*

this way it is fitting for us to fulfill all righteousness" (Matt. 3:15). Fundamentally, Christ's baptism signified His public identification, in His incarnate state, with the sinful human race which He had come to redeem and reconcile to God. This He did by meeting all the demands of the law which were designated for the ultimate redemption of sinful man, though He himself was without sin (II Cor. 5:21). Wesley remarks on these words of Christ:

> It becometh every messenger of God to observe all His righteous ordinances. But the particular meaning of our Lord seems to be, that it becometh us to do (Me to receive baptism, and you to administer it) in order to fulfill, that is, that I may fully perform, every part of the righteous law of God, and the commission He hath given Me.[9]

Clarke's explanation of these words of Christ, "it is fitting for us to fulfill all righteousness," is highly significant:

> It was the initiatory ordinance of the Baptist's dispensation. Now as Christ had submitted to circumcision, which was the initiatory ordinance of the Mosaic dispensation, it was necessary that He should submit to this, which was instituted by no less an authority, and was the introduction to His own dispensation of eternal mercy and truth. But it was necessary on another account. Our Lord represented the high priest, and was to be the High Priest over the house of God. As the high priest was initiated into his office by washing and anointing, so must Christ; and hence He was baptized, washed, and anointed by the Holy Ghost. Thus He fulfilled the righteous ordinance of His initiation into the office of High Priest, and thus was prepared to make an atonement for the sins of mankind.[10]

Ralph Earle says that these words of Jesus in verse 15

> . . . explain why Jesus was baptized. He would go all the way as the Representative of man in his sin and deep need. He stood there that day, not by himself or with John only, but with the crowd. Here was the Incarnation in action, divine love revealed.[11]

The significance of Jesus' baptism by John and the descent of the Spirit upon Him is severalfold. First, as previously noted, it marked the fulfillment of the divine law. Jesus Himself said, "Do not think that I am come to abolish the Law or the Prophets; I did not come to abolish, but to fulfill" (Matt. 5:17).

Second, His water baptism and the descent of the Spirit upon Him signified the transition from the old dispensation of the law to the new dispensation of the Spirit of grace.

---

9. *Op. cit.* (original), p. 24.
10. *Op. cit.*, p. 770.
11. *Wesleyan Bible Commentary*, IV, 22.

Third, it signified the first clear and explicit New Testament witness to the divine Trinity. This witness is admirably stated by Clarke.

> This passage affords no mean proof of the doctrine of the Trinity. That three distinct Persons are here represented there can be no dispute: (1) The person of Jesus Christ, baptized by John in Jordan; (2) The person of the Holy Ghost in a bodily shape (Luke iii.22) like a dove; (3) The person of the Father—a voice came out of heaven, saying, "This is my beloved Son." The voice is here represented as proceeding from a different place to that in which the persons of the Son and Holy Spirit were manifested; and merely, I think, more forcibly to mark this divine Personality.[12]

Fourth, it signified God's special equipment and authorization of Christ for His public ministry and redemptive mission.

Wesley remarks on Matthew's words, "And behold, the heavens were opened, and he [He] saw the Spirit of God descending as a dove ["in bodily form like a dove" Luke 3:22] and coming upon Him,"

> probably in a glorious appearance of fire, perhaps in the shape of a dove, descending, with a hovering motion, till it rested upon Him. This was a visible token of those secret operations of the blessed Spirit, by which He was anointed in a peculiar manner and abundantly fitted for His public work.[13]

Fifth, the "voice out of the heavens" which accompanied the descent of the Spirit upon Christ at His baptism, saying, "This is my beloved Son, in whom I am well pleased," signifies God the Father's confirmation of the divine Sonship of Jesus Christ.

Sixth, the Spirit's descent upon Christ at His baptism was the identification and confirmation of Christ's messianic, divine Sonship to John Baptist, who bore witness of this fact (John 1:29-34).

From henceforth the ministry of Jesus Christ was the execution of the Father's will and purpose in man's redemption (cf. Mark 9:7b; Luke 9:35; Isa. 42:1).

There is a very real sense in which the baptism of Jesus, both by John in water and by the Spirit's descent from heaven upon Him, was the prototype of man's salvation, and the believers' baptism with the Holy Spirit at the first Christian Pentecost (Acts 2:1-4).

D. The Holy Spirit in Relation to Christ's Temptation

Mark's statement, following Christ's baptism, that *"immediately the Spirit impelled Him* to go out into the wilderness" indicates both the urgency and the importance of this event to Christ's life and ministry. He had to deny Satan's usurped authority before He could claim His own rightful, universal authority (cf. Matt. 28:18). For this He required both the power and the direction of the Spirit. Luke likewise emphasizes this event by saying that "*Jesus, full of the Holy Spirit,* returned from the Jordan and was led about by [or, "under the influence of"] the Spirit in the Wilderness" (4:1). Luke's notation that Christ was "led about [or, "under the influence"] of the Spirit" may very well suggest both the variety of temptations, and the shifting positions involved in the temptation to which Christ was subjected in the wilderness. However, Matthew's statement seems to suggest more fully the Spirit's purpose in *impelling* Christ to go into the wilderness than either of the other Gospels. Since Christ had come "to fulfill all righteousness" (3:15) the wilderness temptation was essential to this accomplishment.

The First Adam had met Satan in the Garden and failed in his encounter with the enemy, thus relinquishing his sub-sovereignty over the natural order of the universe, as well as his own relationship to God, to Satan's authority. This tragic failure of Adam constituted the Fall of both man and all that over which God had given him authority, into the hands of Satan. This constituted the very essence of unrighteousness. Christ came "to fulfill all righteousness." However, before He could accomplish His mission it was necessary that He meet the same temptation before Satan's unrightful claims, and assert His own rightful claims to man and the natural order (see Heb. 2:5-10; cf. 4:10). It was the Spirit that "*impelled*" Christ to go into the wilderness to meet Satan's challenge, and it was by *the power of the Spirit* that He came forth from that wilderness ordeal a complete victor over Satan. From that time forth Christ walked in the power and authority of His Spirit-wrought victory over Satan and all the evil forces.

Wesley's remarks on this event are both concise and practical: "After this glorious evidence of His Father's love, He was completely armed for the combat. Thus, after the clearest light and the strongest consolation, let us expect the sharpest temptations."[14]

E. The Holy Spirit in Relation to Christ's Ministry

The Spirit is evident in the ministry of Christ from His baptism to His ascension. No part of His life, teaching, or mighty deeds can be

---

14. *Ibid.*

divorced from the personal presence and power of the Holy Spirit. Where this fact is not clearly stated it is nevertheless assumed. We shall note here only those instances in which it is made explicit.

Luke informs us that following His temptation "Jesus returned to Galilee in the power of the Spirit; and news about Him spread through all the surrounding district" (Luke 4:14; cf. Matt. 4:12, 23-25; 12:15-21; Mark 1:14-15; John 4:43-45). Like a mighty general marching forth from a victorious campaign against a powerful enemy, Jesus comes forth from His encounter with the arch adversary, Satan, a mighty victory in "the power of the Spirit." The news of His divine glory, grace, and power was manifest abroad, or as Luke relates, the "news about Him spread throughout all the surrounding district . . . [and He] was praised by all" (Luke 4:14, 15). He was, as Wesley remarks, "more abundantly strengthened after His conflict."[15] Clarke's practical remark is most apropos: "He who, through the grace of God, resists and overcomes temptation [by the aid of the Spirit] is always bettered by it. This is one of the wonders of God's grace, that those very things which are designed for our utter ruin He makes the instruments of our greatest good."[16]

Barclay thinks that when the expression "and Jesus, full of the Holy Spirit" (Luke 4:1a) is used it has a special significance. While all the great men of God and prophets of the Old Testament received their messages from the Spirit, their experiences of the Spirit were "transitory and spasmodic; with them the Spirit ebbed and flowed." Their reception of the Spirit was on special occasions and for special messages and undertakings. However, Jesus' reception of the Spirit was an abiding and inalienable enduement. Their experience of the Spirit was fragmentary, varied, diverse, partial, and temporary. Christ's experience of the Spirit was permanent.[17] (cf. Heb. 1:1-3.)

That Christ should have begun His ministry in the power of the Spirit is a most noble example for every young person who would serve God effectively in the gospel ministry. No matter how brilliant the mind, how exceptional the talents, how finished the education, or how magnetic the personality, the person who begins his ministry devoid of the power of the Spirit is doomed to defeat and failure as a servant of God. No person can do God's service without the enduement of God's Spirit.

As Christ entered the synagogue at Nazareth and read from the

---

15. *Ibid.*, p. 215.
16. *Op. cit.*, p. 862.
17. *Op. cit.*, p. 23.

prophecy of Isaiah concerning the Messiah and His mission, He confidently identified Himself as the personal fulfillment of that prediction with the words, "Today this Scripture has been fulfilled in your hearing" (Luke 4:21b; see vv. 16-20). As applied to Christ these words of the prophet Isaiah designate Him as empowered and anointed by the Spirit for His gospel ministry to the poor, the liberation of those taken captive by Satan, the illumination of the blind, the elevation of the oppressed, and the declaration of "the favorable [or, "acceptable] year of the Lord" (Luke 4:18-19; cf. Matt. 13:54-58; Mark 6:1-6a). Wesley sees this last reference as "plainly alluding to the year of jubilee, when all, both debtors and servants were set free."[18] With this interpretation Godet agrees when he states that

on the first day of the year of Jubilee, the priests went all through the land, announcing with sound of trumpets the blessings brought by the opening year.[19]

Plumtre says: "It is obvious that both figures, the return from exile and the release at the Jubilee, admirably express Christ's work of redemption."[20]

Christ's Spirit-anointed ministry here at the outset of His mission is a vivid reminder of the ministry of the Spirit as declared by Paul to the Corinthians: "Now the Lord is the Spirit; and where the Spirit of the Lord is, there is liberty" (II Cor. 3:17), and again Paul's declaration of the purpose of his own ministry in Acts 26:18.

F. The Holy Spirit in Relation to Christ's Instruction of His Disciples

In the preparation of His disciples for their ministry, Jesus gave to them certain specific instructions concerning the Holy Spirit. These instructions appear in three different relationships to His followers, in the Synoptic Gospels. One pertains to the Father's gift of the Spirit to them (Luke 11:13), the other two concern the Spirit's ministry in relation to their trials (Matt. 10:20; Mark 13:11, and Luke 12:12).

Barclay emphasizes the importance of the Spirit in the life and ministry of all Christ's disciples. If Christ needed to depend upon the

---

18. *Op. cit.*, p. 216.
19. *Commentary on the Gospel of Luke* (Grand Rapids: Zondervan Publishing House, rep., n.d.), p. 234.
20. "The Gospel According to Luke," *Commentary on the Whole Bible*, ed. C. J. Ellicott (Grand Rapids: Zondervan Publishing House, rep., n.d.) IV, 221.

Spirit then His disciples are even more dependent upon the Spirit than He was.[21] It is highly significant that Jesus follows His discussion with His disciples on the subject of prayer with His assurance of the Father's willingness to bestow the Spirit upon those who ask Him. Christ's own spirit-empowered prayer had moved one of His disciples to request that He teach them to pray likewise (Luke 11:1). In response Jesus gave to them the model prayer, commonly known as "The Lord's Prayer," which has been used by Christians in private and public worship ever since (Luke 11:2-4; cf. Matt. 6:9-13).

He follows this lesson in prayer with an hypothetical situation, the main import of which is intense desire arising out of a desperate need that expresses itself in persistent importunity (Luke 11:5-9). This in turn is emphasized by an exhortation to persistence in prayer (Luke 11:10), and the assurance of the Father's willingness to supply the petitioner's request (Luke 11:11-12). At this point Christ climaxed His instruction by driving home the main thrust of the entire lesson: "If you then, *being evil,* know how to give good gifts to your children, *how much more shall your Heavenly Father give the Holy Spirit to those that ask Him?*" (Luke 11:13). That is, request with an intensity of desire such as He has illustrated in the previous examples.

Three things stand out clearly in this assurance from Jesus to His disciples of the Heavenly Father's readiness to bestow upon them the Holy Spirit. First, importunate prayer is basic to the success of their Christian lives and ministry. Second, the motivation and effectiveness of such prayer is dependent upon the Spirit in their lives (cf. Rom. 8:25-27), and third, it is God's plan and purpose to bestow the Holy Spirit upon all believers. Here is one of the clearest intimations of the effusion of the Spirit upon the disciples of Christ at the first Christian Pentecost that is given in the Synoptic Gospels. Wesley notes a significant gradation in the examples leading up to and including this divine assurance of God's readiness to bestow the Spirit upon the believing disciples. He remarks: "How beautiful is the gradation—a friend, a father, God!"[22]

We can understand the full force of this divine assurance of the Spirit only as it is taken in conjunction with Matthew's account of Christ's words. According to Matthew, Jesus said, "If you then, being evil, know how to give good gifts to your children, how much more

21. *Op. cit.,* p. 24.
22. *Op. cit.,* p. 243.

shall your Father who is in heaven give what is good to those who ask Him!" (Matt. 7:11). We readily agree with Barclay in his comparison of the accounts of Luke and Matthew on this passage.

The gift of the Spirit to believers is the very essence of all God's good gifts to His children. It is not necessary to regard these passages as contradictory. Barclay holds that Jesus may have used both forms of this saying. Thus the Spirit is God's supreme gift, and through the Spirit all other good gifts are received from God.[23]

Wesley likewise remarks that the Holy Spirit is *"The best of gifts, and that which includes every other gift."*[24]

When thus understood, it becomes evident that the Spirit is the divine administrator and dispenser of every blessing and benefit which the believer receives from the Father. Without the Spirit man has no access to God and God has no way of dispensing to man these spiritual blessings. Paul said without equivocation: "if anyone does not have the Spirit of Christ, he does not belong to Him" (Rom. 8:9b).

But an even deeper meaning emerges from these words of Christ, if we take them to intimate the inclusion of the gracious effusion of the Spirit at Pentecost. He spoke these words to His disciples, who as such were born of the Spirit and whose names were entered on the records of God's kingdom (Luke 10:20). Yet Christ characterizes them as "being evil." This characterization we would understand to refer to an *inner condition of heart,* rather than evil in the sense of open rebellion against God. It was not until they received *the fullness of the Spirit* in the Pentecostal effusion that their inner natures were purified from this condition. This gracious act of the Spirit at Pentecost Peter clearly witnessed to in his defense of the gospel for the Gentiles at the church's first general council when he said: "And God, who knows the heart, bore witness to them, giving them the Holy Spirit, just as He also did to us; and He made no distinction between us and them, cleansing their hearts by faith" (Acts 15:8-9).

Paul adds his testimony to this gracious divine provision administered by the Spirit when he says, "that my offering of the Gentiles might become acceptable, sanctified by the Holy Spirit" (Rom. 15:16b).

Important as was the Spirit of Christ's disciples in the areas of prayer and their ministry, another area was yet more crucial. This

---

23. *Op. cit.,* p. 25.
24. *Op. cit.,* p. 243.

was the area in which their faith would be tested to the limit, and in which their fidelity to Christ would depend on the presence and power of the Spirit in their lives. According to Matthew's Gospel, Christ informs them that they will be as sheep among wolves; they will need superior wisdom and purity of life; they will be hauled before the courts and will be scourged; they will be tried before governors and kings for His sake as His witnesses; brother will betray brother and fathers and children will betray each other, even to death, and they will be the objects of the hatred of all unrighteous men (Matt. 10:16-23).

However, Christ gives to them the assurance that in the midst of all these trials to which they will be subjected for His name's sake they have the assurance of being directed and fortified by the Holy Spirit. Christ says:

> But when they deliver you up, do not become anxious about how or what you will speak; for it shall be given you in that hour what you are to speak. For it is not you who speak, but it is the Spirit of your Father who speaks in you" (Matt. 10:19-20; cf Mark 13:9-13).

Luke's description of the indignities and sufferings to which Christ's disciples will be subjected for His name's sake does not differ appreciably from that given by Matthew and Mark, except that it includes the warning against blaspheming the Holy Spirit, which will be considered subsequently (Luke 12:8-12).

The one most important factor of security in their ordeal is to be the Spirit. By His omniscient wisdom and omnipotent power they will be fully equipped to meet every exigency of their lives and ministry. Clarke notes:

> This was an extraordinary promise, and was literally fulfilled to those first preachers of the gospel; and to them it was essentially necessary, because the New Testament dispensation was to be fully opened by their extraordinary inspiration. In a certain measure it may be truly said that the Holy Spirit animates the true disciples of Christ and enables them to *speak*. *Your Father*. This is added to excite and increase their confidence in God.[25]

Barclay notes that God never leaves the Christian believer to do his battles alone. The spirit will help him to "face the unfaceable and do the undoable and to bear the unbearable."[26]

G. The Holy Spirit in Relation to Christ's Expulsion of Demons

Matthew records Christ's first direct personal encounter with Satan, following His temptation in the wilderness, when Christ by

---

25. *Op. cit.*, p. 789.
26. *Op. cit.*, p. 25.

the power of the Spirit expelled a demon from a possessed man during His Perean ministry (Matt. 12:22-30; cf. Mark 3:22-30 and Luke 11:14-23). Matthew states: "Then there was brought to Him a demon-possessed man who was blind and dumb, and He healed him, so that the dumb man spoke and saw" (12:22). However, in verse 28 Christ implies that it was by the "Spirit of God" that He cast this demon out. That both Mark and Luke concur with Matthew's statement in verse 28 is evident from their records in Mark 3:29 and Luke 11:20. The onlookers gave two different interpretations of this event. While they were all amazed at the miraculous deliverance, in the minds of some there arose a suspicion that Christ was the Messiah, "the Son of David" (v. 23). However, the Pharisees, who could not deny the evidence of the miracle, assigned it to the power of *Beelzebul* (or *Beezebul*). On another occasion also the Pharisees, who seemed to be somewhat expert in their knowledge of demonology, designated this Beelzebul "the ruler of the demons" (Matt. 9:34). If this interpretation is valid, then Christ, endued with the power of the Holy Spirit, here again encounters and routs the same Satan over whom He gained the victory in His wilderness temptation immediately following His baptism. That Satan personally should have possessed this unfortunate individual made of it a most extraordinary case. Thus it is not surprising that in this incident alone, where Christ encountered demons, according to the Synoptic records, following His temptation-victory, the Holy Spirit is mentioned as the agent of the expulsion of Satan.

Luke's version of this incident in which he records Christ as saying, "if I cast out demons *by the finger of God*" (Luke 11:20a) need not cause concern. Barclay thinks it unnecessary to argue which of these two forms is original or genuine. He says we are not confronted with "an *either or*," but with "a *both and*." He considers that Christ may have said this many times, and that He likely used both forms of saying.[27]

Barclay further notes that Jesus used these expressions, "*the Spirit of God*" and "*the finger of God*," synonymously. He then calls attention to the significant fact that *the finger of God* occurs in three important connections in the Old Testament, namely, in the creative work of God: "When I consider Thy heavens, *the work of Thy fingers*" (Ps. 8:3); in the special revelation of God where "He gave Moses the two tablets of testimony, tablets of stone, written by *the finger of God*" (Exod. 31:18); and in God's demonstration of His

---

27. *Ibid.*, p. 24.

power in the deliverance of Israel from Egypt, which caused the Egyptian magicians, who failed to match Moses' miracles, to inform Pharaoh that "This is *the finger of God*" (Exod. 8:19). Barclay notes that when Jesus used the expression "*the finger of God*" He referred to the Spirit of God working through Him. Thus it signified that in Christ was the consummation of "the creating, the revealing, and the redeeming power of God."[28] Thus *God's finger* represents His creative, revealing, and redemptive power executed in the affairs of men by the Holy Spirit, who here, as elsewhere, administers the redemptive provisions of Christ.

Clarke thinks that the Spirit may be mentioned here in opposition to the magical incantations of certain Jews who professed ability to cast out devils (cf. Acts 8:9-24; 13:8-12; 19:13-17). What is clearly evident in this remarkable incident is that Satan has been conquered by the power of the Holy Spirit and is now subservient to the will of God. Thus he has no power over believing men beyond the permissive will of God.

Christ's statement, "if I cast out demons by the Spirit of God [which was evident from the possessed man's deliverance], then the kingdom of God has come upon you," clearly implies His destruction of Satan's kingdom on earth and its replacement with the kingdom of God in the hearts of believing men. The expression, "the kingdom of God has come upon you" doubtless suggests the unexpectedness and surprise with which they were encountered with Christ's kingdom rule.

H. The Seriousness of Blasphemy Against the Holy Spirit

The solemn warning of Jesus Christ against the danger of blasphemy against the Holy Spirit is directly related to the preceding incident in which He was accused of casting out the demon by the ruler of demons, *Beelzebul* (cf. Matt. 9:34). Here is one of the most awe-inspiring statements in the entire Bible, or any other literature, in fact. Barclay calls these words "the most terrifying thought in the New Testament."[29] These solemn words came directly from the lips of the Son of God:

> "Therefore I say to you, any sin and blasphemy shall be forgiven men, but blasphemy against the Spirit shall not be forgiven. And whosoever shall speak a word against the Son of Man, it shall be

---

28. *Ibid.*
29. *Ibid.,* p. 26.

forgiven him; but whosoever shall speak against the Holy Spirit, it shall not be forgiven him, either in this age, or in the age to come" (Matt. 12:31-32).

Mark's version of Christ's words is even more weighty when he says: "whoever blasphemes against the Holy Spirit *never has forgiveness, but is guilty of an eternal sin*" (Mark 3:29). And Mark's version is exceeding helpful in understanding *the nature* of this *unforgivable blasphemy*, which is only given implicitly in Matthew and passed over entirely by Luke. Mark explains: "because they were saying, 'He has an unclean Spirit' " (3:30). Clearly Mark's meaning is that the *unforgivable blasphemy against the Holy Spirit* is to assign to Satan the works of the Holy Spirit. There is convincing logic, as well as divine authority, in these awful words. Christ is the only Savior of men. The Spirit is the only administrator of Christ's saving provisions. Satan is the arch enemy of Christ and man's salvation. In this enemy of God and man there is no hope of salvation. Thus to assign to Satan the administrative work of the Spirit is to deprive Him of any possible saving help to man. Since this cuts off any possible access of God to man or of man to God, it leaves man in an utterly hopeless position in relation to God. This was exactly what certain Pharisees were doing when they said, "This man casts out demons only by Beelzebul the ruler of the demons" (Matt. 12:24). They were denying in fact that Christ had ever conquered Satan, and were assigning the superior power to the very emperor of the infernal world, thus making Christ Himself a subservient instrument of the Devil himself, illogical as all this was. Christ intimates this illogic when He says that "Any kingdom divided against itself is laid to waste; and any city or house divided against itself shall not stand. And if Satan casts out Satan, he is divided against himself; how then shall his kingdom stand? (Matt. 12:25b-26). In fact Christ implies that Satan has used better logic than do these Pharisees. Wesley remarks: "Does not that subtle spirit [Satan] know this is not the way to establish His Kingdom?"[30]

Again Christ asks of these Pharisees a question that devastates their accusation that He casts out demons by the ruler of the demons. In effect He says, How can I rob Satan of his subjects unless I have first conquered and bound him? (see Matt. 12:29).

Barclay has a most helpful explanation of this unforgivable sin against the Holy Spirit. He thinks that the expression "son of man"

---

30. *Op. cit.*, 63.

referred to here by Matthew and Luke may not be in reference to Christ at all, but that it may mean just any human being. In this case it is understandable that such a sin against a fellowman would be forgivable, and thus the distinction between a sin against Christ as "Son of man" and the Holy Spirit would disappear.

However, Barclay goes on to point up that the deepest meaning of the sin against the Holy Spirit may consist in resisting His strivings until the person becomes totally insensitive to His appeals. We would heartily agree with Barclay that the person who fears he has committed the sin against the Holy Spirit is one who has not done so. If a man has actually committed this sin he has in large measure, if not entirely, lost his consciousness of sin. If one realizes himself to be a sinner he cannot have committed the sin against the Holy Spirit. For it is the Spirit who creates the consciousness of sin.[31]

I. The Holy Spirit in Relation to the Lordship of Jesus Christ

We come here to the very climax of Christ's teaching concerning the mission of the Holy Spirit. Jesus Christ came to this world to reclaim divine lordship over all men and creation itself, which had been usurped by Satan in the Fall. From the Fall to the completion of Christ's finished redemptive work it was the function of the Holy Spirit to superintend and direct the entire redemptive plan to its culmination in Christ and His redemptive work. When this redemptive work was accomplished, Christ triumphantly announced His succession to the Lordship of the universe by proclaiming that "All authority has been given to me in heaven and earth" (Matt. 28:18). On the basis of this universal authority He then commissioned His disciples to go forth and proclaim His Lordship to the entire race of men (Matt. 28:19-20). This proclamation became the burden of the apostolic witness throughout the Book of Acts, where the Lordship of Jesus Christ is referred to no less than 110 times. This is many more times than any other doctrine of the Christian religion occurs in the Acts record.

In confident assurance of this victory, Jesus subtly brings it to light in His teaching in the temple, according to Mark's record (12:35). The discussion goes as follows:

> Now while the Pharisees were gathered together, Jesus asked them a question, saying, "What do you think about the Christ, whose son is He?" They said to Him "*The son* of David." He said to them, "Then

---

31. *Op. cit.*, pp. 27, 28, 29.

how does David in the Spirit call Him 'Lord,' saying, 'The Lord said to my Lord, "Sit at My right hand, Until I put Thine enemies beneath Thy feet." ' "If David then calls Him 'Lord,' how is He his son?" And no one was able to answer Him a word, nor did anyone dare from that day on to ask Him another question (Matt. 22:14-46).

The heart of this discussion rests in Christ's question in verse 43. "Then how does David in the Spirit [or by inspiration] call Him 'Lord'?"

These words are quoted from Psalm 110:1, which the Jews ascribed to David, and which they recognized as inspired by the Spirit of God. If David said under the inspiration of the Spirit, "The Lord said to my Lord, Sit at My Right Hand" (cf v. 44), then the "My Lord" of David's utterance could not have been his son. Clarke notes well that two points are clear from this argument of Christ: "(1) That David wrote by the inspiration [of the Spirit] of God; and (2) That it is a prophetic declaration of the Messiah."[32] This is the claim that Christ is now making for Himself. If Christ is the son of David by human generation, as they admit, then He is the Lord of the universe by the witness of the Holy Spirit who inspired David to make this utterance. It has been the function of the Spirit to witness to the Lordship of Christ from the first intimations of God's redemptive plan, and that continues to be His function to the end of the age.

J. The Holy Spirit in Relation to Christ's Baptismal Formula

There remains one further function of the Holy Spirit in the Synoptic Gospels, namely, His relationship to the baptismal formula in Christ's commission to His disciples to proclaim His accomplished Lordship over all creation.

The witness of His disciples, who constitute the church of Jesus Christ, is God's method of winning men through Christ's Saviorship to His Lordship. Paul makes this crystal clear when he writes to the Corinthians thus: "We are ambassadors for Christ, as though God were entreating through us; we beg you on behalf of Christ, be reconciled to God" (II Cor. 5:20).

The Synoptic Gospels begin with clear evidence for the Triune God, especially at the Baptism of Jesus, as we have seen. They close with the clear witness of Jesus Christ to the divine Trinity in the baptismal formula which He commissions His disciples to administer

---

32. *Op. cit.*, p. 814.

to those who accept His Lordship in their lives. We shall not here concern ourselves with the critical controversy concerning the genuineness of this trinitarian baptismal formula in Matthew. Insufficient critical evidence has been produced to invalidate it, and we shall assume with the church of the ages that these are words spoken by Jesus to His disciples, and that they are binding upon all of His followers to the end of the gospel age. This formula meets the demands of a document written primarily for Christian Jews by a Christian Jew, that "by the mouth of two or three witnesses every fact may be confirmed" (cf. Deut. 19:15; Matt. 18:16). Thus the Father, the Son, and the Holy Spirit, the Triune God, witness to all that Christ taught and did as of divine origin as recorded in the Synoptic Gospels. No clearer affirmation of the divinity of the Spirit is required than that given in these closing words of Jesus. The words of Clarke are a fitting conclusion to this discussion.

> Again, baptism is not made in the name of a quality or attribute of the divine nature; therefore the *Father,* and the *Son,* and the *Holy Spirit* are not qualities or attributes of the divine nature. The orthodox, as they are termed, have generally considered this text as a decisive proof of the doctrine of the Holy Trinity, and what else can they draw from it? Is it possible for words to convey a plainer sense than do these? And do they not direct every reader to consider the *Father, the Son,* and the *Holy Spirit* as three distinct Persons?[33]

33. *Ibid.,* p. 835.

Chapter 5

The Holy Spirit
in the
Gospel According to John

I. THE IMPORTANCE OF THE HOLY SPIRIT IN THE GOSPEL OF JOHN

The Fourth Gospel is what Barclay calls the "high water mark" of the New Testament teachings concerning the Holy Spirit."[1] It is surprising to note that Walter Thomas Conner in his otherwise excellent book *The Work of the Holy Spirit* does not include a specific treatment of the Spirit in the Gospel According to John, though he does have a chapter on "The Holy Spirit in the Synoptics."[2] The Gospel According to John, more than any other book of the New Testament, except perhaps the Book of Acts, has influenced the thinking of scholars and laymen alike on their understanding of the Holy Spirit.

In this chapter we shall follow the order in which John's record presents the Spirit. However, where his treatment covers materials already dealt with in the preceding chapter on "The Holy Spirit in the Synoptic Gospels" the reader will simply be referred to such treatment, rather than duplicating it in the present chapter.

---

1. *Op. cit.*, p. 30.
2. (Nashville: Broadman Press, 1949), Table of Contents, p. 1.

Perhaps the one distinguishing mark of John's treatment of the Spirit, from that found in the Synoptics, is that his material consists mainly of *Christ's teachings* concerning the Spirit.

The first specific mention of the Spirit encountered in John's Gospel is in relation to John's baptism of Jesus. However, since this remarkable event was treated in the chapter on the Synoptics the reader is referred to that treatment, with the exception of a single comment of importance. In John 1:33 John the Baptist says: "He upon whom you see the Spirit descending and *remaining upon Him, this is the one who baptizes in* (Grk. *en* = "in," "with," or "by"] *the Holy Spirit.*" Richard S. Taylor offers a significant observation on the Greek preposition *en* used by John in this passage. He notes that

> the use of the English preposition "of" implies a corresponding Greek genetive, which is never used in connection with this spiritual baptism. The genitive is found in Matthew 21:25, "the baptism *of* repentance," but *nowhere is there a similar "baptism of the Spirit."* The preposition used is *en,* in, *with,* or sometimes *by,* and usually these days . . . the nomenclature has become almost exclusively *"baptism in the Spirit.* Actually *it is Christ's baptism with the Spirit,* the counterpart of John's baptism with water.[3]

This observation accords well with the place and function of the Spirit throughout the entire Bible. Nowhere does the Spirit function independent of the Father and the Son. His mission in the world is to serve the redemptive interests of and to glorify Christ. Christ makes this clear and specific in His teaching concerning the Spirit in John 16:14 where He says: "He shall glorify Me; for He shall take of Mine, and shall disclose it to you." In this sense there is no such thing as "the baptism of the Holy Spirit," only a "baptism *in, by,* or *with* the Spirit."

II. THE HOLY SPIRIT IN RELATION TO THE NEW BIRTH

The first of Christ's teachings concerning the Spirit, as recorded by John, relates to the new birth, or spiritual regeneration. The account concerns Christ's conversation with Nicodemus, and the record is found in 3:1-25. The basic question concerns the requirements for admission to the kingdom of God. The fundamental answer to that question is a new, or second, birth wrought in man's spiritual nature by the regenerative operation of the Holy Spirit.

Nicodemus was a Jew and understood well the practice and

---

3. Professor of Theology and Missions at Nazarene Seminary, in a letter to the author.

meaning of water baptism. It is at this point of his knowledge that Jesus begins His answer to Nicodemus' quest for salvation. It is of *"water and the Spirit, not the Spirit and water,* by which a man must be born to enter the kingdom of God, Jesus informs His earnest inquirer. Proselytes to the Jewish religion were admitted through water baptism and circumcision, the first symbolizing a rebirth and the second the circumcision of the heart, or purification of the inward nature from the pollution of sin. Thus the water used in his baptism was only an external symbol or emblem of the Holy Spirit.

As by the water the body was washed, cleansed, and refreshed, so in the new birth by the Spirit the soul would be released from its guilt of sin and renewed into a new life in Christ. Here is where the impartation of a new life, the life of God, or properly speaking, immortality, is implanted in the soul of man. Man becomes a new creature because by the regenerative influence of the Spirit moving upon his spirit a new life from above is imparted to him. While the Greek word *bios* is used in the New Testament for man's *natural life,* *zoē* is the word that usually designated the supernatural life imparted to him in the new birth by the regenerative influence of the Holy Spirit (cf. II Cor. 5:17).

Jesus uses the same word for Spirit as He uses for wind, but obviously with a different meaning. The import of His remark to Nicodemus seems to be that just as the natural phenomenon which we call wind is effective, though imperceptible in itself, so the heavenly *pneuma,* or "breath," or the Spirit of God is effective in the spiritual realm in imparting a new life to the soul spiritually dead in trespasses and sin (cf. Eph. 2:1-5; Rom. 8:11).

Wesley remarks incisively on Christ's words to Nicodemus, "so is everyone who is born of the Spirit" (John 3:8b): "The fact is plain; the manner of His operation, inexplicable."[4] Clarke says, "we cannot discern the air itself; we only know that it exists by the effects which it produces . . . the effects [of the Spirit] are as discernible and as sensible as those of the wind, but itself we cannot see. But he who is born of God knows that he is thus born."[5] Paul said: "The Spirit Himself bears witness with our spirit that we are the children of God" (Rom. 8:16); and the apostle John said: "By this we know that we abide in Him and He in us, because He has given us of His Spirit" (I John 4:13).

From Christ's teaching to Nicodemus concerning the work of the Spirit in the new birth we may deduce the following truth. No man

4. *Op. cit.* (reprint), p. 312.
5. *Op. cit.,* p. 904.

can enter the kingdom of God until he is born anew of the Holy Spirit. The new life which he receives in this birth is the very life of God imported by the Spirit. While man cannot comprehend the method by which the Spirit works this miracle of a new creation, he can and will know the effects of that which the Spirit has wrought in his life. The final assurance of his new birth is the inward witness of the Holy Spirit to his human spirit that he is a child of God. Paul writes to the Galatian Christians: "Because you are sons, God has sent forth the Spirit of His Son into our hearts, crying Abba Father" (4:6).

Henry Drummond said the new birth wrought by the Spirit in man dead in his trespasses and sins is like the inanimate soil into which the animate plant sinks its roots, transmutes to it life, takes it up into its living organism, and thus transforms its being and nature.[6] Likewise the living and life-giving Spirit of God penetrates the spiritually inanimate nature of man, imparts to it the new life from God above, takes that nature up into His living self, and transforms it into a new being (cf. II Peter 1:3-4).

In John 3:34 Christ presents yet another great truth, which follows on the new birth by the Spirit. He says "*He gives the Spirit without measures.*" From these words it is clear that Christ means to teach that the Holy Spirit of God is *qualitative*, and *not quantitative*. The Spirit is in no sense bounded or limited by quantitative considerations. He is the representative of the infinite Godhead and as such extends to every location and need of man.

III. JESUS' FREE OFFER OF THE SPIRIT TO ALL BELIEVERS

In John's Gospel 7:37-39 we have one of the most remarkable, and in certain respects most misunderstood, teachings concerning the Holy Spirit. This passage may be best considered by approaching it from four different perspectives. Thus we shall note first *the occasion* of His offer of the Spirit, second, *the condition* of the offer, third, *the effects* of the Spirit received, and finally, *the problem* involved in John's explanation.

A. The Occasion of Christ's Universal Offer of the Spirit

In John 7:37-39 Jesus makes one of His most dramatic statements concerning the Holy Spirit found anywhere in the New Testament.

---

6. *Natural Law in the Spiritual World.*

Likewise, His promise of the Spirit was made under a most dramatic circumstance. John says that it was on the last great day of the feast that "Jesus stood and cried out, saying, 'If any man is thirsty, let him come to Me and drink.' "

The occasion was the Jew's Feast of Tabernacles, and the place was the Temple Court (John 7:14). The Jew's Feast of Tabernacles was a harvest-thanksgiving festival which also commemorated Israel's journey through the wilderness to their promised Canaan land. During this feast the people dwelt in booths commemorating their tent dwellings during the wilderness journey. During the first seven days, Clarke says, "they professed to offer sacrifices for the seventy nations of the earth, but on the eighth day they offered sacrifices for Israel; therefore the eighth day was more highly esteemed than any of the others."[7]

On this *high day* of the feast the multitudes were in the Temple and the surrounding precincts as worshipers and onlookers. The ceremonies were most impressive and opportune for the announcement Christ was soon to make. The High Priest, accompanied by his official retinue, and bearing a silver pitcher from the Temple, proceeded to the pool of Siloam where he filled the pitcher with water and returned through the crowd to the Temple. The accompanying chant of the worshiping throngs lent dignity and significance to the ceremony as they sang the promises of the coming Messiah from the prophecy of Isaiah.

> "Behold, God is my salvation, I will trust and not be afraid; for the Lord God is my strength and song, and He has become my salvation." Therefore you will joyfully draw water from the springs of salvation (12:2-3).

Returning to the Temple, the High Priest poured the water over the altar of burnt offering as an offering to God. May there possibly be in this act the symbolical significance that the water represents the age of the Spirit which supersedes the age of law represented by the altar of burnt-offering on which sacrifice for sins was made?

Barclay sees a threefold symbolism in this ceremony: (1) thanksgiving to God for water in memory of their waterless and thirsty days in the wilderness journey; (2) an "acted prayer" for rain that the harvest would never fail; (3) a forecast or prophecy of the messianic days when they would draw water from the wells of salvation, and the Spirit would be poured on the thirsty souls of men.[8] He thinks

---

7. *Op. cit.*, p. 920.
8. *Op. cit.*, p. 31.

the people all well understood these symbolisms. However, little did they realize that the messianic days were at hand, and that the Spirit would soon be poured out at their Feast of Pentecost.

It was probably as the Priest was pouring the water on the altar of burnt-offering that the people were startled and arrested as the distinct voice of Jesus rang out from the temple courts, "If any man is thirsty, let him come to Me and drink." If it be doubted that so many people could hear the voice of Christ without any modern vocal aids for communication, it will be remembered that Jesus addressed five thousand men by the Sea of Galilee on a mountain-side, with possibly four times that number including the women and children. It was not uncommon for John Wesley to address from ten to twenty-five thousand in a single audience in his day in England, and his journal frequently records that they all heard him distinctly. This entire occasion appears to most remarkably foreshadow the Day of Pentecost, when the mighty effusion of the Spirit would occur.

B. The Conditions of Christ's Universal Offer of the Spirit

The conditions for the reception of the Spirit which Christ announces are threefold. They may be simply stated as spiritual desire, personal willing-obedience, and saving faith in Christ. *"If any man is thirsty, let him come to me and drink.* These first two conditions are absolutely necessary to the reception of any provision of God's saving mercies. However, Jesus lays down a third condition of equal importance, namely, saving faith—"He who believes in me" (John 7:38a).

Jesus once said, when criticized by Pharisees for associating with the tax-gatherers and sinners, "It is not those who are healthy who need a physician, but those who are ill" (Matt. 9:12). By this rebuke we understand Christ to mean that it is only one who recognizes and admits his moral malady, one who is sincerely desirous of a remedy, that He can help. There can be no appropriation of God's blessings without a sincere desire for them. And there can be no reception of Christ or His Spirit without a recognized and confessed need.

But Christ's second condition is as important as the first: "let him come unto me." Indeed, God has taken the initiative in man's salvation by sending His Son to die for us. But He respects the moral freedom and responsibility of man to respond to His initiative. "Come to Me, all who are weary and heavy laden, and I will give you rest" (Matt. 11:28), said Jesus. "Behold, I stand at the door and knock," said the risen Christ, "if any one hears My voice and opens the door, I will come in to him, and will dine with him and he with Me" (Rev. 3:20). God's last invitation to man given in the Bible implies both man's recognized need of God and his obedient response: "And the Spirit and the bride [the church] say, 'Come'. . . . And let the one who is thirsty come; let the one who wishes take the water of life without cost" (Rev. 22:17). Christ's promise is that the Father will give the Spirit to those who ask Him (Luke 11:13). All of these divine utterances, and all others in relation to the question in fact, state or imply the necessary condition of man's personal need and obedient response in order to receive God's Spirit as an inner personal experience. This brings us to the third consideration of this great offer of Christ.

But faith in the divine person and saving efficacy of Christ's redemptive work is also an absolutely essential condition for the reception of the promised Spirit. To the assembled Jews whom Christ addressed, this meant their recognition and acceptance of Him as their long-expected Messiah. But to every man desiring salvation it means personal faith in Jesus Christ as his Savior and Lord (Heb. 11:6). When the foregoing conditions are met the divine response is assured. This brings us to a consideration of the effects of the Spirit upon the recipient.

C. The Effects of the Spirit upon Those Who Receive Him

1. The Spirit Indwells and Purifies the Believer's Deepest Being

Two great truths emerge from Christ's words: "From the innermost being shall flow rivers of living water" (John 7:38b). In the first instance it is clear that this experience of the Spirit which Christ promises is something beyond the usual experience of the Spirit in the Old Testament, with which these Jews were perfectly familiar. In the Old Testament the Spirit was, as we have seen, for the most part an external experience, usually *"a coming upon."* Here He is to be an internal experience of man's deepest spiritual nature. In fact, *He is to dwell in and flow out from man's "innermost being,"* as a fresh, pure stream of water that flows from the mountainside spring by reason of the pressure exerted upon it from within the bowels of the earth.

In fact the Greek word used here by Jesus is *koilias,* a form of *koilia,* which means "belly," "abdomen," or a general term which covers any organ of the abdomen, such as the stomach or womb. *"Ek koilias matros,* means "from birth."[9] In the *KJV* it is rendered "belly," but "innermost being" seems best to express the true meaning of Christ's word. The term "depths of one's being" well expresses the idea. When the Spirit was outpoured upon the disciples on the Day of Pentecost it is said that "they were all *filled with the Holy Spirit*" (Acts 2:4a). If they were *filled with the Spirit* then His presence reached to the deepest recesses of their innermost beings.

We have noted that one possible meaning of the Greek word *koilias,* used by Jesus in verse 38, is "womb." The womb is the source of the production of new life. Is it possible that Jesus may be alluding to this very source of new life, in a spiritual sense, where the Spirit dwells and from which He sheds forth His influence upon others? It was in the womb of Mary that the Incarnation took place. May Christ here have used the word *koilias* intentionally in a figurative sense to represent the area of the Spirit's dwelling in man's innermost being, where his new spiritual life is generated and from which it issues forth? This would certainly make better sense than the crude and illogical *KJV* translation of the word—"belly." It is instructive that Nicodemus uses the same word *koilias,* for womb in his conversation with Jesus in John 3:4.

The foregoing is exceedingly important in understanding the cleansing efficacy of the baptism in the Spirit. Since He is the *Holy Spirit* of God His very *holy* nature will accordingly purify whatever He pervades, and consequently His penetration to the innermost recesses of the believer's being effects the purification of the believer's soul, and thus he is inwardly sanctified by the indwelling personal presence of the *Holy Spirit* (cf. Rom 15:16). Paul's words collaborated this truth when he wrote to the Corinthians: "Do you not know that you are a temple of God, and that the Spirit of God dwells in you . . . the temple of God is holy, and that is what you are" (I Cor. 3:16, 17); and again, "Or do you not know that your body is a temple [or "sanctuary"] of the Holy Spirit who is in you, whom you have from God, and that you are not your own?" (I Cor. 6:19).

Perhaps no one besides the apostle Paul has ever fathomed and described the utmost subconscious regions of the natural man's turbulent condition more adequately than Sigmund Freud, the renowned naturalistic psychologist. Freud describes this region of man's nature, which he calls the *id* as a chaos or "caldron of seething excitement." This is, in Freud's psychological concept, the true

---

9. Souter, *op. cit.,* p. 135.

unconscious reservoir of instinctive impulses characterized by a blind dynamic wishfulness. Freud thinks of this as but a stage in the onward insurgence of the blind, unintelligent, and undirected animalistic evolutional force in man.[10] In Romans 7 Paul recognizes and describes this condition, and then simply denominates it "the sin which indwells me" (Rom. 7:17). Freud diagnoses the condition quite correctly, but he wrongly denominates it and assigns it to a false source, and offers no prescription for its remedy, simply because he knows no remedy. Paul likewise accurately describes the condition, properly denominates it as "indwelling sin," and then prescribes God's remedy for the condition (Rom. 7:25–8:3).

This is, in Wesleyan terminology, experiential sanctification provided in Christ's atonement (Heb. 13:12), wrought in the believer's innermost being by the baptism of the Holy Spirit (I Thess. 5:22-24).

2. The Spirit Flows Out from the Believer's Inmost Being

But a second no less significant implication emerges from these words of Christ, "From his innermost being shall flow rivers of living water." There is here a twofold implication in the Spirit's outflow from man's innermost being. It precludes any possible stagnation of the Spirit-possessed individual's religious experience. It is the assurance of a continuous freshness and cleanness of that experience. This is not to say that sin may not happen to the sanctified, Spirit-filled, but it does mean that sin does not cling to his nature, but is cleansed at once if and when it does occur. It may be illustrated by the water that flows from the spring on the mountainside over the rocks in the channel of its descent to the valley below. Indeed impurities may fall upon the stones over which it flows, but they are washed away without opportunity to gather dirt on the stones. John Wesley clearly taught a progressive sanctification from the moment of conversion, leading up to a crisis experience of entire sanctification, and thereafter a continuous or progressive sanctification following the crisis experience. This issue is most admirably and adequately dealt with in a scholarly article by Bishop Leslie Marston, "The Crisis Process Issue in Wesleyan Thought," *Wesleyan Theological Journal.*[11]

---

10. Norman N. Bonner and Charles W. Carter, "Psychodynamics Versus Evangelicalism," *Wesleyan Theological Journal* (Wilmore, Ky.: The Wesleyan Theological Society, 1968), Vol. 3, No. 1, pp. 67-75.

11. "The Crisis Process Issue in Wesleyan Thought," *Wesleyan Theological Journal* (Concord, Mich: Published by the Wesleyan Theological Society, 1969), Vol. 4, No. 1, pp. 3-15.

However, of no less importance is the influence of the Spirit that flows out of the Spirit-filled life upon others. The influence of the Spirit's outflow from the lives of Spirit-filled men upon individuals and society throughout the Christian era is beyond estimation. This experience impelled Paul to look upon the entire world of humanity as the objects of Christ's saving gospel (Rom. 1:8; Col. 1:6, 23). It was this experience that moved Wesley to see and say that "the world is my parish."

D. The Problem in Christ's Offer of the Spirit

The problem that has puzzled the thinking of many interpreters arises out of John's statement in verse 39: *"the Spirit was not yet given,* because Jesus was not yet glorified." Of course, as we have seen in our study of the Spirit in the Old Testament and in the Synoptic Gospels the Spirit had been given already to many, and on many different occasions. Furthermore, we have Paul's statement: "But if anyone does not have the Spirit of Christ, he does not belong to Him" (Rom. 8:9). To conclude that Christ meant this statement to be taken literally would mean that there were no Christians before the effusion of the Spirit at Pentecost. Such a conclusion would be absurd in the extreme, and would directly contradict Christ's own words concerning His disciples (see John 17:6-16). Since, as we have seen in Christ's instruction of Nicodemus, any man who enters the kingdom of God must be born of, or regenerated by the Spirit, these disciples whom Christ claims as His own, did of necessity have the Spirit in their regenerated experience.

What then does John mean by these apparently strange words? Clarke is exceedingly helpful at this point. He says:

Certain measures [manifestations] of the Holy Spirit had been vouchsafed from the beginning of the world to believers and unbelievers, but that *abundant effusion* of his graces spoken of by Joel, chap. ii. 28, which peculiarly characterized the Gospel times, was not granted till after the ascension of Christ: 1. Because this Spirit in its plenitude was to come in consequence of his atonement; and therefore could not come till *after* his *crucifixion.* 2. It was to supply the place of Christ to his disciples and to all true believers; and therefore it was not necessary till after the removal of his bodily presence from among them. See our Lord's own words, John xiv. 16-18, 26; xvi. 7-15.[12]

12. "The New Testament of our Lord and Savior Jesus Christ," *Clarke's Commentary,* (Nashville: Abingdon Press, rep. n.d.) I, p. 572.

Barclay is in agreement with this interpretation. He sees John as meaning that it was only after Christ's glorification and ascension that the Spirit descended in all His fullness and power upon men, and thus the Spirit's effusion at Pentecost occurred only after Christ's ascension.[13]

This statement of John may be best understood by an illustration taken from another area of experience. Ever since creation atomic power has existed as an essential, though largely hidden and mysterious factor in nature. It is true that the early Greek philosophers had some concept of an atomic universe. Indeed some of their theories appear absurd to us today.

However, a certain group of Greek thinkers known as the Atomists, which included Leucippus and Democritus, arrived at conclusions remarkably similar to the present-day atomic concept of the universe. These thinkers "reached the conclusion that everything in the universe was composed by the uniting in various ways and in various numbers of tiny atoms which were all alike."[14] They saw these atoms as the essential elements and forces of the universe. Through the ages this atomic energy has existed, and there have been occasional obvious manifestations of its presence and power in nature.

However, it was not until the release of two atomic bombs in 1945 to end the Second World War that the full significance of this natural force broke in upon the consciousness of men. That sudden and awful manifestation of nature's power will remain one of the greatest landmarks in human history. In fact it divides history into the preatomic and the postatomic eras. Likewise, the Holy Spirit had been present and active in the world from creation, and occasional occurrences of His existence and activities are evident throughout the Scriptures.

However, it was not until the full manifestation of His *personal presence and power* was released on the Day of Pentecost that it was given to man to understand who and what He was in the plan of God for the redemption of humanity. Barclay significantly remarks: "That is the way in which men enter into the experience of the Spirit."[15] Thus the Spirit's effusion at Pentecost became one of history's greatest spiritual landmarks. The Spirit's manifestation on

---

13. *Op. cit.,* p, 32,
14. S. E. Frost, *The Basic Teachings of the Great Philosophers* (Philadelphia: Blackstone Company, 1942, rep. 1947), p. 7.
15. *Op. cit.,* p. 32.

the Day of Pentecost also divided human history spiritually. It marked the divine witness to the completion of Christ's redemptive work which opened the door to the new era of divine grace to the souls of all men. It was this that John meant as he spoke under divine inspiration those seemingly contradictory and strong words, but which when taken in the foregoing light are perfectly logical and lucid.

IV. THE HOLY SPIRIT IN RELATION TO CHRIST'S DEPARTURE

In John 14, 15, and 16, we have Christ's teaching concerning the coming of the Holy Spirit in relation to His imminent departure from this world to return to His Father in heaven. Barclay calls this "the greatest teaching about the Spirit in the New Testament,"[16] and with this judgment we would agree.

A. The Problem of the Terminology Used for the Holy Spirit in John 14-16

1. The Difficulties of Translating Parakletos

It is significant to note that in every instance in the Synoptic Gospels, and the Gospel According to John up to this point, the Greek word *pneuma,* in one form or another, is used for the Holy Spirit. However, in these chapters Jesus uses a different word for the Holy Spirit four times. That word is *parakletos,* and it occurs in 14:16, 26; 15:26; and 16:7. In other references to the Spirit in these chapters Christ reverts to the use of the word *pneuma.*

The term *parakletos* has caused translators no small difficulty. The *KJV* renders the word "comforter." While this word had its value in the older English, it is much misunderstood today. Clarke notes that the word *comforter* in his day signified "advocate," "defender of a cause," "counselor," "patron," and "mediator," as well as the ordinary sense of the word, such as consolation in distress, trouble or worry, solace, support, assistance, or encouragement under trial. Both Wycliffe (1320?—1384) and Tyndale (1492?—1536) seem to have understood and used the word *comforter* in the sense of strength and enablement, applying it to several different texts such as Ephesians 6:10; I Timothy 1:12; and others.

---

16. *Ibid,* p. 32.

The word *comforter* derives from the Latin *fortis,* meaning "brave." However, for most English speaking people today the meaning of *comforter* is restricted in large measure to this latter common meaning. This limited understanding of the word robs it of much of its richer and broader significance. Among modern versions the *RSV* translates *paraklētos* as "counsellor"; William's translation renders it "the Friend"; Knox renders it "He who is to befriend you"; The Twentieth-Century New Testament renders it "Helper," as does Moffatt; and Philips renders it "someone to stand by you." These and other renderings of the word indicate something of the difficulty encountered in translating the Greek word *paraklētos.*

Clarke's rendering of *paraklētos,* in addition to "Comforter," as an "advocate," a "defender of a cause," a "counselor," "patron" [or], "mediator,"[17] seems to be quite comprehensive and perhaps adequate. Souter notes that *paraklētos,* as used in pre-New Testament times, had "the general sense [of] *one who speaks in favor of another, an intercessor, a helper* . . . and was borrowed by Hebrew and Aramaic."[18] Arndt and Gingrich likewise state that "in the few places where the word is found in pre-Christian and extra-Christian literature it has for the most part a more general meaning: one who appears in another's behalf, mediator, intercessor, helper."[19]

The word *paraklētos* appears in one other place in the New Testament where it is applied to Jesus Christ Himself, and is translated even in the *KJV* as "advocate" (I John 2:1). *Parakalein,* from which *paraklētos* derives, is used in the Greek Septuagint version of the Old Testament in Isaiah 40:1-2, where it is rendered "Comfort," but with the meaning of the impartation of courage and bravery. Thus it would seem that "advocate" or "helper" may be the best understanding of *paraklētos.*

Adam Clarke remarks:

> The Holy Spirit is thus called [*Parakletos = Advocate,* or Helper] because He transacts the cause of God and Christ in us, *explains* to us the nature and importance of the great atonement, shows the necessity of it, *counsels* us to receive it, *instructs* us how to lay hold on it, *vindicates* our claim to it, and makes intercessions in us with unutterable groanings. As Christ acted with His disciples while He sojourned with them, so the Holy Ghost acts with those who believe in His name.[20]

---

17. *Op. cit.,* I, 623.
18. *Op. cit.,* p. 190.
19. William F. Arndt and F. Wilbur Gingrich, *A Greek-English Lexicon of the New Testament* (Chicago: University of Chicago Press, 1957), p. 623.
20. *Op. cit.,* I, 623.

2. The Believers' Need of the Spirit-Advocate in Their Lives

Since the cross, atonement, and victorious resurrection of Jesus Christ will be man's only hope of salvation to the end of the age, so will the presence and function of the Spirit as man's advocate be necessary in the world to the end of the age to apply the benefits of Christ's redemptive work and enable man to appropriate those benefits to his salvation needs. Thus, Christ prays to the Father for His disciples that "He will give you another Helper [*Paraklētŏs,* or, "one called along side to help," or "Intercessor"] that He may be with you forever (John 14:16).

Huffman thinks the word "Helper" may best express the meaning of this word *paraklētŏs,* which Jesus uses here for the Holy Spirit. He says:

> In seeking to discover the meaning of this favorite title for the Spirit, it may be found in the seriousness of the hour in which Jesus employed it. He who had been the Helper of the disciples was about to depart, leaving the disappointed, helpless, disciples behind. He had been everything to them: teacher, guide, preceptor, example, and now he has to be taken from them. They needed not only a comforter, but a helper, in every respect.
>
> Of course these disciples stood greatly in need of comfort, as such, particularly as we see them clinging to a false hope that Jesus would do something entirely different from what He intended to do. They had hoped that Jesus would strike from the necks of the Jews the yoke of Roman domination, and would inaugurate a world kingdom, something which He did not come to do—quite the opposite. As "another helper," the Spirit was to stand beside those who would receive and welcome him, and be to them what Jesus had previously been. No word can better express the meaning of *paraklētos,* than does Helper.[21]

Since Christ is about to leave His disciples, and there are certain needs in their lives which He has met personally, but cannot longer do so in His absence, He gives to them His promise: "I will not leave you orphans; I will come to you" (John 14:18). What are these needs which make necessary the coming of the *Helper-Advocate* whom Christ has promised? Before proceeding to a further examination of the teachings of Christ concerning the Holy Spirit in these chapters, let us note some of the believers' needs which can be met only by the Spirit in Christ's absence from them.

They need further enlightenment and instruction in spiritual matters which the natural, unaided mind cannot comprehend.

21. Jasper Abraham Huffman, *Golden Treasures from the Greek New Testament for English Readers,* 2nd ed. (Marion, Ind.: The Wesley Press, 1951), pp. 79, 80.

They need the aid of the Spirit in recalling and correctly understanding what Christ taught while with them. When it is remembered that Christ wrote nothing of which we have record, and that the earliest of the Gospels was probably not written before about A.D. 60 to 70, or at best not earlier than A.D. 50, it is evident that about a quarter of a century would have elapsed between Christ's departure and the disciples' recording what He said and did while on earth. For such a task to be accomplished with accuracy the inspiration and aid of the Holy Spirit was absolutely necessary. This need, Christ assures His disciples, will be adequately met by the promised Spirit. "But the Helper, the Holy Spirit, whom the Father will send in My name, He shall teach you all things, and bring to your remembrance all that I said to you" (John 14:26).

While the function of the Spirit in enlightening and aiding the minds of Christ's disciples in accurately recalling and reconstructing His earthly life, teaching, and deeds, has great significance in relation to the reliability of the Gospel records, it also has a continuing practical significance.

There can be little doubt from either the Scriptures or the experience of Spirit-animated believers that the indwelling Spirit quickens minds, aids memories, directs the mind to penetrating insights of truth, animates the expression of truth, and in many other ways serves the minds of believers in relation to truth. But perhaps the greatest practical value of the Spirit to the believer in relation to the truth is His illumination of the mind to comprehend the message of revelation given in the Bible. As any author is the best interpreter of a book written by him, so the Holy Spirit is the most reliable interpreter of the Bible, of which He is the divine author.

B. The Teachings of Christ Concerning the Holy Spirit in John 14–16

For many centuries the Jews had looked forward to the messianic age as a time when God's Spirit would be outpoured in a universal manner upon men. The Spirit had been promised by the ancient prophets, by John the Baptist, by the Father, and now by Christ in His final confirmation to these age-long promises.

1. Christ Promises the Spirit as God's Gift to His Followers

Jesus Christ had been God's gift to the world as man's Savior (John 3:16). But the Spirit was to be God's gift to all believers as their sanctifier and preserver in Christ's saving grace. Christ is soon to be taken from them but He reassures them that He "will ask the Father, and He will give you another Helper [Advocate], that He may be with you forever" (John 14:16).

Christ's time on earth was brief, slightly more than thirty years, and His personal presence was restricted in space and time, in considerable measure, by the self-imposed limitations of the human body that He assumed in the Incarnation for the purpose of procuring man's redemption. He had now fulfilled the Father's promised gift of His redemptive mission. He is ready to return to the Father, but they are not to be left orphaned (John 14:18). They are going to receive another, a second personal gift from the Father: "He will give you another Helper."

There are four things that characterize a gift. (1) A gift is the expression of the affection and good will of one party toward another. (2) A gift is gratuitous. It costs the recipient nothing, and it requires no compensation. It cannot be earned by effort or purchased with money. (3) A gift is something to be esteemed, appreciated, treasured, and kept. And (4), to refuse the offer of a gift is an insult to the donor. Barclay is quite right in noting that it is a sad tragedy that so many people are too busy to receive God's offered gift of the Spirit.[22] May it be that Christ's purpose in requiring His disciples to tarry in Jerusalem for ten days between His ascension and the effusion of the Spirit at Pentecost was to heighten their expectation of the promised gift of the Spirit's descent upon them?

2. Christ Promises the Spirit as an Abiding Presence in the Believer's Experience

The Spirit's presence was to be to the believer what it was not possible for His earthly presence to be. In His earthly presence Christ could meet with His disciples, have fellowship with them, and teach them. However, of necessity His relation to them was inconstant and external; nor could it be their universal experience at any given time. Again Christ's presence could not be permanent with His disciples as His ascension was necessary to the completion of his Highpriestly office in the Father's presence. However, all of this and more the Spirit, when given at Pentecost, could be to Christ's disciples.

The Spirit, unlimited by bodily form, could be omnipresent. He could, by His very nature as Spirit be the constant companion of the

---

22. *Op. cit.*, p. 35.

believers' lives. His presence would be the internal experience of the disciples by reason of His indwelling their spiritual natures. And His presence would be an abiding experience as He was to be God's permanent gift to all believers. The effusion of the Spirit at Pentecost was His permanent release upon mankind to the end of the age. The teaching that a time will come in the present age when the Spirit will be withdrawn has no basis in Scripture. Jesus' promise was that the Father would give them another *Helper-Advocate "that He may be with you forever"* (John 14:16).

From the Spirit's effusion at Pentecost to the end of the age every man is confronted with the Spirit, either as an indwelling presence or as an ever-present external rebuke to his unrighteous life. Barclay says that "Because of the coming of the Spirit there is no place in all the world where a man can be separated from Jesus Christ." [23] Indeed he may separate himself from Christ, but there is no circumstance or condition of life capable of separating the Spirit-possessed believer from Christ without the consent of the individual's will (cf. Rom. 8:31-39).

3. Christ Characterizes the Spirit as Truth

First, Christ designates the Holy Spirit "the Spirit of truth" (John 14:17b). In two other instances He inextricably relates the Spirit with *the truth* (John 15:26; 16:13). It is not strange that the Spirit should be designated "the Spirit of truth" when the meanings of both the Holy Spirit and the truth are considered in their basic significance. The Holy Spirit as a member of the Trinity is the very essence of ultimate *truth,* since God Himself is the truth. Since He is not corporeal it cannot be said that He is *fact,* though in our scientific age the term *fact* is often mistakenly identified with truth.

Second, *a fact,* properly speaking, characterizes empirical science, which can never be said to have reached ultimate truth *per se.* From the days of the early cosmological Greek thinkers to the present, the natural order has been recognized as characterized by ever-changing phenomena. One of these early Greek thinkers argued that a natural phenomenon is like a stream of water into which a man cannot step a second time, since what he has placed his foot into once has flown away before he can step into it again. But another countered that it is impossible to step into the same stream of water once, since the

---

23. *Ibid.,* p. 36.

water is flowing away while he is putting his foot into it. We have in our atomic era come to an even fuller realization of the instability, the ever-changing activity of natural phenomena. However orderly this change may be, it is nevertheless constantly changing. Jesus seems to suggest this in His characterization of the wind in His conversation with Nicodemus (John 3:8).

Third, physiology teaches us that the body changes completely in its chemical composition, though not necessarily in its physical form, about every seven years. Consequently something can be called *a fact* only for the instant that the mind perceives its fleeting phenomena. A room is probably never at exactly the same temperature at any two succeeding instances, though we may not possess an instrument capable of registering the very minute differences. And a body is probably never at exactly the same atomic weight in two succeeding instances, though we may not possess a scale sufficiently sensitive to register the differences. Now these observations of changing natural phenomena are properly designated *facts*—and facts they are. But such facts should never be confused with truth *per se*.

Fourth, it has always been recognized by the best thinkers of the ages that behind all of the changing phenomena of the physically perceptible world there must be something that is in itself unchangeable, and that accounts for all orderly change in the universe. And the best and most honest thinkers have admitted that this ultimate *unchangeable,* which accounts for all orderly and purposeful change, is itself God. Thus we never know *truth as such* until God reveals Himself to us.

Fifth, properly speaking, truth belongs to the realm of *revealed religion alone,* since the unaided finite mind cannot attain to God, though it can receive God's revelation (cf. Eph. 3:9). This is the very reason that Pilate, the pagan Roman governor, exclaimed: "What is truth?" in reply to Christ's statement, "for this I came into the world, to bear witness to the truth. Everyone who is of the truth hears My voice" (John 18:37b, 38). Whether his words were uttered in sincerity or dishonest evasion, we cannot be certain. Pilate was worldly minded, and Jesus had said concerning "the Spirit of truth" that "the world cannot receive [Him], because it does not behold Him [or know] Him" (John 14:17). The *truth per se,* which belongs to God alone, is spiritual, and thus should never be confused with empirical, factual knowledge. Paul writes to the Corinthians, concerning this very nature of truth, saying that it is *the wisdom* which none of the rulers of this age has understood; for if they had understood it, they would not have crucified the Lord of glory; but just as it is written, "Things which eye has not seen and ear has not heard, And *which* have not entered the heart of man, All that God has prepared for those who love Him." For to us God revealed *them* through the Spirit; for the Spirit searches all things, even the depths of God (I Cor. 2:8-10).

Paul seems to be thinking in this same vein when he writes to the Romans: "Let God be found true, though every man be found a liar" (3:4). Two considerations emerge from this utterance of the apostle. First, God Himself is *the ultimate* and thus *infallible truth*—the very essence of truth. Second, man, by his very nature, is fallible, subject to error. Paul's word here rendered "liar" (Greek, *pseustēs,* from *pseūsma*) may be "a lie," "falsehood," "untruthfulness," or "undependability."[24] Therefore, while *pseustēs,* here rendered "liar," may signify purposeful prevarication, it may also suggest error of judgment due to the inability of man's natural mind to grasp the truth. In fact Webster gives as one definition of a lie, "an untruth or inaccurate statement that may or may not be believed true by the speaker."[25]

Sixth, man is fallible, and any judgment he renders must finally be tested by the *truth of God* for accuracy. But without a revelation to man of God's truth by "the Spirit of truth" he has no final criterion by which to judge the accuracy of his judgment. And the man of the world cannot receive this revelation because he "cannot receive the Spirit of truth" through whom the revelation of truth comes.

The sum of what Christ here teaches is that without "the Spirit of truth" the world is left in hopeless relativity and consequent skepticism and confusion. What other conclusion can be drawn concerning our present age? If "God is dead," then so is truth, and without truth man is hopelessly lost in a wilderness of relativity, religiously, ethically, and in every other manner. Confusion and despair will reign until man returns to God and receives "the spirit of truth." Clarke says: "God, in the operation of His hands, and the influence of His Spirit, is found everywhere except in the perverted passions of men. In these alone do men of corrupt minds seek Him; here *only* He is *not* to be found; and therefore they become infidels and atheists."[26]

24. Arndt and Gingrich, *op. cit.,* p. 900.
25. A Merriam-Webster, *Webster's Seventh New Collegiate Dictionary.*
26. *Op. cit.,* p. 624.

4. Christ Distinguishes Between the Spirit in Regeneration and Crisis Sanctification

Christ's words in John 14:17, "He [the Spirit of truth] abides with you, and will be in you," have puzzled many interpreters, and produced a variety of interpretations. Perhaps a major problem consists in taking these words too literally. It would seem that the sense of these words may be best understood in the light of an earlier passage where John explains that "the Spirit was not yet given, because Jesus was not yet glorified" (John 7:39).

Jesus was not denying the presence of the Spirit in the lives of the believers in their regenerated state, but rather alluding to the gracious effusion of the Spirit that was to occur at Pentecost. So in these words, "He abides with you, and will be in you," Jesus very evidently means to distinguish between the disciples' experience of the Spirit in His regenerative work and presence in their lives, and the deeper experience of the Spirit's cleansing and filling of their lives in what they will experience in the baptism in the Spirit upon His effusion at Pentecost.

Admittedly a literalist may press the point of distinction between the prepositions *with* and *in* and forge a doctrine of "legal justification" devoid of spiritual life out of the distinction. But such a doctrine can never be harmonized with the general teachings of the New Testament on this subject. By the application of such a literal type of interpretation of Psalm 91:4 it would be possible to reduce the concept of God to a female fowl spreading her feathery wings in protection over her human brood of believers, for the psalmist says, "He will cover you with His pinions, and under His wings you may seek refuge."

5. The Trinity Is Implicit in Christ's Teaching

One of the great truths which emerges from Christ's teaching in these passages is that of the divine Trinity. True, there is no explicit statement concerning the Trinity, and Christ gives no formal definition of the Trinity here or elsewhere. However, the Trinitarian implications are clear. Christ speaks of Himself and His personal relationship and ministry to His disciples. He speaks of the Father and His promises to the disciples. And He speaks freely of the person of the Holy Spirit who is going to take His place as the disciples' *Advocate-Helper* upon His departure from them. Thus, nowhere in

Scripture does the Trinity become clearer than in these teachings of Christ concerning the Holy Spirit.

6. *Christ Teaches that the Holy Spirit Will Be the Divine Witnessing Agent*

It is clear from John 15:26-27 that the witnessing mission of the Holy Spirit is twofold. "When the Helper [Advocate] comes ... " said Jesus, "He will bear witness of Me, and you [the disciples] will bear witness also, because you have been with me from the beginning."

The Holy Spirit will bear witness to the spirits of Christ's disciples that they belong to Him and that He stands in support of them, and in turn He will bear witness through them to the world. Clarke says, "He shall bear His testimony in your souls, and you shall bear this testimony to the world."[27]

The Christian religion is not philosophical speculation. In fact the word *philosophy* appears but once in the entire Bible (Col. 2:8), and the word *philosophers* likewise appears but once (Acts 17:18). In neither case are the terms used in a complimentary sense. Nor is the Christian religion a rationalistic system, though indeed it is reasonable. The Christian religion is a *witness* to the person and redemptive work of Jesus Christ. Anything less than this is not Christian. The Jews understood the significance and value of the witness. The Old Testament is not a record of speculation nor of argumentation. The faith of the Hebrews in God rested in what God had done. Thus history was for them of the utmost importance, since it was a record of God's redemptive acts. It was a witness to their faith of what God had done in their behalf, and it was a confession of this faith in what God would do in the future. The faith of the Jews always pointed in two directions. It looked back to what God had done for them, and it looked forward to what they expected God to do for them. This ever kept alive the faith of the Jews.

Likewise Christianity at its best has fed its faith on the acts of God in history, and on its hope of the future. To deny or minimize the importance of the great historical events of Christianity is to remove the foundation on which the Christian faith rests. To blot out its future hope of God's redemptive acts is to kill the faith. The past and

---

27. *Ibid.*, I, p. 630.

the future acts of God are the abutments upon which the bridge of redemptive faith rests and spans the chasm of despair.

Thus it is the function of the Spirit to keep alive faith in the personal and redemptive work of Christ in the souls of the believers in every age and circumstance. It is in this connection that Christ promised His disciples, "He [The Spirit] will ... bring to your remembrance all that I said to you" (John 14:26b). Paul takes up this theme in Romans and says, "The Spirit Himself bears witness with our spirit that we are children of God, and if children, heirs also, heirs of God and fellow-heirs with Christ" (8:16, 17a).

7. The Spirit Bears Witness to the Believer's Salvation

But the manner in which the Spirit bears His witness of sonship with God in the souls of believers is the persistent question. This must be frankly recognized as the inexplicable factor at base in the Christian experience. It is at this point that Christianity has been divided into *formalism* and *mysticism* at its worst, and perhaps between *imputation* and *imparted righteousness* at best. The witness of God's Spirit to the spirit of the believer is the most intimate personal experience known to man. It is at this point that the greatest of all Personal Spirits, the Spirit of the living God, has a *rendezvous* with the personal spirit of man. And it is at this secret meeting that man's spirit either surrenders to the terms of the Spirit of the universe and allows Him to become Lord of his life, or he refuses those terms of divine Lordship and becomes the sworn enemy of God's righteous Spirit.

Jesus exhorted His followers: "Seek first His kingdom, and His righteousness ... " (Matt. 6:33a). It is impossible to enter the righteous kingdom of God without accepting unconditionally the righteous rule of the King. This is what Paul characteristically designates *death to self, crucifixion with Christ,* and other related terms with identical meanings (see Rom. 6:3-4, 6; I Cor. 11:26; Phil. 3:10; Gal. 2:20; 5:24).

To be sure, each individual is the final court of appeal to what he knows within his personal, private, inner experience. Paul, perhaps better than any other inspired writer, understood and expressed the nature of the depth and intimacy of this meeting of God's Spirit with man's spirit in I Corinthians 2:8-16.

On the subject of the inner witness of the Spirit, Wesley wisely counsels:

I observed many years ago, "It is hard to find words in the language of man, to explain the deep things of God. Indeed, there are none that will adequately express what the Spirit of God works in His children. But perhaps one might say (desiring any who are taught of God, to correct, soften, or strengthen the expression), by the testimony of the Spirit, I mean, an inward impression on the soul, whereby the Spirit of God immediately and directly witnesses to my spirit, that I am a child of God; that Jesus Christ hath loved me, and given Himself for me; that all my sins are blotted out, and I, even I, am reconciled to God."

After twenty years' further consideration, I see no cause to retract any part of this. Neither do I conceive how any of these expressions may be altered, so as to make them more intelligible. I can only add, that if any of the children of God will point out any other expressions which are more clear, or more agreeable to the Word of God, I will readily lay these aside.

Meantime let it be observed, I do not mean hereby, that the Spirit of God testifies this by any outward voice; no, nor always by an inward voice, although He may do this sometimes. Neither do I suppose, that He always applies to the heart (though He often may) one or more texts of Scripture. But He so works upon the soul by His immediate influence, and by a strong, though inexplicable operation, that the stormy wind and troubled waves subside, and there is a sweet calm; the heart resting as in the arms of Jesus, and the sinner being clearly satisfied that God is reconciled, that all his "iniquities are forgiven, and his sins covered."[28]

However real and meaningful the witness of the Spirit may be to the inner being of the believer concerning his sonship, this witness will be outwardly manifest in the fruits of the Spirit, just as a seed that is sown in the ground dies in order to bring forth new life which will manifest itself in a healthy, growing plant that produces fruit after its kind. Failure of the soul to thus respond to its new spiritual environment signifies either arrested growth or a *still-birth*. Though the "fruits of the Spirit" will be dealt with later, it is the question of *how* the Spirit of God witnesses to the believer's spirit that he is accepted into the family of God that concerns us here.

It may be best to simply say that in this realm of personal, private, inner experience the recipient of the Spirit's witness is best qualified to judge. A man may and will inevitably judge the ethical conduct of his fellow men, whether Christians or otherwise, but what takes place between the Spirit of God and the spirit of man within him only God and man are qualified to judge. The ancient inspired writer saw this clearly and said: "God sees not as man sees, for man looks at the outward appearance, but the Lord looks at the heart" (I Sam. 16:7b).

---

28. John Wesley, "The Witness of the Spirit: II," *Sermons* II, 2-4 (S, II, 344-45).

However, this personal, inner witness of the Spirit to the individual is never to be taken as an end in itself in Christian experience. Jesus immediately follows His words, "He [the Spirit] will bear witness of Me" with the assurance to those receiving the Spirit's witness, "and you will bear witness also." Again we note that there is no such thing as a static Christian experience. " 'He who belives in Me. . . . "from his innermost being shall flow rivers of living water." ' But this He spoke of the Spirit, whom those who believed in Him were to receive . . . " (John 7:38-39b; cf. Matt. 28:18-20; Acts 1:8). This outflow of the Spirit's witness to the world through the Spirit-filled disciples of Christ, following their experience at Pentecost, is treated at length in the chapters on "The Holy Spirit in the Expansion of the Church," and "The Holy Spirit's Gift of Communication to the Church."

8. Christ Reveals the Work of the Spirit in Relation to the Unconverted World

Important as is the work and witness of the Spirit in relation to the believer, He also bears an important relationship to the world of unconverted men. This function of the Spirit is made explicit by Christ in His statement:

> "But I tell you the truth, it is to your advantage that I go away; for if I do not go away, the Helper shall not come to you; but if I go, I will send Him to you. And He, when He comes, will convict the world concerning sin, and righteousness, and judgment; concerning sin, because they do not believe in Me; and concerning righteousness, because I go to the Father, and you no longer behold Me; and concerning judgment, because the ruler of this world has been judged (John 16:7-11).

In these words Christ delineates specifically and clearly the three-fold mission of the Spirit in relation to the world of unconverted men. The mission concerns (1) the sin of man, (2) the righteousness of Christ, and (3) the judgment of God.

The word *convict* ("reprove," *KJV*; "convince," *RSV*) which Christ uses to express the Spirit's mission to unconverted men is, according to Huffman, from the Greek word *ĕlĕgchō*, which he states "is a legal term" containing much meaning. Huffman says that

> in the first place it suggests the work of the sheriff, who apprehends the wrongdoer, and brings him into the custody of the law. In the second place, it suggests the office of the prosecutor, who arraigns the criminal at the bar of justice. In the third place, it suggests the

duty of the judge, who pronounces, upon the apprehended and arraigned wrong doer, the verdict of guilty or acquittal.[29]

Barclay sees the import of this word as demonstrating the truth to a man in such a manner that he is compelled to recognize it as the truth, and thus admit his error, and in response accept personally the consequences of the truth of which he is convinced.[30]

Thus, this word carries a forensic significance and belongs to the usage of the law-court, or is of judicature usage. Clarke bears out this thought when he says:

> In all that our Lord says here, there seems to be an allusion to the office of an *advocate* in a cause, in a court of justice; who, by producing witnesses, and pleading upon the proof, *convicts* the *opposite* party of *sin*, *demonstrates* the *righteousness* of his client, and shows the necessity of passing *judgment* upon the accuser.[31]

In each of the threefold expressions or applications of the Spirit's convicting office, Jesus gives an explanation in the following verses.

First, Jesus says that upon His advent the Spirit will *convict the world of sin* (v. 8). Then Christ explains that the sin of which the Spirit will convict man is unbelief in Himself: " . . . because they believe not in Me" (v. 9).

Granted, those who will come first under this conviction of the Spirit will be the Jews, whose Messiah Christ was, but who disbelieved in Him and rejected Him as a malefactor (John 1:11). This is not the full meaning of Christ's words, however. The Greek word *kósmon* (from *kosmos*) used here for the world suggests, in this connection, " . . . the world as apart from God its creator . . . and thus evil in its tendency[32] (cf. I John 2:15; James 4:4; II Peter 2:20). The term is sometimes used synonymously with the inhabited world, or the race of mankind, especially sinful man. It seems to be in this latter sense that Christ uses the word here. Thus there is a universalistic suggestion in Christ's statement, both as to the sinfulness of humanity and the convicting ministry of the Spirit.

But why does Christ designate this convicting ministry of the Spirit, in relation to *sin,* in the singular number, rather than *sins* in the plural? The answer is obvious in Christ's own words, "concerning sin, *because they do not believe in Me.*" Thus it seems that Christ's

---

29. *Op. cit.,* pp. 89, 90.
30. *Op. cit.,* p. 43.
31. *Op. cit.,* I, 633.
32. Souter, *op. cit.,* pp. 138, 139.

meaning is that there is but *one basic, tap-root sin* from which all other sins spring. When that tap-root sin of unbelief in Christ is severed, the entire tree with all of its fruit, fed as they are by the tap-root, will die. Some of the older theologians regarded *pride* as the *basic sin*. But careful examination seems to reveal that pride itself is born of unbelief. Perhaps it is enough to say that when sin is considered psychologically pride is basic to all other sins, but when considered theologically unbelief becomes the basic sin. Certainly a close, if not inextricable relationship exists between the two concepts.

The Greek word used here for sin is *hamartia,* which is the generic word for sin—the root word for sin. This is a collective word which embraces sin both in principle and practice. As a principle it is found in such passages as Romans 6:7; 7:14; and 8:10. As an act it is found in such passages as Matthew 9:6 and I John 3:8. Of the 14 different Greek words used for sin in the New Testament, *hamartia* occurs no less than 170 times, while the other 13 words combined occur only 117.

Thus Christ's use of this word *hamartia,* for the sin which the Holy Spirit came into the world to convict, takes on great significance. Unbelief in Jesus Christ closes the door of salvation and hope to the soul of man. This is the only sin necessary to damn the soul of man here and hereafter. The German theologian Dietrich Bonhoeffer says that unbelief in Jesus Christ is so absolutely basic that it is not possible for any other sin that man might commit, not even suicide itself, to add any guilt to this sin of unbelief in Jesus Christ. Thus unbelief is the sin of all sins, and it is to convince man of this sin and arraign him before the bar of God's righteousness in Christ, and impel him to confess himself a sinner before God, that the Spirit was sent into the world of unconverted men. Huffman says:

> In the last analysis, there is only one *damning* sin, one sin that will stand against man in the day of Judgment and will also separate him, now and here, from all that is good in this world and in the next—the sin of unbelief. Even the sin against the Holy Spirit is basically, and in deepest reality, this sin.[33]

Second, the function of the Spirit in relation to the world is to convince unconverted men of righteousness: "concerning righteousness, because I go to the Father, and you no longer behold Me" (v. 10), said Christ.

---

33. *Op. cit.,* p. 92.

The Greek word translated "righteousness" here is *dikaiosúnē*, "justice," or "righteousness" of which God is the source or author, especially a divine righteousness. Thayer[34] says it means, "The state of him who is such as he ought to be; the condition acceptable to God." It may imply integrity, purity of life, virtue, uprightness, or correctness in thinking, feeling, and acting.[35] It becomes evident that the righteousness of which the Spirit will convict men is the righteousness of Christ.

Christ explains that the Spirit will convict the world of His own righteousness because He returns to the Father not to be seen again by His disciples. Christ's ascension to and acceptance by the Father is to be the Father's validation of all that He taught, did, and claimed to be in His redemptive mission on earth. Had He not remained at the right hand of the Father in His ascension there would have been good reasons to doubt the claims He made for Himself and His redemptive work. However, His acceptance by the Father in His ascension was sufficient evidence to substantiate His claim to be the Son of God. The Jews' faith in God should have convinced them of this, but so does every man have a faith in God, notwithstanding all the attempted denials to the contrary. Barclay notes with significance that the ultimate evidence that Jesus' claims are justified, that Jesus was who He was and what He claimed to be, rests in the validity of His resurrection and ascension.[36]

This is the principal reason the enemies of Christ and Christianity have ever so subtly, persistently, and viciously attacked the Christian faith at the point of Christ's resurrection. Naturally the ascension stands or falls with the resurrection. On this great truth Wesley simply but meaningfully makes Christ say, "But I could not go to Him if I were not righteous."[37]

However, this convicting work of the Spirit is twofold in that it lays upon men convicted of Christ's righteousness an obligation to conform to the righteousness of God as revealed in the person of Christ. This Greek word is translated "righteousness" in Matthew 6:33, where Christ exhorts His followers to "seek first His Kingdom, and *His righteousness* [*dikaiosúnēn*]," and promises that all other things needful to them will be provided (Matt. 6:33). Again the same

---

34. Arndt and Gingrich, *op. cit.,* p. 900.
35. Huffman, *op. cit.,* p. 94.
36. *Op. cit.,* p. 44.
37. *Op. cit.* (reprint), p. 371.

word is used in James 1:20, where the apostle says that "the anger of man does not achieve the righteousness [*dikaiosúnēn*] of God."

In his letter to the Romans, the thesis of which is "The righteousness of God as revealed in Christ and His gospel in relation to the totality of the sin and salvation of all men," Paul makes extensive use of this idea. In fact, at the very outset of this epistle he says, concerning the gospel of Christ, that " . . . in it the righteousness [*dikaiosúnē*] of God is revealed from faith to faith; as it is written, 'But the righteous (*dikaios* = "just in the eyes of God," or "righteous") men shall live by faith' [or, "he who is righteous by faith shall live"] " (Rom. 1:17).

Thus it becomes clear that since it is the work of the Spirit to convict men of sin against the righteousness of God in Christ, it is likewise His function to convict them of God's demands that their lives conform to God's standard of righteousness as revealed in the person of Christ (cf. Matt. 5:48). Christ came not only to reveal God's righteousness, but also to save men from their unrighteousness, and through the work of the Spirit in their lives to cleanse them and recreate God's righteousness in their lives (cf. Rom. 12:1-2). This is the main purpose of Christ's redemptive work, and it is the principal purpose of the Spirit to execute in men's lives Christ's righteous redemptive provisions. Huffman has well said:

> Christ declares of the Holy Spirit, that it is His work to bring about the righteousness of sinful man—by apprehending, prosecuting, and acting as judge, until the sinner, entirely unacceptable to God, and wrong in his relation to God and to his fellow-men, is brought into the right relation to both . . . as sin is a deadly evil from which man is to be delivered as a result of the ministry of the Holy Spirit, so righteousness is a glorious reality into which man is to be brought as a result of the same ministry. It is to be a deliverance from something to something.[38] (See I Thess. 1:9-10.)

In summary, first it is the work of the Spirit to convict men of sin, and second, in the light of the righteousness of the Perfect Man, Christ Jesus, to lead them to salvation in Christ, and perfect them in holiness of heart and life (cf. Heb. 9:24-26; 12:22-24).

Third, the work of the Spirit in relation to the world of unconverted men is to *convict* them "concerning judgment, because the ruler of this world [Satan] has been judged" (John 16:11). The logic of Christ's statement is clear. Since the world of mankind is, as Luther well understood it, divided into two kingdoms, the one under the rule of Satan and sin and the other under Christ and righteous-

---

38. *Op. cit.*, pp. 94, 95.

ness, both cannot stand. Christ has already defeated, and thus judged and condemned, Satan to his eternal doom, through His death and victorious resurrection. All who pay allegiance to this already condemned and doomed ruler of the present evil world automatically fall under the condemnation and doom of Satan and his kingdom. Thus the only hope of sinful man to escape this coming doom is to defect to Christ's righteous kingdom and place himself under the rule of the victorious Christ. There is for the sinner no other hope.

The "many more things" which Christ has to say to His disciples, in John 16:12, which they could not understand then must await their subsequent baptism in the Spirit at Pentecost when the veil will be removed from their minds and they will receive the greater revelation of truth through the Spirit's instruction. Wesley says: "These things we have, not in uncertain traditions, but the Acts, the Epistles, and the Revelation."[39]

---

39. *Op. cit.* (reprint), p. 371.

Chapter 6

The Hebrew-Jewish Pentecost in Relation to the Effusion of the Holy Spirit in Acts 2

I. THE OCCASION AND SIGNIFICANCE OF THE EFFUSION OF THE SPIRIT AT PENTECOST

The Day of Pentecost was, from the Jewish standpoint, an historical landmark occurring fifty days after the Passover, but from the Christian point of view it was and is both an historical landmark occurring fifty days after the death and resurrection of Jesus Christ, and an abiding miracle of the Christian era.

This *first Christian Pentecost,* at which the outpouring of the Holy Spirit occurred, as recorded in the second chapter of the Acts of the Apostles, is the most significant event in the history of man subsequent to the death, resurrection, and ascension of Jesus Christ. In fact all that went before in the ministry and work of Christ, including the atonement made on the cross, the resurrection, and ascension, was validated by the effusion of the Holy Spirit on that occasion. This Christian Pentecost was the *culmination* and *fulfillment* of the redemptive plan. It was God's witness to redemption completed by Christ.

The essence of the *first Christian Pentecost* is recorded in the first four verses of the second chapter of the Book of Acts as follows:

> And when the day of Pentecost had come, they were all together in one place. And suddenly there came from heaven a noise like a violent, rushing wind, and it filled the whole house where they were sitting. And there appeared to them tongues as of fire distributing themselves, and they rested on each one of them. And they were all filled with the Holy Spirit and began to speak with other tongues, as the Spirit was giving them utterance (2:1-4).

A correct understanding of this *first Christian Pentecost,* however, demands that we take note of the historical origin and meaning of the *Day of Pentecost* in the Hebrew-Jewish usage of the term, and then note its relationship to this *first Christian Pentecost* as recorded in Acts 2.

The reader's attention is at once arrested by those introductory words: "And when the day of Pentecost had come [lit., "was being fulfilled"]." What was this Day of Pentecost in the Hebrew-Jewish calendar upon which this unusual spiritual phenomenon occurred? What place did it hold in the life and thinking of the Jews? Why did the divine effusion take place on the occasion of this Jewish feast? These and similar questions present themselves to the mind of the serious reader of the second chapter of Acts.

II. THE ORIGIN OF THE HEBREW-JEWISH PENTECOST AND ITS PREFIGURING OF THE FIRST CHRISTIAN PENTECOST

In consideration of the foregoing questions, an answer is found in part in the catalog of Jewish feasts. The order of these feasts, as set forth by one authority, is both interesting and instructive.[1] According to this source, the Jewish feasts fall into four groups, namely, the *Septenary Festivals* (Cycles of Sabbaths), the *Yearly Festivals,* the *Post-Exilic Festivals,* and *Certain Doubtful Festivals.* Of the *Yearly Festivals* there were three principal ones, namely, the Feast of Passover and Unleavened Bread; Pentecost, or the Feast of Weeks; and the Feast of Tabernacles. Thus the Feast of Pentecost was the second of the three principal annual Jewish feasts. The Day of Atonement was not properly regarded by the Jews as a feast day.

D. Freeman[2] confirms this interpretation. He notes that the "fifty days" of Leviticus 23:16 refer to the number of days from the

---

1. Charles Randall Barnes, ed., *The People's Bible Encyclopedia* (Chicago: The People's Publication Society, 1913), pp. 354ff.
2. "Feast of Pentecost," *The New Bible Dictionary* (Grand Rapids: Wm. B. Eerdmans Publishing Company, 1962), pp. 964, 965.

offering of the barley sheaf at the commencement of the Passover. The fiftieth day marked the Feast of Pentecost. It was called the "feast of weeks" because the intervening time was seven weeks (Exod. 34:22; Deut. 16:10). Freeman states:

> It marks the completion of the barley harvest, which began when the sickle was first put to the grain (Deut. 16:9), and when the sheaf was waved "the morrow after the sabbath" (Lev. 23:11). It is also called *haḡ haqqāsîr*, "feast of harvest," and *yôm habbikkûrîm*, "day of the firstfruits" (Exod. 23:16; Num. 28:26). The feast is not limited to the time of the Pentateuch, but its observance is indicated in the days of Solomon (II Chron. 8:13), as the second of the three annual festivals (cf. Deut. 16:16).[3]

The Feast of Pentecost was observed as a "holy convocation" during which no servile labor was permitted (Lev. 23:21). During the Feast of Pentecost every able-bodied male Israelite was required to appear at the sanctuary. Both sin-offerings and peace-offerings were made to God at this Feast of Pentecost (Lev. 23:17-20). It was also observed as a day of joyful thanksgiving to God for the blessings of grain harvest, accompanied by a sincere reverential fear of the Lord (Deut. 16:15-16; Jer. 5:24).

However, the Israelites' gratitude to and reverential fear of God was also in recognition of their redemption and deliverance from Egyptian bondage (Deut. 16:12). This is evidenced by their sin- and peace-offerings. God's acceptance of their offerings was conditioned upon the removal of their sins and their reconciliation to Him.

Freeman notes that

> in the inter-testamental period and later, Pentecost was regarded as the anniversary of the law-giving at Sinai. . . . The Sadducees celebrated it [Pentecost] on the fiftieth day (inclusive reckoning) from the first Sunday after the Passover (taking the "Sabbath" of Lev. 23:15 to be the weekly sabbath); their reckoning regulated the public observance so long as the Temple stood, and the Church is therefore justified in commemorating the first Christian Pentecost on a Sunday (Whit Sunday).[4]

The New Testament contains only three references to the Jewish Pentecost. The first is found in Acts 2:1 in relation to the effusion of the Holy Spirit, which occurred fifty days following Christ's completed redemptive work. This included forty days during His appearance from His ascension (Acts 1:3), and ten days of the disciples'

---

3. *Ibid.*
4. *Ibid.*

waiting, between Christ's ascension and the outpouring of the Spirit on the Day of Pentecost. This event occurred in about A.D. 30.[5]

The second reference to Pentecost in the New Testament is made by Luke, where he says that "Paul had decided to sail past Ephesus in order that he might not have to spend time in Asia; for he was hurrying to be in Jerusalem, if possible, on the day of Pentecost" (Acts 20:16; c. A.D. 57). Apparently Paul continued to observe this annual feast of the Jews, as he did certain other Jewish customs, though he most certainly recognized its symbolism as having been fulfilled in the descent of the Spirit as recorded in Acts 2. The third reference to Pentecost in the New Testament is found in I Corinthians 16:8 where Paul states his purpose to remain in Ephesus until Pentecost because of the unusual opportunities which presented themselves to him for preaching the gospel there (c. A.D. 54 or 55).

Three different names were generally ascribed to Pentecost by the ancient Hebrews; namely, *The Feast of Weeks,* apparently due to the fact that it was celebrated seven weeks, or fifty days, following the Passover (see Exod. 34:22; Deut. 16:10, 16; II Chron. 8:13; Lev. 23:15, 16); *The Feast of Harvest,* due to the fact that it concluded the harvest of the later grains (Exod. 23:16); and *The Day of First Fruits,* so called because the first loaves which were made from the new grain were offered on the altar at this time (Lev. 23:17).

Whatever may have been the original significance of Pentecost, it appears evident that by the time of Christ the Jews associated it with both the Passover and the giving of the law on Mount Sinai. From Exodus 19 they reasoned that the Decalog was given on the fiftieth day after the Exodus. By the time of the Pentecost recorded in Acts 2 the giving of the law was directly associated with the Feast of Pentecost and the two were celebrated simultaneously (see Deut. 16:6-13). "The Jewish Pentecost was essentially linked to the Passover—that festival which, above all others, expressed the fact of a race chosen [for divine service to reflect God to the nations] while separated from other nations—and was the solemn termination of the consecrated period."[6] The following observation confirms this view of the identification of the Jewish Pentecost with the giving of the Mosaic law: "It [Pentecost] marked the completion of the corn

---

5. This is the date given for Pentecost by both Jack Finegan, *Handbook of Biblical Chronology* (Princeton, N.J.: Princeton University Press, 1964), p. 301, and F. F. Bruce, *Letters of Paul: An Expanded Paraphrase,* (Grand Rapids: Wm. B. Eerdmans Publishing Company, 1965), p. 8.

6. Barnes, *op. cit.,* p. 361.

harvest, and according to the later Jews it commemorated the giving of the law on Sinai."[7]

The precise time for the celebration of the Jewish Pentecost was, according to Leviticus, the fiftieth day from "the morrow after the Sabbath" of the Passover; or, according to Deuteronomy, it was to be celebrated seven full weeks after the sickle was put to the corn. The exact meaning of the word *Sabbath* in this connection is much in dispute among scholars. In any event the time intervening between the Passover and Pentecost was a period of fifty days, and thus accounts for the name of the later feast.

While it is not the author's purpose to elaborate on the Jews' observances of Pentecost, in general it may be noted that the people were exhorted to

> rejoice before the Lord your God, you and your son and your daughter and your male and female servants and the Levite who is in your town, and the stranger and the orphan and the widow who are in your midst, in the place where the Lord your God chooses to establish His name (Deut. 16:11).

The Israelites were also to recall their bondage in and deliverance from Egypt, and they were admonished to keep the divine law (Deut. 16:12). It is also significant and instructive to note, as one authority has observed concerning the Jews' Pentecost, that "From Acts 2:9-11 we infer that, perhaps more than to any other great festival, the Jews came from distant countries to Jerusalem,"[8] perhaps as many as three million, according to one authority.

III. THE MEANING OF THE HISTORICAL PENTECOST
IN RELATION TO THE EFFUSION OF THE SPIRIT
AT THE FIRST CHRISTIAN PENTECOST

The first Christian Pentecost is recorded in Acts 2. As the ancient Hebrew Feast of Pentecost occurred fifty days after the Passover, so the first Christian Pentecost occurred fifty days after the atonement made by Jesus Christ on the cross. As the ancient Passover signified atonement for and deliverance from sin, and the giving of the law on Mount Sinai fifty days later signified God's provision for the moral government of His people, so the atoning death of Christ provided God's remedy for sin, and the effusion of the Holy Spirit, which occurred fifty days later, was God's provision for the writing of His

---

7. J. R. Dummelow, ed., *Commentary on the Holy Bible* (New York: Macmillan Company, reprint, 1951), p. 820.

8. Barnes, *op. cit.*, p. 361.

laws on the hearts of His people (Jer. 31:33; Heb. 8:10). This is made clear by Jeremiah, who prophesies thus:

> "Behold, days are coming," declares the Lord, "when I will make a new covenant with the house of Israel and with the house of Judah, not like the covenant which I made with their fathers in the day I took them by the hand to bring them out of the land of Egypt, My covenant which they broke, although I was a husband to them," declares the Lord. "But this is the covenant which I will make with the house of Israel after those days," declares the Lord, "I will put My law within them, and on their heart I will write it; and I will be their God, and they shall be My people. And they shall not teach again, each man his neighbor and each man his brother, saying, 'Know the Lord,' for they shall all know Me, from the least of them to the greatest of them," declares the Lord, "for I will forgive their iniquity, and their sin I will remember no more" (31:31-34).

The author of the Epistle to the Hebrews makes it clear that the New Covenant prophesied by Jeremiah was instituted by the atoning work of Christ and the baptism of the Holy Spirit (Heb. 8:6-13; cf. Isa. 44:3; Ezek. 11:19; 36:25-29; 37:14; 39:29).

Again, as the Hebrew-Jewish Feast of Pentecost signified the culmination of the harvest season, "fifty days after the putting in of the sickle," so the first Christian Pentecost signified the gracious fruit of the atonement of Christ, a harvest yielding in its initial stages about three thousand converts (Acts 2:41).

Finally, the broad inclusiveness of the participants in this Hebrew-Jewish festival, namely, the children, men, and maid servants, the Levites, the strangers, the fatherless, and the widows, according to Deuteronomy 16:11, is prophetic of the universal scope of the gospel of Jesus Christ through the instrumentality of the Spirit outpoured on the Day of Pentecost (Acts 1:8). One has made the significant observation that "Appropriately, therefore, on this day the gospel harvest begun; and the old Law of ordinances was superseded by the new Law of love."[9]

IV. THE CUMULATIVE PREPARATION FOR THE EFFUSION OF THE SPIRIT AT PENTECOST

A. The Christian Pentecost Fulfilled a Divine Promise and Human Hope

The Christian Pentecost was the fulfillment of an age-old divine promise, and a persistent hope and expectation on the part of the

---

9. Dummelow, ed., *op. cit.*, p. 820.

Jews, as also a longing expressed among the Gentiles. The Hebrew-Jewish Feast of Pentecost was characterized by both retrospect and prospect. In retrospect it commemorated the culmination of the Israelites' deliverance from more than four hundred years of bondage in Egypt. The Passover marked their break with Egypt and the crisis experience that initiated that memorable deliverance.

God's issuance to Moses of His codified moral laws for Israel sealed once and for all time their deliverance from past bondage and signified their covenant relation with Himself for the future. Thus, while the giving of the law closed the door to their past bondage experience in Egypt, at the same time it opened the door to a new and promising future for God's people. It delivered them from bondage, but it also gave the glorious prospect of a new way of life with God (cf. I Thess. 1:9-10). Likewise the atoning death of Jesus signified this twofold perspective. Concerning Christ's last supper with His disciples, Paul quotes Christ as saying: "do this, as often as you drink it, in remembrance of Me. For as often as you eat this bread and drink the cup, you proclaim the Lord's death until He comes" (I Cor. 11:25, 26; cf. Luke 22:14-20).

That the law was never intended by God to be an end-in-itself, but rather a directive to a brighter future prospect of spiritual deliverance provided by God for all men who would believe, the more perceptive leaders of Israel always saw with greater or lesser clarity. It is not necessary to assume that the Old Testament writers understood the developed New Testament theology before they could have a clear understanding and experience a persistent expectation of a future spiritual Deliverer, which was properly designated the messianic hope. The author of the Epistle to the Christian Hebrews places this truth in clear perspective when he says: "For the Law, since it has *only* a shadow of the good things to come *and* not the very form [Greek *eikóna* = "image or likeness"] of things, can never by the same sacrifices year by year, which they offer continually, make perfect those who draw near" (10:1).

Nowhere is the intent or purpose of the law, as given to Moses and commemorated by the Israelites at their annual Feast of Pentecost, made clearer than in the statement of the converted Jew, the apostle Paul. "Before faith came," says Paul, "we were kept in custody under the law, being shut up to the faith which was later to be revealed. Therefore the law has become our tutor [lit., "a child conductor," mar.; Grk. *paidagogòs*] to lead us to Christ that we might be justified by faith" (Gal. 3:23-24). This child conductor was "a boy-leader, a slave or freeman who attends and guards a boy to and from, sometimes also in school, and looks after his moral character expecially.[10]

Again, the author of the Epistle to the Hebrews sets in clear perspective the relation of the law, as given to Moses and commemorated at Pentecost, to its fulfillment in Christ and His redemptive provision and purpose for all believing men. That relationship is best expressed in the author's own graphic description.

> For you have not come to *a mountain* that may be touched and to a blazing fire, and to darkness and gloom and whirlwind, and to the blast of a trumpet and the sound of words which *sound was such that* those who heard begged that no further word should be spoken to them. For they could not bear the command, "IF EVEN A BEAST TOUCHES THE MOUNTAIN, IT WILL BE STONED." And so terrible was the sight, *that* Moses said, "I AM FULL OF FEAR AND TREMBLING." But you have come to Mount Zion and to the city of the living God, the heavenly Jerusalem, and to myriads of angels, to the general assembly and church of the first-born who are enrolled in heaven, and to God the judge of all, and to the spirits of righteous men made perfect, and to Jesus the mediator of a new covenant, and to the sprinkled blood, which speaks better than *the blood* of Abel. See to it that you do not refuse him who is speaking. For if those did not escape when they refused him who warned *them* on earth, much less shall we *escape* who turn away from Him who *warns* from heaven. And His voice shook the earth then, but now He has promised, saying, "YET ONCE MORE I WILL SHAKE NOT ONLY THE EARTH, BUT ALSO THE HEAVEN." And this expression, Yet once more," denotes the removing of those things which can be shaken, as of created things, in order that those things which cannot be shaken may remain. Therefore, since we receive a kingdom which cannot be shaken, let us show gratitude, by which we may offer to God an acceptable service with reverence and awe; for our God is a consuming fire (12:18-29).

As a revelation of God's character and a directive for man's conduct, the twofold nature of the moral law, as given to Moses (Exod. 20:1-17; Deut. 5:1-21), is clearly evident. The first four commandments of the Decalog direct man's moral conduct in relation to God, while the last six commandments direct man's moral responsibility to his fellow men. The first four codify man's religious conduct; the last six his social conduct. Could it be that the "two tablets of stone" upon which the commandments were written represent respectively this religio-social division of the Decalog? That most, if not all, of these moral directives were known to men, with greater or lesser clarity, from the moral constitution of man (see

---

10. Souter, *op. cit.*, p. 186.

Rom. 2:14-15), and even from nature itself (see Ps. 19) appears evident. However, because of the obscurities imposed by the Fall, their clear codification in the Decalog became necessary.

That these constitutional moral laws were yet to be brought out into bold relief through their fulfillment in Christ's redemptive work the New Testament makes clear. Where the Old Testament had *faintly anticipated* (cf. Deut. 6:4-6 with Matt. 22:37-40 and Mark 12:29-31), the New Testament *explicitly reveals* Christ's redemptive work in relation to man's moral nature.

This may be illustrated by the photographer's chemical bath that brings the image out in the print. Though indistinct, broken, and blurred by the Fall, nevertheless the natural, and certainly the political image of God in man was not completely effaced, notwithstanding the fact that the moral image was lost entirely. The descent of the Spirit at Pentecost would again restore that moral image. This is made explicit in the Epistle to the Hebrews thus: "And the Holy Spirit also bears witness to us; for after saying, 'This is the covenant that I will make with them after those days, says the Lord: I will put My laws upon their heart, and upon their mind I will write them'" (Heb. 10:15-16; cf. 8:10; Jer. 31:33).

That the law contained a covenant, which was conditional, as well as an unconditional divine promise, becomes clearly evident in both the Old and the New Testaments. The covenant relationship is explicitly expressed in the Decalog. God's covenant-promises here are based upon man's obedience to His commands. Man's violation of the commandments abrogates the divine covenant-promises, just because they were conditional.

On the other hand, *God made certain unconditional promises concerning His provision of salvation for man.* Paramount among those promises was the messianic Savior, Jesus Christ. Nothing that man or devils could do could prevent the fulfillment of God's promises of a Savior from sin for fallen man. The promise of God from Genesis 3:15 to its fulfillment in the victory of the cross and resurrection of Christ rested upon no other condition than the integrity of God's own character. The author of the Epistle to the Hebrews quoting from Genesis 22:15-18, states: "For when God made the promise to Abraham, since He could swear by no greater, He swore by Himself" (6:13f.).

Likewise God's gift of the Holy Spirit at Pentecost was the fulfillment of an age old *promise,* conditioned only upon God's own veracity and immutability. Both promises would have been fulfilled without regard to man's response, as these were unconditional *promises* and not *convenants per se.* However, the *benefits of the provisions* of these fulfilled promises were and are *conditioned on man's response.* Thus the divine-human relationship becomes *a new covenant.*

The Christian Pentecost was the fulfillment of the promise of the Mosaic law (Gal. 3:21-22; 4:4-6, 25, 26, 31). It was the fulfillment of the promise of the prophets (Acts 2:16-18, 21). It was the fulfillment of the promise of God the Father (Luke 24:29). It was the fulfillment of the promise of John the Baptist (Matt. 3:11). And it was the fulfillment of the promise of Christ Himself (Acts 1:8).

B. The Christian Pentecost Culminated Ages of Preparation

From the initial brooding of the Holy Spirit over chaos, producing an orderly cosmos, to His mighty manifestation on the Day of Pentecost, God had progressively prepared the world for this culminating event (Gal. 4:4-6). Likewise, the Christian Pentecost was the culmination of Christ's preparation for that event (John 17:4; 19:30; Matt. 28:18-20; Acts 1:8).

The Christian Pentecost was the culmination of the disciples' preparation (Acts 1:14). They had been converted (John 17:6, 8-9, 11-12). They had been regenerated by the Spirit (John 3:5-7; Rom. 8:9; John 17:6, 14-16). They had become the recipients of Christ's final promise that they would be endued with the power of the Holy Spirit (Acts 1:8). They were disillusioned of their mistaken hope that Christ was to establish a temporal, material kingdom on earth in their day (Acts 1:6-12).

The Christian disciples were united in prayer, purpose, and faith as they awaited the fulfillment of the promise of the Spirit (Acts 1:14, 21). The interesting Greek word from which "one accord" *(KJV)* is derived (Acts 1:14), which describes the unity of the disciples, is *homothumadon,* a word occurring ten times in the Book of Acts, and only once elsewhere in the New Testament (Rom. 15:6). It is compounded by *homos,* meaning "together or in unison," and *thumos,* which suggests "to rush along" or "to breathe violently." The English expression that best translates the Greek *homothumadon* is "one accord." While this is not a musical term as such it has a musical significance suggesting "to agree in pitch and tone."

Thus, varied though these disciples were in background, culture, positions, and personalities, they were *united in "one accord"* of devotion, purpose, faith, and expectancy of the fulfillment of the promise of the Spirit. They were *united,* but not *formalized;* they were *diverse* but not *divided;* they were a harmonious spiritual orchestra, notwithstanding the great diversity of the instruments that made up that human orchestra.

The 120 disciples awaiting the effusion of the Spirit included such diverse individuals as the impetuous and vacillating Peter; the hot-tempered James and John ("sons-of-thunder"), who at one time wished to burn up the Samaritans (Luke 9:53-54); the empirically disposed, "doubting Thomas"; Matthew, a former publican of dubious honesty; Simon Zealotus, a former member of a guerilla outlaw gang (Greek, *sikarios*), who likely had committed murder; Mary, the mild and affectionate mother of Jesus; undoubtedly the wealthy and cultured Mary, mother of John Mark; likely Mary Magdalene of former ill repute, out of whom Jesus had cast seven devils; possibly the "woman of Samaria" who met Jesus at Jacob's well; and the brothers of Jesus who belatedly believed on Him—to mention only a partial number of the list of those now gathered in "one accord" awaiting the fulfillment of the promise of the Spirit.

The actual location of the Christian disciples at the occurrence of the effusion of the Spirit on the day of Pentecost is neither finally certain nor important. That the disciples resorted to an upper room for prayer, and to await the fulfillment of the promise, we learn from Acts 1:13, 14: "And when they had entered, they went to the upper room, where they were staying. . . . These all with one mind were continually devoting themselves to prayer. . . ." Some have thought that they were in the upper chamber where they ate the last supper with the Master before His crucifixion. Others, including G. Campbell Morgan, believe they were in a compartment of the Temple. It seems more likely that they were in a private home, probably that of Mary the mother of Mark. The latter position is favored by Clarke.

Of far greater significance than the place are the persons who first experienced the Christian Pentecost. This initial Christian Pentecost was not the experience of non-Christian Jews living in Jerusalem, nor of the masses of non-Christian Jews gathered from the fifteen nations named in Acts 2 for the Jewish Pentecostal festival. Nor was it the experience of the proselytes to the Jewish faith from the Gentile world, to say nothing of the Gentile world itself. Indeed the divine effusion was to have its influence on these unconverted peoples, but not until the disciples were inwardly purified and fully possessed by the Holy Spirit.

The *they* of Acts 2:1 who experienced the outpouring of the Spirit at this first Christian Pentecost were those Christian disciples enumerated in Acts 1:13, 14. Indeed Luke gives the total number of believers present at this time as "about a hundred and twenty," though there were many others elsewhere (I Cor. 15:6). In His high priestly prayer, as recorded in John 17, Jesus had prayed for these disciples. In that prayer He declared that they belonged to God, that He had kept them (except Judas, "the son of perdition"), and that they were not of this world, even as He was not of this world (John 17:16). The witnessing mission of His disciples given in Matthew 28:18-20, is reiterated in the last commission to them by Christ (Acts 1:8).

Thus the recipients of the first Christian Pentecost were the saved disciples of Jesus Christ, regenerated by the Holy Spirit, separated from the world, and designed by Christ to become the living evangels of His lordship to all men, subsequent to their baptism with the Spirit at Pentecost. And thus this Christian Pentecost cannot be properly regarded as "the birthday" of the Christian Church, as some have asserted. Christ had brought the church into existence during the days of His flesh. He had called out and saved these disciples who now waited for their baptism with the Holy Spirit. Thus the outpouring of the Spirit at Pentecost may be regarded as the *consecration, dedication,* or *inauguration* of the Church of Christ, rather than its birthday. Thus, it was the body of living believers in Christ who first experienced the mighty effusion of the Spirit at Pentecost, as recorded in Acts 2:1-4.

Upon those Christian disciples there descended "from heaven," as Peter explained, the fulfillment of Joel's divinely inspired prophecy.

> This is what was spoken of through the prophet Joel: "And it shall be in the last days, God says, 'That I will pour forth of My Spirit upon all mankind; And your sons and your daughters shall prophesy, And your young men shall see visions, And your old men shall dream dreams; Even upon My bondslaves, both men and women, I will in those days pour forth of My Spirit and they shall prophesy. And I will grant wonders in the sky above, And signs on the earth beneath, Blood, and fire, and vapor of smoke. The sun shall be turned into darkness, and the moon into blood, Before the great and glorious day of the Lord shall come. And it shall be, that every one who calls on the name of the Lord shall be saved' " (Acts 2:16-21).

Chapter 7

The Baptism with the Spirit in the Pentecostal Experience

I. THE DIVINE PURPOSE IN THE EFFUSION OF THE SPIRIT AT PENTECOST

A. Pentecost Fulfilled the Scripture Promises

The preparations and promises of the ages concerning the future Age of the Spirit came to their culmination and fulfillment on the Day of Pentecost with the mighty effusion of the Holy Spirit. This was what the prophets had foreseen, what John the Baptist had promised (Matt. 3:11), what Jesus Christ and His Father had promised, and it was that for which the Jewish nation and the disciples of Christ had earnestly hoped and waited. It was what the whole world of mankind needed. It was what God the Father provided. It was the manifestation of Christ's victory over the arch enemy of God and man that made possible the return of the Spirit to His God-intended habitat, the sanctuary of man's soul, from which he had been evicted by man's disobedience in the Fall ages before. It was, in a sense, the homecoming of the Holy Spirit. It was redeemed man's day of jubilee. It was the fulfillment of the time of which Malachi, the last of the prophets, spoke when he said:

> Behold, I am going to send My messenger, and he will clear the way before Me. And the Lord, whom you seek, will suddenly come to His temple; and the messenger of the covenant, in whom you delight, behold, He is coming, says the Lord of hosts. But who can endure the day of His coming? And who can stand when He appears? For He is like a refiner's fire and like fullers' soap. And He will sit as a smelter and purifier of silver, and He will purify the sons of Levi and refine them like gold and silver, so that they may present to the Lord offerings in righteousness (Mal. 3:1-3).

It was the day of which Jesus spoke when He said: "And behold, I am sending forth the promise of My Father upon you; but you are to stay in the city *until you are clothed with power from on high*" (Luke 24:49). It was the fulfillment of Christ's last words of promise to His disciples: "But you shall receive power when the Holy Spirit has come upon you; and you shall be My witnesses both in Jerusalem, and in all Judea and Samaria, and even to the remotest part of the earth" (Acts 1:8).

B. Pentecost as Interpreted in Wesleyan Theology

However, the interpretation of the meaning of what happened on that memorable Day of Pentecost when the effusion of the Spirit occurred has been a matter of wide difference of opinion among the various theological scholars of the Christian church. These differences of interpretation by the three main schools today have been sharply pointed up in a significant article entitled, "Who is the Holy Spirit?" by William M. Greathouse, President of Nazarene Theological Seminary. He writes of these differences of interpretation as follows:

> First of all, we must recognize differences of interpretation which distinguish advocates of the Spirit-filled life.
> Wesleyans believe that Pentecost brings heart purity and perfect love. Keswickians place emphasis upon the victory and power of Pentecost. Pentecostals and neo-charismatics see speaking in tongues as the sign of the Spirit's infilling.
> Some of these distinctions are partly in the realm of emphasis and terminology, while others reach to the very heart of the Christian experience. In order to point up these distinctions I shall attempt a thumbnail summary of each.
> *The Wesleyan View*—From our Wesleyan perspective the pentecostal baptism with the Holy Spirit purges the heart of the believer from sin, perfects him in God's *agape* love, and thereby empowers him for effective Christian witness. We penitently acknowledge, however, that many of us have not paid the full price for such a genuinely pentecostal experience. Too often we have settled for a loveless, passionless profession of holiness which belies the New Testament.

Under the impact of the Spirit's moving in our times many of us who call ourselves Wesleyan are coming to see clearly that the heart of holiness is to be *filled, cleansed, and indwelt by the Holy Spirit,* and, further, that the baptism with the Spirit is a *baptism of love.* Some of us are becoming increasingly concerned that we relate Pentecost to evangelism, without modifying our historic insistence that the baptism with the Spirit personally connotes entire sanctification.

The Keswick View—Closely related to the Wesleyan teaching, and yet distinct from it at certain points, is the viewpoint associated with the famous Keswick Convention which dates from 1875 in Keswick, England.

The Keswick teaching lays stress upon the Christian's being filled with the Spirit as essential to a life of spiritual victory and Christlikeness. Although these teachers stress "the crucifixion of self" and the "cleansed life," they differ with Wesleyans as to the possibility of the destruction of sin in the believer's life. The indwelling Spirit is generally seen as counteracting "the old nature" which remains until death.

In practical emphasis, however, the Keswick message is quite close to the Wesleyan. The differences may be more in words than in reality. For if a person has really died to sin and self and has been truly baptized with the Holy Spirit, he is sanctified in the New Testament sense.

A great many of those who teach and profess the Spirit-filled life would come somewhere within this school of interpretation. One strength of this position is its strong emphasis upon the Christian's obligation to *maintain* a Spirit-filled relationship and give a Spirit-filled witness to Christ.

The "Pentecostal" View—A third point of view is the "Pentecostal," now being strongly urged also by the neo-Pentecostal and neo-charismatic advocates of the Spirit-filled life. Many Roman Catholic priests, nuns, and laymen identify with this position which, until the early 1960's, was largely limited to the small Pentecostal churches and sects.

Here the weight of stress is not upon the purifying or perfecting work of the Spirit baptism, but upon the personal and emotional aspect of this Pentecostal effusion and the accompanying evidences of tongues-speaking.

Whereas both the Wesleyan and Keswick schools see *holy love* as the one unmistakable evidence of the Spirit's full indwelling, the "Pentecostal" insists that speaking in tongues is the indisputable sign. The former place primary stress upon the graces of the Spirit, the latter upon His *gifts.*

These differences of emphasis generally lead to two entirely different concepts of the Spirit-filled life. Wesleyans and Keswickians place heavy stress on the *ethical* manifestations of the Spirit's presence. "Pentecostals" tend to overemphasize *physical* manifestations. Here are distinctions which may lead to real differences.

Wesleyans object that the theory and practice of contemporary charismatics fail to meet biblical standards at three points:

1. They tend to advocate an *unscriptural reception* of the gift of

tongues. In many cases, psychological manipulation is used to induce glossolalia.

2. They place *an unscriptural evaluation* on this gift, putting it at the top of the list rather than near the bottom, as does Paul.

3. They make an *unscriptural claim* that speaking in tongues is the evidence of the baptism with the Holy Spirit. While some charismatic teachers admit that one may be baptized with the Holy Spirit without the accompanying evidence of speaking in tongues, I have not found any who did not say that every Spirit-filled believer is potentially a tongues-speaker and that he should exercise this gift in order to know the rich meaning of the Spirit-filled life.

The crucial question, then, is: What is the Christian experience of the Holy Spirit? What is the authentic sign of His presence and working in the life of the believer and the Christian community? What dangers, if any, attend a Spirit-centered theology?

The prior question is: Who *is* the Holy Spirit? How does the New Testament refer to the Spirit? It is the Wesleyan understanding of the Bible that He is preeminently the Spirit of Christ, in and through whom *Christ himself* comes to the church to indwell, sanctify, and continue His ministry of reconciliation, until He is revealed at the end of the age to consummate His kingdom.[1]

In this chapter we are concerned first with the Spirit's manifestation in divine *power* as symbolized by the heaven-sent "noise like a *violent* ["*mighty*," *KJV, ASV, RSV*], *rushing wind* [which] filled the whole house where they were sitting" (Acts 2:2).

II. THE SPIRIT'S POWER IN THE PENTECOSTAL EXPERIENCE

A. The Purpose of the Spirit's Power in the Pentecostal Experience

A major emphasis of Christ's promise of the Holy Spirit to His disciples just before His ascension was on divine power. This emphasis is set in proper perspective in the marginal reading of the *KJV* on Acts 1:8: "Ye shall receive the power [Greek, *dunamis* = lit. "physical power," "force," "might"], of the Holy Spirit coming upon you." God's power is in His divine personality, and is never divorced from nor exercised independent of His personality. This same idea is also inherent in the name Comforter, or better Paraclete (Greek, *parakletos* = a "helper," "succorer," "aider," "assistant,"—J. H. Thayer[2])

---

1. "Who is the Holy Spirit?" *Herald of Holiness*, Vol. 61, No. 10; Official organ of the Church of the Nazarene (Kansas City, Missouri: Nazarene Publishing House, May 10, 1972), pp. 8-12. Used by permission.

2. *A Greek-English Lexicon of the New Testament* (New York: American Book Company, 1889, copyright 1885, Harper & Brothers), Art., "Paraklētos."

used by Christ four times to designate the Holy Spirit in the Gospel According to John just before His ascension (14:16, 26; 15:26; 16:7). Likewise the power of the Holy Spirit is suggested in the symbolization of the Spirit as "a violent, rushing wind" at Pentecost in Acts 2:2. But power is also manifested in the first mention that is made of the Spirit in the Bible. He is the creative power which brought cosmic order out of the chaotic primal substance as He was "moving over the face of the water" (Gen. 1:2).

There appears to have been a twofold purpose in the divine phenomenon described by Luke as "a noise like a violent [or, mighty], rushing wind" (Acts 2:2) on the day of Pentecost. First, it was intended to stimulate the faith of the disciples for all that was to follow. Second, its purpose was to arrest the attention of the masses of people assembled in Jerusalem for the Jewish Pentecost and thus provide audience for the inspired apostolic preaching which was to result initially in the conversion of about three thousand people (see Acts 1:41-42).

Power has ever been the passion of man. Nor does the realization and exercise of power appear to have been absent from God's plan and purpose for man. He gave His divine commission to man immediately following creation: "Be fruitful and multiply, and fill the earth, and *subdue it:* and rule [or, "have dominion"] over the fish of the sea and over the birds of the sky and over every living thing that moves on the earth" (Gen. 1:28; cf. Ps. 8). A review of man's material and intellectual achievements through the ages would bear conclusive testimony to the near fulfillment of that commission.

But there are two important realms in which man, devoid of the Spirit of God, has sadly failed to fulfill the commission to *"subdue . . . and have dominion,"* namely, the realms of the spiritual and the moral. The writer of the Wisdom literature expressed this truth when he said, "He who rules his spirit [is greater] than he who captures a city" (Prov. 16:32b). Man has, through the exercise of his native abilities, become a giant; but in the absence of God's Spirit from his life he often becomes a *morally insane* giant; a giant who, devoid of God, will inevitably destroy himself by his own powers. It is an inner divine power that man requires if he is to fulfill God's purpose in his existence. For this power Paul prayed for the church universal (Eph. 3:14-16). John declared concerning the importance of the Spirit's power in the life of man: "greater is He who is in you than he who is in the world" (I John 4:4b).

B. The Priority of the Spirit's Power in the Pentecostal Experience

The "noise like a violent [or, "mighty"] rushing wind" on the Day of Pentecost is vividly suggestive of the power (*dúnamis,* from which the English word "dynamite" comes) of God in His relation to man. This *"violent,* [or, "mighty"] rushing wind," "from heaven" is the symbolical fulfillment of Christ's words to His disciples: "And behold, I am sending forth the promise of My Father upon you; but you are to stay in the city until you are clothed with power [*dúnamis*] from on high" (Luke 24:49). James B. Walker points up the highly significant truth of the necessity of the manifestation of divine power for the establishment of men's faith in God in every new situation where a clear and correct understanding of his nature and attributes do not exist. Such was the case with the Israelites after more than four hundred years of bondage in idolatrous Egypt. J. B. Walker states that

> By the miracles of Egypt the false views and corrupt habits of the Israelites were, for the time being, in a great measure removed. Previously they had believed in a plurality of Gods; and although they remembered the God of Abraham, yet they had, as is evident from notices in the Bible, associated with His attribute of almighty power . . . many of the corrupt attributes of the Egyptian idols. Thus the idea of God was debased by having grovelling and corrupt attributes superinduced upon it. By miraculous agency these dishonorable views of the Divine character were removed—their minds were emptied of false impressions in order that they might be furnished with the true idea and the true attributes of the Supreme Being.[3]

Walker is on solid premises when he notes that

> Man cannot, in the present condition of his mind, believe that religion has a divine origin, unless it be accompanied with miracles. The necessary inference of the mind is, that if an infinite Being acts, His acts will be superhuman in character, because the effect, reason dictates, will be characterized by the nature of its cause.[4]

> In view, therefore, of existing circumstances, two things were necessary, on the part of God ["not in view of God's attributes, but in view of man's nature and circumstances"], in order to give any revelation to the Israelites;—First, that He should manifest himself by miracles, and—Second, that those miracles should be of such a character, as evidently to distinguish them from the jugglery of the magicians, and to convince all observers of the existence and omni-

---

3. *God's Wisdom in the Plan of Salvation;* formerly the *Philosophy of the Plan of Salvation,* rev. ed. (Butler, Indiana: The Higley Press, 1958), 56.
4. *Ibid.,* p. 45.

presence of the true God, in contradistinction from the objects of idolatrous worship. Unless these two things were done, it would have been impossible for the Israelites to have recognized JEHOVAH as the *only* living and *true* God.[5]

In full recognition of the foregoing principle, before Christ commissioned His disciples to carry out their world-wide witness He assured them of *His absolute authority* both *in heaven* and *on earth* (Matt. 28:18). He then promised them the availability of His power through His accompanying presence, by the Holy Spirit whom He would send, even to the end of the age (Matt. 28:20). Every new movement of God in relation to human redemption has been inaugurated by an initial demonstration of the power of God's Spirit over the existing powers. This is a fact well authenticated by the history of Christian missions throughout the centuries.

Such was the case at the deliverance of Israel from Egypt; at the entrance of the Israelites into their promised land; and at the beginning of the public ministry of our Lord. And such is the case at the inauguration of the Christian church by the baptism in the Spirit at Pentecost; and at each new step in the progress of the church on its triumphal march throughout the first Christian century. Likewise, at the entry of the gospel into each new land of missionary endeavor during the past two thousand years there have been accompanying demonstrations of divine power. Paul's review of the initial entry of the gospel into the pagan city of Thessalonica well exemplified this principle. Says he, "for our gospel did not come to you in word only, *but also in power [dunámei]* and in the Holy Spirit and with full conviction . . . " (I Thess. 1:5a).

C. The Necessity of the Spirit's Power in the Pentecostal Experience

Logically and theologically speaking, omnipotence is an essential note of the Judeo-Christian God. With the validity of this attribute man's concept of and faith in God stands or falls. The very philosophical designation of God is *the absolute,* and to be absolute He is necessarily all-powerful. To deny God's absolute power is to deny His divinity, but this is only to transfer divinity to another absolute, even though that absolute may be rationalism, or some other characteristic of *humanistic man.*

It is at this point that man has often erred in his thinking. An occurrence of the denial of God's *infinite power* is seen in the

---

5. *Ibid.,* pp. 49, 50.

thinking of such an influential, modern, liberal Christian scholar as Edgar Sheffield Brightman, lately of Boston University. This religious philosopher seemed compelled to reduce his conception of God to the *finite* before he was able to attempt a solution to the ills of the world. However, when he had thus reduced God to the finite he neither had any divine solution to the ills of humanistic man nor had he any *really personal* God—not even the philosopher's God of the absolute. In limiting God he implied something greater than God, and thus made a transfer of divinity from the God of Christianity to a finite god of his own intellectual conceiving. And thus again, man creates God in his own image. The fatal weakness of Christianity in modern times has been due in large measure to man's concept of *a limited God,* a notion which is consequent upon a limited concept of and faith in God. It was said of Jesus on a certain occasion that "He did not do many miracles ["works of power"] there because of their unbelief" (Matt. 13:58). Unbelief in God's omnipotence inevitably restricts the exercise of His power among men.

D. The Personality of the Spirit's Power in the Pentecostal Experience

In the concluding chapter of Matthew's Gospel, the author represents Jesus, following His death and resurrection, as prefacing the Great Commission to His disciples with a claim to "all authority" (Greek, *exousia* = "absolute authority, power," esp. "moral authority"). Jesus says: "All authority ["power"] has been given unto Me in heaven and on earth" (Matt. 28:18). The words of the resurrected and ascended Christ, given to John, correspond with the foregoing declaration. Christ declared to John: "I have the keys [representing His authority] of death and of Hades" (Rev. 1:18). Jesus follows up His claim to all authority with the commission to His disciples, "Go *therefore,* and make disciples of all the nations . . . " (Matt. 28:19a), after which He gives to them the assurance: "And, lo, I am with you always, even to the end of the age" (Matt. 28:20b).

The relationship of Christ's claim to "all authority," and the promise of His accompanying presence with the disciples, "even to the end of the age," to the promise of Acts 1:8 is at once evident. In the latter passage Luke records Christ's commission to His disciples: "But you shall receive power when the Holy Spirit has come upon you; and you shall be my witnesses . . . even to the remotest part of the earth" (Acts 1:8). The second passage is a corollary of the first. The

Holy Spirit is what Samuel Chadwick calls the "Other Self of the Christ"[6] who indwelt Christ's disciples after their baptism in the Spirit on the Day of Pentecost, to the limit of their spiritual capacities. H. Orton Wiley[7] takes an identical position.

The power of the Spirit is not an impersonal gift or influence of Christ to His disciples. Rather, that power is the power of the divine personality of Christ revealed in the person of the Holy Spirit, indwelling the hearts and lives of the Christian disciples who were baptized in the Spirit at Pentecost. Thus man has only as much of divine power as he has of the Spirit's divine personality. God does not give His power to His followers; He gives Himself, and His power is in His personality. Thus, to preach the gospel of Jesus Christ is to preach the *personal power* of God. To preach, in the true sense of the term, is to *witness* to the person and work of Christ by the power of the Holy Spirit. Said Paul: "I am not ashamed of *the gospel,* for it *is the power of God* for salvation to every one who believes" (Rom. 1:16; cf. Rom. 10:10).

E. The Adequacy of the Spirit's Power in the Pentecostal Experience

The first significance of the baptism in the Spirit is a personal experience of the infinite power of God (Acts 2:1-4). It is a new manifestation and demonstration of the Spirit's power that the present-day spiritually anemic church needs most if she is to save herself from her present impotence and fulfill her mission to this generation.

It is in recognition of the need and adequacy of the Spirit's power that Paul offers his great prayer for the Christian church universal.

For this reason I bow my knees before the Father from whom every family in heaven and on earth derives its name, *that He would grant you,* according to the riches of His glory, *to be strengthened with power [dunámei] through His Spirit in the inner man* (Eph. 3:14-16).

Let it be noted that this great prayer finds its fulfillment in the church's experience of the baptism in the Holy Spirit. Thus Paul's petition to the Father that the church may be *strengthened with power through his Spirit in the inner man,* coupled with his benediction, "Now to Him who is able to do exceeding abundantly beyond all that we ask or think, *according to the power* [the power of the

---

6. *Op. cit.,* p. 21.
7. *Christian Theology* (Kansas City, Missouri: Nazarene Publishing Company, 1941 ed.), II, 311.

Holy Spirit] *that works within us*" (Eph. 3:20), finds its fulfillment in the inevitable consequence of the personal indwelling of God's Spirit.

The recognized inadequacy of man to face the pressures of life, evils, and problems of this day, or any day, will be met only when the adequacy of God's power through the Spirit is recognized, confessed, and appropriated. God's ability for the ills of man in this evil world is to be found in the power of the indwelling Holy Spirit. When the church or the individual turns again to tap that resource, the Spirit's power will be released for the Christian life and witness for the salvation of a world that is presently threatened with destruction through atomic or hydrogen energy, if not by anarchy.

F. The Practicality of the Spirit's Power in the Pentecostal Experience

The application of the divine power of the personal indwelling presence of the Holy Spirit in the life of the sanctified Christian believer is multifold. Only a few select suggestions of those practical applications can be considered here.

First, the indwelling Spirit's power is the assurance of the sanctified Christian's victory over the powers of temptation and sin. It is this assurance that the apostle John had in mind when he wrote, "You are from God, little children, and have overcome them: because *greater is He who is in you than he who is in the world*" (I John 4:4). Again, the apostle Paul sets forth the assurance of this spiritual victory through the indwelling presence of the Holy Spirit most forcibly in Romans 8 (see vv. 31-39).

Second, the power of the Spirit is an effective enablement to the execution of the Christian witness. Said Jesus, "But *you shall receive power, when the Holy Spirit has come upon you: and you shall be my witnesses* both in Jerusalem, and in all Judea and Samaria, and even to the remotest part of the earth" (Acts 1:8). Of the early disciples, subsequent to their baptism in the Spirit at Pentecost, Luke wrote: "And *with great power the apostles were giving witness* to the resurrection of the Lord Jesus: and abundant grace was upon them all" (Acts 4:33). The indwelling presence of the Holy Spirit is quite as much an enabling to witness by a consistent, righteous, exemplary life as by oral testimony. Each validates the other (cf. II Cor. 3:2-3).

Third, the efficacy of the Spirit's power for the endurance of persecution is well exemplified by the first Christian martyr, Stephen

(Acts 7:54-60). Repeatedly in the early chapters of the Acts of the Apostles we read of the spiritual victories of the apostles through the enabling presence of the Holy Spirit in the experiences of most extreme and severe persecution.

Fourth, the expulsion of demons by the Spirit-filled apostles dots the pages of first-century Christian history. A notable failure of such an attempt in the name of Jesus, but in the absence of the indwelling presence of the Holy Spirit, is that of the sons of Sceva at Ephesus (Acts 19:14-17).

It is noteworthy that a special office of demon expulsion was established in the early church, and that such an officer was appointed for each of the main churches.

Fifth, the Spirit's power for healing in the first-century church was quite as much in evidence as is demon expulsion. The Acts of the Apostles is replete with instances of divine healings at the hands of the Spirit-filled apostles. There is the healing of the lame man at the Gate-Beautiful, leading to the Temple, at the hands of Peter (Acts 3:1-10). Many were healed at Jerusalem under the ministry of Peter (Acts 5:16). There were many healings under the Spirit-filled ministry of Philip in Samaria (Acts 8:5-8). A lame man was healed under the ministry of Paul at Lystra (Acts 14:8-10). The father of Publius was healed through Paul's ministry on Melita (Acts 28:8).

Sixth, even death was forced to give up its victims at the command of these Spirit-filled servants of the Lord. Dorcas was restored to life at the hands of Peter at Joppa (Acts 9:36-42). Paul was stoned and left "supposedly" dead at Lystra, but he revived and resumed his work for God (Acts 14:19-22). At Troas a boy fell from the window of a building where Paul was preaching and, in the words of Luke, "was picked up dead" (Acts 20:9). However, Paul was instrumental under the power of the Spirit in restoring the lad to life. Paul would seem to be thinking of both the healing of the body and the final resurrection when he said, "But if the Spirit of Him who raised up Jesus dwells in you, He who raised Christ Jesus from the dead will also give life to your mortal bodies through His Spirit who indwells you" (Rom. 8:11).

To recognize the power and function of the Holy Spirit in the divine healing of the physical body is not, however, to suppose that physical healing is a provision of Christ's atonement in the same sense as the salvation of men's souls. At this point certain extreme charismatics have seriously erred and done great damage to the cause of Christ. Indeed, every benefit of God to man is through Christ's atonement. However, whereas the salvation of every man is God's will and provision through Christ's atonement (John 3:16), such cannot be said of divine healing. The absurdity of such a doctrine becomes evident when it is considered that such would eliminate the very possibility of death, unless by accident or suicide, especially for Christians. No such a possibility is taught or exemplified in the Bible, and Christian history and experience do not support such a position.

It is far from adequate to contend that since God has allotted to man "three score years and ten" (seventy years), a universal healing is provided to, but not beyond, that life span. Many have been disillusioned and injured in their faith in God when they have been urged to believe for healing against every evidence and indication that such was the will of God for them, and then time and experience indicated otherwise. Christ made no such promises, and the apostle Paul witnessed that God's will proved that His grace was sufficient to enable him to bear his sufferings, even when he entreated God for healing (II Cor. 12:7-10).

Furthermore, it cannot be successfully denied that sickness and suffering have sometimes been used of God for the spiritual and moral benefit of certain people to the glory of God. This is not to say that salvation comes through man's suffering rather than Christ's, but rather that suffering is often a means by which God reveals His greater grace and the believer is benefited through such revelation.

Seventh, the Spirit was given to the followers of Christ that they might be able to live for Him. The Spirit was not simply an instrument of power by which the Christians might perform marvelous feats. He was and is *the living divine presence* dwelling within Christ's sanctified disciples, enabling them to live lives that exemplified the grace of God. He is, as Paul expressed it so beautifully, "Christ in you, the hope of glory" (Col. 1:27b).

III. THE SPIRIT'S PURIFYING EFFICACY
IN THE PENTECOSTAL EXPERIENCE

Luke records that with the effusion of the Spirit on the Day of Pentecost "there appeared to them tongues as of fire distributing themselves, and they rested [or, "remained"] on each one of them" (Acts 2:3). John the Baptist predicted this aspect of the Pentecostal experience when he said:

> "I baptize you in water for repentance; but He who is coming after
> me is mightier than I, and I am not *even* fit to remove His sandals;

He Himself will baptize you with the Holy Spirit and fire. And His winnowing fork is in His hand, and He will thoroughly clean His threshing floor; and He will gather His wheat into the barn, but He will burn up the chaff with unquenchable fire" (Matt. 3:11-12).

There are two things about this first Christian Pentecostal phenomenon of *"tongues as of fire"* which especially arrest the reader's attention, namely, its meaning and its administration.

A. The Meaning of the Tongues of Fire in the Pentecostal Experience

In the Pentecostal effusion God was manifesting or revealing Himself *primarily* to the believing disciples of Jesus Christ who on that memorable occasion "were all together in one place." They had withdrawn from the life of normal activity and had dedicated themselves in faith to the pursuit and execution of Christ's command to wait for the fulfillment of the promise that the Spirit would be outpoured (Luke 24:49). At last their hopes that Christ was to establish a material, earthly kingdom in their day were forever gone (see Acts 1:6-14).

They were now in earnest and purposeful pursuit of the inner spiritual kingdom which Christ had promised to them (cf. Matt. 6:33). Before the inward uncontested reign of Christ could be fully realized in their lives there must be an inner purification, a purification of the inner nature of the sinful self, a spiritual and moral renovation of every secret chamber of the soul that nothing foreign or opposed to the nature of God might remain within. It was God's purpose that His disciples should be so inwardly purified that they might declare their independence of the domain of sin and Satan as did Christ when He said, "The ruler of the world [Satan] is coming, and he has nothing in me" (John 14:30). There was to be no claim foreign to the claim of Christ upon nor within the lives of these disciples of Jesus.

For the purpose of this inner purification God revealed Himself to the waiting disciples under the symbol of "tongues ["flames"] as of fire." Consistently throughout the Scriptures, fire is employed as a symbol of divine purification. Fire is also a Biblical symbol of the holiness and justice of God. Thus God revealed Himself to His servants in ancient times (Deut. 4:24; Ezek. 1:4; Exod. 3:2; 19:18; Isa. 6:4; Dan. 7:10).

Malachi predicted the coming and the work of Christ under the symbol of fire.

"The Lord, whom you seek, will suddenly come to His temple; and the messenger of the covenant, in whom you delight, behold, He is coming," says the Lord of hosts. "But who can endure the day of His coming? and who can stand when He appears? For *He is like a refiner's fire* and like a fullers' soap: And *He will sit as a smelter and purifier of silver,* and *He will purify the sons of Levi and refine them like gold and silver,* so that they may present to the Lord offerings in righteousness" (3:1b-3).

Likewise in His post-ascension and second coming appearance, Jesus is represented by John the revelator under the symbol of fire: "His eyes were like a flame of fire; and His feet were like burnished bronze, when it has been caused to glow in a furnace . . . and His face was like the sun shining in its strength" (Rev. 1:14, 15, 16). The prophet Jeremiah represents God as saying: " 'Is not my word like fire?' declares the Lord . . . " (23:29).

Finally, God Himself is represented by the author of the Letter to the Hebrews under the symbol of fire: "Our God is a consuming fire" (12:29). Thus it was God the Holy Spirit in *"consuming fire"* who manifested Himself in "tongues as of fire" to the disciples on the Day of Pentecost, purifying their inner spiritual natures in preparation for His habitat in their lives. Their souls were to be His sacred sanctuary here in this world.

B. The Spirit's Administration of the Tongues of Fire in the Pentecostal Experience

The administration of the "tongues as of fire distributing themselves" at Pentecost likewise arrests attention. Luke informs us that "Suddenly there came from heaven a noise like a violent [or, "mighty"], rushing wind . . . [which] filled all the house where they were sitting" (Acts 2:2). Then there was the general or mass appearance of fire, this pillar of fire *distributed itself* among them individually, and individualized tongues of fire rested upon each one of the disciples in particular (Acts 2:3). Thus while Pentecost was initially a sudden general manifestation of God's Spirit to the company of waiting, believing, expectant disciples, as the Spirit began to administer His purifying efficacy to them He did so on an individual and personal-need basis. The following is a pertinent observation on this passage: "St. Luke means that the tongues or flames of fire appeared first in one mass over the assembled church, and then divided, one flame or tongue settling upon the head of each disciple"[8]

---

8. Dummelow, ed., *op. cit.,* p. 820.

This fire—symbolized in unity—so *diversified* and *individualized itself* as to meet, on an individual and personal basis, the heart condition and need of each of the 120 disciples at the same time. And, just so, God the Holy Spirit normally deals with His children in saving and purifying efficacy. There may be, and frequently is, a general manifestation of the Spirit's presence to God's people, but at the same time the dealings of the Spirit, and the administration of His grace, are always on an individual and personal basis. The tongues symbolized fire (Matt. 3:11). The fire was both a unity and a plurality. The tongues, or flames, were many, but the fire was *one* (I Cor. 12:13).

Finally, at the first great general Christian council held at Jerusalem in about A.D. 48/49,[9] Peter, speaking in defense of the gospel for the Gentiles, declared that their heart-purification was on the same basis as that of the disciples at Pentecost. Said Peter, "And God, who knows the heart, bore witness to them, *giving them the Holy Spirit,* just as He also did to us; and He made no distinction between us and them, *cleansing their hearts by faith* (Acts 15:8, 9). Lange's *Commentary* is in harmony with Peter's interpretation of this event when it says: "It now appears that God has given His Holy Spirit to these people . . . and thereby He has cleansed and sanctified them."[10] There may very well be an allusion to the moral cleansing or sanctification of these people in the divine revelation given to Peter in his trance on the housetop at Joppa when God told him: "What God has *cleansed,* no longer consider unholy" (Acts 10:15b).[11]

Writing of the relation of water baptism to the Baptism in the Holy Spirit, Clarke says: "the stress should be laid on the *thing* signified—the Holy Ghost, to *illuminate, regenerate, refine,* and *purify* the heart. With this sprinkling or emersion are equally efficient: without this, both are worth nothing."[12]

Thus, the tongues of fire were the manifestation of the Spirit's personal, purifying presence to the inward, impure natures of the disciples, making them inwardly clean in preparation for His complete and uncontested possession and dominion of their lives. In the

9. Jack Finegan, *A Handbook of Biblical Chronology* (Princeton: Princeton University Press, 1964), p. 321.
10. John Peter Lange, ed., *Commentary on the Holy Scriptures* (New York: Charles Scribner's Sons, 1866), V, 206.
11. "The New Testament of Our Lord and Savior Jesus Christ," *Clarke's Commentary,* I, 683.
12. *Ibid.*

midst of the general manifestation of the Spirit's presence there was an individualization, or personal manifestation, providing for the personal conditions and needs of each disciple.

Consequently, while this purification or sanctification of the disciples' inner natures was primarily negative, it was a necessary and adequate divine provision for the positive work which was to immediately follow, namely, the complete possession of their entire beings by the personal presence of the Holy Spirit, giving them power over sin, the world, and the devil, and energizing them with a dynamic spiritual passion for the proclamation of the gospel of Christ to all men throughout the world of their day.

IV. THE FULLNESS OF THE SPIRIT IN THE PENTECOSTAL EXPERIENCE

A. The Spirit's Fullness Restores Spiritual Union

Luke informs us that following the Spirit's manifestation to the disciples in His power and purity, "they were all *filled* with the Holy Spirit . . . " (Acts 2:4a).

It was God's evident purpose in the creation of man to personally indwell him by His Spirit. The Fall evicted the Spirit of God from the heart of man. Redemption through Christ provided a means of reconciliation between an offended God and offending man. However, reconciliation, important and essential as it is, is not enough to completely restore fallen man and satisfy the heart of God. He purposes to indwell and fully possess the life of redeemed man.

Before such an unrivaled establishment of God's Spirit in man's life can be realized, the inward nature of polluted and perverted desires and affections must be cleansed. "Therefore Jesus also, that He might sanctify the people through His own blood, suffered outside the gate" (Heb. 13:12). God's purpose in this great cleansing work provided for the soul of converted man by Christ is set forth by Paul in his first letter to the Thessalonian Christian converts thus: "For this is the will of God, your sanctification" (I Thess. 4:3a).

However, the moral and spiritual cleansing of a personal Pentecost is not an end in itself. Rather it is a means to a greater end, or a God-ordained goal. That great purpose of God is the personal indwelling and control of His believing children by His Holy Spirit. This purpose of God, to be realized through the sanctification of His redeemed children, is beautifully expressed in the Letter to the Hebrews thus: "For both He who sanctifies and those who are sanctified are all from one Father; for which reason He is not ashamed to call them brethren" (2:11). Such a purpose is likewise expressed by Christ in His high-priestly prayer for His disciples.

> Sanctify them in the truth; Thy word is truth . . . that they may be one, just as we are one; I in them, and Thou in me, that they may be perfected in unity, that the world may know that Thou didst send me . . ." (John 17:17, 22, 23).

Thus it is evident that this great redemptive purpose of God in Christ was initially realized on the Day of Pentecost when the disciples "were all filled with the Holy Spirit," and were reunited in their spirits with the Spirit of God. Their sancification had its inception in their regeneration, and it had its developmental continuation following their crisis experience at Pentecost.

B. The Spirit's Fullness Completes Spiritual Regeneration

But the question may be fairly asked, Was not the Spirit of God *in* these disciples from the time of their conversion before Pentecost? That such was the case no careful student of the Word of God would attempt to deny. The regenerative work of God in the lives of penitent believers is the work of the Holy Spirit. Jesus declared to Nicodemus: "Truly, truly, I say to you, unless one is born of water and the Spirit, he cannot enter into the kingdom of God. That which is born of the flesh is flesh; and that which is born of the Spirit is Spirit" (John 3:5, 6). Likewise Paul declared, " . . . you are not in the flesh but in the Spirit, if indeed the Spirit of God dwells in you. But if anyone does not have the Spirit of Christ, he does not belong to Him" (Rom. 8:9).

It is especially noteworthy in Christ's instruction of Nicodemus that "water," which may here very well suggest "water baptism," and thus signify the "baptism of repentance," precedes the Spirit in Christ's word order. This order characterizes Christ's own "water baptism" by John, which was followed by the descent of the Spirit upon Him, though it is not to be supposed that Christ's baptism in the Jordan by John involved repentance. Rather it signified Christ's representation of sinful men in the redemptive plan. This appears evident in His own words to John: "Permit it at this time; for in this way it is fitting for us to fulfill all righteousness" (Matt. 3:15). John the Baptist maintains this order, likewise, when he places his baptism of repentance before Christ's baptism with the Holy Spirit (Matt. 3:11). It is in fact the New Testament order throughout.

There is no phase of the redemptive work that can be divorced from the direct operation of the Spirit of God. Jesus declared that even the work of conviction for sin in the world was to be the function of the Holy Spirit (see John 16:7-11). Christ further declared that there can be no true worship apart from the Spirit of God. He said that "God is spirit and those who worship Him must worship in spirit and truth" (John 4:24).

C. The Spirit's Possession Provides Divine Control

It will be noted that after His death and resurrection, and in conjunction with the Great Commission, which was not to be carried out until after Pentecost, Jesus "breathed on them [His disciples], and said to them, 'Receive the Holy Spirit' " (John 20:22). Like the apostle's explanation of Christ's promise of the Spirit in John 7:38-39, these words of Jesus must be understood in the light of the effusion of the Spirit at Pentecost. They cannot be taken as indicating that these disciples of Christ had not been born of the Spirit, or regenerated, before Christ spoke these words in John 20:22. To thus interpret them either makes Christ contradict Himself, or resolves conversion into legal justification which provides no spiritual life for the believer. Either position is totally out of harmony with Christ's teaching concerning the Holy Spirit.

The divine outpouring of the Holy Spirit on the Day of Pentecost cannot be separated from the Great Commission. "But you shall receive power when the Holy Spirit has come upon you; and you shall be My witnesses" (Acts 1:8) said Jesus. If their witnessing mission could not begin until Pentecost was a reality in the lives of the disciples, then the Christian Pentecost could not become a reality in their lives until the outpouring of the Holy Spirit on the Day of Pentecost. Nor is there any indication in Christ's words, "He abides with you, and will be in you" (John 14:17), that the Holy Spirit had not become the vital principle of their new lives in Christ. Rather the utterance is a prediction of that *fullness of the Spirit* which they were to experience on the Day of Pentecost. Chadwick says, with profound insight, "The change from *with* to *in* marks the transition from one dispensation to another."[13] It is indeed the difference between the personal, physical presence of Christ with His disciples and what His spiritual, inward, abiding presence through the person

---

13. *Op. cit.,* p. 44.

of the Holy Spirit would be as a result of the divine effusion at Pentecost. Again Chadwick says:

> There is often some confusion in the interchange of terms, and the elimination of the middle factor. The Son comes in the coming of the Spirit, and abides in the soul in the presence of the Spirit; and in the coming of the Son through the Spirit the Father comes and abides also. "He will come. . . . I will come. . . . We will come" all refer to the Coming of the Spirit as promised in our Lord's farewell talk with His disciples (John 14:16-23). In their relation to the human soul the Father and the Son act through and are represented by the Holy Spirit. And yet the Spirit is not merged in either the Father or in the Son. There is absolute unity with perfect distinction of Persons in the Trinity. They are never confused in the unity nor divided in the distinction. Each is Divine and all are one.[14]

The difference between the relationship of the Holy Spirit to the converted and regenerated disciples before Pentecost and the sanctified disciples after Pentecost may be better understood by an illustration, though the following illustration is not to be taken in full extension, or in any literal physical sense.

Should a man stand on the shore of the Atlantic Ocean with a five-gallon pail which had been used as a tar container, and to the inner walls of which a quantity of tar still adhered, he would be unable to *fill* such a pail with the exhaustless water of the Atlantic Ocean. This inability would not be due to lack of sufficient water but to the fact that a foreign substance adhered to the walls of the pail and thus displaced in part the pail's capacity for water. Even though water should be poured into the pail from the ocean until the pail ran over, *it still would not be filled with water,* since the foreign substance would displace in part its capacity for water. However, a melting of the residue of tar and a thorough cleansing of the pail from this foreign substance would make it possible to *fill* the pail with water.

While sin is in no sense a physical substance, such as the tar, it is a self-centeredness and selfishness which displaces man's capacity for God. Likewise a regenerated but unsanctified Christian may possess the Holy Spirit of God in his life, but he may never be *filled with the Holy Spirit* in the ethical sense until the fiery baptism with the Spirit (Matt. 3:11) has so cleansed and purified his inner nature from impure motives and doublemindedness that God, by the Holy Spirit, may *fill* his heart and life with His own holy presence.

In this sense it is proper to say that the cleansed believer is *filled*

---

14. *Ibid.,* pp. 44, 45.

with the Holy Spirit. As a regenerated disciple of Christ he has the Holy Spirit in his inward life, but he cannot be *filled with the Holy Spirit* in the ethical sense, until he has experienced the crisis of an inner cleansing by a personal spiritual Pentecost, or baptism of the Spirit, in which the Holy Spirit pervades and purifies his inner nature thoroughly by His own holy presence (cf. Ps. 51:2). "They were all filled with the Holy Spirit" immediately after, and not before, "there appeared to them tongues as of fire . . . [which] rested on each one of them."

Paul well understood the cleansing importance of Pentecost's provision and prayed the following prayer for the Christians at Thessalonica, who had *"turned to God from idols to serve a living and true God,* and to wait for His Son from heaven" (I Thess. 1:9-10): *"Now may the God of peace Himself sanctify you entirely;* and may your spirit and soul and body be preserved complete, without blame [*though not without fault*] at the coming of our Lord Jesus Christ. Faithful is He [the Spirit] who calls you [*to sanctification*], *and He also will bring it to pass"* (I Thess. 5:23-24).

V. SOME PROBLEMS IN THE WESLEYAN VIEW OF THE BAPTISM IN THE HOLY SPIRIT IN RELATION TO SANCTIFICATION

That there are certain problems in the traditional and contemporary Wesleyan views on the baptism in the Holy Spirit and its relation to entire sanctification must be frankly admitted.

A. The Problem of Neglected Emphasis upon the Baptism in the Spirit

One of the problems that faces the Wesleyan position on the baptism in the Holy Spirit is that it has had a minor emphasis by the Christian church throughout most of church history. This is indeed difficult to understand in the light of the distinctive and positive emphasis given the subject in the teachings of John the Baptist, Christ, and the New Testament writers. This problem is made the more complex when it is remembered that the baptism in the Spirit is the only distinctively Christian baptism taught in the New Testament.

Certainly water baptism is taught in the New Testament, but it is not peculiar to the New Testament. It is well known that Judaism baptized its proselytes into the Jewish faith. John the Baptist's baptism of repentance is well known. However, it cannot be said that John's baptism was a Christian baptism. He himself did not regard it as such. He was careful to prevent his disciples from confusing his promissory water baptism with its ultimate fulfillment in the baptism with the Holy Spirit (Matt. 3:11). He personally recognized his baptism with water to be but part of his preparatory mission for the coming Messiah, and His *ultimate* baptism with the Spirit. F. F. Bruce recognizes this fact when he says that John's baptism was "a baptism of expectation rather than one of fulfillment as Christian baptism now was. . . . It appears that their Pentecostal enduement with the Spirit transformed the preparatory significance of the baptism which they already received into the consummative significance of Christian baptism."[15]

Important as was John's baptism, as is witnessed by Jesus' submission to it, nonetheless it must not be confused with that toward which it pointed. The promise must not be confused with its fulfillment, or the shadow with its reality in the baptism with the Holy Spirit. As Robert A. Mattke well says: "The baptism of [or, "in"] the Holy Spirit is the baptism of baptisms; it is the one [and only] baptism spoken of by Paul in company with 'One Lord, one faith . . . One God and Father of all, who is above all, and through all, and in you all' " (Eph. 4:5, 6; I Cor. 12:13).[16]

In the light of the foregoing evidence for the baptism in the Spirit as the ultimate and distinctive Christian baptism it is indeed hard to understand the persistent neglect of the subject by the mainline churches. Earle expresses the same problem when he says: "It is difficult to understand the *almost universal neglect* in the Christian Church of the baptism of the Holy Spirit."[17] There is no want of evidence in church history for emphasis upon water baptism, and there are few doctrines upon which there have been greater differences of theological positions or opinions; further, there are few over which there have been more frequent or severe theological controversies. These have sometimes involved problems not more important

15. "The New International Commentary on the New Testament," *Commentary on the Book of Acts* (Grand Rapids: Wm. B. Eerdmans Publishing Company, 1954), p. 386.
16. "The Baptism of the Holy Spirit as Related to the Work of Entire Sanctification," *Wesleyan Theological Journal* (Published by the Wesleyan Theological Society, Vol 5, No. I, 1970), p. 23.
17. Ralph Earle, *The Gospel According to Mark* (Grand Rapids: Zondervan Publishing House, 1957), p. 30.

than the "modes" of water baptism. Here, incidentally, Wesleyanism in general has experienced little difficulty as any one of the three modes of water baptism (sprinkling, pouring, and emersion) have been considered valid by most Wesleyan groups.

This unaccountable neglect of one of the greatest provisions and teachings of the Chrisitian faith has left the door wide open for false emphases and perversions of this great truth by the cultists and those who have grossly misunderstood its true meaning and purpose. Thus this may well be another example of an observation made by Jan Karl Van Baalen that the modern cults represent "the unpaid bills of the Christian church."[18]

B. The Problem of Wesley's Apparent Reluctance to Use the Term "Baptism in the Spirit" in Relation to Sanctification

Wesleyans face an even greater problem in relation to their teachings on the baptism in the Spirit when it is noted that this is a term sparingly used by the Wesleys, as also by John Fletcher in America. Various reasons are given for this lack of emphasis. Mattke says:

> Worthy of consideration is the suggestion that Wesley did not want to enter the controversies associated with this terminology. As he charted a course between Pietism on the one hand and Anglicanism on the other, the use of such a vocabulary did not suit his purpose of stressing the practical aspects of perfect love in the life of a Christian.[19]

In this connection Dr. Mildred Wynkoop's observation is noteworthy:

> Among the very many terms he [Wesley] used for entire sanctification, never did he call it the baptism of the Holy Spirit or any like term because of the danger of seeking the Holy Spirit for some accompanying gift or emotion instead of seeking Christ and His will. *Wesley's ethical insights are seen in the fact that he does not point us to the gifts of the Spirit but to the fruits of the Spirit.*[20] (Italics added.)

Charles C. Brown, however, gives quite a different reason for Wesley's neglect in the use of this terminology in relation to sanctification. He says that "even the Wesleyan theologians were so far misled by the technical theologians that they failed to put proper

---

18. *Chaos of Cults* (Grand Rapids: Wm. B. Eerdmans Publishing Company, 1948), p. 17.

19. *Op. cit.,* p. 24.

20. *Foundations of Wesleyan Arminian Theology* (Kansas City: Beacon Hill Press, 1967), p. 112.

emphasis on the baptism of the Holy Spirit."[21] Another opinion
expressed by Herbert McGonigle, an English Wesleyan pastor-scholar,
asserts, "it is evident that Wesley had not clearly thought through all
the implications of this aspect of perfect love."[22] McGonigle then
continues:

> It is my personal conviction that the holiness people, particularly in
> the present day have, consciously or unconsciously, followed Wesley
> in their reticence to make full use of that grand, scriptural phrase,
> "the baptism of the Holy Ghost." This reticence has helped twen-
> tieth-century Pentecostalism to practically usurp the term and use it
> for its own purpose. Surely the distinctive hallmark of those who, in
> a New Testament and Wesleyan sense, are sanctified wholly, is that
> they have been baptized with the Holy Ghost and fire."[23]

Another contemporary English Wesleyan scholar criticizes Wesley
at this point when he says that Wesley does not "link the doctrine
enough (as Paul does) with the cross and the Holy Spirit."[24]

Perhaps it is sufficient to note that Wesley was a reformer whose
mission was to revive and reemphasize the great New Testament
doctrine of sanctification, or heart purity eventuating in perfect love,
as Luther's mission had been to revive the New Testament doctrine
of justification by faith. However, he was also a child of his time in
that he was much influenced by the theological currents of his day.
Seldom has any reformer had more than one great emphasis that was
distinctive from the currents of his time.

Usually reformers relate everything else to their distinctive emphasis. By so doing they change the course of history. With Martin
Luther it was "justification by faith alone"; with Wesley the major
emphasis was upon "heart purity, or sanctification resulting in perfect love for God and man."

Certain things are important to note concerning Wesley, however.
First, He did place great emphasis upon the person and work of the
Holy Spirit in relation to entire sanctification, even if he failed to use
the terminology of "baptism in the Spirit." A single quotation from
one of his sermons makes his position crystal clear. Wesley says:

> I believe the infinite and eternal Spirit of God, equal with the Father
> and the Son, to be not only perfectly holy in Himself, but the

21. *The Meaning of Sanctification* (Anderson, Indiana: Warner Press, 1945),
p. 114.
22. "Pneumatological Nomenclature in Early Methodism," *Wesleyan Theological Journal*, Vol. 8, Spring 1973 (Published by the Wesleyan Theological
Society), p. 70.
23. *Ibid.*, p. 71.
24. W. E. Sangster, *The Path to Perfection* (New York: Abingdon-Cokesbury
Press, 1943), p. 44.

> *immediate cause of all holiness in us;* enlightening our understand-
> ings, rectifying our wills and affections, renewing our natures, unit-
> ing our persons to Christ, assuring us of the adoption of sons, leading
> us in our actions, *purifying and sanctifying our souls and bodies, to a
> full and eternal enjoyment of God.*
> *There can be no point of greater importance to him who knows that
> it is the Holy Spirit which leads us into all truth and into all holiness,*
> than to consider with what temper of soul we are to entertain His
> divine presence; so as not either to drive Him from us, or to
> disappoint Him of the gracious ends for which His abode with us is
> designed; which is not the amusement of our understanding, but *the
> conversion and entire sanctification of our hearts and lives.* [25] (Italics
> added.)

In the second place, the author knows of no instance in which
either Wesley or Fletcher ever spoke or wrote against the use of this
terminology of "the baptism in the Spirit." In the third place, both
in John Wesley's sermons and his brother Charles' hymns, the Spirit
is given a very large place in the work of sanctification, or heart
purity, and the planting of perfect love in the believer's heart. A
fourth consideration is that Wesley consistently emphasized the
practical, as opposed to the emotional, aspects of the Spirit's work in
sanctification. With Wesley the heart of man was cleansed from
inbred sin that it might be filled with the perfect love of God for true
spiritual worship and acceptable service for God to men. In Wesley's
view sanctification was never an end in itself but the means to the
ethical integration of the entire person.

A fifth important consideration is Wesley's heavy emphasis upon
"the inner witness of the Spirit" to justification and sanctification.
On the Spirit's witness to justification Wesley wrote:

> By the testimony of the Spirit, I mean, an inward impression on the
> soul, whereby the Spirit of God immediately and directly witnesses
> to my spirit, that I am a child of God; that Jesus Christ hath loved
> me, and given Himself for me; and that all my sins are blotted out,
> and I, even I, am reconciled to God. [26]

Likewise on the Spirit's witness to sanctification Wesley says:

> Q. But how do you know, that you are sanctified, saved from your
> inbred corruption?
> A. I can know it no otherwise than I can know that I am justified.
> "Hereby know we that we are of God (in either sense), by the Spirit
> that He hath given us."
> We know it by the witness and by the fruit of the Spirit. And, First,
> by the witness. As, when we were justified, the Spirit bore witness
> with our spirits that our sins were forgiven, so when we were

25. John Wesley, "On Grieving the Holy Spirit," *Sermons* (J. VII, 485-486).
26. Wesley, "The Witness of the Spirit," *Sermons* II, 2-4 (S. II, 344-45).

sanctified he bore witness, that they were taken away. Indeed, the witness of sanctification is not always clear at first (as neither is that of justification); neither is it afterward always the same, but like that of justification, sometimes stronger and sometimes fainter. Yea, and sometimes it is withdrawn. Yet, in general, the latter testimony of the Spirit is both as clear and as steady as the former.[27]

By the witness of the Spirit it is clear that Wesley meant an inner personal witness to the soul, giving assurance of sins forgiven and a heart made clean by the operation of the Holy Spirit.

Roy S. Nicholson, a well-known Wesleyan scholar, finds a wealth of Wesleyan-Holiness theology in the voluminous collection of the Wesleys' hymns.[28] This is indeed a Wesleyan source much overlooked.

C. The Problem of the Misrepresentation of Wesleyan Teaching on the Baptism in the Spirit

Wesley gives little place in the witness of the Spirit to outward signs or manifestations apart from the Scriptural fruits of the Spirit. At no time did Wesley ever teach or countenance emotional extravagance as evidence of the work of the Spirit. One searches in vain, either in Wesley's own writings or the history of his time, to find any evidence of outward signs such as "tongues speaking" having been taught or practiced by Wesley. Whenever emotional extravagances appeared in his meetings Wesley was quick to discourage such or direct them into practical Christian channels of service. On the passage in Acts 2:38 Wesley remarks:

> The gift of the Holy Ghost does not mean, in this place, the power of speaking with tongues; for the promise of this was not given to all that were afar off, in distant ages and nations; but rather the constant fruit of the Spirit, even righteousness, and peace, and joy in the Holy Ghost."[29]

Early American Methodism was quite as free from any evidence of "tongues speaking" as was its English father and founder, John Wesley. Francis Asbury, the father of American Methodism, followed closely in the steps of Wesley. His evangelistic methods and church

27. John Wesley, *A Plain Account of Christian Perfection* (Louisville, Ky. Pentecostal Publishing Company, rep. n.d.) p. 37.
28. "The Holiness Emphasis in the Wesleys' Hymns": *Wesleyan Theological Journal.* Vol. 5-No. 1, Spring 1970 (Published by the Wesleyan Theological Society), pp. 149-61.
29. *Op. cit.* (reprint), p. 401.

administration were sane and constructive at all times, and, like
Wesley, he emphasized the fruits rather than the gifts of the Spirit.
Peter Cartright, one of the greatest pioneer evangelists and church
planters of nineteenth-century American Methodism, though personally dynamic and sometimes even vociferous, would never allow
any "tongues speaking" in any of his meetings. His autobiography
reveals that there were times of high emotion in some of his meetings, but if anyone attempted to speak in "tongues" he immediately
silenced him or expelled him from the meeting.[30]

The National Holiness Association has from its inception, as "The
National Camp-meeting Association for the Promotion of Christian
Holiness" at Vineland, New Jersey, in 1867, to the present time
emphasized the "Baptism in the Holy Spirit" as the means of the
believer's crisis experience in sanctification. "Tongues speaking,"
however, has never been recognized by this organization as in any
way related to this crisis experience. Nor has "tongues speaking" ever
been given any place in the NHA, known as The Christian Holiness
Association since 1971.

Delbert R. Rose, the official historian of the Christian Holiness
Association, has taken Joseph H. Smith as the most typical representative of this movement in his book, *A Theology of Christian
Experience: Interpreting the Historic Wesleyan Message.*[31] Smith
was born in 1855 and lived until 1946. He began his ministry with
his first sermon in 1876 at the age of nineteen years and continued
preaching until very near the end of his life. For more than seventy
years Joseph H. Smith was recognized as the leading expositor of the
doctrine and experience of Christian holiness in America. As a young
man the author was privileged to hear Smith in the later years of his
life. In the ministry of this great Christian and expositor of the
doctrine of Christian Holiness no place was ever given for the
practice of "speaking in tongues" as an evidence of the baptism in
the Holy Spirit, or in any other relation to the doctrine and experience of Christian holiness. It simply is not true to historical facts to
relate Pentecostal "tongues speaking" in its origin to Methodism or
the National Holiness Association.

None of the standard Wesleyan-Holiness churches, such as the
Wesleyan Methodist (1843), the Free Methodists, the Church of the

30. *The Autobiography of Peter Cartright* (Nashville: Abingdon Press,
rep. ed.).
31. *A Theology of Christian Experience: "Interpreting the Holiness Wesleyan
Message* (Minneapolis: Bethany Fellowship, Inc., 1965).

Nazarene, which originated about the turn of the century, and the Pilgrim Holiness church, which came into being about the same time, the Salvation Army, or any other non-Pentecostal holiness church has been characterized by "tongues speaking," either in doctrine or practice. That excessive emotionalism sometimes characterized the meetings of these Wesleyan-Holiness movements and churches is not to be denied. However, two things are important to note. First, emotionalism and the claim to speaking in an "unknown tongue" as the evidence of the baptism of the Holy Spirit are in no sense identical, or even necessarily related. Second, excessive emotionalism has in no way been confined to the Wesleyan-Holiness groups.

The so-called Great Awakening under the ministry of Jonathan Edwards was sometimes characterized by extreme emotional manifestations, as witnesses the reaction to his famous sermon, "Sinners in the Hands of an Angry God." Extreme emotionalism sometimes characterized Charles G. Finney's revivals. The religious emotionalism of the American frontier probably reached its highest pitch in the famed Cane Ridge Revival. However, this movement was begun by Presbyterians and other Calvinistic groups rather than those of Methodistic affiliation. Only later did any Methodists join in this movement. But even at the Cane Ridge Revival there is no evidence of "tongues speaking" *per se.* The use of the expression "Pentecostal-like manifestations" by a contemporary Pentecostal writer in his description of these movements[32] is quite misleading. The expression is obviously intended to lead the reader to conclude that these meetings were characterized by "tongues speaking." The historical evidence for this is wanting.

On the other hand, this same writer is quite correct in his observation that "tongues speaking" characterized the early Mormons and Shakers in America. However, neither the Mormons nor Shakers were Methodistic, or any part of the Wesleyan-Holiness movement.

Furthermore, any attempts to trace "Pentecostal tongues speaking" to Methodistic origins through the Topeka, Kansas, and Azusa Street Mission outbreak of this phenomenon lacks convincing evidence, even when the mere historical facts are subjected to careful scrutiny. Wherever any of the Wesleyan-oriented churches were drawn into the vortex of this aberrant fanaticism of the time, the

---

32. Vinson Synan, *The Holiness Pentecostal Movement in the United States* (Grand Rapids, Wm. B. Eerdmans Publishing Company, 1971), pp. 25, 26.

work of such Wesleyan groups declined or disappeared. However, in the areas unaffected by this aberrant movement the progress of the Wesleyan-Holiness churches continued to grow and prosper. "Tongues speaking" as an evidence of the baptism in the Holy Spirit has never been recognized as Biblical by any of the Wesleyan-Holiness denominations. Any attempt to establish this position, whether for the greater respectability of Pentecostalism or otherwise, comes near, if it is not actually, to a falsification of history.[33]

Mattke is quite correct when he observes that

> In our contemporary situation, it would appear that we who support the Wesleyan-Arminian theological position are found somewhere between two extremes: namely, between the evangelicals who generalize the baptism of [in] the Holy Spirit and the Pentecostals who particularize this aspect of the Spirit's work. While there seems to be no problem as to the fact of this baptism, theologians do have difficulties identifying the time when this baptism occurs, describing the nature of it and finding a suitable terminology that is generally understood.[34]

VI. SOME CONCLUSIONS CONCERNING THE RELATION OF THE BAPTISM IN THE HOLY SPIRIT TO SANCTIFICATION

A. John Fletcher's Position on the Baptism in the Spirit in Relation to Sanctification

Though he expresses something of the same reticence that Wesley manifested in relation to the use of the terminology of the baptism in the Spirit designating sanctification, John Fletcher, nevertheless, leaves little doubt concerning his personal position in the matter. In the work of the Spirit in regeneration, Fletcher calls the Spirit a "monitor," whereas in the crisis experience of sanctification he designates Him a "Comforter." Fletcher says:

> If you mean a believer completely baptized with the Holy Ghost and with fire, in whom he that once visited as a Monitor now fully

33. *Ibid.*, pp. 92, 95ff., 106-109, 116-119, 123, 136, 143, 148, 221.

A somewhat similar unsupportable position is taken by Frederick Dale Bruner in his book *A Theology of the Holy Spirit* (Grand Rapids: Wm. B. Eerdmans Publishing Company, 1970). Bruner is of the Reformed faith, but he like Synan attempts, unsuccessfully, to show Pentecostalism to be an outgrowth of the Methodistic-Holiness movement. An incisive critique of Bruner's work is given by George A. Turner under the title, "An Evaluation of John R. W. Stott's and Frederick Bruner's Interpretations of the Baptism of the Holy Spirit," *The Wesleyan Theological Journal.* Vol. 8, Spring 1973 (Published by the Wesleyan Theological Society, and available from Delbert R. Rose, Asbury Theological Seminary, Wilmore, Kentucky).

34. Mattke, *op. cit.*, p. 25.

resides as a Comforter, you are right; the enmity ceases, the carnal mind and body of sin are destroyed, and "God is all in all" to that just man "made perfect in love."[35]

McGonigle makes a rather strong case for Fletcher's use of the terminology of "baptism in the Holy Spirit" in relation to sanctification. He informs us that

> Most of what Fletcher says concerning the baptism of the Holy Spirit is found in his "Last Check to Antinomianism," the "Check" dealing with the exposition and defense of Christian perfection. He says that the experience of love as described in I Corinthians 13 is the consequence of the baptism of [in] the Holy Ghost. He sees Christ's prayer, "that they may be perfected," being answered on the day of Pentecost. . . . Fletcher clearly relates the work of the Holy Spirit to the experience of entire sanctification and does not hesitate to call it "the baptism of the Spirit." Fletcher had no question that his interpretation of Christian perfection was identical to Wesley's and he defends his own use of the term "baptism of the Spirit." We should remember that Wesley reviewed all the "Checks" and particularly recommended the last "Check."[36]

Fletcher and Wesley may have been somewhat reticent in their use of the terminology of the baptism in the Spirit as synonymous with the crisis experience of sanctification due to their desire not to detract from the Spirit's work in regeneration. They regarded the Spirit as the agent of man's regeneration, as also of the believer's crisis experience of cleansing, and in his "developmental sanctification" to the end of his life.

It is important to note that from the days of Fletcher and Wesley to the present, the responsible Wesleyan scholars who have followed in their theological train have understood them to teach that the crisis experience of sanctification is a work of the Holy Spirit wrought in the heart of the believer subsequent to his regeneration by the Spirit. Further, with Fletcher and Wesley, these scholars have believed and taught that both regeneration and sanctification receive the inner witness of the Spirit, if not immediately upon believing, certainly eventually, without any other outward evidence than the fruits and graces of the Spirit in their lives.

B. Wesley's View of the Spirit in Relation to Personality Integration

Wesley has the following interesting comment on Paul's prayer for sanctification in I Thessalonians 5:23-24, when he speaks of "Spirit and soul and body." He says:

---

35. John Fletcher, *Works*, 4 vols. (New York: Carlton and Porter, 1851), I, 167.

36. McGonigle, *op. cit.*, pp. 68, 69.

Of the three here mentioned, only the last two are the natural constituent parts of man. *The First is adventitious,* and the supernatural gift of God, to be found in Christians only. [Webster defines the word *adventitious* = "added extrinsically and not inherent or innate."] That man cannot possibly consist of three parts, appears hence: The soul is either matter or not matter: there is no medium. But if it is matter, it is part of the body: if it is not matter, it coincides with the spirit.[37]

Whether one accepts Wesley's interpretation on this question will depend on whether he holds the psychological view of dichotomy or trichotomy. Obviously Wesley held the former. However, in the contemporary functional psychology we do not meet the problem that faced Wesley in his day. If, however, Wesley's position is correct, then what Paul prayed for these Thessalonian Christians was that they be sanctified wholly with a view to the unification and preservation of their bodies and souls in responsible ethical harmony with the Spirit of God which they had received in their experience of regeneration (see I Thess. 1:3-10).

C. Wesley and the Crisis-Process Issue in Sanctification

On the question of the "Process-Crisis Issue" in sanctification, Wesley is clear in his teaching that sanctification begins initially at conversion, or regeneration, continues to a crisis experience of complete heart cleansing, and thereafter continues in developmental sanctification until death. On this issue Wesley says:

Neither dare we affirm, as some have done, that all this salvation is given at once. There is indeed an instantaneous as well as gradual work of God in His children; and there wants not, we know, a cloud of witnesses who have received in one moment either a clear sense of the forgiveness of their sins or the abiding witness of the Holy Spirit. But we do not know a single instance in any place of a person receiving, in one and the same moment, remission of sins, the abiding witness of the Spirit, and a clean heart.[38]

On the question of the time of "entire sanctification" Wesley says further:

A man may be dying for some time, yet he does not, properly speaking, die till the instant the soul is separated from the body; and in that instant he lives the life of eternity. In like manner he may be dying to sin for some time, yet he is not dead to sin until sin is separated from his soul; and in that instant he lives the full life of

---

37. Wesley, *Notes, op. cit.,* p. 763.
38. Wesley, *Plain Account of Christian Perfection,* pp. 8, 9.

love. And as the change undergone when the body dies is of a
different kind, and infinitely greater than any he had known before,
yea, such as till then it is impossible to conceive; so the change
wrought when the soul dies to sin is of a different kind, and
infinitely greater than any before, and than any can conceive till he
experiences it. Yet he still grows in grace and in the knowledge of
Christ, in the love and image of God, and will do so, not only till
death but probably to all eternity.[39] (see Heb. 12:22-24.)

D. A Word of Caution Concerning the Use of Wesleyan Terminology Relating to the Holy Spirit

Mattke offers the following wise word of caution in relation to the
use of Wesleyan terminology concerning the ministry of the Spirit.

> Another necessary task is that of sharpening our own definitions.
> For instance, the baptism of [in] the Holy Spirit is oftimes equated
> with the scripture phrase "filled with the Holy Spirit." These two
> phrases as they appear in Scripture do not always have the same
> meaning. After acknowledging his indebtedness to Daniel Steele,
> Delbert Rose says, "there were fulnesses of the Spirit before the Day
> of Pentecost, but these were not the Pentecostal baptism with the
> Holy Spirit."
> The first example is that of a "Charismatic Fullness" which preceded
> the Day of Pentecost. The Angel said of John the Baptist, "He shall
> be filled with the Holy Ghost, even from his mother's womb (Luke
> 1:15).
> Luke writes that both Elizabeth and Zacharias were "filled with the
> Holy Ghost" (1:41, 67) in a pre-Pentecost sense.
> A second type is called an "ecstatic Fullness." This is a temporary
> emotional fulness which is characterized by a fulness of joy such as
> Jesus mentioned in John 16:24. Luke records [in Acts] that the
> Christians at Antioch in Pisidia "were filled with joy, and with the
> Holy Ghost" (13:52).
> The "fulness" which Daniel Steele equates with the baptism of the
> Holy Spirit is an "Ethical Fulness." When Peter reports the Jerusa-
> lem-Pentecost and the Caesarean-Pentecost he emphasizes the fact
> that in both cases the result of the baptism was the "purifying their
> hearts by faith" (Acts 15:8-9).[40]

Thus we conclude, with those who have attempted to understand
Wesley's theology of the Holy Spirit in relation to his doctrine of
perfect love or entire sanctification, that though his terminology was
often varied, he nevertheless regarded the Holy Spirit as the agent of

39. *Ibid.*, pp. 24, 25. *Note:* Bishop Leslie R. Marston has a most excellent
treatment of "The Crisis-Process Issue in Wesleyan Thought" in the *Wesleyan
Theological Journal*, Vol. 4, No. 1, 1969 (Published by the Wesleyan Theological
Society), pp. 3-15.
40. Mattke, *op. cit.*, p. 30.

man's salvation in all of its many aspects from conviction through regeneration and sanctification to final glory. If for reasons perhaps best known to himself he did not always use the terminology familiar and sacred to modern day Wesleyans, they are nevertheless quite correct in concluding that Wesley meant theologically and experien-

---

41. Certain important studies on Wesleyan thought have appeared since this book has gone to press which can receive only brief mention here.

Among the foregoing is H. Ray Dunning's "Biblical Interpretation and Wesleyan Theology," *The Wesleyan Theological Journal*, Vol. 9, Spring 1974 (Lakeville, Ind.: Published by the Wesleyan Theological Society, 1974). In this significant article Dr. Dunning makes a scholarly case for Wesley's interpretation of New Testament Scripture as the fulfillment of Old Testament prophecy, rather than the commonly held literalistic view that Old Testament prophecy is primarily predictive rather than messages directed to the people and situations of the prophets' times. Thus Wesley's hermeneutic avoids, in Dunning's view, the occurrence of inconsistencies that seem to appear between what the Old Testament prophets said and what is found in the New Testament. This approach seems to harmonize with the "Double Aspect" view of Old Testament prophecy and thus does much to solve certain serious problems in the harmonization of Old Testament prophetic messages with their New Testament fulfillment.

Another provocative study by Donald W. Dayton appears in the foregoing number of *The Wesleyan Theological Journal* under the title of "Asa Mahan and the Development of American Holiness Theology." While Dayton makes a sincere and commendable attempt to solve the problem of Wesley's apparent reticence to make adequate use of the Biblical terminology of "The Baptism in the Holy Spirit" in relation to the redemptive work of sanctification, he seems to fail to take account of several very important factors involved in the issue. Among these are certain issues of Wesley's own time which have been noted in the foregoing chapter. Nor does Dayton take sufficient account of the significant scholarly works of such writers in this area as Timothy Smith's *Revivalism and Social Reform* (Abingdon, 1957) in which Smith shows an earlier and more extensive emphasis upon the person and ministry of the Holy Spirit in the nineteenth-century holiness movement than Dayton allows. Perhaps Dayton also assigns greater credit to Asa Mahan and the Oberlin School for the "supposed shift of emphasis" to the work of the Spirit in relation to sanctification than the evidence may support. It has been shown in this chapter that both Wesley and Fletcher did give a very large place to the person and work of the Spirit in relation to sanctification, even though Wesley did not make specific use of the terminology of "Baptism in the Holy Spirit." However, a yet more serious problem in Dayton's position seems to arise out of his apparent tendency to overstate his argument, even sometimes to the almost total neglect of the place of the Spirit in the work of redemption. In doing this it seems that the Book of Acts is relegated to a place of minor importance in the New Testament record. Indeed it is true that the function of the Spirit was and is ever to focus attention upon the person and redemptive work of Jesus Christ. But to deny the function of the Spirit as the executive of the Godhead in the practical application of Christ's redemptive work to man's saving need is to seriously overlook, if not to deny, the specific teachings of Christ Himself concerning the person and ministry of the Holy Spirit as found in such crucial passages of Christ's teachings as Chapters 14-16 of John's Gospel and Acts 1:8, as also John the Baptist's

tially essentially the same Biblical truth as they believe and teach. If Wesley's followers have improved upon the structure and expression of his vital doctrine of "crisis and progressive sanctification" as included in the ministry of the Holy Spirit, Wesley himself would be the first to commend them for their service of love to God and man.

---

testimony in Matthew 3:11-12, and many other New Testament teachings concerning his Spirit.

Further, Dayton's emphasis seems to come seriously near to a practical, though not necessarily doctrinal, denial of the divine trinity.

Dayton's conclusions sometimes appear to lack the degree of objectivity that might be desired in such a crucial study. Finally it is highly regrettable that Dayton should have appealed for support for his position to the seriously unreliable historical position of Vincent Synan's work *The Holiness Pentecostal Movement in the United States* (Eerdmans, 1971). As has been pointed up earlier in this chapter, Synan attempts, quite unsuccessfully, to produce an apologetic for "Tongues-Speaking-Pentecostalism" by supposing early American Methodism, and particularily the National Holiness Association (now renamed the Christian Holiness Association) to have been the forerunners and parents of the contemporary "Tongues-Speaking-Pentecostalism." Dayton should have noted that even Synan, notwithstanding his foregoing unsatisfactory argument, admits that the earliest occurrence of "tongues-speaking" in American history was among the Mormons and Mother Ann Lee's Shakers, neither of whom were in any way related to Methodism or the holiness movement. This practice has never had any place or part in the standard Wesleyan-Holiness movement in America, as it did not in the English Wesleyan revival of the eighteenth century.

Tongue movements

Chapter 8

The Spirit's Gift
of Communication
to the Church[1]

I. THE NECESSITY OF THE SPIRIT'S GIFT
OF COMMUNICATION TO THE CHURCH

The first Christian Pentecost was accompanied by a miracle of communication. Concurrent with the effusion of the Spirit on that memorable occasion, the historian Luke informs us that the Christian disciples "began to speak [or, "speak out"] with other tongues as the Spirit was giving them utterance" (Acts 2:4b). The polyglot multitude gathered at Jerusalem for the Jews' annual Feast of Pentecost afforded these Spirit-filled disciples of Christ their first great opportunity to witness to the death, resurrection, and universal Lordship of Jesus Christ.

The gift of the law to Moses on Mount Sinai, the gift of His Son through the Incarnation at Bethlehem, and the gift of the Holy Spirit with His varied manifestations at the first Christian Pentecost consti-

---

1. This chapter is appropriated in part, with certain revisions, from an article by the author entitled, "A Wesleyan View of the Gift of Tongues in the Book of Acts," published in *The Wesleyan Theological Journal*, Vol. 4–No. 1 (Published by the Wesleyan Theological Society, 1969), by permission of the editor.

tuted God's three most benevolent acts toward man. It is with the third and last of these three divine gifts, the gift of the Spirit, but especially His gift of communication to Christ's first-century disciples, that we are particularly concerned in this chapter.

Luke records that when "the sound [as of a violent, rushing wind] occurred, the multitude came together, and were bewildered, because they were each one hearing them speak in his own language [or "dialect"]." Some estimates of the number present on this occasion run as high as three million people.[2] Luke simply designates them a "multitude," which means a great number, a crowd, or a throng, without even suggesting a possible number. It is stated of the reaction of this multitude that they were "amazed and marveled" that these Galilean disciples were actually speaking concerning the "mighty deeds of God" in the languages of those present who represented no less than fifteen different nations into which the Jews of the dispersion were born and where they lived.

II. THE MEANING OF THE SPIRIT'S GIFT OF COMMUNICATION TO THE CHURCH

A. The Spirit's Gift of Communication Justified

Concerning the Greek word used here for "tongues" (*glossais*), Thayer says, "the gift of foreign tongues."[3] It is a logical, moral, and Biblical necessity that any purported miracle should demonstrate its moral purpose and value in order to validate its claim to the miraculous. Harris Franklin Rall has well said that "within Christian writings . . . miracles must be judged by the principles of the Christian faith and according to their moral meaning and spiritual value."[4] On the basis of this principle, the divine miracle of the gift of different languages at Pentecost, as recorded in Acts 2, was amply justified by the fruits of the gospel proclaimed through these media, in that about three thousand persons from the assembled multitude were converted to Christ and added to the church (v. 41).

---

2. John Matthews, *Speaking in Tongues* (John Matthews, Publisher 1925), p. 20.

3. *Op. cit.*

4. *New Testament History: A Study of the Beginnings of Christianity* (New York and Nashville: Abingdon-Cokesbury Press, 1914), p. 145.

B. The Spirit's Gift of Communication Defined

It must be faced in all honesty from the very outset that the word *unknown,* in relation to the Bible "gift of tongues," does not occur in the original Greek of the New Testament, nor is it used in the standard modern versions. It is italicized in the *KJV*, indicating that it was added by the translators, and that misleadingly, in a futile attempt to clarify the meaning of the word *tongues.* Thus, properly speaking there is no "unknown tongue" in the original language of the New Testament. The Greek word *glossa,*[5] meaning "a tongue," "a language," or "a nation of people distinguished by their language," is consistently used in its various forms throughout the New Testament, except where the Greek word *dialekto* (dialect), meaning "conversation, speech, discourse or language . . . the tongue or language peculiar to any people" (Thayer) is employed. Indeed, on occasion Paul uses the Greek word *phonon,* but only to signify "a sound" and never a language as such. After noting that Paul is not always uniform in his use of words, Harvey J. S. Blaney, Chairman of the Division of Graduate Studies at Eastern Nazarene College, says,

He . . . uses three different words which are translated "tongues" in most versions of the New Testament. They are *dialekton, glossa* and *phonon.* The second is used almost exclusively in the present chapter (I Cor. 14). The last [*phonon*] is used to denote mere sound, while the other two are used to denote a language which is peculiar to a people and distinct from that of another. Thus *glossa* always means a language unless another meaning is signified. Paul indicated his meaning in the present usage by offering an analogy to the tongues at Corinth.

When a bugler blows an uncertain military call, the soldiers do not know whether to turn in for the night or fall in for battle (I Cor. 14:8). From this we draw three premises: The speaking in tongues at Corinth was unintelligible (v. 13), the purpose of speaking should always be communication. Whether in prayer or song (v. 15), praise (v. 17), or in public address (v. 27), one should make use of his mind as well as his inner spirit (v. 15) and it should be done for the purpose of mutual edification.[6]

Webster defines the word *tongue* as "The power of communication through speech. . . . Act of speaking; esp., a spoken language"; and the new *Random House Dictionary* defines a tongue as "the

---

5. Thayer, *op. cit.*

6. Harvey J. S. Blaney, "St. Paul's Posture on Speaking in Unknown Tongues," *Wesleyan Theological Journal,* Vol. 8, Spring 1973 (Published by the Wesleyan Theological Society), p. 56.

language of a particular people, region, or nation, i.e., the Hebrew tongue; a people or nation distinguished by its language" (Isa. 66:18; Rev. 5:9). Hence a tongue, in this sense, is an articulate, intelligible speech or language used for the purpose of communicating symbolized ideas or judgments from one person to another.

This definition of a tongue accords with the Biblical use of the word throughout the New Testament, except in the case of certain perversions that occurred in the church at Corinth. These will be considered later. With the occurrence of the divine gift of languages at Pentecost the disciples "began to speak with other tongues, as the Spirit was giving them utterance" (Acts 2:4), and the multitude exclaimed, "How is it that we each hear them in our language to which we were born? . . . We hear them in our own languages speaking of the mighty deeds of God" (Acts 2:8, 11).

C. The Spirit's Gift of Communication Practicalized

It was the more amazing to the multitudes that they should hear the disciples speaking to them distinctly and intelligibly in their varied languages since these men were Galileans, and presumably uneducated and provincial. F. F. Bruce remarks on this occurrence that:

> The reversal of the curse of Babel is probably in the narrator's mind. . . . The Galilean dialect was so distinctive and difficult for non-Galileans to follow that the disciples released from the peculiarities of their local speech and their sudden capacity for speaking in tongues understood by the motley crowds then in Jerusalem could not fail to be remarked. When once the attention of the people had thus been attracted, Peter seized the opportunity to stand up with the other Apostles, and addressed all who were within earshot.[7]

Again, in the case of Cornelius' household, it is said that the Jews accompanying Peter heard them speak with tongues (*glossais,* "languages") and magnify ("extolling," *RSV*; "exalting," *NASV*; "acclaiming the greatness of God," *NEB*; "glorifying," Phillips) God (Acts 10:46). One observes:

> It was a gracious accommodation to man that God provided the miracle in the realm of languages. . . . Whatever sophistication any of us may acquire in using other languages, we will always find a special interest in a message given to us "in the tongue in which we were born." That is to say, even if the polyglot multitude in Jerusalem might have "made some sort of sense" out of a one-language presen-

---

7. "Acts," *The New Bible Commentary,* ed. F. Davidson (Grand Rapids: Wm. B. Eerdmans Publishing Company, 1954), p. 902.

tation on the Day of Pentecost, the impact would have been immeasurably less than it was. This suggests . . . God's adaptation of His dealing in our human involvement in the "mother tongue."[8]

Marvin R. Vincent notes that the "other tongues" of Acts 2:4 means

strictly *different,* from their native tongues, and also different tongues spoken by the different apostles. . . . The Spirit kept giving them the language and the appropriate words as the case required from time to time. It would seem that each apostle was speaking to a group, or to individuals. The general address to the multitude followed from the lips of Peter.[9]

To the objection that this was not so much a miracle wrought on the disciples, as a miracle of hearing wrought on the listeners, Wesley replies:

The miracle was not in the ears of the hearers (as some have unaccountably supposed) but in the mouth of the speakers. And this family praising God together, with the tongues of all the world, was an earnest that the whole world should in due time praise God in their various tongues as the Spirit gave them utterance. Moses, the type of the law, was of a slow tongue; but the gospel speaks with a fiery and flaming one.[10]

Clarke's comment on "To speak with other tongues" is illuminating.

At the building of Babel the language of the people was confounded, and in consequence of this they became scattered over the face of the earth. At this foundation of the Christian Church, the gift of various languages was given to the apostles that the scattered nations might be gathered, and united under one Shepherd and Superintendent of all souls. *As the Spirit gave them utterance.* The word seems to imply such utterance as proceeded from immediate inspiration and included oracular communication.[11]

Bengel observes that the disciples, under the influence of the Holy Spirit, began

to speak languages of which they had been before entirely ignorant. They did not speak now and then a word of another tongue, or stammer out some broken sentence, but spoke each language as

8. Harold B. Kuhn (Professor of Philosophy and Religion, Asbury Theological Seminary), in a letter to the author.

9. *Word Studies in the New Testament* (Grand Rapids: Wm. B. Eerdmans Publishing Company, rep. 1957), I, 449.

10. John Wesley, *Explanatory Notes upon the New Testament* (London: Epworth Press, reprint 1954), p. 396, n. 4.

11. Adam Clarke, *Commentary on the Holy Bible: One-Volume Edition,* abridged by Ralph Earle from the original six-volume edition (Grand Rapids: Baker Book House, 1967), p. 960.

readily, properly, and elegantly as if it had been their mother-tongue. They spoke not from any previous thought, but *as the Spirit gave them utterance.* He furnished them with the matter as well as the language.[12]

Likewise, when this phenomenon occurred at Ephesus, Luke states that "they began speaking with tongues and prophesied" (Acts 19:6). Both Clarke and Matthew Henry take the position that this "prophesying" was preaching in the miraculously given "tongues" (*glossais*-"languages") to people who could not have heard and understood the gospel message distinctly otherwise at that time.

III. THE RATIONALE FOR THE SPIRIT'S GIFT OF COMMUNICATION TO THE CHURCH

A. The Rationale for the Spirit's Gift of Communication at Pentecost

The Spirit's gift of languages at Pentecost was necessary to meet the demands of the opportune situation that existed at Jerusalem at the Feast of Pentecost, where fifteen different linguistic groups, with possibly as many as three million people, were present. Most of these would soon return to their respective homes and countries to carry with them the gospel which they had heard at Pentecost (Acts 2:5-8).

1. The Jews' Obligation to Attend the Annual Feasts at Jerusalem

William G. Blaikie notes that these Jews, "unable to pay due regard to the ordinances of Moses in the different countries of their dispersion . . . seem to have made very great effort to come to Jerusalem to the annual festivals."[13] Fifteen different nations were represented at the Jerusalem Pentecost, into whose countries Jews of the dispersion (*Diaspora*) had been born, and whose languages they spoke, together with many gentile proselytes to the Jews' faith, and "God-fearers" from among the gentiles.

The objection that the "multitude" of the dispersion would not have come to the Feast of Pentecost had they not known they would get much from a one-language observance can hardly be sustained.

---

12. Bengel, *One Volume Commentary* (Grand Rapids: Baker Book House, reprint 1972), comment on Acts 2:4.

13. *A Manual of Bible History* (New York: Ronald Press Company, 1940), p. 369.

First, it was expected, if not actually legally required, of every Israelite to attend these feasts at Jerusalem and thus appear before the Lord, if such was within his ability.[14] Second, religious worship is a greater influence on men than religious language, important as is the latter. Third, as a parallel, every faithful Moslem is required once in his lifetime, if at all possible, to make the pilgrimage to Mecca (the Haj), and longs to do so. "In case of incapability a Moslem may send a substitute on this sacred duty."[15] Certainly a vast percentage do not understand intelligibly the Arabic language, even though they may have memorized sections of the Koran. And even a greater number have *no* knowledge of the Arabic language used in the religious services at Mecca.

2. *The Relation of the Dispersions to the Languages at Pentecost*

The *Diaspora* is a term referring to the Jews who were scattered throughout the ancient world during and following the Exile. In all, there were five of these dispersions which took place before the coming of Christ. The first occurred in about 722 B.C., when the ten northern tribes of Israel were conquered by the Assyrians, taken into exile, and eventually scattered among the nations.

The second occurred in about 586 B.C., when the southern kingdom was defeated and the Jews were carried into captivity by the Babylonians, and subsequently planted in separate colonies throughout the whole of the 127 provinces of the Persian empire, all the way from India to Africa, by the Persians who succeeded the Babylonians (Esther 1:1; 3:8-15). The Jews of the northern kingdom never returned from their exile, and only a small percentage of those from the southern kingdom returned to Palestine after some seventy years of exile. Concerning the other three pre-Christian Jewish dispersions, Benjamin W. Robinson states:

> During the third century B.C., when Egypt controlled Palestine, Jews migrated in large numbers to Alexandria, so named after Alexander the Great. There they formed a considerable colony in the city, adopted the Greek language, and translated the Old Testament into Greek. In the second century B.C., when Syrian power became dominant in Palestine, the Jews migrated northward and settled in large numbers around Antioch. They went farther into Cilicia, following the line of march of Alexander over into the cities

---

14. Dummelow, ed., *op. cit.*, p. 821.

15. Robert Ernest Hume, *The World's Living Religions* (New York: Charles Scribner's Sons, 1924), p. 229.

of Asia Minor, Macedonia, and Greece. After Pompey and the Roman armies conquered Palestine in the first century B.C., the dispersion of the Jews gradually reached to the ends of the Roman Empire.[16]

The foregoing observations are an illuminating commentary on Paul's great declaration: "But when the fulness of the time came, God sent forth His Son, born of a woman, born under the Law, in order that He might redeem those who were under the Law, that we might receive the adoption of sons" (Gal. 4:4-5).

In order to comprehend the fuller significance of the necessity for the miracle of other languages on the Day of Pentecost, it is necessary to examine briefly the character of the hearers to whom the gospel was preached at the Jerusalem Feast of Pentecost, as recorded in Acts 2. Luke states: "Now there were dwelling in Jerusalem Jews [some omit the word "Jews"] devout men from every nation under heaven" (Acts 2:5, *RSV*). Thus this vast multitude would have consisted of the Jerusalem and Judaean Jews and proselytes who resided more or less permanently in Jerusalem. However, as previously noted, there was also a vast host of the Jews, together with their proselytes and God-fearers, present from the lands of the dispersion.

The language problem at Pentecost, represented by this "multitude," is suggested by the presence of "Parthians," "Medes," "Elamites," and Mesopotamian Jews, from the nations beyond the Roman Empire and the influence of Rome, where the Israelites had been carried captive and scattered by the Assyrians and Babylonians in about 722 and 586 B.C. (cf. II Kings 17:6). These Jews had by the first century lost the use of the Hebrew language and had adopted the languages of the countries into which they were born.[17] "Mesopotamia," the chief Jewish center of which was Babylon, famed for its rabbinical schools, and formerly the point of the "confusion of tongues" at the halting of the construction of the Tower of Babel, receives special notice by Luke.

"Judea," probably as distinguished from Galilee, the home of Christ's disciples, was naturally represented. "Cappadocia," "Pontus," "Asia," "Phrygia," and "Pamphylia" represented the countries of Asia Minor from which foreign-born Jews and proselytes had come to Pentecost. "Egypt," where according to Philo, the famed Greco-Jewish philosopher of Alexandria, a million Jews resided and

---

16. *The Life of Paul* (Chicago: University of Chicago Press, 1928), p. 9.

17. Elmer W. K. Mould, *Essentials of Bible History* (New York: Ronald Press Company; 1951), p. 524.

formed a large part of the population of the city and imbibed much of the Hellenic culture including language, having been lured there by Alexander the Great, sent its representatives to the Jerusalem Pentecost.

North African "Libya," and the north African Greek city of "Cyrene," a quarter of whose great population consisted of Jews with full citizenship rights, who had been sent there by Ptolemy Soter, also sent representatives to the Jerusalem Feast of Pentecost. There were present those of the synagogue of the Cyrenians who disputed with Stephen on the occasion of his martyrdom (Acts 6:9). Christian representatives of Cyrene first bore the gospel to the Greek population of Antioch of Syria (Acts 11:20).

A Christian prophet in the Antioch church, Lucius of Cyrene, played an important part in launching the first Christian missionary journey of Paul and Barnabas (Acts 13:1). "Strangers" and "sojourners from Rome," both "Jews" and "proselytes," were present. And finally, inhabitants of the large Mediterranean Island of "Crete," and of the "Arabian peninsula" are named as being present at Pentecost. All of these Jews, together with their proselytes and God-fearers, had come for the Pentecostal feast.

3. *The Linguistic Composition of the Multitude at Pentecost*

These Jerusalem Jews, strangers, Hellenistic Jews, Gentile proselytes, and God-fearers exclaimed, "we hear them in our tongues speaking the mighty deeds of God" (Acts 2:11). Even if it should be allowed that Luke's reference to "dialects" indicates local variations in the Greek and Aramaic languages, as some questionably hold, it is necessary to note that dialects may and often do vary so greatly as to amount practically to different languages, as far as the effective communication of the gospel of Christ is concerned. Therefore, a miracle of speaking would be necessary to cover these varied dialects at Pentecost, to say nothing of the distinct languages that were represented.

Second, besides the Jerusalem and Hellenic Jews present at Pentecost, there were many "proselytes" and "God-fearers." A proselyte was an individual of non-Jewish nationality who had come to see in the Jewish religion the true way of worship, and was fully converted to the Jewish religion and accepted all its regulations as binding upon him, including circumcision. The "God-fearer" resembled the proselyte in being of non-Jewish nationality, and in his conviction of the spiritual truth of the Jew's monotheism and noble ethical ideals, but he was unlike the proselyte in that he did not submit to the elaborate Jewish ceremonialism and strict legalistic requirements. Nor was he willing to assume the social disadvantages imposed upon gentile proselytes to Judaism.

"God-fearers" did, however, readily accept the Christian faith which was not shackled by the Jewish requirements, and thus they constituted the greater percentage of the Christian converts from the synagogues of the empire, as also those in Jerusalem.[18] Consequently, while a God-fearer was permitted to worship in the Jews' synagogue, he was regarded by the Jews as ceremonially unclean and was considered an outsider. These "God-fearers" were found both in Jerusalem and out in the countries of the empire and even beyond Rome. The total of the Jewish communities outside Jerusalem may have reached 150 by the time of Paul, Benjamin W. Robinson thinks.[19]

Earle states concerning Acts 2:7, in which the multitude at Pentecost recognized the Christians who spoke in their respective dialects as Galileans, that "Galileans were noted as narrow provincialists. It was doubly remarkable, therefore, that they were speaking many different languages"[20] (cf. Matt. 26:73; Mark 14:70; Luke 22:59). Earle further remarks that the expression,

> "Our own language," is literally "our very own dialect." While these were evidently all Jews in religion, they had been born and brought up in different lands, and the language of their own locality constituted their mother tongue.[21]

Likewise Boyce W. Blackwelder states:

> At Pentecost the speakers were Galileans (2:7). Their natural languages were Aramaic and Koine Greek. The audience was composed of Jews and proselytes (2:10) who had assembled at Jerusalem for the feast of Pentecost. These visitors knew (for the most part) Aramaic and Koine Greek, but there were local dialects used in the various countries from which they had come. To their amazement these pilgrims heard the Galileans declaring the things of God in the manifold dialects of the Diaspora. Under the impetus of the Holy Spirit, each Christian was speaking in a language that he had not acquired, and it was understood immediately by representatives from the land familiar with it. . . .
> Thus Jesus' promise, given in connection with the Great Commis-

---

18. *Ibid.*
19. *Op. cit.*, p. 10.
20. Charles W. Carter and Ralph Earle, *The Acts of the Apostles*, rev. ed. (Grand Rapids: Zondervan Publishing House, 1973), p. 31.
21. *Ibid.*

sion, that believers would speak in *kainais glossais* (Mark 16:17)—[if this passage should be genuine], was demonstrated at the Pentecost Feast when the disciples presented the gospel to strangers in their own vernacular. The linguistic ability imparted on that occasion was symbolical of the universality of the gospel (cf. Mark 16:15; Matt. 28:19; Luke 24:47; Rev. 5:9; 10:11; 14:6). It showed that God's revelation is not limited to the Jews nor the Hebrew language (cf. Joel 2:28-32).

The Lucian account leaves no doubt about the intelligibility of the utterances. Three times it is stated that the disciples were heard speaking in the definite dialects of the listeners (Acts 2:6, 8, 11). In verse 11, the dative of the strong possessive pronoun *hemetrais* is used with the *glossai* as the hearers call the vocal expressions "our own languages." Each listener recognized immediately the indigenous dialect of his native land (v. 8).[22]

Some scholars think there were about 250 synagogues in Jerusalem. The Millers note that by A.D. 70 Jerusalem had scores of synagogues and that they were also found in such rural towns as Nazareth (Luke 4:16-30), with many located in cities such as Damascus (Acts 9:20). These authorities state that estimates run as high as four to seven million Jews of the Diaspora who had more than a thousand synagogues by this date.[23] Another authority states: "The Rabbinical writers say that there were 480 synagogues in Jerusalem; and though this must be an exaggeration, yet no doubt all shades of Hellenistic and Aramaic opinions found a home in the common metropolis."[24]

These assembled multitudes at Pentecost heard the Galilean disciples preaching Jesus, His resurrection and consequent universal lordship, "the mighty deeds of God" (Acts 2:11), "We each hear them in our own language to which we were born" (Acts 2:8b).

From the foregoing it becomes evident that this initial occurrence of "tongues" is to be understood as the use of the *bona fide* languages and/or dialects of the people present at Pentecost when the Spirit was outpoured who otherwise would have been incapable of hearing intelligibly the good news that Jesus Christ was risen (Acts 2:22-41), and that they were spoken by men who themselves were ignorant of the languages which they were using. It has been well said that "we see in this event, which seemed to obliterate the barriers of

22. "The Glossolalia at Pentecost," in *Vital Christianity* (Anderson, Ind.: Warner Press, March 10, 1963), p. 6.
23. Madeline S. Miller and J. Lane Miller, *Harper's Bible Dictionary* (New York: Harper and Brothers, Publishers, 1955), p. 717.
24. W. J. Conybeare and J. S. Howson, *The Life and Epistles of Saint Paul* (Hartford, Conn.: S. S. Scranton and Company, 1899), p. 56.

nationality and language, a reversal of the separation and confusion of tongues"[25] (cf. Gen. 11:1-9).

The language problem in the Roman Empire and regions beyond Rome has long constituted one of the major difficulties in understanding the divine gift of languages as that phenomenon appears in the New Testament. The Koine Greek has been considered the universal language, the lingua franca of the ancient world, in the first century. This is especially true in the East, though Latin was the government language of the West. However, it must be recognized that vast numbers of people out in the provinces could not communicate intelligibly in Greek, and they were thus dependent upon their native dialects for a meaningful understanding of the gospel.

The miracle of the proclamation of the gospel in the different languages of those present at the Jews' Pentecost, which resulted in the great spiritual awakening that followed the effusion of the Spirit, appears to have anticipated the fulfillment of Christ's Great Commission (Matt. 28:18-20; Acts 1:8). This is further suggested by the universal representation of redeemed humanity which is so vividly depicted in the Book of Revelation (5:9-10; 7:9-10).

4. The Testimony of the Church Fathers and Prophets to the Genuineness of the Gift of Languages at Pentecost

The gift of languages at Pentecost was God's extraordinary provision, as well as on other occasions subsequently. Almost all of the early church fathers, including Origen (185?-254?), Chrysostom (347?-407?), Theodoret (396-457), Gregory of Nyssa (331-394), and Gregory of Nazianzus (329-457), understood this miraculous gift of tongues to consist of *bona fide* languages, or dialects, given for the purpose of evangelizing the nations. The proclamation of the "mighty deeds of God," primarily the resurrection of Jesus Christ from the dead and His universal lordship, was made intelligible to the people of the fifteen nations enumerated in Acts 2 by reason of the miracle of languages. The result was that about 3,000 people were initially converted to Christ and added to the church (Acts 2:41). This event in itself is sufficient to establish the fact that the divine gift of languages on the day of Pentecost was for the purpose of evangelization.

In accord with the evangelistic purpose of the gift of languages on the Day of Pentecost is the prediction of Isaiah, which prediction

25. Dummelow, *op. cit.*, p. 82.

looks ultimately to the Gospel Age, and probably embodies Pentecost itself. Says the prophet: "The time cometh, that *I will gather all nations and tongues;* and they shall come, and shall see my glory. And I will set a sign among them . . . and they shall declare my glory among the nations" (Isa. 66:18, 19, *ASV*). Also it is in conjunction with the Great Commission that Mark records the promise of the phenomenon of "new tongues" (*glossais*-"languages"), though the genuineness of this passage is highly suspect (16:15-17).

There are but two other clear references to the gift of tongues in the Book of Acts, and both of these afford an adequate justification for the gift by reason of the evangelistic opportunities they presented.

B. The Rationale for the Spirit's Gift of Languages at Caesarea

At Caesarea the household of Cornelius, a "God-fearer" (Acts 10:22), was baptized in the Spirit and spoke with tongues (*glossais*-"languages," Acts 10:46) in which they glorified or exalted God. Cornelius was a Roman centurion, or more likely a captain of a cohort, having from 300 to 600 soldiers under his command. These soldiers were recruited from various parts of the Roman Empire and consequently represented a wide variety of linguistic backgrounds. Thus through this gift of tongues the message of the gospel could be conveyed more intelligibly to them in their own languages by this miraculous gift of God.

On this Caesarean incident Clarke remarks: "They had got *new hearts* as well as *new tongues,* and having believed with the heart unto righteousness, their tongues made confession unto salvation; and God was magnified for the mercy which He had imparted."[26]

Upon the manner in which the Spirit was given at Caesarea Clarke says:

> Probably it was in the same way in which it had been given on the Day of Pentecost. For as they spoke with languages, which was the effect of the descent of the Spirit as flaming tongues on the heads of the disciples on the Day of Pentecost, it is very likely that the same appearance now took place. . . . The Holy Spirit, and its various gifts and graces in the same way and in the same measure in which He gave them to us Jews.[27]

Henry and Scott comment on Acts 10:46 thus:

---

27. *Ibid.,* p. 767.

26. "Commentary and Critical Notes," *The New Testament of Our Lord and Saviour Jesus Christ,* p. 769.

They spoke with tongues which they had never learned. They magnified God, they spoke of Christ and the benefits of redemption, concerning which Peter had been preaching to the glory of God. . . . Whatever gift we are endowed with, we ought to honor God with it, and particularly the gift of speaking.[28]

C. The Rationale for the Spirit's Gift of Languages at Ephesus

The third and last occurrence of the gift of languages in the Book of Acts is found in 19:6. This was at Ephesus, where Paul laid his hands upon the twelve disciples and they were baptized in the Holy Spirit and spoke with other tongues (glossais-"languages") and prophesied. Ephesus was a great linguistic as well as a religious and cultural center comprised of people from all over the ancient world. The principal attraction was the worship of Diana, or Artemis, the multi-breasted Asiatic fertility goddess.

The twelve disciples who were baptized in the Spirit and spoke with tongues at Ephesus most likely became the twelve elders of the Ephesian church who subsequently helped Paul evangelize western Asia Minor during his approximate three-year stay at Ephesus. Thus these languages in which they spoke would have enabled them to accomplish their evangelistic mission. This interpretation has Clarke's support:

They received the miraculous gift of different languages: and in those languages they *taught* the people the great doctrines of the Christian religion: for this appears to be the meaning of the word *proefateuon*, prophesied, as it is used above (v. 6).[29]

Henry and Scott agree with Clarke's interpretation of Acts 19:6.

They spoke with tongues, and prophesied, as the apostles did, and the first Gentile converts (Acts 11:17-18). They had the spirit of prophecy, that they might understand the mysteries of the kingdom of God themselves; and the gift of tongues, that they might preach them [the mysteries] to every nation and language.[30] (See Matt. 28:18-20; Acts 1:8; Rev. 5:9-10; 7:9-10.)

At each of the three foregoing occurrences of the miraculous gift of languages (at Pentecost, Caesarea, and Ephesus) their need for the effective evangelization of the polyglot unconverted peoples sufficiently justified the miracle. However, each of these occurrences also

---

28. "Matthew—Acts," *Commentary on the Holy Bible* (Grand Rapids: Baker Book House, reprint 1960), p. 472.

29. *Op. cit.*, p. 842.

30. *Op. cit.*, p. 505.

constituted a new ethnic and geographic challenge for the introduction and spread of the new Christian religion.

At Pentecost the polyglot Jews, including proselytes and God-fearers, were confronted with the gospel in the languages intelligible to them. At Caesarea the Roman gentile world, represented by the ubiquitous Roman military forces, received the gift of languages that they might effectively spread the new faith that they had received. At Ephesus the Asian gentiles may well have represented the great ancient Greek and non-Roman Asiatic world. As Artemis, or Diana, an imported Asiatic fertility goddess whose image was at Ephesus, was worshiped by "all Asia and the world" (Acts 19:27, *ASV*), so from Asia Minor the gospel might spread to all Asia and the ancient world.

Peter identifies in every respect the manner, as also the matter, of the effusion of the Spirit at Caesarea with that at Pentecost in Acts 2. When reporting to the Jerusalem church what had happened at Caesarea, Peter said specifically: "And as I began to speak, *the Holy Spirit fell upon them, just as He did upon us at the beginning* [or, "at Pentecost"] " (Acts 11:15). As if to make this identification more explicit, Peter continues: "*God therefore gave to them the same gift as He gave to us also* [the gift of the Spirit] after believing in the Lord Jesus Christ, who was I that I could stand in God's way?" (Acts 11:17).

IV. THE HOLY SPIRIT IN RELATION TO THE GIFT OF TONGUES, GENUINE AND SPURIOUS, AT CORINTH

A. The Strategic Location of Corinth

The situation at Corinth probably furnishes a better example of the need for the Spirit's gift of various languages for communicating the gospel than at any other location where the phenomenon occurred. Corinth was a famous commercial seaport of southern Greece where people from all parts of the ancient world met. Within the church at Corinth there would quite naturally have been people from many nations of the Roman Empire.

B. The Tongues Problem at Corinth

The tongues problem at Corinth arose more than twenty years after the initial gift of language occurred at the Jerusalem Pentecost.

Paul was thoroughly familiar with the Jerusalem Pentecostal and the Caesarean event through his associations with Peter and others who had been present when those momentous events occurred. Furthermore, Paul was personally involved in the occurrence at Ephesus and at Corinth. Nowhere does he attempt to make any distinction between any of these later occurrences of "tongues," where he considers them genuine, and the initial occurrence at Pentecost.

Had there been differences in the genuine manifestation of tongues at the later events, it is most improbable that Paul would have failed to indicate such differences. Therefore it is safe to assume that the occurrence of the gift of tongues as described by Luke in Acts 2 is the norm by which the three subsequent New Testament occurrences must be interpreted, insofar as they were genuine, bona fide gifts from God.

C. The Different Aspects of the Tongues Situation at Corinth

That Paul was forced to deal with the "tongues" problem at Corinth in at least four different aspects appears evident from the account in I Corinthians 12–14.

1. The Bona Fide Gift of Languages at Corinth

From the standpoint of its polyglot situation, with its myriads of commercial, marine, military, governmental, tourist, philosophical, and general transient population from all over the Roman Empire and far beyond, Corinth far surpassed Ephesus, Caesarea, and even Jerusalem, where the phenomenon of "tongues" had occurred previously. Consequently there is good reason to assume that a bona fide gift of different languages may have occurred in the church at Corinth to meet the need for evangelizing this transient population. Thus there existed at Corinth a situation that justified and validated the miraculous gift of languages for evangelization purposes as at Jerusalem, Caesarea, and Ephesus.

2. The Visitors of Foreign Languages at Corinth

Paul may well have been dealing with another factor also at Corinth. The evidence seems quite conclusive that in certain instances in the Corinthian situation Paul is simply giving instructions concerning transient visiting believers from other parts, who knew only their own native languages which were foreign to the Corinthian Greek-speaking church. That such existed is evident from the problem that arose at Lystra which was most likely due to faulty communication by reason of the inability of the natives to speak or understand any language other than the Lycaonian (see Acts 14:11).

Moved by the Spirit of the meeting, these foreign Christian visitors would wish to worship by vocalizing their prayers, by giving witness to Christ, or by delivering an exhortation. Paul instructs such persons to worship in silence before God, unless there should be present an interpreter of their language, lest their unintelligible language seem to the Corinthian believers like heathen gibberish (*bar bar*), or the babblings of a madman (I Cor. 14:11).

3. The Possibility of the Use of the Hebrew Language at Corinth

Another factor, as some have pointed up, including Matthew Henry, may have been a special divine gift of an understanding of the deeper insights into the Hebrew language of the Old Testament, which was, for the most part at least, a dead language by that time. Thus for the Christian teachers to read, by divine enabling, Scripture in their archaic languages would have constituted an "unknown tongue" to the listeners, without an interpreter equally inspired to translate the meaning into the language of the people.

4. The Perversions of the Gift of Tongues at Corinth

The tongues problem at Corinth obviously consisted in a confusion and consequent counterfeiting of the genuine, miraculously bestowed gift of bona fide languages, such as was experienced at the Jerusalem Pentecost, at Caesarea, and at Ephesus. Some Corinthian Christians apparently introduced into the church elements of the unintelligible, ecstatic utterances used by the worshipers of Aphrodite and Cybele at Corinth, and elsewhere in the ancient world. Many in the church at Corinth had doubtless worshiped at the shrines of the lustful goddess Aphrodite Pandemos and Cybele before their conversion to Christianity. In this worship trances and ecstatic experiences, accompanied by unintelligible and meaningless utterances, were common.

Some in the church at Corinth may have heard about, or even observed, the bona fide gift of languages, and then confused the phenomenon with the ecstatic "unknown utterances" at the pagan shrines. Having been addicted to the latter, they carried these pagan practices into the church, where they sought to display their misdirected talents in competition with those who spoke with the genuine gift of languages to witness to people of foreign speech who were present in their services. It is not strange that they should have done so when it is remembered that Paul had to deal with other pagan practices also which were brought into the church at Corinth by those former worshipers of Aphrodite Pandemos and Cybele, including idolatrous worship, sexual immorality, gluttony, rivalry, strife, and other evil practices. Thus these subjective, if not sometimes demoniacal, ecstatic experiences with which Paul dealt in his Corinthian correspondence were either intentional or ignorant counterfeits of the genuine, divinely given experiences of bona fide languages (see I Cor. 12:1-3).

Concerning these aberrations at Corinth Mould says:

> Paul had the good sense to try to divert this type of experience away from a mere expenditure of emotional froth into an ethical channel (the edification of others) and to bring it under the control of reason (I Cor. 14:19, 26). . . . The principle of control which Paul emphasizes is the principle of love (I Cor. 13). . . . In Paul's thought the most genuine manifestation of the Spirit is to be observed in the Christian life of ethical integrity and altruistic service. This same principle of ethical and rational control, Paul applies to other types of ecstatic experience, as in II Corinthians 12.[31],[32]

D. The Apostle Paul's Personal Linguistic Ability Set Against the Corinthian Tongues Situation

Paul's statement in I Corinthians 14:18 that "I thank God, I speak in tongues more than you all" has caused many interpreters considerable difficulty. However, this may well imply his versatile linguistic ability as a veteran missionary among many different linguistic situations in Asia Minor and Europe, as possibly elsewhere. This is the reasoned interpretation of Adam Clarke, the prince of Wesleyan interpreters. Clarke says:

> He understood more languages than any of them did; and this was indispensably necessary, as he was the apostle of the Gentiles in general, and had to preach to different provinces where different dialects, if not languages, were used. In the Hebrew, Syriac, Greek,

---

31. *Op. cit.*, pp. 521, 522.
32. See the author's treatment of the "tongues" problem at Corinth in his "Introduction" to I Corinthians and the "Exposition of I Corinthians 12-14" in the *Wesleyan Bible Commentary* (Grand Rapids: Wm. B. Eerdmans Publishing Company, 1965), Vol. V.

and Latin, he was undoubtedly well-skilled from his education; and how many he might understand by miraculous gift we cannot tell. But even literally understood, it is very probable that he knew more languages than any man in the church at Corinth.[33]

In reply to the question, "Did Paul speak in unknown tongues?" Blaney says:

> The exclusiveness of the Corinthian manner of religious expression (unknown tongues) made them feel superior to those who did not speak that way (I Cor. 14:36). And so Paul decided to boast a little for himself. You speak in a tongue which no one can understand and are proud of yourselves; but I speak in languages more than all of you; and five words that I speak intelligently to instruct others is worth more than 10,000 words of what you utter unintelligibly for your own sakes. Paul could say this because he spoke Hebrew, Greek, Latin, and probably Aramaic. Also, he had communicated the gospel to multitudes more than all of them put together. And so to credit Paul with speaking in unknown tongues is quite out of keeping with what we know of him and his stress on intelligent speech and the moral and spiritual effects of the Spirit's work.[34]

E. A Lucid Translation of I Corinthians Chapters 12–14

A well-known New Testament scholar and exegete, Boyce W. Blackwelder, has given us a most excellent English translation from the Greek of Chapters 12 through 14 of I Corinthians in his book, *Letters from Paul: "An Exegetical Translation.* Because of the lucidity of this Greek scholar's rendition of this difficult and much misunderstood section of Paul's writing, Blackwelder's translation is reproduced here as a fitting conclusion to the problem of "tongues" at Corinth.

---

33. *Commentary on the Holy Bible: One-Volume Edition,* abridged from original six-volume edition by Ralph Earle (Grand Rapids: Baker Book House, 1967), p. 1118.
34. Blaney, *op. cit.,* p. 57.

I Corinthians
Chapter 12

Now concerning spiritual manifestations, brothers, I want you to be adequately informed. [2] You recall that when you were pagans you used to be swept away whenever the impulse happened to seize you,[a] to idols that could impart no knowledge. [3] Let me give you the criteria for testing spiritual expression: No one speaking under the influence of the Spirit of God declares "Jesus be cursed!" And no one is able to say "Jesus is Lord!" except by the influence of the Holy Spirit.

---

[a] Cf. 10:20.

[4] There are varieties of gifts, but they are from the same Spirit. [5] And there are varieties of ministries, but it is the same Lord [who enables us to serve]. [6] And there are varieties of activities, but it is the same God who energizes every person. [7] To each one is given the manifestation of the Spirit with a view to the common good. [8] To one is given, by the Spirit, discourse characterized by wisdom. To another, discourse characterized by knowledge according to the same Spirit. [9] To another, [extraordinary] faith[b] by the same Spirit. To another, gifts to heal different kinds of diseases[c] by the one Spirit. [10] And to another, the working of miracles.[d] And to another prophecy.[e] And to another, the ability to discriminate between true and false spirits,[f] To another, various languages. And to another, interpretation of languages. [11] But all these are imparted by the one and same Spirit, who distributes them to each individual exactly as He chooses.

[12] For just as the [natural] body is one and has many members, and all the members, though many, constitute one body, so it is with Christ [in whom all believers are one]. [13] Indeed, by means of one Spirit all of us—whether Jews or Greeks, whether slaves or free men—were baptized into one body, and all were given to drink of one Spirit. [14] So, the body does not consist of one member but of many.

[15] If the foot were to say, "Because I am not a hand, I am not part of the body," it would not cease being part of the body. [16] If the ear were to say, "Because I am not an eye, I am not part of the body," it would not cease being part of the body. [17] If the entire body were an eye, how could anyone hear? If the entire body were an ear, how could anyone smell? [18] But the fact is, God has placed the members—every one of them—in the body just as he wished.

[19] If the whole were just one part, how could there be a body? [20] Actually there are many members, but there is only one body. [21] The eye cannot say to the hand, "I do not need you"; nor can the head say to the feet, "I do not need you." [22] On the contrary,[g] the members of the body which seem to be weaker are certainly necessary, [23] and those parts which we regard as less honorable are the ones which we surround with more abundant honor.[h] And the least presentable parts are treated with special consideration [24] which our more presentable parts do not require.

But God has formed the body in such a way that special dignity has been given to the [seemingly] inferior parts, [25] in order that there may not be any discord in the body, but that the members should exercise mutual concern for one another. [26] So if one member suffers, all the members suffer with it; if one member is honored, all the members rejoice with it.

[27] Now you—the congregation—are a body in relation to Christ,

---

[b] Cf. 13:2; Matt. 17:20; 21:21; Mark 11:22-24.
[c] Literally, *gifts of cures.*
[d] Literally, *operations of powers.*
[e] Or, inspired preaching or teaching, Cf. 14:3.
[f] Literally, *discernings of spirits.* Cf. I John 4:1.
[g] Literally, *but by much more.*
[h] Or which we clothe with special care.

and each member has his function to perform. [28]And God has placed in the church first, apostles; second, prophets; third, teachers; next, miraculous powers; then gifts of cures, abilities for rendering assistance, capacities for leadership, facility in various languages. [29]All are not apostles, are they?[i] All are not prophets, are they? All are not teachers, are they? All are not workers of miracles, are they? [30]All do not have gifts of cures, do they? All do not speak in foreign languages, do they? All do not interpret, do they? [31][j]Earnestly desire[k] the greater gifts, and yet I want to show you a way that far surpasses them.

---

[i]Every question in this and the following verse is introduced by the Greek negative particle *mē*, which indicates that in each instance the answer *No* is expected.
[j]This verse might well be placed with chapter 13.
[k]Cf. v. 11.

I Corinthians
Chapter 13

If I spoke with the eloquence of men and even of angels, but lacked love,[a] my oratory would amount to no more than unimpressive loquacity.[b] [2]And if I had prophetic insight and knew all the secret truths and all the knowledge [available to man], and if I could exercise the widest range of faith—even to move mountains—but had not love, I would be nothing. [3]And if I gave away all my possessions, and actually sacrificed my body to be burned, but had not love, it would profit me nothing.

[4]This love [to which I refer] is long-suffering and kind. It is not envious. It does not put itself on display. It is not arrogant. [5]It does not express itself in a rude manner. It is not selfish. It is not irritable. It keeps no record of evil [done to it]. [6]It does not rejoice over wrong-doing but it rejoices with the truth. [7]It does not unnecessarily expose anyone.[c] It is eager to believe the best [about everybody]. It tries to find love in every situation. It perseveres in all circumstances.

[8]Love will never lose its preeminence.[d] Where there are prophetic activities, they will be terminated. Where there is eloquent speech, it will cease. Where there is knowledge, it will be transcended. [9]Indeed, our knowledge is only partial, and our prophesying[e] is partial. [10]But when that which is perfect comes, all that is partial will be superseded.

[11]When I was a child, I used to talk like a child, I used to think like a child, I used to make plans like a child; but now that I have become a man, I have given up permanently the ways of a child.

---

[a]The Greek word for love used throughout this chapter is *agapē*, which denotes God's love made known in Christ and shed forth into the believer's heart by the Holy Spirit (cf. Rom. 5:5).
[b]Literally, *I have become a noisy gong or a rattling cymbal.*
[c]Literally, *It puts a roof over everything.*
[d]Literally, *Love never fails.*
[e]Or, preaching.

[12] Actually, at the present we see only dim reflections as if we were looking in a mirror, but then [we shall see] face to face. Now I know in part, but then I shall know as fully as I myself am known. [13] And so faith, hope, and love remain—these three—but the greatest of these is love.

I Corinthians
Chapter 14

Keep pursuing divine love[a] [as your foremost aim because it is indispensable], yet continue to be zealous for spiritual endowments, especially for the gift of persuasive preaching.[b] [2] He who speaks in a foreign language[c] speaks not to men but to God, for no one[d] understands him. But by the Spirit[e] he declares revealed truths.[f] [3] However, the one who preaches persuasively addresses men [in a way that brings] edification and admonition and consolation. [4] He who speaks in a foreign language edifies himself, but the persuasive preacher builds up [the spiritual life of] the church. [5] Now I might wish[g] that all of you could speak in foreign languages. But I much prefer you to be persuasive preachers.[h] He who preaches persuasively renders a more useful service than he who speaks in foreign languages—unless, of course, the latter interprets [what he says], so that the church may receive benefit.[i]

[6] Now, brothers, if I come to you and speak in foreign languages,

---

[a] Greek, agapē.

[b] Literally, *but rather that you may prophesy.*

[c] Corinth was a flourishing commercial city, with harbors on two seas. Its population came from all parts of the known world, hence the members of the church there would reflect many languages and dialects.

[d] "No one" is not to be taken in the absolute sense. The speaker would understand and give the interpretation (cf. vv. 5, 6, 13-17). The whole context indicates that anything spoken under the impetus of the Holy Spirit is intelligible. A difficulty might arise because of the languages used, but not because of the absence of meaning.

[e] Cf. 2:13; Acts 2:4.

[f] Literally, *mysteries.*

[g] Or, I wish. The Greek verb *thelō* is the form of both the subjunctive and the indicative. In the present context it seems to be the subjunctive, i.e., it expresses a hypothetical statement.

[h] Reiteration of preference stated in v. 1.

[i] Paul is dealing with young converts, many of whom were former pagans. Some faults of their pre-Christian experience were re-appearing or, more probably, had not yet been overcome. The Corinthians needed to understand the nature of spiritual gifts, and to escape the perils of false expressions. Pagan worship was characterized by frenzied, ecstatic utterances over which reason had no control. Paul does not approve unreasoning emotionalism. His purpose is to lead the Christian believers completely away from the old cultic behavior patterns. To this end he writes in a diplomatic manner and takes a positive approach, emphasizing the qualities and procedures which are paramount in the new life.

what good can I do you unless my words convey some meaning either by revelation, or by knowledge, or by clear preaching, or by teaching? [7] It is the same with inanimate things,[j] such as the flute or the harp—if they do not make a distinction in the notes, how can the melody be recognized?[k] [8] Again, if a military trumpet does not sound a clear signal, who will prepare himself for battle? [9] So it is with you—unless you speak clearly, how will anyone know what you say? Actually, you will be speaking into the air.

[10] There are, we may say, many different kinds of speech in the world, and none is without meaning. [11] If, however, I do not know the significance of the language [being spoken], I am a stranger to the speaker and the speaker is a stranger to me. [12] So with you, since you are eager for spiritual manifestations, strive especially for excellence in edifying the church.

[13] This is why anyone who speaks in a foreign language should pray that he may interpret [what he says to his hearers]. [14] If I pray[l] in a foreign language, my spirit prays but my understanding produces no fruit [for the benefit of others]. [15] What is the inference of what I have been saying? I will pray with the spirit but I will also pray so as to be understood[m] [by my listeners]. I will sing with the spirit but I will also sing so as to be understood[m] [by my listeners[n]].

[16] Otherwise suppose you are giving thanks [to God] in spirit [only], how can the person who is not conversant [with the language you use] say Amen to your thanksgiving if he does not understand what you are talking about? [17] Indeed you give thanks in a manner edifying to yourself,[o] but the other person receives no benefit [unless he understands what you say]. [18] I thank God that I might speak[p] in foreign languages more than all of you. [19] Nevertheless, in church I would rather speak five words which are understood,[q] in order that I might instruct others,[r] than [to speak] ten thousand words in a foreign language.

---

[j] Literally, *with lifeless things giving a sound.*

[k] Literally, *how can what is played on the flute or on the harp be known?*

[l] A third class condition. It expresses a hypothetical statement, not a declaration of fact.

[m] Literally, *with the understanding also.*

[n] Indicated by vv. 16-19.

[o] Literally, *you yourself give thanks well.* This implies that the speaker is benefited, hence understands what he says. Paul nowhere sanctions meaningless utterance.

[p] Or, I speak. The Greek verb *lalō* is the form of the indicative as well as the form of the subjunctive. In this context (note especially v. 19) it seems to be subjunctive. Cf. same idiom with *thelō* in v. 5. Paul was a versatile linguist. From his cultural background and schooling he learned Hebrew, Aramaic, Greek, and, probably, Latin. As the Apostle to the Gentiles his evangelistic tours carried him into provinces where many local dialects were spoken.

[q] Literally, *five words with my understanding.*

[r] Thus Paul explains what he means by speaking with the understanding.

[20] Brothers, do not be children in your thinking. Be babes where malice is concerned, but in your thinking be mature. [21] In the Law[s] it stands written, "By men of foreign languages and through the lips of strangers I will speak to this people, and not even then will they listen to me, says the Lord."[t] [22] This shows that foreign languages are a sign[u] not to those who believe but to those who do not believe, whereas the clear presentation of God's word[v] is intended not for unbelievers but for believers.

[23] Consequently, if the entire church meets together in one place, and all speak in foreign languages, and uninformed persons or unbelievers come in, will they not say you are crazy? [24] But if everyone proclaims God's word clearly,[w] and some unbeliever or uniformed person comes in, he is convicted by all, he is searched out by all, [25] he sees himself as he is.[x] And so he will bow down and worship God, confessing, "Truly God is among you!"

[26] What are the implications of what I have been saying, brothers?[y] When you meet together, each one has [a contribution to make]: a hymn, a teaching, a revelation, a discourse in a foreign language, or an interpretation. Let all things be done with a view to [the] upbuilding [of the church]. [27] If any speak in a foreign language, let only two or at the most three, speak, one at a time, and let someone interpret what is said.

[28] However if no interpreter is present,[z] let the one who would speak in a foreign language keep silent in the church, and let him speak to himself and to God. [29] Let two or three prophets speak,

---

[s] Here *the Law* refers to the Old Testament Scriptures as a whole. Cf. John 10:34; 12:34; 15:25; Rom. 3:19.

[t] Cf. Isa. 28:11-12. Israel heard God's word, delivered plainly by the prophets, but refused to obey. As a result, divine judgment is pronounced upon the rebellious people and God says they will be conquered by barbarous strangers whose language they cannot understand. The prediction was fulfilled by the Assyrian invasion (cf. 2 Chron. 28:16ff.). That historical incident is analogous to the situation to which Paul applies it. He points out that just as words spoken in strange speech did not lead the Hebrews to obedience, so speaking in foreign languages will not profit the Corinthians.

[u] Not a convincing sign, but one which does not favorably impress unbelievers (cf. v. 23). For other instances of *sēmeion* as a *sign* with a negative effect, cf. Luke 2:34; John 2:18; Matt. 12:39; 16:4.

[v] Literally, *prophecy.*

[w] Literally, *But all prophesy.* Expression in foreign languages has value only through the aid of another gift, i.e., interpretation, whereas persuasive preaching is of first importance because unaided it sets forth the gospel.

[x] Literally, *the secrets of his heart are exposed.* Cf. Heb. 4:12-13.

[y] Literally, *What therefore is it, brothers?*

[z] This implies that a person needing an interpreter is able to ascertain in advance whether or not an interpreter is present. This could not be done if nonhuman or heavenly languages were involved; for if that were the case the interpretation would have to come as a special disclosure in each instance, hence a speaker could never be certain that he should present a message.

and let the others consider carefully what is said. [30] And if anything is revealed to another who is sitting by, let the first speaker yield to him. [31] For you can all declare God's message[a] one by one, so that all may learn and be encouraged.

[32] The spirits of inspired men are under the control of the inspired men[b]! [33] For God is not [the Author] of disorder but of peace, as [he is] in all the churches of the saints.[c]

[34] Let the women maintain silence in the churches. They are not permitted to disturb the decorum of worship, [d] but are to be submissive even as also the Law says.[35] And if they wish to learn about something, let them ask their own husbands at home. For it is a shame for a woman to disturb the decorum of worship. [36] Was it with you that the word of God originated? Or are you the only people it has reached?

[37] If anyone claims to be a prophet or to have any spiritual endowment, let him acknowledge that what I am writing to you is a command of the Lord. [38] But if anyone disregards this, he should be disregarded. [39] So then, my brothers, be eager to preach persuasively,[f] and do not forbid anyone who has the gift of speaking in foreign languages to exercise it. [40] But let everything be done in a proper and orderly manner.[35]

---

35. Boyce W. Blackwelder, *Letters from Paul: An Exegetical Translation* (Anderson, Indiana: © Warner Press, Inc.), pp. 62-68. Used by written permission of the author, and Dr. Harold L. Phillips, Editor-in-Chief, Warner Press, Inc.

---

[a]Literally, *prophesy*.

[b]That is, their emotions and speech are governed by their understanding and their will. The violent possession which often seized heathen spokesmen and overpowered their reason and self-consciousness is foreign to the motivation of the Holy Spirit.

[c]This last clause may be connected with vs. 34. The thought would then be: As in all the churches of the saints, let the women maintain silence in the meetings.

[d]Literally, *they are not permitted to continue speaking;* i.e., whispering and asking their husbands questions during church services. This interpretation is suggested by the present infinitive of the onomatopoetic verb *laleō*, and by the permissive arm of the antithesis contained in v. 35.

[e]No such prohibition is found in the Mosaic Law, hence the Law here refers to the Old Testament in general (as in v. 21) which subordinates woman to man in the account of creation (Gen. 2:21-23), and by the primeval pronouncement given in Genesis 3:16.

[f]Or, to prophesy

V. SOME CONCLUSIONS CONCERNING THE SPIRIT'S GIFT OF COMMUNICATION TO THE CHURCH

The occurrence of the miracle of other tongues (languages) at Pentecost and subsequently is manifold in its significance.

First, the miracle was wrought in and through the Christian disciples by the divine energy of the Holy Spirit, by whom they were *filled* on that occasion (Acts 2:4).

Second, it was administered in a practical way through the disciples under the superintendence of the Holy Spirit (Acts 2:46), and thus it consisted of Spirit-inspired "utterances," and not of a miracle of hearing by the multitude, as some have mistakenly supposed.

Third, it was made necessary by the presence of the multitudes speaking some fifteen different languages and/or dialects at Pentecost, who could not otherwise have heard intelligibly the gospel of Christ's resurrection from the dead, which provided salvation for them (Acts 2:11, 32-36).

Fourth, it consisted of correct and intelligible bona fide languages and/or dialects which were clearly understood by the hearers (Acts 1:8, 11, 37).

Fifth, it served as the vehicle for God's message that produced in many of the hearers the divinely intended result of repentance unto salvation (Acts 2:37-39).

Sixth, it was instrumental in bringing about the conversion of approximately 3,000 hearers at Pentecost who were baptized and added to the Christian church (Acts 2:41).

Seventh, it was attested as a genuine miracle by its value manifested in the spiritual enlightenment, conviction, and conversion of this large number of converts.

Eighth, Luke's record in Acts 2 is the most clearly definitive account of the "gift of tongues" which we have in the New Testament. Though tongues are referred to definitely in three other recognized, genuine New Testament passages (Acts 10, 19, and I Cor. 12-14), it is only in Acts 2:1-11 that the meaning is made explicit. Here it is manifestly a divinely given vehicle of linguistic communication for the evangelization of the multitudes in a situation that demanded and justified it, and as a token of the universal message and mission of the Christian gospel.

Ninth, while I Corinthians was probably written somewhat earlier than Acts (I Cor. between A.D. 54-57 — Acts c. A.D. 63), the question of tongues did not arise at Corinth until nearly a quarter of a century after its occurrence at Pentecost. Luke, the author of Acts, was the companion and fellow worker of Paul during most of his second and third missionary journeys, as also during his two-year Caesarean imprisonment, and on his voyage to Rome and imprisonment there. Consequently it is most certain that Paul would have supplied him information for the Acts record covering those periods when Luke was not with him (especially on Acts 10 and 19). Thus Paul would naturally have approved the interpretation of the events that Luke recorded, though Luke may have gotten his information concerning Pentecost and other events up to the appearance of Paul at Troas from other sources, unless indirectly through Paul (see Acts 8:1-4; 9). In any event his thorough acquaintance with Paul's views on the subject of "tongues," as also other theological issues, seems almost certain. There is absolutely no Biblical evidence of any difference of opinion between Luke and Paul on this "tongues" question, or any other issue in fact. Therefore, on the basis of these facts we would concur with Blackwelder when he says,

> We may assume that the viewpoint of Acts is decisive for what Paul writes in I Corinthians [on "tongues"].
> Some *expositors* begin by attempting to reconstruct the situation at Corinth and then either try to make Luke's account fit what they surmise occurred at Corinth or suggest that there were two different categories of the gift of tongues. Such an approach is unsatisfactory, for it is Luke who describes what the gift was. Paul writes [to the Corinthians] to correct false ideas regarding it. Therefore, if we are to avoid speculation about speaking in tongues, we must get our bearings from the basic treatment which is given in Acts 2:1-11 . . . if the true gift of *glossolalia* is manifested, it will be according to the pattern of Acts 2:4-11.[36]

Blackwelder is on solid ground when he denies that there is any Scriptural evidence that anyone under the influence of the Holy Spirit ever spoke in an "unknown tongue."[37] Since *glossais* means "languages," and languages are means of person-to-person communication, they will necessarily be known to some people.

Tenth, that the gift of languages, as recorded in Acts 2, was for evangelization purposes, rather than for the personal edification of the believer, as is claimed by advocates of the "unknown tongues" doctrine, is further evident from the absence of any mention of tongues in Acts 2 beyond its initial employment in preaching the gospel to the polyglot multitudes present at the Feast of Pentecost. Peter's quotation of Joel's prophecy of the Spirit's effusion makes no reference whatsoever to tongues as a concomitant of the Spirit's

---

36. These facts are evidenced by Luke's use of the personal plural pronoun "we" in his Acts record indicating his presence with Paul at those stages of his travels and missionary work. See the "we" sections in Acts 16:10-17; 20:5-18; 21:1-18; 27:1—28:16.

37. Boyce W. Blackwelder, "Glossolalia at Pentecost," *Vital Christianity, op. cit.,* p. 6.

effusion (see Acts 2:17-21). Any claim that the Samaritans spoke in tongues on the occasion of their baptism in the Spirit is purely gratuitous, and thus unwarranted as far as the Scriptural record reveals.

After the approximately 3,000 converts had been baptized and were received into the fellowship of the church (2:41), no further mention of tongues is found in relation to these believers in the Acts record. Indeed they were edified in the apostles' "doctrine," "fellowship," "breaking of bread," "prayers," acts of charity, rejoicing, "singleness of heart," and by "praising God," with resultant profound spiritual and moral influence on their non-Christian neighbors. This beneficent influence produced converts to Christianity among them daily (2:42-47), but nowhere is there further mention of tongues among these converts. Nor was there further need for tongues now that the multitudes at Pentecost had heard the gospel distinctly and intelligibly in their own languages, a large percentage of whom must have returned to their respective homes following Pentecost.

Eleventh, a careful examination of the structure of Peter's sermon on the Day of Pentecost, as recorded in Acts 2, clearly reveals that the burden of his message concerned the crucifixion and the resurrection of Jesus Christ with His consequent universal Lordship, facts which were designed of God to produce repentance and saving faith in the minds and lives of his hearers (Acts 2:22-40). It is only Luke, the author of Acts, and not Peter, who records that the disciples spoke forth the gospel by miraculous aid in the various languages of the people present. Harold Ockenga has well said that "Peter's Pentecostal Sermon centers in the death and resurrection of Jesus Christ, not speaking in tongues." This concern with the death, resurrection, and Lordship of Jesus Christ likewise characterized Peter's subsequent sermons, as also those of Stephen and Paul. There is no evidence that the thought of "tongues" was in any of their minds, if we are to judge from the contents of their recorded sermons. Peter's words, "he has poured forth this which you see and hear" (Acts 2:33) necessarily refer to the transforming effects of the gospel on the hearers under the Spirit's energy, which they observed ("you see"), and the fact that they heard distinctly the gospel in their own languages ("and hear"; cf. Acts 2:11).

Twelfth, thus it may be reasonably allowed, within the foregoing framework of interpretation, that the divine gift and use of languages

---

38. *Ibid.*

in Jerusalem at Pentecost signified the beginning of the universal missionary program of the gospel as it is set forth clearly by Christ in Acts 1:8, though Christ does not there, nor anywhere else in fact (unless Mark 16:16-17 be credited as genuine), mention "tongues" in any relationship to redemption or the gift of the Spirit, or in any other manner. One may fairly ask why Christ never once mentions "tongues" in relation to the promised gift of the Spirit which John treats so fully in his Gospel, Chapters 14-16, if God intended this phenomenon as an evidence of the gift of the Holy Spirit? It should be noted that *the Spirit* is not mentioned in Mark 16:16-17, even if this passage should be considered genuine. Nor is there any mention of tongues in connection with the descent of the Spirit upon Jesus at His baptism (Matt. 3:16; John 1:32-33), nor by John the Baptist in his prediction of the baptism in the Spirit in Matthew 3:11. Therefore we conclude that wherever "tongues" occur in Scripture they are to be understood as genuine languages for communicating the gospel, except where perversions of this phenomenon occurred at Corinth.

Chapter 9

The Effects
of the Spirit's Effusion
upon the Multitudes
at Pentecost

I. THE MULTITUDES' REACTION TO THE SPIRIT'S EFFUSION

The immediate reaction of the multitudes present at the Jews' Feast of Pentecost, when the Holy Spirit's presence was marvelously manifest, was, in general, twofold. On the part of many, perhaps by far the larger number, the reaction was negative. However, out of the vast multitudes which may have aggregated as many as three million, about three thousand were moved to a positive reaction of sincere inquiry, repentance, and saving faith in Jesus Christ as the long-expected Messiah-Savior.

Concerning the multitudes in general, Luke records that upon hearing the "noise like a violent, rushing wind" (Acts 2:2), that came from heaven ("when the sound occurred") this vast throng "came together," likely in an excited manner in and about the Temple. Their initial reaction was "bewilderment" as they heard these Galilean disciples speaking their several different languages and dialects. "They were amazed and marveled" at what they heard. Luke amplifies and emphasizes their general reaction by saying, "they continued in amazement and great perplexity, saying to one another, 'What does this mean?' "

Before Peter or any of the apostles could expound to them the meaning of the miraculous occurrence, certain of the multitude drew the hasty conclusion that the apostles were intoxicated on "sweet wine" (v. 13). How far their sensibilities were dulled and deadened by long rejection of light and truth is evident from four considerations of their negative reaction to the Spirit's manifestation. First, men do not get intoxicated on unfermented, "new" or "sweet wine" (v. 13b). Second, nine o'clock in the morning was not the time for a company of men to be intoxicated, as Peter replies (v. 15). Third, their frank admission that the Galilean apostles were speaking distinctly and intelligibly their various languages and dialects does not support their charge of intoxication. Intoxicated men do not speak even their own native languages distinctly (vv. 6, 11). Fourth, the nature and quality of their speech was not that of intoxicated men. They were "speaking of the mighty deeds of God" (v. 11b), principally the resurrection of Jesus Christ from the dead.

That the far greater percentage closed their minds against the truth of God proclaimed by Peter and the other apostles appears evident from the record that only about 3,000 of the vast throng were converted, plus the subsequent stubborn rejection of these non-Christian Jews in Jerusalem as the apostles continued to proclaim the Christian message in Jerusalem. As the ultimate judgment upon their willful rejection of the illumination and power of the Spirit at Pentecost, their city and nation were destroyed by the Romans in A.D. 70. And so must men ever suffer the judgments of God and time when they willfully reject the way of truth and righteousness.

II. THE THREE THOUSAND CONVERTS UNDER THE SPIRIT'S EFFUSION AT PENTECOST

Within the vast multitude that witnessed the Spirit's effusion at Pentecost there were about 3,000 whose reaction was positive. These recognized the truth of the apostles' message and were brought under the Spirit's powerful influence. Consequently, they repented and believed on Jesus Christ as their personal Savior and Lord. That these initial converts at Pentecost were, for the most part at least, prior converts to Judaism from among the gentiles appears most likely. They were Hellenist Jews in that they were gentile proselytes and God-fearers who, like the Ethiopian nobleman converted under Philip's ministry, had accepted the truth of the divine revelation concerning the Messiah revealed in the Jews' Old Testament. It is to these approximately 3,000 converts to the Christian faith, on the Day of Pentecost, under the Spirit's influence that we now direct our interest.

A. The Genuineness of Their Conversion to Christianity

The some three thousand converts to Christianity following the effusion of the Spirit at Pentecost may best exemplify the converts of the first century in general. It has often been said that a stream of water is purest at its source. Since the first Christian Pentecost is the life-giving source of the church's fountain of spiritual vitality, it is quite natural and right that we should look there for God's model for the church of all time.

Concerning these converts to Christ on the Day of Pentecost, Luke says:

> So then, those who had received his word were baptized; and there were added that day about three thousand souls. And they were continually devoting themselves to the apostles' teaching and to fellowship, to the breaking of bread and to prayer. And everyone kept feeling a sense of awe; and many wonders and signs were taking place through the apostles. And all those who had believed were together, and had all things in common; and they *began* selling their property and possessions, and were sharing them with all, as anyone might have need. And day by day continuing with one mind in the temple, and breaking bread from house to house, they were taking their meals together with gladness and sincerity of heart, praising God, and having favor with all the people. And the Lord was adding to their number day by day those who were being saved (Acts 2:41-47).

This is not to assume that we will find there an ideal church, since it was constituted of human beings not essentially different from those constituting the body of Christ in every age. Of those first Christians it could be said by Paul, as of Christians in every day and age: "we have this treasure in earthen vessels, that the surpassing greatness of the power may be of God and not from ourselves" (II Cor. 4:7). There were defects in the vessels then as now. However, notwithstanding the imperfections of the vessels, God filled them with His Spirit and used them to His glory. To this Spirit-filled church we now give consideration.

B. Their Ready Acceptance of the Message of Truth

"So then, those who had received his word were baptized" (Acts 2:41a). Another rendering of these words says, "who *gladly*" (Greek, *asmenos*), or "had welcomed" (Greek, *apodxamenoi*) "his word were baptized."[1]

The manner and circumstances under which any people receive the special divine revelation may influence extensively and intensively the entire character and subsequent life of the converts. Jesus recognized this when He spoke the familiar parable of the sower (Mark 4:3-20). His hearers ranged all the way from those in whose lives the Word had no effect whatsoever, through those who heard readily and even gladly, but whose superficial faith quickly withered away under trial, to those in whose lives the Word took root and grew for a time and gave promise of a fruitful harvest, until choked out by the cares of time and their earthly life. Finally, there were those in whose lives the seed of God's Word germinated, struck deep root in fertile soil of responsive character, and bore various degrees of fruit, ranging from thirty through sixty to a hundredfold. One New Testament writer speaks of certain persons in whom "the word they heard did not profit them, because it was not united by faith in those who heard" (Heb. 4:2). To his Thessalonian converts Paul wrote that the gospel had not reached them in ordinary language, but under the power and conviction of the Holy Spirit (I Thess. 1:5). Furthermore, he reminds these converts that they had *"received the word in much tribulation* with the joy [or inspiration] of the Holy Spirit" (I Thess. 1:6).

While the Acts record in Chapter 2 indicates no opposition to the gospel or persecution of the converts initially on the Day of Pentecost, beyond the mockery of certain Jews who accused the Christians of being intoxicated because of their conduct under the influence of the Spirit, severe persecution was soon to set in against them by the unbelieving Jews. Only much later, and possibly not until the Neronian persecution, if William Ramsey is correct, did the Roman civil authorities intentionally and actively participate in their persecution. Such an exception was the execution of James and the intended execution of Peter by Herod Agrippa I, grandson of Herod the Great and nephew of Herod Antipas I, as Roman procurator of Judea from A.D. 41-44, who fell under the pressure to curry favor with the ruling Jewish Sanhedrin in order to make good his rule in Judea. Having inherited the murderous dispositions of his grandfather and uncle, he did not scruple to kill James and intend a like fate for Peter in order to "please the Jews" and thus enhance his standing with them. He deferred to their scruples, observed their regulations, and

---

1. George R. Berry, *Interlinear Literal Translation of the Greek New Testament*, p. 317.

was careful to avoid offense in every respect. It was this disposition toward and deference to his Jewish subjects that elicited his persecution of the Christians, expressed in the beheading of James and his intended, but divinely foiled, execution of Peter during the Jewish Feast of the Passover at Jerusalem (Acts 12:1-23). Thus Herod's persecution cannot be considered persecution by the secular authorities *per se,* but rather one executed under deference to Jewish pressure.

The second apparent secular persecution did not occur until somewhat later, on Paul's second missionary journey, at Philippi when he, together with Silas, was beaten and imprisoned. However, this was clearly a case of mistaken identity on the part of the Roman officials at Philippi, and incidentally a mistake that might well have cost them their lives had they been reported to Rome. Luke tells that story in Acts 16:16-40.

However, the absence of any record of direct persecution on the Day of Pentecost does not exclude severe opposition to the Christians that was soon to follow. No sooner had the new spiritual life movement at Jerusalem, resulting from the effusion of the Spirit at Pentecost, begun to manifest itself in a practical manner than the jealous Jewish Sanhedrin took measures to suppress it. This was the first recorded persecution, and it was instigated at the hands of the Sadducees, the most influential, though numerically smaller, party in the Sanhedrin, and the chief priests. It was occasioned by the healing of the lame man at the Beautiful Gate, plus Peter's subsequent sermon (Acts 3:1–4:31). The second persecution was incited by the Hellenist Jews, though it too was executed by the Jewish Sanhedrin, eventuating in the illegal martyrdom of Stephen and the extensive and severe persecutions of the Christians under the leadership of the mad persecutor Saul, until his conversion (Acts 6:9–8:1; 9:1, 2, 29). What other persecution these Christians at Pentecost and immediately following Pentecost may have suffered we are not told in the Acts record. We know only that large numbers must have been disinherited, deprived of their possessions, and socially ostracized, for Luke records that Christian love moved those who had possessions to provide for the needs of those who were made destitute by reason of their acceptance of the Christian faith (Acts 4:32-37).

If it may be allowed that the author of the Letter to the Hebrews was referring to these first Christian converts at and following Pentecost, then his description of the trying circumstances under which they embraced the Christian faith is highly significant in this context. He bids them, remember the former days, when, after being enlightened, you endured a great conflict of sufferings, partly, by being made a public spectacle through reproaches and tribulations, and partly by becoming sharers with those who were so treated. For you showed sympathy to the prisoners, and accepted joyfully the seizure of your property, knowing that you have for yourselves a better possession and an abiding one (10:32-34).

Indeed, the message that Peter preached on the Day of Pentecost, as also in his second sermon, as well as Stephen's defense before the Sanhedrin, was rife with cutting accusations that brought pungent conviction upon these Jews for their responsibility in having crucified the Lord of glory. However, they were outwitted by God in Christ's resurrection from the dead on the third day (Acts 1:22; 2:24; 3:12-26; 4:8-12; 7:1-54).

It was in the face of this *bitter-sweet message* of the gospel of Jesus Christ delivered under the power and pungent conviction of the Holy Spirit that these early Christian converts had received the Word and were baptized (Acts 2:41). An easy entry into the kingdom of God has sometimes resulted in quite as easy an exit from that kingdom for many professors of Christian conversion. In recognition of this fact Christ exhorted His listeners to "Strive to enter by the narrow door; for many, I tell you, will seek to enter and will not be able" (Luke 13:24).

It was to the church at Ephesus that Paul wrote, reminding them of the effective work of God in their lives. "In Him, you also, after listening to the message of truth, the gospel of your salvation—having also believed ["in Him," mar.] , *you were sealed in Him with the Holy Spirit of promise, who is given as a pledge* ["*down payment.*" mar.] *of our inheritance,* with a view to the redemption of God's *own* possession, to the praise of His glory" (Eph. 1:13-14). It is these Ephesian Christians who *exemplify* the work of God by His Spirit in the lives of the believers at Pentecost. They are genuine samples of the church following the effusion of the Spirit at Pentecost, though their conversion occurred sometime subsequent to that event.

C. Their Joyful Confession of the Christian Faith

Their baptism was their clear-cut confession of faith which sealed their testimony to a saving relationship with Christ before their unbelieving Jewish countrymen, before God, and in their own hearts and lives. It was their outward confession of God's work of grace that had wrought the miracle of salvation within their inner beings.

With Paul they could say meaningfully: "With the heart man believes, resulting in righteousness, and with the mouth he confesses ["*to salvation*," mar.], resulting in salvation" (Rom. 10:10). Identification with Christ and the Christian community through the public rite of baptism was both obedience to Christ's command (Matt. 28:19), and the outward seal of their inward faith in Christ's saving mercy. It was the *hallmark* of their conversion to a living faith in Christ from their former loyalty to the now dead system of Jewish legalism. This was an act well understood by their unbelieving Jewish countrymen, and one that sharply and permanently marked the Christian community as distinct from Judaism. They now belonged to the "new and living way" (Heb. 10:20), to the "new" or "third race," as they were sometimes designated in distinction from the Jews and Gentiles, according to Adolph Harnack and Hans Leitzman.

The Jews of the first Christian century were no strangers to the rite of baptism. It was, in fact, commonly practiced by them as the condition of a proselyte's conversion to the Jewish faith. Thus baptism in the name of Jesus Christ signified a Jew's conversion to the Christian faith and his identification with the new Christian community.

When a Jew received baptism in the name of Christ he was usually forthwith disowned and disinherited by his family and excluded from all communication with his countrymen as far as possible. Thus no person would have forfeited these privileges and endured such shameful and painful persecution except on the clearest and fullest conviction of the validity of the Christian faith.

Again, Christian baptism was an effective deterrent against apostasy. This Christian baptism signified their renunciation of Judaism with all the personal, religious, and political advantages which that religion afforded. Consequently there arose the indispensable necessity of full identification with those who professed the faith of the new Christian religion. It became not only their new way of life, but their *only* way of life. There was no middle ground once they had accepted Christian baptism. Since it is the fact and significance of baptism with which we are here concerned, the controversial question of the mode will be passed over in silence, as Luke does not afford any significant clue to that problem. It is of the greatest importance to note that they were buried with Christ in baptism—thus dead to their former identifications and way of life—that they might be resurrected with Him into this "new and living way" (Heb. 10:20).

D. Their Immediate Identification with the Christian Believers

"there were *added* that day about three thousand souls (persons) (Acts 2:41).

It was as natural that these new converts to Christianity should have automatically identified with the Christian community in Jerusalem as that a newly born human baby or animal should be instinctively drawn to its mother for nourishment and protection, or that steel should manifest its affinity for the attraction of the powerful magnet. There is just reason for questioning the genuineness of the faith and experience of anyone who rejects or neglects identification and fellowship with the body of Christ into which he has been spiritually born. An unwillingness to identify with and assume responsibility for church membership with its fellowship, discipline, support, and service is certain to indicate a deficiency, if not a marked declension of Christian faith.

It would seem, in the face of the adverse circumstances with which these early converts to Christianity were confronted, that they possessed an exceptionally high and clear concept of the church as the body of Christ. Their temporal security had been taken away from them. Their real security was now vested in the spiritual. They were joined through the Spirit as integral organs to the body of Christ, the church, of which Christ Himself is the inseparable and indestructible Head. While united *in Christ*, to use a frequently recurring Pauline prepositional phrase, the church as the body of Christ is as indestructible as is Christ the Head of that body. In recognition of this fact Paul exclaimed exultantly, "For we know that if the earthly tent [lit., "our earthly house of the tent"] which is our house ["our body"] is torn down, we have a building from God, a house not made with hands, eternal in the heavens" (II Cor. 5:1).

Great as was the number of converts on the Day of Pentecost, their identification with the body of believers is of greater importance. On the expression, "*there were added* . . . about three thousand souls ["persons"]," Clarke has the following pertinent observation.

> *They went over from one party to another.* The Greek writers make use of this verb (*prosetefasan*) to signify that act by which cities, towns, or provinces *changed their masters,* and *put themselves under another government.* So these 3,000 persons left the scribes and Pharisees, and put themselves under the teachings of the apostles, professing the Christian doctrine, and acknowledging that Christ was come, and that he who was lately crucified by the Jews was the promised and only Messiah; and in this faith they were baptized.[2]

---

2. *Commentary on the Holy Bible*, p. 962.

It is not to be supposed that all these 3000 converts were the direct products of Peter's sermon on the Day of Pentecost. Rather evidence and reason indicates that all the Spirit-baptized apostles and disciples were busily engaged in witnessing to the multitudes in various parts of the city in a manner that produced mass conviction. Jesus had promised His disciples that when the Spirit came He would

> convict the world concerning sin, and righteousness, and judgment; concerning sin, because they do not believe in me; and concerning righteousness, because I go to the Father, and you no longer behold me; and concerning judgment, because the ruler of this world (Satan) has been judged (John 16:8-11).

The time of the fulfillment of this promise had arrived, and the result of the Spirit's operation on and through the disciples of Christ bore fruit in such conviction as resulted in 3000 additions to the church in a single day. Such mass conversions in the church at its inception anticipated by 2000 years the contemporary "Church Growth Movement" of the McGavran school, or the earlier "Nevius Method" that proved phenomenally successful in Korea.

III. THE COMMUNION OF THE CHRISTIAN CONVERTS UNDER THE SPIRIT'S EFFUSION AT PENTECOST

Five items stand out in the communion of these disciples under the influence of the Holy Spirit; namely, (1) the constancy of their devotion; (2) their eagerness to learn of the Christian way; (3) the genuineness and warmth of their Christian fellowship; (4) their sacred observance of the sacraments; and (5) their fervent and faithful practice of prayer. All of these characteristics belong intrinsically to the church of Christ that is born and controlled by the Spirit. The following words of Luke will express these characteristics: "And they were continually devoting themselves to the apostles' teaching and to fellowship, to the breaking of bread and to prayer [or, "the prayers"]" (Acts 2:42).

A. Their Communion in the Christian Faith

"They were continually devoting themselves." The expression "continually" ("continued steadfast") comes from the Greek verb *proskartareo,* which signifies "to attach oneself to," "to wait on," or "to be faithful to someone," like a boat that always stands ready for use. But it further suggests progress—to busy oneself with, or to be busily engaged in or devoted to some activity, as also to persevere in something. The expression is found again in Acts 1:14 and 2:46.

One cannot examine the Acts record of those post-Pentecostal Christians without being profoundly impressed by their sincere and unrelenting devotion to the worship and service of Christ. Imprisoned, threatened, beaten, and even in the face of the martyrdom of some of their members, they nevertheless pressed on undaunted in their devotion to Christ. Scattered abroad by severe persecution that took the life of one of their most valiant and promising leaders, Stephen, they went about ["everywhere"] preaching the Word ["bringing good tidings"] (Acts 8:4). Like water dashed upon flaming gasoline, violent opposition and cruel persecution served only to spread the holy flame beyond Jerusalem and Judea to the pagan regions beyond, rather than extinguish or even diminish it. They were thoroughly committed Christians, and they were Spirit-motivated Christians. They exemplified the spirit of the great apostle of Christianity, Paul, who himself practiced the exhortation he gave his fellow Christians at Corinth:

> Run in such a way that you may win. And everyone who competes in the games exercises self-control in all things. They then *do* it to receive a perishable wreath, but we an imperishable. Therefore I run in such a way, as not without aim; I box in such a way, as not beating the air (I Cor. 9:24b-26).

Or again, as Paul urged upon Timothy, his spiritual offspring: "Fight the good fight of faith; take hold of the eternal life to which you were called, and you made the good confession in the presence of many witnesses" (I Tim. 6:12).

Little wonder that with such an undaunted faith this Spirit-filled apostle of Christianity could say, even while incarcerated in the prison of one of the most wicked emperors who ever sat upon the throne of the Roman or perhaps any other empire, and awaiting the executioner's cruel beheading-knife,

> I am already being poured out as a drink-offering, and the time of my departure has come. I have fought the good fight, I have finished the course, I have kept the faith; in the future there is laid up for me the crown of righteousness, which the Lord, the righteous judge [*not Nero the unjust judge*], will award me on that day, and not only to me, but also to all who have loved his appearing (II Tim. 4:6-8).

There in his Roman confinement awaiting death for his faith in Christ and the proclamation of His gospel, Paul could say triumphantly: "Remember Jesus Christ, risen from the dead, descendant of David, according to my gospel; for which I suffer hardship even to imprisonment as a criminal, *but the word of God is not imprisoned*" (II Tim. 2:8-9).

These Spirit-filled Christians were motivated by a clearly perceived purpose—a divinely revealed *telos*, or goal, toward which they unflinchingly moved with resolve and precision. By their pagan compatriots, as also by their fellow-Christians, they were recognized as a new community, a new or third race in fact, motivated by an inward spiritual compulsion and a fixed purpose to make Christ known to all men as the only Savior and Lord. The King James translators six times capitalized the word *Way* in the Book of Acts, thus making it a proper noun characterizing the first-century Christians as a people powerfully motivated by the indwelling Spirit and a consuming desire to see their fellow men brought to Christ. And the Hebrew Epistle's author, writing in the latter part of the first century, denominates this Spirit-filled Christian company, "*a new and living way*" (10:19). Soon after the ascension of Christ the term "disciple" fell into disuse by reason of Christ's bodily absence. In derision the Jews then gave them such names as "Galileans," "The Poor" (*Ebionim*), and "Nazarenes"; the last term persisted longer than many others and was extended widely, notwithstanding its derisive intention. Among their self-designations were "God's people," "Israel in Spirit," "The Seed of Abraham," "The Twelve Tribes," "The Servants of God," "The Chosen People," "Believers," "Saints," "Brethren," "The Church of God," the "New Israel," and "Friends." The three most characteristic titles, and those that reflect the socio-religious solidarity of the new Christian movement, were "Saints," "Brethren," and "The Church of God," or "Church of Christ." "Brethren," or "Brethren in the Lord," as a title, seems most significantly to relate these early Christians to the family of God, as also to their anticipated future kingdom of God. Unfortunately, after the third century this title fell into disuse in large measure, except for ecclesiastics. "Christians" appears to have become the most persistent name designating the followers of Christ. However, one other name, which appears not to have become more than semi-technical, but which was highly significant in describing the characteristics of these Spirit-filled believers, was "*Miles Christi*," or "a soldier of Christ." Paul freely used, and may have originated, this term, which was employed widely and variously.[3]

---

3. See Adolph Harnack, *The Mission and Expansion of Christianity*, II, 125-233.

B. Their Communion in Christian Instruction

"They were continually devoting themselves to the apostles' teaching," Luke informs us of these Spirit-filled disciples of Christ.

Teaching (Greek *didaxá*) is closely linked with fellowship. For those Christians who are eager to learn there is a fellowship of learning between the teacher and those taught—a mutual sharing of spiritual insights and information. Desire for spiritual knowledge is a natural result and concomitant of the new life in Christ. These 3000 converts, newly born into the Christian life, quite naturally devoted themselves to the pursuit of the knowledge of the Lord. Of them it could be said, with Peter, "Like newborn babes [who] long for the pure milk of the word, that by it you may grow in respect to salvation, . . . [when] you have tasted the kindness of the Lord" (I Peter 2:2-3). They bore a close affinity to another company of believing Jews at Berea of whom Luke records that they "were more noble-minded than those in Thessalonica, for they received the word with great eagerness, examining the Scriptures daily, to *see* whether, these things [which Paul had preached to them] were so" (Acts 17:11).

While the word *doctrine* has taken on a somewhat unsavory connotation in relation to religion in modern times, suggesting to many minds fixed and inflexible religious beliefs, the original and real meaning of the word is simply "a teaching." Certainly all progress in grace will be accompanied by new and progressive knowledge received through a faithful and diligent search for truth. It is noteworthy that the great success of the Christian religion in Korea is traceable in large measure to the diligence with which the Korean Christians have devoted themselves to the study of the Bible. Jesus once said: "Search the Scriptures, because you think that in them you have eternal life; and it is those that bear witness of me" (John 5:39). Important as are the illumination and inspiration of the Holy Spirit in the life of the Christian for his soundness in the faith and protection from being led astray into error, he stands in need of instruction in the fundamental principles of the Christian religion. These early Christians steadfastly adhered to the apostles' teachings which produced among them a unity of belief and spirit.

A humble, teachable spirit is a certain evidence of the genuineness of Christian faith. A chief characteristic of an alert and developing child is question-asking. And Jesus said: "Truly I say unto you, unless you are converted and become like children, you shall not enter the kingdom of heaven" (Matt. 18:3). There is no greater need in the church today than that of doctrinal teaching, or clear Biblical exposition of divine truth. Such preaching is largely a lost art in the contemporary pulpit with the resultant spiritually anemic condition of much of modern Christianity. A most interesting observation was made at the great Methodist conference held in Europe a few years ago. Many of the lay preachers, especially, from the Methodist churches in England, reported that large numbers of their people had entered into a new relationship with the Lord under the special moving of the Spirit of God. Though they were enjoying their new spiritual life, these reporters said, they were unable to explain or clearly understand what had happened to them. Thus it had become necessary for the ministers to preach to them doctrinal sermons to define and explain the meaning of what they had already experienced in the Spirit. A desire to know more about Christ will always characterize a people possessed of the Spirit of God (John 14:26; 16:13-15).

On the negative side, Adam Clarke's remarks, based upon Paul's message to Timothy, sound prophetically fresh in the light of the conditions characterizing many churches today. To Timothy Paul wrote: "The time will come when they will not endure sound doctrine; but *wanting* to have their ears tickled, they will accumulate for themselves teachers in accordance to their own desires; and will turn away their ears from the truth, and will turn aside to myths" (II Tim. 4:3-4).

Adam Clarke's comment, in his somewhat quaint manner of expression, on the foregoing passage, is highly significant and worthy of note at this juncture.

> There is a time coming to the church when men will not hear the *practical* truths of the Gospel, when they will prefer speculative opinions, which either do no good to the soul, or corrupt and destroy it, to that wholesome doctrine of "deny thyself, take up thy cross, and follow me," which Jesus Christ has left in His church. *But after their own lusts*—For *these* they will follow, and hate those *preachers* and that doctrine by which they are opposed. *Shall heap to themselves teachers*—They *will add one teacher to another, run and gad about after all,* to find out those who insist not on the necessity of bearing the cross, of being crucified to the world, and of having the mind that was in Jesus. In this disposition interested men often find their account, they set up for teachers, "And widen and strew with flowers the way, down to eternal ruin," taking care to sooth the passions and flatter the vices of a trifling, superficial people. *Having itching ears*—endless curiosity, an insatiable desire of *variety*; and they get their ears tickled with the *language* and *accent*

of the person, abandoning the *good* and *faithful preacher* for the *fine speaker.* And *they shall turn away their ears from the truth—* The truth strips them of their vices, sacrifices their idols, darts its lightnings against their easily besetting sins, and absolutely requires a conformity to a crucified Christ; therefore *they turn their ears away from it. And shall be turned unto fables*—Believe any kind of stuff and nonsense; for, as one has justly observed, "Those who reject the truth are abandoned by the just judgment of God to credit the most degrading nonsense."[4]

C. Their Communion in Christian Fellowship

Luke records concerning these Spirit-filled Christians: "And they were continually devoting themselves to the apostles' . . . fellowship" (Acts 2:42). The Greek word used here for "fellowship" (*Koinonia*) is especially rich in meaning. Its literal meaning is "a partnership." Thus these new converts had entered into a sacred, spiritual partnership with those who had initiated them into the new order of the regal, sacredotal-priesthood" (Rev. 1:6; I Peter 2:5, 9). They were now brothers and sisters and fellow members of the apostolic church. They shared the plight and poverty of others who had embraced the Christian faith under the influence of the Holy Spirit (cf. Rom. 15:26; II Cor. 8:4; 9:13; Heb. 13:16). But this fellowship also suggests reciprocity, or a common interest in and sharing of property and experiences. Like the generous Christians at Philippi, of whom Paul later remarked, "in view of your *participation* in the gospel from the first day until now" (Phil. 1:5), this Spirit-filled community of believers was spiritually and socially involved. They anticipated by two millenniums the *Christian* social *involvement* so much emphasized in recent decades, but much of which lacks the spiritual dynamic of these early disciples of the Lord. They had come to "know Him [Jesus Christ], and the power of His resurrection and the fellowship [or, "participation in"] of His sufferings, being conformed to His death" (Phil. 3:10). It was a fellowship of the Christian faith, in the deepest sense of that term (cf. Philem. 6).

But quite beyond the sharing of temporal blessings and possessions this community of believers enjoyed a spiritual fellowship, or perhaps better, a fellowship of the Spirit—the Holy Spirit who indwelt them all alike. Paul suggests such a common spiritual communion when he writes, "God is faithful, through whom you were called into

---

4. "The New Testament of Our Lord and Saviour Jesus Christ," *Clarke's Commentary*, II, 637.

fellowship with His Son, Jesus Christ our Lord" (I Cor. 1:9). Paul likewise speaks of this fellowship when he writes to the Philippian Christians about their "encouragement in Christ," their "consolation of love," *their "fellowship of the Spirit,"* and their "affection and compassion" for each other (2:1). John portrays a full-orbed picture of this fellowship when he writes: "What we have seen and heard we proclaim to you also, that you also may have *fellowship* with us; and indeed our *fellowship* is with the Father, and with His Son Jesus Christ" (I John 1:3). Theirs was the experience of which John further wrote: "If we walk in the light as He Himself is in the light, we have *fellowship* with one another, and the blood of Jesus Christ His Son cleanses us from all sin" (I John 1:7). Thus this sacred Christian fellowship was characterized by mutual relations between all the members of this great new body of believers. It was a fellowship where all carnal differences, prejudices, and feelings had been cleansed away by the sanctifying presence of the Holy Spirit in their lives. It was a fellowship in which each and all realized themselves the common recipients of God's unmerited favor in Christ; in which all were warmed and anointed by the precious presence of the Holy Spirit; in which the spiritual eyes of all were turned in adoration and worship upon the risen, ascended Savior at the right hand of the Father in heaven; in which all entertained a common hope of eternal life through Christ their Lord.

D. Their Communion in the Christian Sacrament

Writing of their communion of holy sacrament, Luke says: "And day by day continuing with one mind in the temple, and breaking bread from house to house, they were taking their meals together with gladness and sincerity of heart" (Acts 2:46). There is some uncertainty about the meaning of this passage. If it included what became known as the Eucharist, or The Lord's Supper, or otherwise the Holy Communion, it evidently included more than that—perhaps that which became known as the Love Feast (cf. I Cor. 11:20-29; Jude 12).

The early Christians, following the first Christian Pentecost, continued for a time to worship in the Jewish Temple at the stated periods and they seem to have been regarded as a sort of "new life movement" within the Jewish faith (cf. Acts 3:1-26). However, as soon as the universal implications of the Christian gospel became evident, a sharp cleavage between Judaism and Christianity developed. This developing cleavage may already be evident in the fact that the fellowship and worship of these believers took place in their homes rather than the Temple, as is indicated in Acts 2:46 (cf. Acts 12:12; 18:7; 20:20; Rom. 16:5; Philem. 2).

If the Holy Sacrament, or Lord's Supper, is here indicated, then it signified the faith and devotion of Christ's disciples, as well as their mutual fellowship. The sacrament was a form of witness that looked three ways, namely, to the finished work of Christ on the cross, His

present living presence with His disciples, and to His promised second coming (see I Cor. 11:24-26). It was a form of witness to the faith of the believers in Christ. The Communion appears to have been served at every worship service of the disciples at the outset, or perhaps every day (Acts 2:46). Later, however, this order was changed to once a week, on the "first day," or Sunday (Acts 20:7). This Communion evidently took place following the *Agape*, or love feast. However, because of certain abuses that entered the *Agape* at Corinth especially, Paul instructed that the *Agape,* and possibly the Communion, be conducted in their homes rather than at the place of common worship (see I Cor. 11:17-34; cf. Jude 5-16).

However, other interpreters view the meaning in a somewhat different light. Clarke, for instance, thinks that the reference may be to companies of these Christians contiguous to each other who frequently had their meals together at their respective homes or lodgings upon return from public worship. The expression "from house to house" (Greek, *Kát Oikon*) seems best translated, "in the various private homes." While the *KJV* translates it "from house to house," as does the *NASB*, Moffett says, "in their own homes," as also the *RSV*. Thus, though they had all things in common, each family maintained its private home while probably entertaining numbers of those ostracized by their Jewish families because they had embraced the Christian faith. The expression "breaking bread" must be understood as taking their meals together. Specifically, however, it signifies the Jewish custom of breaking by hand their thin, hard, dry bread, rather than our familiar custom of cutting or slicing our soft loaves of bread. Thus the expression "breaking bread" would be the equivalent of our *taking or eating our meals.*

However, more important than the foregoing is the spirit in which they carried out these practices. Contrary to common Jewish practices, they were free from the severity of religious feasts that often bordered on, if they did not reflect, a form of asceticism. On the other hand, they were not given to special feasts, such as later developed with the gluttonous among the affluent members of the church at Corinth, to the embarrassment of the poor and slave members. Moderation and simplicity seem to have been the order of their conduct in this situation, as always becomes genuine, vital Christian deportment. In fact the word sometimes translated "sincerity" (Greek, *afelatati*) is best translated "simplicity." Contentment, gladness, spiritual joy, singlemindedness, and mutual respect and confidence graced their Spirit-liberated and filled new lives and fellowship in Christ.

E. Their Communion in Christian Prayer

"And they were continually devoting themselves to prayer [lit., "prayers"]" (Acts 2:42). In *anticipation* of the fulfillment of Christ's promise of the power of the Spirit which they were to receive for their effective witness to the world (Acts 1:8), the 120 disciples prayed unitedly, persistently, and believingly for ten days until the mighty event of the outpouring of the Spirit occurred, resulting in the conversion of about 3000 persons. Luke records: "these all with one mind were continually devoting themselves to prayer" (Acts 1:14). In their church business session which called for the choice of a successor to Judas to complete the apostolate, Luke says, "They prayed, and said, 'Thou, Lord, who knowest the hearts of all men, show which one of these two Thou hast chosen to occupy this ministry and apostleship from which Judas turned aside to go to his own place" (Acts 1:24-25). It is not the purpose here to consider whether they ascertained aright the will of God in their choice of Judas' replacement. The fact remains that they earnestly prayed for God's will in the matter.

Until the sharp cleavage occurred between the Jews converted to Christ and the unbelieving Jews, the disciples apparently continued to follow the customary Jewish observance of regular, daily, recognized prayer periods in the Temple. It was on such an occasion that the lame beggar at the Gate Beautiful was healed under the faithful ministry of two disciples as, in the words of Luke, "Peter and John were going up to the temple at the ninth *hour* [i.e., 3 P.M.], the hour of prayer" (Acts 3:1).

When arrested by the Jewish Sanhedrin, tried, forbidden to speak further to the people in the name of Jesus, threatened, and released, Peter and John returned to the company of believers, where they made their report of the Sanhedrin's prohibitions laid upon them.

Then Luke records that *"when they had prayed,* the place where they had gathered together was shaken, and they were all filled with the Holy Spirit, and *began* ["began anew"] to speak the word of God with boldness. . . . And with great power the apostles were giving witness to the resurrection of the Lord Jesus, and abundant grace was upon them all" (Acts 4:31, 33).

When an economic problem concerning equality of provisions for the Christian Hellenists' widows with the Christian Jews threatened the unity of the church, the twelve apostles declared their devotion *"to prayer,* and to the ministry of the word" (Acts 6:4), and then judiciously selected seven qualified laymen who were "full of the Spirit and wisdom" (Acts 6:3) to look after these temporal affairs, "and *after praying,* they laid their hands on them" in a consecration service, and consequently "the word of God kept on spreading" (Acts 6:6, 7).

In the hour of the young church's severest trial, the illegal martyrdom of her greatest Christian, Stephen, at the hands of the Jewish Sanhedrin, these Spirit-filled disciples prayed (Acts 7:55). Luke tells of this severe crisis that fell upon the church: "And they went on stoning Stephen as he called upon *the* Lord and said 'Lord Jesus, receive my spirit!' And falling on his knees, he cried out with a loud voice 'Lord, do not hold this sin against them.' And having said this, he fell asleep" (Luke 7:59-60). However, Stephen's death by martyrdom was not without its victorious sequel, for says Luke, "On that day a great persecution arose against the church in Jerusalem; and they were all scattered throughout the regions of Judea and Samaria, except the apostles. . . . [And] *those who had been scattered went about preaching the word"* (Acts 8:1, 4). Consequently we soon learn of churches having sprung up in various parts of Palestine, in Damascus, Antioch, Rome, and numerous other regions.

But doubtless the greatest single victory resulting from Stephen's gracious prayer, which so closely resembles that of his Lord's on the cross, and his victorious spirit in death, was the eventual conversion of the church's most determined and vicious enemy, Saul. It has been observed, not without significance, that if Stephen had not prayed Saul would not have been converted. Luke records that history-changing event in three chapters of Acts, namely 9, 22, and 26. As always, Luke is faithful in recording the function of the Spirit in this life-transforming experience of Saul when Ananias informed him that he should receive his sight and be filled with the Holy Spirit (Acts 9:17-18).

While it was the ineradicable barb of conviction resulting from Stephen's prayer in his hour of martrydom that had been driven deep into Saul's spiritual consciousness that eventually brought that mad persecutor to prostrate submission before the conquering Christ, it was the prayers of Saul himself (Acts 9:11), and those of the disciple Ananias at Damascus, that brought him eventually to his spiritual resurrection and new life in Christ, and made of him the greatest apostle of the Christian faith that the world has ever known.

In the midst of the great Samaritan awakening under Philip's Spirit-filled ministry, the Jerusalem church sent Peter and John there, who upon arrival "prayed for them, that they might receive the Holy Spirit" (Acts 8:15); and "then they began laying their hands on them, and they were receiving the Holy Spirit" (Acts 8:17).

At Joppa Peter prayed over the dead body of the widow Dorcas and commanded her to arise, with the result that she was restored and presented alive and well to her friends and loved ones, and many were converted to the Christian faith (Acts 9:36-42).

It was following Peter's noon-day, house-top prayer at Joppa, and the simultaneous prayer of Cornelius at Caesarea, that Peter experienced the unusual vision from God that shattered his Jewish prejudices against the gentiles and led him to that army officer and his household-barracks where the first marvelous outpouring of God's Spirit upon the gentiles was experienced (Acts 10:9-48).

It was the Holy Spirit who prepared Peter to receive the messengers sent to him from the gentile Cornelius (Acts 10:20), and it was the same Spirit who fell upon those gentiles as Peter preached to them salvation through the death and resurrection of Jesus Christ, a fact which caused amazement in the minds of those Jews who had accompanied Peter (Acts 10:44-45). That the spiritual significance of the outpouring of the Holy Spirit on these gentiles was identical with that of the effusion at Pentecost as recorded in Acts 2, is attested by Peter's declaration, on the occasion of his defense of the gospel for the gentiles at the Jerusalem Council. In that rehearsal he says: "And God who knows the heart, bore witness to them, *giving them the Holy Spirit, just as He also did to us;* and He made no distinction between us and them, *cleansing their hearts by faith*" (Acts 15:8-9). Thus, as the effusion of the Spirit upon the disciples at Pentecost wrought purity of heart within them, so the hearts of these gentile believers at Caesarea were cleansed by His gracious personal manifestation at the close of Peter's message to them. One is reminded of Christ's words to His disciples: "You are already clean because of the word which I have spoken to you" (John 15:3). *"While Peter was still speaking these words,* the Holy Spirit fell upon all those who were listening to the message" (Acts 10:44), "cleansing their hearts by faith" (Acts 15:9b). A purported baptism with the Spirit that does not purify the Christian's heart of the sinful, corrupt nature within is a spurious experience indeed, and such does not come from God, regardless of the external manifestations or significations that may accompany such an experience. The manifestation of the personality of the Holy God to the inner nature of man's unholy heart inevitably consumes the sinful nature of that heart and recreates it in His likeness (cf. Ps. 51:10). If it is asked whether these gentiles were sanctified by God's spirit on the occasion of this effusion, it may be replied that the time factor intervening conversion and cleansing is never an important matter with God. That they believed unto salvation through Peter's spoken message (the Word of God) before their inward natures were cleansed by the Spirit is obvious. With God there need be no time factor between faith unto salvation and faith for the purification of the believer's heart by the Spirit. The important facts are that *they did believe unto salvation* and that *their hearts were purified by the Holy Spirit* in response to their faith. The accompanying manifestation of "tongues" (languages), as recorded here, is dealt with in another connection.

Whatever God's purpose may have been in allowing Herod to execute James, it was the fervent prayers of the church assembled in the home of Mark's mother, Mary, that saved Peter from a like intended fate (Acts 12:5, 12), with another resultant upsurge of spiritual life and evangelical fruitage (Acts 12:24).

The gentile missionary career of the apostle Paul, extending as it did over three great journeys, if not a fourth, and into most parts of the Mediterranean world, had its inception in a church prayer meeting at Antioch in which the Holy Spirit both *selected* the missionaries and *sent* them on their mission (Acts 13:1-3). With prayer and fasting Paul also dedicated the selected elders to oversee the churches which he had established on that first missionary journey (Acts 14:23).

At Philippi Paul met with a company of "God-fearers" at their *prayer resort* by a riverside (Acts 16:13), subsequently delivered a demon-possessed girl from her evil enslavement, and was consequently beaten and imprisoned together with Silas, through mistaken identity. However, at midnight a prayer and praise service by Paul and Silas eventuated in an earthquake that set the prisoners free, and consequently brought about the conversion of the jailer and his household, and eventually established one of Paul's most prized churches at the city of Philippi (Acts 16:16-40).

At Ephesus the twelve disciples received the baptism of the Holy Spirit through the instrumentality of Paul's prayer ministry (Acts 19:6). The question of their state of grace, what this baptism with the Spirit signified in their Christian experience, and the problem of their speaking with tongues (languages) and prophesying is dealt with in another connection. Luke's touching account of Paul's last meeting with these Ephesian elders at Miletus is climaxed with the words, "And when he had said these things he knelt down and prayed with them all" (Acts 20:28).

At Tyre, likewise, Luke records the touching incident of Paul's parting with the disciples as "they all, with wives and children, escorted us until we were out of the city. And after *kneeling down on the beach and praying,* we said farewell to one another" (Acts 21:5), and this in the face of the fact that they had warned him, by the promptings of the Spirit, not to go to Jerusalem (Acts 21:4).

Following the shipwreck at Malta, Paul witnessed the healing of the father of Publius, a leading official of the island, in answer to his prayers and laying on of his hands (Acts 28:8).

In Nero's prison at Rome, while awaiting trial and eventual execution, Paul records some of his greatest prayers. Among these prayers, and perhaps the greatest of them, is that recorded in one of his prison Epistles, (Eph. 3:14-21). In this same Epistle he records his most eloquent exhortation concerning prayer: "With all *prayer* and *petition pray at all times in the Spirit,* and with this in view, be on the alert with all perseverance and *petition* for all saints" (6:18). Likewise, the apostle James presents a magnificent discourse on the effectiveness of prayer in his Epistle (5:13-20).

F. Their Communion in Joyful Thanksgiving

The Spirit-filled Christians were "praising God and having favor with all the people." There is always a correlation between Christian, Spirit-filled joyfulness and Christian influence upon the unconverted.

A Spirit-filled people are always a joyful people. In ancient times Nehemiah said to Israel, "The joy of the Lord is your strength" (8:10); and the psalmist exultantly exclaimed: "In thy presence is fulness of joy" (16:11). Likewise, Isaiah prophesied: "You will *joyously* draw water from the springs of salvation" (12:3). Jesus declared that the purpose of the believers' abiding relationship with Him was that His joy might be in them, and *that their joy might be made full* (John 15:11). Paul defined the kingdom of God itself as consisting of "righteousness and peace and *joy* in the Holy Spirit," and says he, "he who in this way serves Christ is acceptable to God and approved by men" (Rom. 14:17-18). Again, the apostle declares that joy is prominent among the *fruits of the Spirit* (Gal. 5:22).

A chief characteristic of the early Methodists was their hymnody. Wherever Methodists were found they were joyfully singing praises to God. And the hymnology of Charles Wesley has hardly, if indeed ever, been excelled in the history of Christianity. Likewise, the early Christians were a people who sang joyfully under almost every circumstance of life. Thus the church inaugurated at Pentecost began its existence by "praising God." On the contrary, Paul makes clear that the terrible degeneracy of mankind, as described in Romans 1:18-32, had its inception in the fact that men "did not honor Him [God] as God, *or give thanks*," with the consequence that "they became futile in their speculations, and their foolish heart was darkened" (Rom. 1:21). When man becomes unthankful to God the light of heaven goes out in his life and he is left to grope helplessly in darkness. When praise to God characterizes believing men, the light of God's Son will not fail to shine upon them.

When Peter and John were arraigned before the Sanhedrin, following the healing of the lame beggar at the Gate Beautiful (Acts 3), and were forbidden with severe threats to speak any more in the name of Christ, they returned to the assembled church, where *prayers of praise* were offered to God, after which they resumed their ministry effectively without fear (Acts 4:23-31). The powerful witness of these Spirit-filled, praiseful apostles released God's special favor and power upon them and their ministry (Acts 4:33). When arrested and arraigned before the Sanhedrin a second time for their preaching Christ's resurrection, the apostles were not only warned but severely flogged and disgraced, but when released, Luke relates, "they went on their way from the presence of the Council, *rejoicing* that they had been considered worthy to suffer shame for His name" (Acts 5:41).

Converted under the tactful ministry of Philip near Gaza, as he was directed of the Spirit, the God-fearing treasurer of Candace, Queen of Ethiopia, "went on his way *rejoicing*," after having been baptized by the evangelist, while "the Spirit of the Lord snatched Philip away" for other service (Acts 8:39). When Peter made his report to the church at Jerusalem concerning the effusion of the Spirit upon the gentiles at Caesarea, they, when convinced that it was a genuine, divine work *"glorified God,* saying, 'Well then, God has granted to the Gentiles also the repentance that leads to life' " (Acts 11:18). Just cause there was indeed to praise God for opening the door of salvation to the gentiles. Barnabas, when he visited the new community of believers at Antioch in Syria and "witnessed the grace of God" upon them, was profoundly moved with sincere gratitude and *"rejoiced"* (Acts 11:23).

When the gentiles at Antioch of Pisidia learned that they were included in Christ's redemptive scheme they too "began *rejoicing and glorifying* the word of the Lord" (Acts 13:48). And though persecuted and driven out of Antioch through the instigation of the envious Jews, Paul and Barnabas "were continually *filled with joy and with the Holy Spirit"* (Acts 13:52).

Following the decision of the first general council of the church to admit the gentiles to membership with a bare minimum of legal requirements (Acts 15:20, 29), this decision was delivered to the church at Antioch, and "they *rejoiced* because of its encouragement" (Acts 15:31).

At Philippi when the apostles were shamefully beaten and imprisoned, through misidentification, Luke records that at "about midnight Paul and Silas were *praying and singing hymns of praise* to God" (Acts 16:25), with the result that an earthquake was precipitated to open the prison doors and release the apostles and the other listening prisoners. The jailer, shocked to the point of intended suicide at his feared escape of the prisoners, was forthwith brought into the Christian faith by Paul. Then, together with all his household, he *"rejoiced greatly,* having believed in God with his whole household" (Acts 16:34).

Paul was praiseful to God to the end of his career. As he touched land enroute to Rome for his trial before Nero, he was met by certain Christian believers who had come as far as Appii Forum, about forty-four miles from Rome, to greet and escort him to the capital. Upon seeing these welcome friends Paul *"thanked God* and took courage" (Acts 28:15). Likewise the New Testament Epistles are replete with notes of praise to God. It has been said that Paul's letter to the Philippians might well be summed up in the words: "I *rejoice.* Do you *rejoice*?" To the Thessalonian Christians Paul wrote: "You . . . received the word in much tribulation with *joy of* [lit., "inspired by"] *the Holy Spirit"* (I Thess. 1:6b).

In the light of the praiseful disposition of these early Spirit-filled Christians, it is little wonder that Luke could record that they had "favor with all the people." It has been said that if Christians praised God more the world of unbelievers would doubt Him less. Paul exhorted the Ephesian Christians to *"be filled with the Spirit,* speaking to one another *in psalms* and *hymns* and *spiritual songs, singing* and *making melody* with your hearts to the Lord; always *giving thanks* for all things in the name of our Lord Jesus Christ to God, even the Father" (5:18b-20).

G. Their Communion in Generosity

Luke records of these post-Pentecostal, Spirit-filled Christians,

> All those who had believed were together, and had all things in common; and they began selling their property and possessions, and were sharing them with all, as anyone might have need (Acts 2:44-45).

Paul wrote to the Corinthians saying, "Now the Lord is the Spirit; and where the Spirit of the Lord is, there is liberty" (II Cor. 3:17). Liberty and liberality are but different forms of the same word. Webster defines generosity as "liberality in giving." Thus we may say that the spirit of liberality of these believers was the result of their liberation by the Spirit from all selfish inhibitions, for a generous expression of their Christian love toward their fellows in need. While these words of the apostle are framed in the context of personal salvation that liberates from the bondage of spiritual blindness, they are nonetheless applicable to the total personality, including temporal possessions. This includes the spirit of unselfish compassion and generosity toward all men in need. It has been well said that a stingy Christian does not exist. Jesus placed heavy emphasis upon the spirit of generosity, and in at least one instance He made it the test for entry into the kingdom (Matt. 25:31-46).

There are two types of giving. One is characterized by reckless, lavish, and often wasteful distribution of valuable resources. This kind of liberality is unwise and often harmful to the recipients, as well as impoverishing the donor. It may rob people of their self-respect and initiative. It sometimes makes them dependent when they should be helped to become self-sufficient. Furthermore, it is a waste of resources that should be used for better purposes. Individuals, institutions, and even governments are sometimes guilty of such prodigious distribution of resources, which is totally unrelated to Christian generosity.

On the other hand Christian liberality is the result of the Spirit's influence upon the totality of the personality, stirring the emotions to empathetic identification with genuine human needs, liberating the will to meet those needs, and illuminating the mind to intelligently distribute resources in accordance with existing needs. Such was the character of the generosity that motivated these Spirit-filled believers. Twice Luke emphasizes that their giving was in relation to the existing needs. He says: "they were sharing . . . with all, *as anyone might have need*" (Acts 2:45b); "they . . . distributed to each, *as any had need*" (Acts 4:35b). This was also the principle that guided the early church in the distribution of goods to the Hellenist widows who had complained of inequalities, as Luke gives the record in Acts 6:1-6. Luke further points up three beneficent results of this Spirit-motivated liberality. First, he says, "with great power the apostles were giving witness to the resurrection of the Lord Jesus"; second, "abundant grace was upon them all"; and third, "there was not a needy person among them" (Acts 4:33, 34). Likewise, in relation to the wise distribution of supplies to the needy Hellenist widows, Luke informs us that "the word of God kept on spreading; and the number of the disciples continued to increase greatly in Jerusalem, and a great many of the priests were becoming obedient to the faith" (Acts 6:7).

Among evangelicals there has often been too great a tendency to interpret the "liberty of the Spirit" in terms of emotional expression in worship, and sometimes in terms of unrestrained emotional demonstrations, to the neglect of the more important significance of liberality in giving and in service to needy humanity. It is never the God-intended function of the Christian or the church to become a saving agency for God, rather the Christian and the church should represent God, in relation to temporal resources and material possessions, as His exchequer. It was the often repeated dictum of John Wesley, the father of Methodism, that Christians should make all they can, and save all they can, in order that they might give all they can. This was also Wesley's personal guiding principle in relation to temporal goods. It was this spirit that motivated these early Spirit-filled Christians, and it is this spirit that should motivate all Christians in all times.

Chapter 10

The Holy Spirit
in the
Expansion of the Church

I. THE CHURCH'S NUMERICAL ADVANCE
UNDER THE INFLUENCE OF THE SPIRIT

Whatever the traditional merits of small beginnings may be, such cannot be ascribed to the Christian church inaugurated at the first Christian Pentecost. The historian Luke is specific in noting that as a result of the descent of the Holy Spirit and the subsequent preaching of Peter and other disciples, about 3000 converts *"were added that day"* to the existing company of the disciples of Christ (Acts 2:41).

The secret of the powerful influence of these Christian disciples upon their non-Christian fellows obviously was due to the mysterious presence of the Holy Spirit in their lives. Luke suggests this in his record.

> And everyone kept feeling a sense of awe; and many wonders and signs were taking place through the apostles. . . . And the Lord was adding to their number day by day those who were being saved (Acts 2:43,47b).

However, should this arithmetical figure strike anyone as seeming to be hyperbolic he must prepare himself for even greater mathematical calculations of the rapid increase of the church at Jerusalem and beyond. Luke notes shortly after Pentecost that "many of those who heard the message ["word," mar.] believed; and the number of the men came to be about five thousand" (Acts 4:4). That these 5000 men constituted the aggregate of male believers, including the initial pre-Pentecostal disciples, plus the 3000 converts on the Day of Pentecost and onward, is probable. The Greek word (*agenēthē*) seems to indicate that the total number of believers at this point reached about *five thousand*. However, even allowing this interpretation, Luke's specific designation of "five thousand *men*" may well suggest only the male complement of believers, without accounting for women and children converts to the faith (cf. Matt. 14:21). If this should be true then we are completely at a loss to estimate the total number of believers, beyond the approximate 5000 *men* mentioned by Luke, at this time. The continued rapid increase of the faith following the effusion of the Holy Spirit at Pentecost is indicated by such notations in Acts as, "Now at this time while the disciples were *increasing* in *number*" (Acts 6:1a); "And *the word of God kept on spreading;* and *the number of the disciples continued to increase greatly* in Jerusalem, and *a great many of the priests were becoming obedient to the faith*" (Acts 6:7); "So the church throughout all Judea and Galilee and Samaria . . . *continued to increase*" (Acts 9:31); "but the word of the Lord *continued to grow and to be multiplied*" (Acts 12:24). A national-scale acceptance of the Christian faith by the Samaritans under Philip's preaching seems intended by Luke's words: "Now when the apostles in Jerusalem heard that *Samaria had received the word of God,* they sent them Peter and John" (Acts 8:14; cf. Luke 8:13; Acts 11:1; 17:11; I Thess. 1:6; 2:13; James 1:21).

II. THE CHURCH'S VICTORIOUS ADVANCE OVER OBSTACLES BY THE POWER OF THE SPIRIT

Obstacles served only as challenges to greater progress for these Spirit-filled followers of Christ. The cynical mockings of the unbelieving Jews on the Day of Pentecost provoked Peter to a clarification and defense of God's "mighty acts" in relation to the Scriptures (Acts 2:13-40). The material poverty of Peter and John challenged them to draw upon the resources of the Spirit to meet the needs of the indigent beggar framed so piteously in the expensive and ornate Gate Beautiful leading to the magnificent Temple of worship (Acts

3:1-12). Report has it that ages later in the thirteenth century, when the church had grown large and wealthy, the Pope remarked to Thomas Aquinas, as they viewed the church's hoarded wealth in the coffers of St. Peter's in Rome: "Thomas, no longer can the church say, as Peter and John said to the beggar at the Beautiful Gate, 'Silver and gold have I none.' " Upon this the Angelic Doctor replied, "Nor can the church any longer say to the crippled beggar, 'In the name of Jesus Christ the Nazarene, arise and walk!' "

These Spirit-filled disciples boldly defied the demands of the opposing Jewish Sanhedrin, and its infliction of painful persecution, to continue saturating Jerusalem with the message of Christ's resurrection from the dead. Arrested by the Sanhedrin for having preached in the Temple the resurrection of Jesus Christ, imprisoned overnight, and then arraigned before the Jews' court the next day, Peter and John were demanded to answer "by what power, or in what name [they had] done this? Then Peter, *filled with the Holy Spirit,*" courageously answered their charges and defended the gospel of Jesus Christ as man's only hope of salvation. Upon being ordered by the court not to speak further in the name of Christ, Peter and John left it to the judgment of the court as to whether it was right to obey man or God. Released by the Sanhedrin, the apostles returned to their Christian companions and reported the decision of the court. Immediately they engaged in prayer, reiterated the forecast of David, who spoke under the inspiration of the Holy Spirit concerning the opposition that would arise against the gospel, and called God to witness the court's threats. And then they prayed that they might continue to "speak Thy word with all confidence." In response to their courageous and confident prayer, "the place where they were gathered together was shaken, and *they were all filled with the Holy Spirit,* and began to speak the word of God with boldness. . . . And with great power the apostles were giving witness to the resurrection of the Lord Jesus, and abundant grace was upon them all" (Acts 4:1-33).

Again as the cause of Christ was prospering, many were being healed, demons were being cast out, and "multitudes of men and women were constantly added to their number" (Acts 5:14). The high priest and the Sadducees, "filled with jealousy," again arrested and imprisoned the apostles, who were released by an angel of the Lord and were found preaching again in the Temple early the next morning. Arrested and arraigned again before the Sanhedrin, they were forbidden to preach further in the name of Jesus. Conversely,

Peter delivered a courageous charge against the Jewish elders for having rejected and crucified Christ, whom God raised from the dead for the remission of their sins. Peter then declared, "And we are witnesses of these things; and so is the Holy Spirit, whom God has given to those who obey Him" (Acts 5:32). Though warned by Gamaliel, a Pharisee member of the Sanhedrin, to take care as to how the court treated these men lest they be found to be fighting against God, the Council nevertheless "flogged them and ordered them to speak no more in the name of Jesus, and then released them" (Acts 5:40). However, the apostles returned directly to their ministry in the name of Jesus "rejoicing that they had been considered worthy to suffer shame for His name" (Acts 5:41-42).

Persecution has seldom accomplished its purpose to prevent a Spirit-filled ministry from advancing the cause of Christ. Some years ago the *Nature Study Magazine* published an account of the attempts of certain northern European oyster gatherers to save their oyster beds from the starfish who were destroying them. The starfish were seined out of the oyster beds and piled in heaps on the shore. However, the stench of decaying starfish became unbearable to the townspeople, and consequently it was decided to run the starfish through a chopping machine and return them to the ocean to be washed away with the tide. The result was most disappointing, as each piece of the dismembered starfishes developed into a new living starfish. Thus they multiplied their problems instead of eliminating them! Likewise, each opposition and persecution wielded against these Spirit-filled early Christians only served to challenge them to more intensive efforts to make Christ known, with the result that the church was greatly increased, instead of being extinguished as their enemies intended.

Even the invasion of the church's ranks by the sinister monster of hypocrisy in the persons of Ananias and his conniving wife Sapphira was turned, under the judgment of God, to the advancement of the church (Acts 5:1-16).

Under the Spirit's wisdom and direction, threatening internal church problems were solved in such a manner as to accelerate the church's influence and advancement (Acts 6:1-7). Even the martyr's crown placed upon Stephen's head by the enemies of Christ served only to spread the faith to new regions and eventually bring about the conversion of Saul, the most vicious persecutor the church had yet confronted, and transformed him into history's greatest witness to the faith (Acts 7:54—8:4; 22:20). Likewise, the martyrdom of

James at the hands of cruel King Herod, and the subsequent deliverance of Peter from a like intended fate, is followed by Luke's victorious statement: "But the word of the Lord continued to grow and to be multiplied" (Acts 12:24).

The apostle Paul, *"filled with the Holy Spirit,"* rebuked the opposing apostate Jewish priest, Elymas the sorcerer at Paphos, which action resulted in the conversion of Sergius Paulus, the proconsul of Cyprus, and thus the gospel was planted on that island (Acts 13:6-12).

III. THE CHURCH'S COURAGEOUS ADVANCE INTO THE GENTILE WORLD, UNDER THE INFLUENCE OF THE SPIRIT

At Caesarea Peter witnessed an unusually effective effusion of the Holy Spirit upon the gentiles of Cornelius' household. This also most likely extended to the entire barracks of some 600 soldiers, if Cornelius actually was a captain of a cohort rather than a centurion in command of 100 soldiers, as is thought by some scholars (Acts 10:34-48).

At Antioch of Syria Barnabas found a flourishing church. This body of believers was evidently the result of the witness of disciples who went there when the Christians were scattered during the persecution that followed Stephen's martyrdom (Acts 11:19-24). Barnabas' ministry at Antioch became exceedingly fruitful, as Luke records: "for he was a good man, and *full of the Holy Spirit* and of faith. And *considerable numbers* [lit., "multitudes"] *were brought* [lit., "added"] to the Lord" (Acts 11:24). It was also noted that others had made their way to Phoenicia and Cyprus where the Jews were evangelized, apparently with success (Acts 11:19). Antioch became the first Christian church to launch a major missionary witness to the gentile world, and subsequently it became the great missionary base of the first century. Adolph Harnack noted that by the end of the second century the Antioch Christian community had a membership of approximately 200,000. From Antioch the city state of Edessa, to the east of Antioch, was evangelized and almost the entire city state became Christian. Luke informs us that as Paul and Barnabas evangelized at Antioch of Pisidia on the second "sabbath *nearly the whole city assembled* to hear the word of God" (Acts 13:44). Notwithstanding the fact that the apostles were eventually driven from Antioch by the unbelieving Jews, Luke says that "when the Gentiles heard this they began rejoicing and glorifying the word of the Lord . . . *and the word of the Lord was being spread through the whole region*" (Acts 13:48, 49).

At Derbe, following the stoning of Paul at Lystra by the pagans, at the instigation of the jealous Jews from Antioch and Iconium, it is recorded that the apostles *"made many disciples"* (Acts 14:21). However, the opposition met at Lystra, where Paul was stoned and left for dead, did not preclude the success of the gospel message. It was here at this time that the young man Timothy, who became one of Paul's most intimate and trusted co-workers to the end of his life, was converted to the Christian faith. Apparently it was to the home of Timothy that the apostles resorted following the persecution (Acts 14:20). Outward bound on his second missionary journey, Paul found this promising young convert at Lystra growing in the faith "and well spoken of by the brethren who were in Lystra and Iconium," thus indicating that there evidently had been a considerable number of converts in these cities during the first visit by Paul and Barnabas, notwithstanding Jewish opposition and pagan persecution (Acts 16:1-3).

Upon their return from the first missionary journey, Paul and Barnabas recounted to the church at Antioch the phenomenal success of their mission to the Gentile world, as suggested by Luke: "They began to *report all things that God had done with them* and how He had opened a door of faith to the Gentiles" (Acts 14:27). Again when called to Jerusalem for the first general Christian council that settled the conditions on which the gentiles were to be admitted to church membership, these missionary apostles reported to the entire council "all that God had done with them" (Acts 15:4b). Peter indicated something of the magnitude of the success of the first mission to the gentile world when he said to the council, "And God, who knows the heart, bore them witness, *giving them the Holy Spirit,* just as He also did to us [the Jews]; and He made no distinction between us and them *cleansing their hearts by faith*" (Acts 15:8-9).

Upon his arrival at Philippi Paul found a door of access for the gospel in the person of one of the many gentile God-fearers scattered throughout the Roman empire. This person was "Lydia, from the city of Thyatira, a seller of purple fabrics, a worshiper of God [who] was listening; and the Lord opened her heart to respond to the things spoken by Paul. And . . . she and her household . . . [were] baptized" into the Christian faith (Acts 16:14-15a). That Lydia became an influential factor in the church that Paul established at Philippi seems evident from Luke's record (see Acts 16:15, 40).

Even the shameful flogging and imprisonment of Paul and Silas at Philippi, through misrepresentation and misidentification, turned out to the furtherance of the gospel as the Philippian jailer and his entire household believed on Christ and were baptized into the faith (Acts 16:30-34). Here at Philippi, in spite of persecution and suffering, Paul's most prized church was established (see Paul's letter to the Philippians).

The success of the gospel at Thessalonica is indicated by Luke, who tells us that when Paul preached the gospel in the synagogue there "some of them [the Jews] were persuaded and joined Paul and Silas, along with a great multitude of the God-fearing Greeks and a number of the leading women" (Acts 17:4). The further success of the gospel at Thessalonica is clearly indicated in Paul's two letters directed to this church at a later time. He commends them for the exercise of the three greatest Christian virtues—their *"work at faith* and *labor of love* and *steadfast hope* in the Lord Jesus Christ" (I Thess. 1:3; cf. I Cor. 13:13). Further, Paul reminds them that they had "turned to God from idols to serve a living and true God" (I Thess. 1:9b). The genuineness of their faith and extensiveness of their service is indicated by Paul as he commends them for their exemplary Christian conduct and evangelizing activities. Paul says: "you became an example to all the believers in Macedonia and Achaia. For the word of the Lord has sounded forth from you, not only in Macedonia and Achaia, but also in every place your faith to God has gone forth, so that we have no need to say anything" (I Thess. 1:7-8).

At Berea Paul found a more noble-minded class of Jews in the synagogue than those who had opposed him at Thessalonica, who "received the word with great eagerness, examining the Scriptures daily, to see whether these things were so" (Acts 17:11).

Even at Athens, the renowned center of Greek philosophy and learning, where Paul made his famous defense before the Areopagus on Mars Hill, the gospel had its powerful effects. Luke closes this account by noting that "some men joined him [Paul] and believed, among whom also was Dionysius the Areopagite and a woman named Damaris and others with them" (Acts 17:34). The conversion of a member of the august Areopagus, the Supreme Court of Athens, every member of which was required to have served as Archon, or mayor of Athens, was of no small consequence, not to mention others who believed.

At Corinth Paul first met resistance to the gospel as he preached in the Jewish synagogue. However, when he transferred his campaign to

2 of 360...

the house of Titus Justus, a God-fearer who lived near the synagogue, "Crispus, the leader of the synagogue, believed in the Lord with all his household, and many of the Corinthians when they heard were believing and being baptized" (Acts 18:8). That the gospel won a large number of adherents during Paul's eighteen months' ministry there is evident from correspondence with the church at Corinth in his first and second letters to the Corinthians, notwithstanding the fact that Corinth became the apostle's most serious problem church.

Certainly the gospel harvest at Ephesus during Paul's ministry there was surpassed by no other part of the gentile world, unless possibly at Antioch. Here in western Asia Minor the apostle found the twelve imperfectly instructed disciples of Christ who received Christian baptism and *the baptism with the Holy Spirit* under Paul's ministry (Acts 19:1-7). These initial objects of Paul's ministry at Ephesus may have become the twelve elders of the Ephesian church who assisted him in the evangelization of the whole of western Asia Minor during his ministry at Ephesus (see 21:17-38). The polyglot nature of the people of western Asia Minor afforded ample justification for the miraculous gift of tongues (Greek, *glossais* = "languages") that accompanied their baptism with the Holy Spirit (Acts 19:6). They at once put to practical use this miraculous endowment by prophesying, or preaching the gospel of Christ.

Clarke gives the weight of his testimony to this position thus:

> They [the Ephesian twelve] received the miraculous gift of different languages; and in those languages they *taught* to the people the great doctrines of the Christian religion; for this appears to be the meaning of the word *Proefateuon, prophesied.*[1]

Matthew Henry significantly remarks:

> This was indeed to introduce the gospel at Ephesus, and to awaken in the minds of men an expectation of some great things from it; and some think that it was further designed to qualify these twelve men for the work of the ministry, and that these twelve men were the elders of Ephesus, to whom Paul committed the care and government of the church. They had the spirit of prophecy, that they might understand the mysteries of the kingdom of God themselves, and the gift of tongues, that they might preach them to every nation and language.[2]

In support of this interpretation, the world renowned scholar F. F. Bruce says:

1. *Clarke's Commentary: The New Testament of Our Lord and Saviour Jesus Christ* (New York: Methodist Book Concern, n.d.) I. 842.

2. *Commentary on the Whole Bible* (New York: Fleming H. Revell Co., n.d.), VI, comment on Acts 19:6,7.

> Ephesus was to be a new centre of the Gentile mission—the next
> in importance after the Syrian Antioch—and these twelve disciples
> were to be the nucleus of the Ephesian church. By this exceptional
> procedure, then, they were associated in the apostolic and mission-
> ary task of the Christian Church.[3]

Certainly, while there is found no basis in this incident for the
interpretation of an "unknown tongue," there is strong evidence for
a valid conclusion that what occurred was a miraculous divine gift of
bona fide languages designed for the enablement of these Spirit-filled
Christian disciples to preach Christ to the polyglot peoples of one of
the greatest centers of the ancient world.

After three months of fruitful ministry in the Jewish synagogue at
Ephesus, Paul was forced to withdraw with his disciples to the
lecture hall of a philosopher whose name was Tyrannus. Here for two
years he held forth, "so that all who lived in Asia [i.e., *the west coast
province of Asia Minor*] heard the word of the Lord, both Jews and
Greeks. And God was performing extraordinary miracles [or, "works
of power"; cf. Acts 8:13] by the hands of Paul" (Acts 19:10b-11).

An incident of interference occurred here which, though demoni-
cally designed to thwart the evangelistic efforts of Paul, turned out
to the acceleration of the gospel ministry (Acts 19:13-17). Thus
Luke could record that as a result of this thwarted incident,

> Fear fell upon them all and the name of the Lord Jesus was being
> magnified. Many also of those who had believed kept coming,
> confessing and disclosing their practices. And many of those who
> practiced magic brought their books together and *began* burning
> them in the sight of all; and they counted up the price of them and
> found it fifty thousand pieces of silver [Greek, *drachma* = about 20¢,
> for a total of approximately $10,000.00]. So *the word of the Lord
> was growing mightily and prevailing* (Acts 19:17b-20).

The admission of Demetrius, the silversmith, that Paul had turned
many from idolatry at Ephesus and all of the province of Asia, and
even endangered the craft of the silversmiths who made idols to the
world-renowned goddess, Artemis [*Roman, Diana*], at Ephesus is a
monumental witness to the effectiveness of the gospel at Ephesus
and throughout the province of Asia (Acts 19:23-27). The seven
churches of Asia, described in the early chapters of the Book of
Revelation, were the results of these evangelizing efforts at and from
Ephesus.

En route to Jerusalem on his last visit, Paul found and visited with

---

3. "The New International Commentary on the New Testament," *Commentary on the Book of Acts*, p. 387.

Christians at Tyre (Acts 21:3-6), Ptolemais (Acts 21:7), and Caesarea, where the evangelist Philip had settled with his family of four virgin daughters who were all prophetesses (Acts 21:8-9).

Thus throughout the Book of Acts Luke records the triumphs of the gospel as it was proclaimed under the power and inspiration of the Holy Spirit in whom these early Christians were baptized. This Spirit-filled church was an effective witnessing church to the end of Luke's Acts record where Paul, its greatest apostle, a prisoner of Christ in Nero's prison at Rome, could write to Timothy, his son in the gospel, "I suffer trouble, as an evil doer, even unto bonds; *but the word of God is not bound*" (II Tim. 2:9, *KJV*).

IV. THE CHURCH'S AMAZING CONQUESTS UNDER THE INFLUENCE OF THE SPIRIT

How seriously these early disciples took the obligation laid upon them by Christ in His Great Commission, following the effusion of the Spirit at Pentecost, may be seen by reference to the evidence of their accomplishments. One is amazed to read in Paul's letter to the Romans, written about A.D. 54/55, according to Jack Finegan,[4] but according to Bruce in A.D. 57[5]; but in the event within approximately twenty-five to thirty years after Pentecost, that already the gospel had penetrated the world of that generation. Paul says: "First, I thank my God through Jesus Christ for you all, because your faith is being proclaimed throughout the whole world" (Rom. 1:8).

Even though it should be granted that Paul's "whole world" was but the limits of the Roman Empire, yet the accomplishment of such a feat as the spreading of the gospel throughout that colossal political structure in approximately a quarter of a century following the effusion of the Spirit at Pentecost staggers the imagination. Such an accomplishment is eloquent testimony to the effectiveness of those early disciples of Christ who were animated by the Holy Spirit. However, again in his Colossian letter Paul writes: "the gospel, which has come to you, just as in all the world also it is constantly bearing fruit and increasing" (1:5, 6). But yet again Paul says to this same church, "the hope of the gospel that you have heard . . . was proclaimed in all creation under heaven" (Col. 1:23).

---

4. *Handbook of Biblical Chronology* (Princeton, N.J.: Princeton University Press, 1964), pp. 121, 122.
5. *The Letters of Paul: An Expanded Paraphrase* (Grand Rapids: Wm. B. Eerdmans Publishing Company, 1965), p. 179.

Nor does Paul stand alone in his testimony to the wide outreach of the gospel in the early church. Justin Martyr, writing shortly after the close of the first Christian century, states:

There is not a single race of human beings, barbarians, or whatever name you please to call them, nomads or vagrants or herdsmen living in tents, where prayers in the name of Jesus the crucified are not offered up.[6]

And again this same authority states:

Through all the members of the body is the soul spread; so are Christians throughout the cities of the world.[7]

While Tertullian lived and wrote at a slightly later date (A.D. 160-230), yet his memorable tribute to the far-reaching influences of the Christian religion reflects the success of the first-century Christian evangel.

We the Christians are but of yesterday. Yet we have filled all the places you frequent—cities, lodging houses, villages, townships, markets, the camp itself, the tribes, town councils, the palace, the senate, and the forum. All we have left you is your temples.[8]

Again we read:

Behold, every corner of the universe has experienced the gospel, and the whole ends and bounds of the world are occupied with the gospel.[9]

Writing of the rapid spread of the gospel in the days of the cruel Emperor Nero, a contemporary of the apostle Paul, Lactantius, observes:

This belief, that the original apostles had already preached the gospel to the whole world, is therefore extremely old. . . . The belief would never have arisen unless some definite knowledge of the apostles' labours and whereabouts (i.e., in the majority of cases) had been current. Both Clemens Romanus and Ignatius assume that the gospel had already been diffused over the world. . . . Finally, as the conception emerges in Hermas, it is exceptionally clear and definite; and this evidence of Hermas is all the more weighty, as he may invariably be assumed to voice the opinions which were widely spread and commonly received. On earth, as he puts it, there are twelve great peoples, and the gospel has already been preached to them all by the apostles.[10]

6. Adolph Harnack, *The Mission and Expansion of Christianity in the First Three Centuries*, II, 24 ff.
7. *Ibid.*
8. *Ibid.*
9. *Ibid.*
10. *Ibid.*

Many more testimonies of Biblical and extra-Biblical writers could be added as evidence that these disciples of Jesus Christ caught a vision under the powerful illumination of the Spirit that impelled them irresistibly to proclaim the glorious gospel of Jesus Christ to the ends of the earth. The experience of the baptism of the Spirit then, as always, set on fire the hearts of those first-century Christians with a passion that could not be satisfied as long as a creature remained who had not heard of Christ and His saving provisions.

Thus, the significance of the baptism with the Holy Spirit at the inauguration of the Christian church, as in the life of Christians in every subsequent age, lies in the manifestation and demonstration of the *infinite power* of God to the inward spiritual life of redeemed man. The Spirit produces a purification of his inner nature from the principle of sin by the heavenly-fire baptism. The nature and being of redeemed and sanctified man is fully possessed by the personal presence of the Holy Spirit, revealing and executing the Lordship of Christ in his life. The Spirit inwardly fortifies his soul against the outer attacks of evil. And finally, the purpose is realized in the quickening and inspiring of the individual and the church to *vital personal witness* to the indwelling presence of Christ, who is both Lord and Savior of the world. Such a personal baptism of the Spirit is the greatest need of every member of the church of Jesus Christ today, as in every day. Such an experience would release anew "the power of God unto salvation" upon a world that today threatens to destroy itself by its own self-created powers over which it has lost moral control. Will the church of Jesus Christ experience again the baptism of the Spirit that would transform its life, and that of the present age?

If those first-century Spirit-filled Christians could carry the gospel to the inhabited world of their day, limited as they were in means of transportation and communication, what could the church of today do with all of its modern means of transportation and communication, by way of evangelizing the modern world, if it were likewise possessed of the Holy Spirit of the living God, as were those early Christian believers? Whenever the church of Jesus Christ has been baptized, purified, possessed, empowered, energized, and directed by the Holy Spirit of the living God, the citadels of sin and Satan have not been able to stand before her invincible spiritual forces. And so will it ever be with the church of Jesus Christ.

As a fitting conclusion to the influence of the Spirit upon these first-century Christians in their extention of the gospel into the world of their day, we here quote the following significant account published under the caption, "Pentecostal Power."

High in the Pyrenees French scientists have built the world's largest solar furnace. This amazing furnace, with its complex of nearly 20,000 mirrors, can concentrate enough sunlight to create temperatures in excess of 6,000 degrees F.

"Anchored against a reinforced concrete office and laboratory building, the huge concave mirror [alone] consists of 8,570 individual reflectors. For the furnace to operate efficiently, these small (18 inches square) mirrors must be precisely adjusted so that their light will converge exactly at the parabola's focal point 59 feet in front of the giant reflector" (*Time*, May 18)

"It takes only a minute for the powerful light from the reflector to cut a fiery hole through a 3/8-inch-thick steel plate" (*Ibid.*).

In Acts 2 we have the familiar account of Pentecost. On that day the rays of the Sun of righteousness were focussed in the lives of 120 of His disciples. After a ten-day period of adjustment, they met in the upper room with one accord, rightly related to the risen Lord and to one another.

In this way they were able to catch the rays of the Spirit of the glorified Christ and to focus them with burning intensity upon the world around them.

This is the secret of Pentecost. The disciples did not originate the flame of the Spirit; rather they reflected it and relayed it. In and through their lives the beam of heavenly light was focussed both upon Judaism and paganism, and they thus had an influence and impact for God.

Let each member of the Church today become adjusted to the Spirit of God. Let each one seek to be a reflector of that flame. Then together believers will accomplish great things for God.

Let us pray the prayer of the hymn writer:

"Oh, that on me the sacred fire
Might now begin to glow,
Burn up the dross of base desire,
And make the mountains flow."[11]

---

11. T.S. Rendall, Editor and Author *The Prairie Overcomer*, No. 9, Vol. 43 (Three Hills, Alta., Canada: Prairie Bible Institute Publishers, Sept. 1970). Used by permission.

Chapter 11

Graces and Gifts
of the Spirit
in Paul's Epistles

I. INTRODUCTION

By the very nature of the variety of teachings, both implicit and explicit, concerning the Holy Spirit in the New Testament Epistles written by Paul, it seems the better part of wisdom to consider these teachings topically rather than somewhat historically, as in the previous chapters. This is not to assume that the Epistles present the Spirit in contradiction to the previous Biblical writers. Rather the presentation is simply fuller and more complete. It might be said, in a general sense, that what we have in the Epistles is the fruit of the Spirit from the spiritual tree that was planted, grew, and came to maturity in the Old Testament, the Gospels, and Acts.

While the teachings of Peter and the other apostles concerning the Holy Spirit in the Epistles are extremely important, it is Paul who gives to us the most extensive and perhaps the richest teaching concerning the Spirit in all the New Testament. In the light of this consideration we shall note first what the Spirit means to Paul in relation to the Christian faith and life.

II. PAUL'S CONCEPT OF THE SPIRIT AND HIS ACTIVITIES IN THE CHRISTIAN'S LIFE

A. The Spirit Is Essential to Man's Salvation

Adoption into the family of God is made possible through the agency of the Spirit (Rom. 8:14-16). Through the agency of the Spirit we are assured of our acceptance into God's family and can call Him our heavenly Father (Gal. 4:6).

For Paul the Holy Spirit is the agency of the sinner's justification by faith before God (Rom. 3:24; 14:17). In both the foregoing passages cited, a form of the Greek word *dikaios* is used, though translated "righteousness" in Romans 14:17, and "justified" in Romans 3:24. This word *dikaios* means "just in the eyes of God," or "the righteousness of which God is the source."[1]

While it is by faith that the repentant sinner is justified (Rom. 3:24; 5:1), it is through the agency of the Spirit that he enters into the righteousness of God (Rom. 14:17). This means not only that God for Christ's sake reckons the sinner to be righteous (*imputed righteousness*), but more than that, it is the function of the Spirit to *impart* the righteousness of God to the believer. Paul writes to the Philippians: "work out your salvation with fear and trembling; *for it is God who is at work in you,* both to will and to work for His good pleasure" (Phil. 2:12b, 13). And Peter writes: "Seeing that His divine power has granted to us *everything pertaining to life and godliness* . . . in order that by them *you might become partakers of the divine nature,* having escaped the corruption that is in the world by lust" (II Peter 1:3, 4).

Thus in this Greek word *dikaios,* from which our English word *justification* derives, there is represented, in Paul's usage, as also Peter's and others, the idea of regeneration or the Spirit-imparted life of God to the believer, beyond the idea of *reckoned* or *imputed* righteousness. To stop with legal justification is to leave the sinner forgiven but spiritually dead, but justification in the New Testament sense is something more than justice. It is forgiveness and the Spirit's inwrought righteousness of God in the soul of man. David understood this in his penitential prayer in Psalm 51, and Christ made it plain to Nicodemus in John 3. It is also the position of the apostles in the Epistles.

---

1. Alexander Souter, *A Pocket Lexicon to the Greek New Testament* (Oxford: At Clarendon Press, rep. 1966), p. 68.

This is indeed the best of good news, and it is the work of the Spirit to witness to the believer inwardly that it is true, and that he may confidently rely upon the Spirit's witness. It is only as we daily rely upon the trustworthiness of the Spirit's witness that we can experience His power to overcome the temptations of Satan and the subtle enticements to sin. Likewise, it is only as we rely upon His presence and power within us that we can bear fruit to God's glory. Barclay designates the Spirit as "the liaison officer of the good news of God"[2] between God and the believer's soul. The hymn writer has well expressed it as follows:

> Breathe on me, breath of God;
> Fill me with life anew,
> That I may love what Thou dost love,
> And do what Thou wouldst do.

This conviction of Paul is doubly emphasized by the apostle in three specific questions which he puts to his Galatian converts who were being alienated from Christ by the Judaizers. First, he asks: "This is the only thing I want to find out from you: Did you receive the Spirit by the works of the law, or by the hearing with faith? Are you so foolish? Having begun by the Spirit, are you now being perfected by the flesh? . . . Does he who provides you with the Spirit and works miracles among you, do it by the works of the Law, or by hearing with faith?" (3:2-3, 5).

B. The Spirit Is Essential to the Christian Life

Paul regards the Holy Spirit as absolutely essential to the Christian faith and life. This truth he makes plain in the Epistle to the Romans when he writes. "But if anyone does not have the Spirit of Christ, he does not belong to Him" (8:9b).

It is not surprising that Paul should have considered the Spirit so essential to the Christian faith and life when it is remembered that he himself began his Christian life in the Spirit. After having been smitten blind and rendered helpless by Christ on the Damascus road, Paul was approached by Ananias in Damascus with the words: "the Lord Jesus . . . has sent me so that you may regain your sight, and be filled with the Holy Spirit. And immediately there fell from his eyes something like scales, and he regained his sight, and he arose and was baptized" (Acts 9:17b, 18).

---

2. William Barclay, *The Promise of the Spirit* (London: The Epworth Press, 1960), pp. 72, 73.

For Paul there is no such thing as a Christian devoid of the Holy Spirit in his life. For him the Christian life is living activity in the Spirit (Gal. 5:16). Paul admonishes: "If we live by the Spirit let us also walk by [or, "follow"] the Spirit" (Gal. 5:25). For Paul the whole Mosaic legal system is fulfilled and completed by the Spirit (Rom. 7:6; 8:1-4). For Paul the Holy Spirit is the Spirit of Christ in the life of the believer (Rom. 8:9-14ff.; II Cor. 3:17; 6:16; Gal. 4:6). Paul said: "For to me, to live is Christ . . ." (Phil. 1:21; cf. Gal. 2:20). But Paul recognizes the Holy Spirit as Christ's representative on earth, and therefore the Christian life is dependent upon the presence of the Spirit in the life of the believer. Nothing could be clearer than this from Paul's own words: "Now *the Lord is the Spirit* . . ." (II Cor. 3:17). This is not to be taken as a theological statement from the pen of Paul in relation to the Trinity. He was, as Barclay notes, " . . . speaking from experience and his experience was that to possess the Spirit was nothing less than to possess Jesus Christ."[3]

C. The Spirit Is Essential to Christian Service

Paul was at heart a missionary, and thus a man of action. He exceeded by far all other Christians of his day in the extent of his travels, and experienced by far more adventures than any other Christian. In eighteenth-century England, John Wesley was to the British Isles in his missionary labors what Paul was to the Mediterranean region. Both were men of the Spirit and men of action. During his lifetime Wesley covered 250,000 miles on horseback, preached to audiences in the open air of up to 25 thousand people, planted churches everywhere he went, produced a voluminous quantity of literature, including a complete set of notes on both the Old and the New Testament running to over 3500 pages.[4] Both men were dynamic rather than crystalized systematic or propositional theologians, simply because both were men of the Spirit.

Spirit is never at rest, and therefore the Holy Spirit was ever the motivating force in all of Paul's life and activities. The deity and

---

3. *Ibid.*, p. 68.
4. This includes Wesley's little known extensive *Explanatory Notes Upon the Old Testament* (Bristol: Printed by William Pine in Wine-Street, 1767), in three volumes which run to over 2600 pages, plus his well known *Expository Notes Upon the New Testament* (London: The Epworth Press, rep. 1954), which number about 1050 pages.

personality of the Spirit held a prominent place in Paul's thinking, preaching, and writing. For Paul the Holy Spirit was the Spirit of God (Rom. 8:9; cf. I Cor. 3:16). The Spirit is an essential person of the Godhead (II Cor. 13:14; cf. Matt. 28:19). He exercises His prerogatives in the bestowal of gifts upon believers (I Cor. 12:4-11); He reveals the Father's will to Christ's followers (I Cor. 2:10-12); He instructs believers in the things of God (I Cor. 2:13). He honors and blesses the witness of believers to Christ (I Cor. 2:4; I Thess. 1:5). He sets the Christians in battle array against evil (Gal. 5:16-26). He crucifies the evil motivations and deeds of the body in believers (Rom. 8:13). He terminates the reign of sin in the lives of believers and exercises over them the reign of grace (Rom. 6;12-14). He effects a progressive moral transformation in the lives of believers (II Cor. 3:18). He liberates believers for spiritual activities (Rom. 8:2, 5-8; II Cor. 3:17; cf. Gal. 5:1).

D. The Spirit Is Essential to Christian Worship

For Paul the Holy Spirit activates the church's worship (Phil. 3:3). He produces unity and fellowship in the church (Eph. 4:3-4; Phil. 2:1-2). Through the Spirit the believers are baptized into the body of Christ (I Cor. 12:12-14). The Spirit communicates gifts to the church (I Cor. 12:4-11) (of this more will be said presently). And for Paul, as also the other New Testament writers, the Holy Spirit is the effective agent in the sanctification of believers (Rom. 15:16).

For Paul it is by the mediation of the Spirit that all men have access to God (Eph. 2:18). As an old Chinese custom where professional mediators arranged engagements and marriages between men and women of different families, so the Spirit introduces men to God, and even makes intercession for them (Rom. 8:26-27), and then bears witness to their acceptance by God (Rom. 8:16-17). The Greek word which Paul uses for access in Ephesians 2:18 is *prosagogēn,* the verb form of which is *proságo.* This is a most interesting word which means "to lead to, or bring to"; characteristically, "I bring a subject into the presence of a king"; "present to"; "introduce" (I Peter 3:18); "I approach" (Acts 27:27)."[5] Thus the Spirit introduces, or presents, the believer to the king of the universe. Man has no other access to God than through Christ by the mediation of the Spirit (cf. Rom. 6:23; Phil. 4:19).

---

5. Souter, *op. cit.,* p. 218.

E. The Spirit Is Essential to Christian Fruitbearing

Paul sees other benefits, in addition to God's righteousness, bestowed upon the believer by the Spirit. One of these benefits is *peace*, "peace . . . in the Holy Spirit" (Rom. 14:17b; cf. 5:1). Peace is the deepest and most universal desire of the human heart. Christ was called the "Prince of Peace" by the prophet (Isa. 9:6). He came to this world to make peace by the blood of His cross (Col. 1:20). He left His blessing of peace with His disciples. It is the function of the Spirit to implant this peace of God provided by Christ in the hearts of believers (Phil. 4:7).

Again, *joy* is as naturally the result of peace as fruit is of the tree that bears it (Rom. 14:17). The Spirit who implants peace in the believer's heart consequently produces a joyful reaction. Paul calls this "joy in the Holy Spirit" (Rom. 14:17b).

Contrary to popular usage, *hope* is a stronger word than *faith,* though not as strong as *love*. In his trilogy in I Corinthians 13:13 Paul lists faith first, hope second, and love third, and then characterizes these three Christian virtues as the abiding elements of the Christian life (cf. Rom. 15:13; Gal. 5:5; I Thess. 1:3).

Freedom is likewise an essential characteristic of the Christian experience and life. This moral freedom is also imparted to the believer by the Spirit (II Cor. 3:17; cf. Gal. 5:1).

As the Spirit was first manifested in *power* at Pentecost (Acts 2:2), just as He was promised by Christ before His ascension (Acts 1:8), so Paul sees the Spirit as an inner dynamic in the life of believers for Christian life and service (Rom. 8:9, 10; I Cor. 3:16-17; Eph. 5:18; I Cor. 6:19). It is also the function of the Spirit to *lead* the believer, and he walks in the Spirit (Gal. 5:16, 18, 25) and in the Spirit he stands fast (Eph. 6:10-18). Barclay notes that the Spirit imparts wisdom for the defense of the faith in argument, power to witness to it in life and service, and moral courage to keep it when under attack.[6]

F. The Spirit Is Subject to Offense

A truth often overlooked is that the Spirit is a divine person sensitive to offense and subject to being grieved. Against this danger Paul is careful to warn believers (Eph. 4:30), as he is to warn them against *quenching the Spirit* (I Thess. 5:19). It is noteworthy that

---

6. *Op. cit.,* p. 82.

Paul's warnings against *grieving* and *quenching* the Spirit, in the foregoing references, are warnings related to the Spirit's work of sanctification in the believer's experience and life.

The Spirit may be grieved by an unforgiving spirit, bitterness of soul toward fellow-men, unholy anger, dishonesty, slander, gossip, or impurity of thoughts, actions, and words.

Paul's warning against quenching the Spirit has a different context. Here in I Thessalonians 5:19, Paul's admonition, "Do not quench the Spirit," is immediately followed by another closely related admonition, "do not despise prophetic utterances" (v. 20). To disregard the voice of the Spirit heard in the sound proclamation of God's truth, to reject admonitions of the Spirit, to neglect the promptings and checks of the Spirit will quench and eventually extinguish the flame of the Spirit, especially as these relate to the Spirit's purpose to lead the believer into the deeper experience of cleansing, or sanctification (vv. 23-24).

III. THE *GIFT*, AND THE *GIFTS* OF THE SPIRIT

A. The Greek Passion for Gifts

The Greeks considered themselves the most gifted of all ancient peoples, and in certain respects this was not an exaggerated self-estimate. Certainly in the areas of art, architecture, athletics, philosophy, poetics, language, elocution, and rhetoric they were unequaled in the ancient world. Their ability to perform was unmatched, but their weakness lay in the absence of ability to organize, direct, and conserve their accomplishments. They were able to master almost everything but themselves.

This is well illustrated by Aristotle's influence over Alexander the Great. Philip employed the great philosopher Aristotle to tutor his son Alexander when the latter was a promising but impassioned and undisciplined lad of thirteen years. Aristotle tried diligently to make of Alexander a great man. Later, however, he observed that he had succeeded in teaching the boy to conquer almost everything but himself. It was this one fatal deficiency that accounted for his ultimate personal defeat after he had conquered most of the ancient world.

In this respect the Corinthian Greek Christians were the heirs of Alexander who manifested greatness in so many areas of his life and work, but in the end failed ignominiously in the area of self-discipline. The Greeks conquered the ancient world, but then were themselves conquered and made slaves by the Romans' practical genius. Likewise the absence of self-discipline was the great problem which Paul faced in the Corinthian church.

B. God's Unmeasured Gift of the Spirit

Two things concerning the Spirit become obvious as we read the New Testament Epistles. The first is that the Holy Spirit is God's gift to believers who constitute the church of Jesus Christ. The second is that the Spirit bestows His gifts upon the church.

Earlier in John's Gospel (3:34) we met Christ's statement that God "gives the Spirit without measure." This suggests first the generosity of God's love. But in the second place it suggests the very qualitative, as opposed to the quantitative, nature of the Holy Spirit. In the third instance it suggests the finitude of the Spirit.

Earlier we noted in our study of the Spirit in the Old Testament, the Gospels, and Acts, that the Spirit has in some sense always been God's gift to man. This was especially evident in Acts at Pentecost. But this divine gift of the Spirit, as it emerges in the Epistles, has a special significance. This gift is severalfold in its characteristics.

Paul's great prayer for the church universal, as recorded in Ephesians 3:14-21, is concerned primarily with the petition that God would bestow His Spirit upon the believer: "That He would grant you, according to the riches of His glory, to be strengthened with power through His Spirit in the inner man" (Eph. 3:16). Not as in the Old Testament where in the usual manner the Spirit "came upon" certain individuals temporarily, does the apostle request, *but that He may be the inner, strengthening and abiding experience* of the church (Eph. 3:16-17). Paul's prayer is in perfect harmony with the prayer of Christ to the Father that His disciples may receive the gift of the Holy Spirit for their lives and ministry (John 14:16-18).

Paul implies that the Holy Spirit is God's gift to the believers for their personal sanctification (I Thess. 4:7), and then says: "Consequently, he who rejects this [provision of sanctification, v. 7] is not rejecting man but the God who gives His Holy Spirit to you" (I Thess. 4:8). No greater gift has God provided for the believer than the Holy Spirit as his personal sanctifier. This is the one gift necessary for entrance into heaven, without which no one will meet God in peace (Heb. 12:14).

God gives His Spirit to the believer that by Him the "love of God [may be] *poured out within our hearts"* (Rom. 5:5). Thus Paul suggests the lavishness of God's generosity in this most precious of all divine gifts to His believing children. There is no other way of knowing "the breadth and length and height and depth" of God's love in Christ, which surpasses all other ways of knowing, than as it is *"poured out within our hearts"* in the person of the Spirit (see Eph. 3:18-19).

Barclay emphasizes this divine generosity by calling attention to two Greek words employed by Paul in this connection. The first is found in Galatians 3:5 where Paul says: "He then who provides you [or, "ministers to you with the Spirit"]." Here the word *provides* or *ministers* is represented by the Greek verb *epichorēgein*. In Philippians 1:19 Paul speaks of "the provision [or, "supply"] of the Spirit of Jesus Christ," and uses the Greek noun *epichorēgia*. These Greek words are great words with an important history. Their chief importance, Barclay thinks, suggests "generosity, lavishness, abundance."[7] He notes that in due time this Greek word *choregia* takes on greater meaning. It came to be used in marriage contracts where the husband promised to supply his wife with all the necessities of life according to his ability. It was used in relation to supplying soldiers in battle with all necessary equipment. It was used to describe man's natural or constitutional endowments for the demands of life; and to express man's equipment to meet the demands of duty and honor in life.[8] This generous, divine supply of the Spirit for all the necessities of the believer's life in this world is reflected in the loving generosity of a human father who supplies all the necessary provisions of life for his children. Such is God's gift of the Spirit to His believing children. Several other passages in the Epistles likewise emphasize the gift of the Spirit.

Paul informs the Corinthian church that ". . . each one is given the manifestation of the Spirit for the common good" (I Cor. 12:7). Thus God's gift of the Spirit is never for personal enhancement or aggrandizement, but something to be shared with the whole body of believers for their edification.

When writing to the Galatians Paul informs them that the promise of the gift of the Spirit is received through faith (3:14). John writes to the believers that the assurance of an abiding relationship in God is attested by the fact that *"He has given us of His Spirit"* (I John 4:13).

---

7. *Ibid.*, p. 64.
8. *Ibid.*, pp. 64-65.

C. The Spirit's Administration of the Gifts in the Church[9]

The New Testament makes abundantly clear the distinction between God's *gift* of the Spirit to believers, and the *gifts* which the Spirit bestows upon believers. It is the latter with which we are concerned at this juncture. However, before examining these Spirit-gifts, it is well that we take brief notice of an important distinction that must be made between such gifts as the Spirit may *bestow* upon a believer, and those natural or constitutional gifts that may characterize an individual, but which may be realized only when awakened and developed under the influence of the Spirit who has been given to him by God.

There is frequently much confusion at this point, and admittedly the distinction is not always easy to make. Certainly when considered in a very broad sense, both the talents or abilities constitutional to an individual, and the special endowments by the Spirit are the gifts of God, perhaps in the sense that life itself is a gift of God. But when considered more definitively there is a marked difference between the two. In consideration of what may be termed natural or constitutional gifts, the gift of the person of the Spirit may illumine, quicken, and nurture these potentialities in an individual to the development of greater usefulness, whereas without the presence of the Spirit in the life of an individual such potentialities may remain dormant throughout life and thus never serve any useful purpose.

The foregoing may be illustrated by the great Sahara Desert in North Africa, which constitutes a third of the area of this second largest continent on the globe, with its nearly twelve thousand square miles. The Sahara has remained practically uninhabited and fruitless for centuries unknown. However, scientific analysis reveals that the soil of the Sahara is among the most fertile in the world and that if water could be brought from the subterranean sources to the surface for irrigation purposes it could be converted into one of earth's most productive areas. The potential is there, but it lacks the necessary conditions for the development of that potential.

Likewise, natural, potential gifts are present in many, and perhaps most, lives. It is the presence of the gift of the Spirit that is necessary to awaken, nurture, and develop those potentialities. Probably a far greater percentage of what are commonly called the gifts of the

9. Much of the following discussion on "The Gifts of the Spirit" is reproduced from the author's treatment of this subject in the *Wesleyan Bible Commentary* V. 196-204 and 409-411.

Spirit fall into this category than are in the class of *special endue-ments* by the Spirit. But, we repeat, it is not always easy to make this distinction because, in large measure at least, it is often impossible to evaluate the potential of any person until such potential has been actualized in his life. Nor can the individual himself evaluate his own potential until it is actualized in response to the right challenge. No instrument, psychological or otherwise, has ever yet been devised to measure the potential of an individual, and probably there never will be one.

However, whether *natural endowment,* awakened by the gift of the Spirit, or *special enduements* of the Spirit, the Scripture makes frequent reference to what are designated the gifts of the Spirit. We shall now examine some of the more prominent of these gifts found in the epistles.

Among the most important of the Spirit's gifts found in the epistles is the list recorded by Paul in I Corinthians 12:1-11. Here Paul begins his delineation of the spiritual gifts in this comprehensive list with the introductory words: "Now concerning spiritual *gifts,* brethren, I do not want you to be unaware" (I Cor. 12:1). Then he continues: "there are varieties of gifts, but the same Spirit . . . but to *each one* is given the manifestation of the Spirit for the common good" (I Cor. 12:4, 7).

Certain clear implications emerge from these introductory words of the apostle. First, at Corinth, as even today, there was a serious misunderstanding of the gifts of the Spirit. "I would not want you to be unaware," or improperly informed, Paul says at the outset. Second, all the gifts are through the Spirit (v. 4), and therefore these gifts all depend upon the believer's possession of the Spirit. Without the Spirit there are no gifts from God for man.

A third consideration is that no one possesses all of the gifts, though the gift or manifestation of the Spirit is for all believers. Fourth, all of the Spirit's gifts are for the benefit and edification of the entire body of believers—the church of Jesus Christ—"the common good" (v. 7). Fifth, therefore, none of the gifts of the Spirit are private, in the sense of being given to an individual for his exclusive personal benefit. They are *gifts for the benefit of the Church.* Therefore, *no one person* has a monopoly upon any of the Spirit's gifts.

The catalog of gifts of the Spirit as given by Paul in I Corinthians 12:8-11 includes nine specific gifts. These are (1) "the word of widsom," (2) "the word of knowledge," (3) "faith," (4) "gifts of healing," (5) "effecting of miracles," (6) "prophecy," (7) "distinguishing of spirits," (8) *various* kinds of tongues" (languages), and (9) "interpretation of tongues" (languages). We shall consider each of these gifts of the Spirit in a somewhat orderly manner.

D. The Spirit's Manner of the Bestowal of Gifts (I Cor. 12:1-3)

The word *gift* is somewhat in question, but it appears to make little difference, as the Greek word *pneumatikon* (intermediate gender) "could accordingly denote 'spiritual men' or 'spiritual things.' "[10] Generally it is understood to denote things or gifts, though there may be exceptions to the rule. Persons are often mentioned in the context, but the gifts are exercised by people. Instead of the commonly used Greek word for spiritual gifts, *charisma,* Paul uses *pneumatikos* in this connection.

That the Corinthians had a serious deficiency in their understanding of this important subject of spiritual gifts is clearly indicated by Paul's introductory words. *I would not have you ignorant* ("unaware"), or have you continue in ignorance. That verse 2 suggests a potential, if not actual, relationship between the Corinthians' present misuse of spiritual gifts and their former pagan practices is evident from Paul's cautionary reminder that they were formerly "blindly hurried,"[11] or emotionally "moved" (*RSV*), "led astray by demons"[12] (10:19f.) *to those dumb idols.* That they had been made the captive slaves of the demons that led them to their own worship through the dumb idols is evident in the expression "however you might be led," or "however they chose to lead you."

Vain is man's boast of moral freedom when he is the slave to Satan through his sinful passions. There may be a gentle hint in Paul's reminder, "ye were led astray to *dumb* idols" at their *ecstatic unintelligible utterances* to which they are emotionally given, and which bear certain marks of identity with their former *dumb* idols (cf. 10:20-21). The meaning seems to be that "they were led from time to time." The imperfect tense with the indefinite particle signifies that they were led away habitually, or whenever the occasion might arise.

10. Leon Morris, *The First Epistle of Paul to the Corinthians* (Grand Rapids: Wm. B. Eerdmans Publishing Company, 1958), p. 166.
11. Vincent, *op. cit.,* p. 255.
12. Archibold Thomas Robertson, *Word Pictures in the New Testament* (New York: Harper and Brothers, 1931), IV. 167.

In the light of the previous observations on the extent of moral and spiritual degeneracy with some of the Corinthian Christians, including factions, false pride, incest, fornication, gluttony, drunkenness, and demon worship, it would not be surprising that someone should have been taken over by a demon spirit and in an emotional trance be made to anathematize, or curse Christ. No man knows what he may do when he has given over his rational powers to another. James Moffatt says on verse 3:

> It is indeed possible that the reference may be to an incoherent outburst in some *glossolalia* cry, as the man unconsciously screamed a phrase caught up from his normal experience. Such a phenomenon is not uncommon in hysteria or in the babbling of patients under a drug, when sub-consciously they utter things quite out of keeping with their real selves.[13]

Conversely, it is only by the Holy Spirit's revelation to a man that he can sincerely say *Jesus is Lord*. This is a divine revelation, not a human discovery. This is the Spirit's disclosure to man's inner spiritual self by the Spirit (Matt. 16:16-17).

E. The Spirit's Variety of Gifts (I Cor. 12:4-11)

1. All Spiritual Gifts Issue from One and the Same Spirit

Paul sets forth three categories of *diversities* or "varieties" in I Corinthians 12:4-6. They are (1) *diversities of gifts* (v. 4), (2) *diversities of ministrations* (v. 5), and (3) *diversities of working* or "effects" (v. 6).

Paul makes clear (v. 4), first, that no one Christian is divinely endowed with all God's gifts. Different gifts characterize different Christians. Second, he shows that all God's many spiritual gifts issue from the same Holy Spirit. He is the custodian and administrator of God's gifts. The Corinthians had conceitedly displayed and employed their gifts in furthering the factional spirit in the church. The possession and exercise of gifts had become a competitive matter with them. Paul reminds them that all genuine spiritual gifts are from the one Holy Spirit, and He does not oppose Himself. He has the same ultimate purpose in the bestowal of all His gifts.

Verse 5 emphasizes the "varieties of ministries, and the same Lord." In customary logical form Paul places Christ (*Lord*) between

---

13. *An Introduction to the Literature of the New Testament* (New York: Charles Scribner's Sons, 1911), p. 179.

the Spirit and the Father. While ministries can be understood as either service to Christ or the ministries of Christ through the believers, the latter seems more likely. Christ calls different individuals with different personalities, abilities, and talents. He, by the Spirit, dwells in and works through the channels of their varied personalities (cf. John 15:16). But it is the same Lord working in all.

The manifest effects of the various divine gifts working in and through the variety of redeemed human personalities are actually the operations of God's energy in the believers. God is all-powerful, power is energy, and energy is always active and acting toward some given end. God's gifts can never be separated from His personality. His gifts to men are the diversified manifestations of His own personal power. He *is* His gifts. Therefore, He is the same Father-God working by His many manifestations through the varied personalities of all His children. Consequently, there can be no place for boasting, divisions, or rivalry among God's people. "All one body we!"

Paul makes the operations or workings of divine energy and the effects of those workings identical. This is correct because God is what He does, and He is present in all His workings. Therefore, His servants need not concern themselves about visible results from their efforts. They need only be concerned that their gifts are God-given and empowered. The effects are the personal workings of God.

2. The Spirit's Gifts Are Impartially Bestowed

The personality of the Holy Trinity is clearly implied in this passage—the *same Spirit,* the *same Lord,* the *same God* (Father). In the unity of the Trinity there are diversities of gifts, of ministrations, and of effects or workings (cf. John 5:17).

Paul indicates that all Christians, not just a few privileged persons, receive God's gifts ("*to each one is given,*" v. 7). God's Spirit manifests Himself to every believer, and His manifestation is the assurance of God's gifts. The benefits of His manifest presence look two ways. The recipient is spiritually benefited, and all are benefited to whom the Spirit manifests Himself through the believer He possesses. All God's blessings are for the benefit of all His people—"for the common good" (v. 7).

3. The Spirit Awakens and Activates the Believer's Natural Abilities

Paul's distinction between *the word of wisdom (sophīa)* and the *word of knowledge (gnōsis)* in I Corinthians 12:8 is most challenging.

Knowledge as used here means "the highest intellectual excellence." *Wisdom (sophia)* refers to supernatural mysteries, or the knowledge of God that transcends human attainment, no matter how great that attainment may be (cf. Eph. 3:19). Paul says that it is the function of the Spirit to illumine, purify, and activate the believer's natural mental powers to their highest possible intellectual attainments in all areas of knowledge. But he recognizes the limitation of the human mind even at its best. It has its ceiling. It is finite. Therefore the Spirit, who searches and knows the mind of God, reveals to the illuminated, purified, and activated mind of the Spirit-possessed believer the higher wisdom *(sophia)* of God (cf. I Cor. 2:9-14; I John 2:27).

God places no premium upon ignorance, and He does not reveal to man what he is able to discover for himself by his natural intellectual powers. He wants all believers to be at their intellectual best, and the Spirit will help them to this end (cf. Rom. 12:1-2; Eph. 4:23). But He also recognizes, and wants man to recognize, man's dependence upon God for the higher wisdom (the divine *sophia*) which can only be had by the revelation of the Spirit. Thus Paul places human and divine knowledge in their proper relations. Paul's use of the term *word* in relation to *wisdom* and *knowledge* signifies utterance or communication.

Man cannot think except in some kind of symbols to give form to thought. Words are symbols or signs of ideas. Therefore the highest human knowledge and divine wisdom are possible to man only as they can be symbolized in his mind. Man understands best that which he is able to communicate to others. Therefore the Spirit illumines his mind and helps him to attain symbols *(words)* for understanding and communicating to others *wisdom* and *knowledge*. Paul may here intend to set in contrast "intelligible words for purposes of communication" with the *"unintelligible tongues"* which were so highly prized by some of the misdirected Corinthians. There have been great minds in human history possessed of vast natural knowledge, but the greatest minds of the ages have been those that were illumined and inspired by God's Holy Spirit. They had access to man's *knowledge* plus God's wisdom.

4. The Spirit's Gifts Are Related to Faith

That in verse 9 Paul is referring to something different from natural, or even evangelical or fiduciary (trustful) faith is evident. This is very evidently a special kind of faith by which God works miracles through certain believers, but not all—to another (or certain ones) *faith*. The ordinary kinds of faith cannot be regarded as the gifts of God, except in a very general sense, as air and lungs are God's gifts to man. Breathing, however, is man's use of those gifts. Faith, in the evangelical sense, is man's response to the divine initiative. There has been much confusion at this point. On the commonly misunderstood passage in Ephesians 2:8, it is interesting that the *NASB* rendering correctly makes the demonstrative pronoun "that" to refer to the salvation procured by faith and thus the antecedent of "the gift of God." F. F. Bruce notes that the demonstrative pronoun "that" is neuter in the Greek (*touto*), and that "faith" is a feminine noun (*pistis*), and thus these facts, combined with other considerations, suggest that Paul's reference is to "the whole concept of salvation by grace through faith that is described as the gift of God." He further states that this was John Calvin's interpretation of Ephesians 2:8, though he notes that many of Calvin's followers have taken faith itself as the gift of God.[14] It should be noted, however, that Calvin's followers are not alone in this misinterpretation of the passage since some even of Wesleyan persuasion have fallen into the same error. For two reasons Paul cannot be referring to saving faith in this passage. First, evangelical or saving faith is not a gift, in the sense of direct impartation from God, but rather man's obedient response to God's offer of the gift of salvation. Second, were it evangelical faith then salvation would not be God's universal offer to men, because the faith of verse 9 is given only to some. Consequently it must be regarded as a special gift for service rather than for salvation. Robertson says concerning this faith: "Not faith of surrender, saving faith, but wonder-working faith like that in 13:2"[15] (cf. Matt. 17:20; 21:21; Heb. 11:33). Likewise Vincent says: "Not *saving* faith in general, which is the common endowment of all Christians, but *wonder-working* faith."[16] This is also the position of Dummelow.[17]

5. The Spirit's Gifts Include Divine Healing

Closely linked to this wonder-working faith are the *"gifts of healing."* That there have been and are individuals especially en-

14. *The Epistle to the Ephesians, A Verse by Verse Exposition* (New York: Fleming H. Revell Company, 1961), pp. 51, 52.
15. Robertson, *op. cit.*, p. 196.
16. Vincent, *op. cit.*, p. 256.
17. *Op. cit.*, p. 913.

dowed with the gifts of healing (note the *gifts* here is plural) is well known. On the miraculous side it should be noted that the direct divine intervention in physical disorders requires less faith to accept than the spiritual conversion of an individual, for the simple reason that the latter involves a moral will which God will never violate, while the former does not involve such. God could heal the human body of a person not committed to Him without violating a moral principle, while He cannot save man's soul without his surrender.

It would seem, however, that these gifts of healing may involve much more than direct divine intervention, important as that is. That there are Christian men and women whose natural aptitudes better qualify them for specific branches of medical science and service than their fellows is evident. And that God should call these individuals into various fields of medical service is both Scriptural and logical. Luke was such a physician. Few Christians have greater opportunity to serve God than those who minister to the sick. Christian doctors, nurses, counselors, and psychiatrists exercise their gifts by "the one Spirit" who endows ministers to preach or teachers to teach. And none of the *gifts* has any Christian meaning or value except as it is exercised in *faith*. There are no effective Christian gifts apart from faith.

To some it is given to perform miraculously (v. 10), while others serve in a less spectacular manner. There are Christian specialists in medicine who accomplish cures that are rightly regarded as miraculous. There are evangelists whose special gifts move multitudes to Christ, while other good men stand by and marvel at such power which they themselves seem not to possess. There are Christian businessmen who are endowed with unusual financial ability which they use to God's glory. There are gifted teachers whose lives are used in an extraordinary way for the instruction of their fellows. There are religious administrators who serve in their areas with superhuman skill.

6. The Spirit's Gifts Include Prophecy

The "*gift of prophecy*" (v. 10), in the New Testament sense, is more often forthtelling or preaching than foretelling future events. That prophecy, in this sense, is the very special enduement of God to certain chosen individuals is too well known in Christian history to require emphasis. The line of gifted Christian prophets is long and illustrious from Peter and Paul through Luther, Wesley, Whitefield, Edwards, Moody, and on to Graham, to mention but a few. And the gift will go on to a long line of others. Prophecy is the greatest of the instrumental gifts, as it is the means by which Christ's saving grace is made known to men.

7. The Spirit's Gifts Include Spiritual Discernment

The gift of *"discernings of spirits,"* or "distinguishing of spirits" (*NASB*), is one of the most important of the Christian gifts if the church is to be saved from wreckage. Of it Vincent says: "Discerning between the different prophetic utterances, whether they proceed from the true or false spirits"[18] (cf. I Tim. 4:1; I John 4:1, 2). Robertson remarks: "A most needed gift to tell whether the gifts are really of the Holy Spirit and supernatural (cf. so-called 'gifts' today) or merely strange, natural or even diabolical"[19] (I Tim. 4:1; I John 4:1f.). Dummelow says: "Power to recognize whether a man were a true or a false prophet."[20]

8. The Spirit's Gifts Include Languages

Here begins Paul's first and only reference to *tongues* in any of his writings (I Cor. 12:10—14:40). In Chapter 12 the subject is mentioned in three verses, namely, 10, 28, and 30. Here, as in I Corinthians 12:10, 28, Paul uses the Greek word *glossai,* which properly means "languages," to express this gift. It signifies articulate speech for the purpose of communication, or the conveyance of ideas from the speaker to the listener. In I Corinthians 12:30 a less complimentary Greek word is used which may signify mere chatter or babble.

Thus "to another *various* kinds of tongues" means that the Spirit bestows upon some ("another") the miraculous ability to speak languages foreign to them for the same reason that He bestows the other gifts enumerated in this section: "But to each one is given the manifestation of the Spirit for the common good" or for the benefit of the entire church. None of these gifts, not even the gift of languages (*tongues*), is divinely intended for personal profit.

The word *unknown* which appears in the *KJV* does not occur in the Greek text, nor in any of the better translations. The New Testament knows nothing of an unknown tongue. Thus the *kinds of tongues* refer to a special gift of languages divinely bestowed upon

---

18. *Op. cit.,* p. 250.
19. Robertson, *op. cit.,* IV, 170.
20. Dummelow, *op. cit.,* p. 913.

some individuals to facilitate the preaching and teaching of the gospel where it was linguistically necessary.[21]

9. The Spirit's Gifts Include Interpretation of Languages

The gift of *the interpretation of tongues* is not bestowed upon the same individuals as are the *kinds of tongues*. Anyone who has been dependent upon interpreters in foreign countries, as the writer has, well knows that efficient interpretation is a special gift that few possess. Education and facility in one's own language are not sufficient in themselves to constitute a good interpreter. Spiritual insight and inspiration often play a far more important role in efficient interpretation than simply a thorough knowledge of two languages. Hodge argues convincingly and conclusively for this interpretation of verse 10.[22]

10. The Spirit's Gifts Issue from His Personality

All of the aforementioned gifts derive from the same source. They are all the workings of the Spirit in different individuals. The Spirit is Himself God's gift to the believer. He fills each believer with His own divine person and influence (Acts 1:8; 2:1-4), and then manifests Himself through the native abilities and talents of each believer. The individual believer furnishes the human mold. The Spirit fills the mold with His presence and energy. Thus in reality the gift is one and the same to all believers, namely, the gift of the Spirit. The gifts are, for the most part at least, the native abilities of the believers through which the Spirit manifests Himself. Consequently, the gifts are as varied as are believers, but they are all made effective by the same Spirit: "One and the same spirit works all these things" (v. 11).

The beautiful variegated rainbow of lights that plays on the Horseshoe Falls of Niagara from the Canadian side at night all issue from the same dynamo. The beautiful harmony of colors playing on the falling waters is produced by the variegated screens through which the *one* and *same light* is filtered. Just so the Holy Spirit is God's gift to all His children. The varied manifestations are but His workings through their varied personalities.

---

21. For an extended description of the problem of "tongues" at Corinth the reader is referred to Charles Hodge, *An Exposition of the First Epistle to the Corinthians* (Grand Rapids: Wm. B. Eerdmans Company, n.d.), pp. 237-308.
22. *Ibid.*, pp. 247-252.

F. The Spirit's Gift of Ministers to the Church

1. The Purpose of the Spirit's Gift of Ministers to the Church

In his letter to the Ephesians, which is most likely a cyclical letter and thus intended for the church universal (see Eph. 3:14-15), Paul presents and delineates the duties of five church offices and officers which are the gifts of the Spirit to the church of Christ. These gifts in order include (1) *"apostles,"* (2) *"prophets,"* (3) *"evangelists,"* (4) *"pastors,"* and (5) *"teachers."* These offices should likewise be viewed in descending order with *apostles* heading the list. Paul is less concerned with the individual gifts treated in the Corinthian church, and more concerned with the official, functional gifts in the church at Ephesus. This is due, it would seem, first, to the differences that characterize the two church situations, and second, to the fact that the Ephesian epistle is a cyclical epistle and thus bears universal and permanent significance for the church in all ages. On the other hand, in his treatment of the gifts of the Spirit in I Corinthians 12, the apostle seems to indicate in Chapter 13 that these are, in part at least, temporary gifts which will eventually cease. This is particularly true of the gift of "prophecy," in the sense of prediction, of the special gift of tongues, or language, and the special gift of knowledge, in the absence of the recorded revelation given in the New Testament which the Corinthian Christians did not as yet have. Could it be that in his words, "When the *perfect* is come, the partial will be done away" (I Cor. 13:10), Paul is alluding to the completion of the recorded New Testament revelation which will take the place of their special temporary knowledge given directly by the Spirit's revelation? Be this as it may, the gifts of the Spirit set forth in Ephesians 4:7-13 are very evidently intended as the Spirit's gifts to the church for all time to the end of the age,

Paul here names five specific functional *gifts* of the Spirit to the church in Ephesians 4:7-13. Bruce notes that these gifts to the church by the ascended Christ are to individual Christians to serve her spiritual needs, while the gifts of the Spirit in I Corinthians 12:4ff. "are endowments bestowed by Him upon individual Christians, which they are expected to exercise in the Church"[23] (cf. I Cor. 12:28). Thus Christ's ministers, as here described, are the Spirit's gifts to the church (cf. I Cor. 3:5, 21, 22). They are, Paul

---

23. Bruce, *op. cit.,* p. 84.

seems to say, the Spirit's superior gifts to the church. One has said,

the emphasis of the passage [v. 11] lies upon the truth that the ideal Ministry is a Ministry of spiritual power . . . the "gifts" are all alike in this, that they are given by the just-ascended Lord; they are Pentecostal gifts. This calls attention supremely to the witnessing work of the Christian Ministry.[24]

2. The Spirit's Gift of Apostles

In Paul's catalog here of the Spirit's gifts to the church, *apostles* came first (cf. Eph. 2:10; 3:5). *He gave some* of the especially qualified members of the church as apostles, *or to be apostles.* Vincent states,

the distinguishing features of an apostle [in the New Testament sense] were, a commission directly from Christ: being a witness of the resurrection: special inspiration: supreme authority: accredited by miracles: unliminted commission to preach and to found churches.[25]

3. The Spirit's Gift of Prophets

Prophets form the second order of the divine gifts to the church. A prophet in the New Testament sense was one who uttered inspired truth, whether this was a prediction (see Acts 21:10-11; II Thess. 2:1-12), a doctrine, or an exhortation (see I Cor. 14:4). Thus every preacher of the New Testament era to the present time who is inspired and moved by God's Spirit to fulfill these functions is a New Testament *prophet.* They are distinguished from teachers by the fact that they are preachers and expounders of God's truth (cf. I Cor. 12:10). Eadie states:

They were inspired *improvisatori* in the Christian assemblies—who, in animated style and under irresistible impulse, taught the church, and supplemented the lessons of the apostles, who, in their constant itinerations, could not remain long in one locality. Apostles planted and prophets watered; the germs engrafted by the one were nurtured and matured by the other. What the churches gain now by the spiritual study of Scripture, they obtained in those days by such prophetic expositions of apostolic truth (cf. I Cor. 14:3, 22, 24, 25).[26]

---

24. Hadley C. G. Moule, "Ephesian Studies," *Cambridge Bible* (Cambridge: Cambridge University Press, 1907), pp. 198, 199.
25. Vincent, *op. cit.,* p. 389.
26. An excellent treatment of this subject is given by John Eadie, *Commentary on the Epistle to the Ephesians* (Grand Rapids: Zondervan Publishing House, n.d.), pp. 298, 299.

4. The Spirit's Gift of Evangelists

The third order of gifts to the church is *evangelists*. These Vincent simply designates "travelling missionaries."[27] The word *evangelist* is used only three times in the New Testament; in this passage, in Acts 21:8 of Philip, and in II Timothy 4:5 as a description of one phase of the ministry of Timothy. Eadie thinks that *evangelists* may have served in an auxiliary capacity to the apostles. He regards them as:

> furnished with clear perceptions of saving truth, and possessed of wondrous power in recommending it to others. . . . Passing from place to place with the wondrous story of salvation and the cross, they preached Christ on man's acceptance, their hands being freed all the while from matters of detail in matters of organization, ritual and discipline (I Cor. 4:17; 16:10).[28]

Wesley regarded *apostles, prophets,* and *evangelists* as being the "extraordinary officers, while *pastors* and *teachers* were the ordinary officers."[29]

5. The Spirit's Gift of Pastors and Teachers

Pastors fall into the apostles' fourth category of the Spirit's gifts to the church. But some scholars hold that *pastors* and *teachers* form one category of church officers and thus the two words should be taken together to designate both aspects or functions of one office. Eadie holds that this dual office "comprised government and instruction, and the former being subordinate to the latter."[30] He further holds that nothing certain is known of early church government and that much of the writing on this subject is "but surmise and conjecture." Church government, he thinks, varied considerably from one Christian community to another, and such as existed devolved upon the teachers and elders of the church.[31]

The unity of these two offices is further supported by the absence of the Greek article from *teachers*. Thus the two go together. No man is truly a pastor who cannot teach. Conversely, the teacher of religion is dependent upon the knowledge derived from pastoral experience.

---

27. Vincent, *loc. cit.*
28. Eadie, *op. cit.*, pp. 302, 303.
29. John Wesley, *Explanatory Notes Upon the New Testament* (London: The Epworth Press, rep. 1954), p. 713.
30. Eadie, *op. cit.*, p. 306.
31. *Ibid.*

The purpose of the spiritual gifts in relation to the maturity of the church is treated in a twofold manner by Paul (vv. 12-16). The gifts are declared first as intended *for the perfecting of the saints, unto the work of ministering,* or service for Christ. In the second place, they are designed for *the building up of the body of Christ.* We shall note these in their order.

God never rests short of the perfection of *His* work. When creation was completed and God reflected upon it and pronounced it perfect, He saw that "it was very good" (Gen. 1:31). He then, but not until then, "rested from all his work which God had created and made" (Gen. 2:3). So God could not rest until the believers, *saints,* were, as Paul wrote to Timothy, "equipped for every good work" (II Tim. 3:17b). J. B. Phillips' translation is an illuminating commentary on these words: "The scriptures are the comprehensive equipment of the man of God, and fit him fully for all branches of his work."[32]

A saint in the New Testament epistle is, as Moule has observed, "just the Christian as he should be; the disciple assumed to be true to Christ and (Rom. 8:9) possessed of His Holy Spirit."[33] He is a member of the church or body of Christ who may or may not hold a public office in the church. He has been saved by Christ and exists as a member of Christ's church for service to and for Christ: *unto the work of ministering.* This is the principle Paul lays down for every Christian, whatever may be the details of the *pastor-teacher* to equip the individual members of the church for their practical service for Christ. Thus the members of the church that are alive in Christ will be spiritually animated and actively engaged in a service of witnessing for Christ in a multitude of ways (cf. I Thess. 1:3, 8).

When the gifts of the ministry (v. 11) exist as ends in themselves they will defeat their own purpose and the purpose of Christ for them. When they exist for the *perfecting of the saints* that the church may become an equipped and active agency in the work of Christ they will serve their God-intended purpose. Priscilla and Aquila were such active lay members of the church who rendered invaluable service to the cause of Christ (Acts 18:26). Moule remarks, " 'Prophet, evangelist, pastor-teacher,' are, *in the rule* of the Master's will, necessary to 'the saints' for their 'work of service'; as

---

32. J. B. Phillips, *The New Testament in Modern English* (New York: The Macmillan Company, 1958), p. 460.

33. H. C. G. Moule, "The Epistle of Paul the Apostle to the Romans," *Cambridge Bible* (Cambridge: The University Press, 1899), p. 200.

on the other hand 'the saints' are utterly indispensable to the full work of the Christian minister."[34]

In the second place, Paul moves in the passage from the church in service to Christ to the character of the Christian community: *unto the building up of the body of Christ*. Indeed the character of the church is determined by the character of its individual members. The prevalence of mature and stable individual members determines the maturity and stability of the church. Paul never views the church as a static institution, but always as a growing, developing, spiritual organism moving toward the ultimate ideal of a mature, stable, adult perfection that excludes all error, doctrinal and practical, and that embodies in principle and practice the truth of God revealed in the gospel of Jesus Christ (cf. Heb. 12:22-23).

Indeed, the absolute attainment of this ideal is reserved for the next world, but its relative realization is the present possibility and purpose of God for His people. Paul is here concerned primarily with time rather than eternity. The church is presently in the process of upbuilding—a present spiritual manhood or maturity attainable en route to the ultimate maturity of the next life. This present maturity in Christ is analogous to the human maturity intended by the father who says, for the encouragement of his son under difficult circumstances, "Be a *little man*." Paul's ideal is that the church should be God's "little mature man now," that it may be God's "big mature man then" in the next world.

In the remainder of this passage Paul makes Christ the central focus of all that he has previously said concerning the ministry, saints, the body, and the Christian community. In Him, and only in Him, all of these may realize their perfection. The body has its individual members with their respective functions, but each member exists and functions by virtue of its relation to the head, which is Christ (cf. John 15:1-13), and its relation to the other members of the body. Thus the one requisite of spiritual life and effective service is union with Christ the Head, and harmony and co-ordination with the other members of the body of Christ. Love alone makes all this possible.

The gifts of the Spirit extend beyond the professional ministry, such as preaching, praying, pastoral counseling, and teaching, important as these are. Paul indicates that every function of the church requires the gift of the Spirit for successful operation. The craftsman

---

34. *Ibid.,* p. 202.

who plans and constructs the church building, the church secretary, the church custodian, and the administrator all require the gift of the Spirit and are honored alike by God in their service. Barclay notes that we have erected a false spiritual aristocracy which must be abandoned in the light of the fact that *"ministry* simply means *service."* Thus any gift that we possess is a gift of the Spirit and should be placed on the altar of service to God.[35]

G. The Spirit's Unification of the Gifts
(I Cor. 12:12-31)

1. The Unity of the Spirit's Gifts Gives Meaning to Their Variety

In the previous consideration Paul has emphasized the variety of spiritual gifts. He now emphasizes the unity within that variety. The Corinthian church prided itself in its great variety of gifts. It had little to boast about in its unity. Paul seeks to show that without the unity the multiplication of gifts is meaningless.

The human body serves to illustrate the principle of unity in the body of Christ (I Cor. 12:12). No member in itself constitutes the body. Nor will all the members, unless properly related one to the other in the body, constitute a body. The body is more than the sum of its parts—*it is a body*—an emergent from the proper relation and harmony of all the parts, even as water is an emergent from H_2O. Water is something more than H_2O. It is *water,* and if it is reduced to its chemical components it ceases to be water. The spiritual body, the body of Christ—the church—is like that. It is only the church when all the members are harmoniously related and functioning in unison. This is made possible by the living soul of the church—the Holy Spirit.

2. The Church is Constituted Christ's Body Through the Baptism in the Spirit

The church is made a spiritual body through the baptism in the Spirit. Through that glorious baptism Jews and Greeks, slaves and freemen, women and men, wise and simple, rich and poor, are all made one in the body of Christ—each has become a partaker of the spiritual water of life (cf. John 7:37-39).

No one member constitutes the body. It requires all the members

---

35. Barclay, *op. cit.,* pp. 83, 84.

to make a whole body, and each in his own position and function is as essential and important to the completion of the body as any other member. The foot is no less a part of the body than the hand, though its function is vastly different. The distinction of the ear from the eye makes it no less a part of the body. If any one member such as the eye or the ear, were the whole of the body, regardless of its individual perfection, it would not constitute a body as such (v. 17).

3. *The Variety of the Spirit's Gifts Is Essential to the Unity of Christ's Body*

The divine design and purpose for Christ's church is evident in verse 18. He has the blueprint for His church (the spiritual body); He needs a great variety of materials to complete and perfect that structure. He knows best just where and how each believer will best fit into that master plan for His church. It is only as all the members submit themselves to His purposes that He can complete a unified and harmonized spiritual body (cf. Rom. 12:1-2). One member cannot constitute the body; the members are many and varied, but they are one body in Christ.

The weaker members of the body, and those accounted as of lesser importance, are, Paul asserts, very necessary, perhaps even more important in some respects than the stronger members. All the citizens are necessary to the body social and politic. This kind of argument should have humbled the proud and encouraged the humble in Corinth.

Morris thinks that Paul is referring to clothing in I Corinthians 12:23. The reason seems to be that because of the uncomeliness of certain parts of the body they are clothed to hide their uncomeliness, and the more comely parts of the body are left exposed. By reason of their clothing, however, the uncomely members are made to appear more beautiful than those parts that remain exposed. Thus the paradox is resolved.[36] True modesty is the most beautiful of all virtues. What it would hide is often made the more attractive. Practically applied and taken seriously, this argument should serve effectively against nudist tendencies in contemporary society.

The wisdom of God takes over and arranges the member in the body in such ways that the less honorable members actually become

---

36. Morris, *op. cit.*, pp. 176, 177.

the more honorable. Not infrequently, by reason of lesser self-esteem an individual realizes greater need of being clothed upon by the power and glory of God, and thus God can and does sometimes give greater honor to the lesser members than to the greater.

4. The Mutual Care of the Members Is Essential to the Unity of Christ's Body

From perfection of arrangement of the members in the body for harmony of appearance and function, Paul now advances to the mutual care and consideration of the members for one another. If each member cares for the other member, if each suffers with another suffering member, if each rejoices when one member is honored, then there will be no place for nor danger of factional rivalry within the church. It is interesting to note that Paul does not say that all are honored when one is honored, though this is true to a degree, but that all rejoice when one is honored. They rejoice in his honor. This is the true, unselfish, outgoing Christian spirit. If taken seriously it would be a sure remedy for many, if not most, internal church problems.

5. The Spirit's Gifts to the Church Are Complementary for the Perfection of Christ's Body

In verse 27 the apostle comes to the crux of the whole argument. All else has pointed to this end. The Corinthian Christians, as all Christians, are members of the church—Christ's body. Each has his respective place in that body, and each has his own importance and honor in the body. But each is but a part of the body. No one is the whole body, no matter how important he may consider himself to be. Each needs the other. The members complement one another to perfect the body of Christ, the church.

In I Corinthians 12:28-31 the apostle brings the logical conclusions of his argument directly to bear upon the church situation at Corinth. He shows the comparative importance of each office within the church, and concludes that just as all cannot be the same member of the body, just so, not all have the same office and function within the church. The offices within the church are then set forth in a descending order of importance. It is interesting that some offices which the Corinthians have been emphasizing as the most important, and have been striving to obtain, are the ones Paul places lowest in the descending scale. This might well give pause to office seekers in the church today.

The order of these church offices is determined by God—they are appointed by the Spirit. But the officers are also appointed by the Spirit to fill the offices, and thus they are not self-appointed. This further eliminates any grounds for strife. There is no point in striving for that which is apportioned in the form of gifts from God. Just as He has arranged the members in the natural body, so He arranges the offices in the spiritual body, the church. They are not chosen by the members, but they are "appointed" or *set* in the church.

First, *apostles* head the list. They were the vanguard of the gospel—the pioneer missionaries—the custodians of the authentic gospel of Christ. They were the evangels, and they rank first in order of importance.

Second, *prophets* follow apostles in importance. Prophets were *forthtellers* or preachers in the New Testament sense, for the most part, *rather than foretellers* or predictors of the future, as in the usual Old Testament sense. Such prophecy might be a temporary function, or permanent. It came more and more to be considered permanent, and prophets came to fill the place of pastors.

Teachers take third place. This indicates their importance. This was likely due in part to the difficulty of obtaining books, Morris thinks. He says: "The cost of hand-copied books was high, so high that, according to A. Q. Morton's estimate, 'a gospel represents in papyrus alone a year's wages and a New Testament about eight year's pay of a skilled workman.' "[37]   Naturally few could afford to own the Scripture. Thus they were dependent upon teachers for direct instruction.

Fourth in the list are *miracles,* not as an office but a function under the divine Spirit. Fifth, *gifts of healing* are listed. Paul mentions *helps* as sixth. The exact meaning is somewhat in doubt; however, such functions as deacons and deaconesses may well have been in his mind. *Administrations* or *governments* follow as seventh in the list. The eighth item is *kinds of tongues,* or different languages. The ninth, *Interpretations,* is related to *tongues.* Paul's purpose in listing *governments* and *tongues* last and lowest in the catalog of offices may be due to the fact that the Corinthians made them the most important, and thus their excessive emphases upon speaking and striving for the mastery over others caused most of the trouble in

---

37. *Ibid.,* p. 179.

the church. This thirst for predominance and power over others has ever been one of the greatest plagues upon Christianity and the church. Thus Paul indicates that no office or function is for everyone. This is doubly true of "tongues," over which they have striven and which have caused so much trouble in the church. Now Paul exhorts them to desire rather the higher and better gifts, those that head his list. Then from these he promises to show them *a most excellent way,* the way of Christian love treated in chapter 13. This they needed most, and of this gift, or rather *fruit* of the Spirit, they had the least. It was the most neglected characteristic of Christianity in the Corinthian church, even as it has ever been in the Christian church.

---

38. One of the best treatments of "Spiritual Gifts" which the present author has seen is found in an article of this title by Dr. Stanley D. Walters published in *The Preacher's Magazine,* Volume 49, Number 1 (Kansas City, Mo.: Beacon Hill Press of Kansas City, January 1974). Walters bases his treatment upon Romans 12:6-8; Ephesians 4:11-12; I Corinthians 12:8-10, 28, 29-30; and I Peter 4:10-11. His analysis of the scriptural gifts is threefold; I. The Variety of Gifts; II. The Purpose of the Gifts; III. The Hierarchy of Gifts. Highlighting this excellent treatment, Walters states: "In fact, each Christian's gifts will probably be in the area of abilities which he already possesses." He brings Rudolf Otto to the support of this position where Otto says, " 'mysterious heightenings of talents and capacities' already possessed by the believer" (*The Kingdom of God and the Son of Man,* 1943, p. 340).

Chapter 12

The Fruit and Guarantee
of the Spirit
in Paul's Epistles

I. THE *FRUIT* OF THE SPIRIT DISTINGUISHED
FROM THE *GIFTS* OF THE SPIRIT

That the "fruit of the Spirit" is something different from "the gifts of the Spirit" Bible scholars are generally agreed. Upon this distinction the New Testament is clear. The Spirit and His gifts are bestowed by God upon believers. The fruit of the Spirit in the lives of believers is the result of His presence within them and the gifts He bestows upon them.

While three explicit references to the "fruit of the Spirit" are found in Paul's Epistles, various implicit references are also present. In each instance the word *fruit* occurs in the singular number. Some of the modern versions render the passage in Ephesians 5:9 as "the fruit of the light." However, the KJV has it "the fruit of the Spirit." Since some of the Greek texts say *karpòs toū pneúmatos* ("fruit of the Spirit"), this text will be considered in reference to the "fruit of the Spirit."

Concerning the relation of the "gifts of the Spirit" to the "fruit of the Spirit" Wesley wisely remarks:

Whether these gifts of the Holy Ghost were designed to remain in the Church throughout all ages, and whether or no they will be restored at the nearer approach of the "restitution of all things," are questions which it is not needful to decide. But it is needful to observe this, that, even in the infancy of the Church, God divided them with a sparing hand. Were all even then prophets? Were all workers of miracles? Had all the gifts of healing? Did all speak with tongues? No, in no wise. Perhaps not one in a thousand. Probably none but the teachers in the Church, and only some of them (I Cor. xii. 28-30). It was, therefore, for a more excellent purpose than this, that "they were all filled with the Holy Ghost."

It was, to give them (what none can deny to be essential to all Christians in all ages) the mind which was in Christ, those holy fruits of the Spirit, which whosoever hath not, is none of His; to fill them with "love, joy, peace, long-suffering, gentleness, goodness" (Gal. v. 22-24); to endue them with faith (perhaps it might be rendered *fidelity*), with meekness and temperance; to enable them to crucify the flesh, with its affections and lusts, its passions and desires; and in consequence of that inward change, to fulfil all outward righteousness; to "walk as Christ also walked," in "the work of faith, in the patience of hope, the labour of love" (I Thess. i. 3).[1]

II. LOVE, THE TAPROOT OF THE FRUIT OF THE SPIRIT

The theme of I Corinthians 13 is divine love, or "the more excellent way." Paul's purpose is to show how this divine love, which is wrought in the believer by the Spirit, is outworked in the "fruit of the Spirit" in the lives of Christians. This thirteenth chapter of I Corinthians begins and ends with what Henry Drummond called *The Greatest Thing in the World*," divine love.[2]

First Corinthians 13 is not a digression, as some have supposed, from Paul's central theme of the "gifts" and "graces" of the Spirit. It is, rather, the climax or summit of that theme. From this summit all the gifts and graces of the Spirit may be viewed and set in proper perspective and correct relationships. It is the mountain top from which the surrounding foothills can be seen with clear and correct vision and understanding. It is "the most excellent way." It is the summit toward which Paul has moved with care and wisdom to bring his spiritually dull Corinthian converts, that they might see with him that no one of the foothills or lesser peaks of the surrounding terrain is in itself the summit of the Christian life. These Corinthian Christians, like many others since their time, were disposed to accept a

---

1. John Wesley, "Scriptural Christianity, 2-4" *Sermons* (S, I, 92-94).
2. *The Greatest Thing in the Word* is the title of Drummond's little classic, an exposition of I Corinthian 13, now published by various companies and available at most religious book stores.

part and regard it as the whole. Paul wanted them, as God wants all Christians, to see and understand the Christian faith in larger perspective—the perspective of love, for "God is love." Paul presents the Christian faith here as a religious philosophy in which all of the parts find their unity and meaning in the all-embracing love of God. Adolph Harnack regarded I Corinthians 13 as "the greatest, strongest, deepest thing Paul ever wrote." Every great thinker of the ages, and perhaps most lesser thinkers, has at some point in his life and thought asked the question, What is the greatest, the most important, the most real and enduring thing in life or the universe? While a great variety of answers have been given to this question, it is Paul's answer in I Corinthians 13 *only* that satisfies the demands of man's mind.

III. THE TRIADIC CLUSTER OF THE FRUIT OF THE SPIRIT

A. The Three Triads of the Fruit of the Spirit (Gal. 5:22-23)

In Romans 14:17 Paul contrasts the constituents of the kingdom of God, "righteousness and peace and joy in the Holy Spirit," with the dissipating, transitory pleasures of life's experiences apart from God. This triad of *righteousness, peace,* and *joy* issues from the believer's life in the Spirit. Dayton remarks:

> The kingdom of God has to do with relationship to the King . . . this reflects itself most deeply in the intensely personal qualities of *righteousness, peace, and joy in the Holy Spirit.*[3]

Clarke remarks on the *fruit of the Spirit,* as implied by Paul in this verse, that the righteousness consists in,

> Pardon of sin, and holiness of heart and life. *And peace.* In the soul, from a sense of God's mercy; peace regulating, ruling, and harmonizing the heart. *And joy in the Holy Ghost.* Solid spiritual happiness, a joy which springs from a clear sense of God's mercy, the love of God being shed abroad in the heart by the *Holy Ghost.* In a word, it is happiness brought into the soul by the Holy Spirit, and maintained there by the same influence. This is a genuine counterpart of heaven: *righteousness* without sin, *peace* without inward disturbance, *joy* without any kind of mental agony or distressing fear.[4]

Wesley says concerning Romans 14:17:

> True religion does not consist in external observances. But in *righteousness*—The image of God stamped on the heart: the love of God

3. *Wesleyan Bible Commentary,* V, 87.
4. *Commentary on the Holy Bible,* p. 1080.

and man, accompanied with the *peace* that passeth all understanding, *and joy in the Holy Ghost.*[5]

In Ephesians 5:9 Paul says "the fruit of the light [or Spirit] consists in *all goodness,* and *righteousness* and *truth.*" This expression, and the idea it represents, is counterbalanced by Paul's reference in Ephesians 5:11 to the "unfruitful works of darkness." The first, the fruit of the Spirit, issues from the lifegiving vine into which believers are grafted (cf. John 15:1, 5). The second, or "unfruitful works of darkness," represents the empty meaninglessness of a lifeless deception. Concerning Paul's words here, Moule remarks:

> *all goodness,* every form of all that is the pure opposite of evil, *and righteousness,* holy regard of the rights of others, in respect of both honesty and purity, *and truth,* the deep reality and sincerity of purpose which is the one possible basis for a right life.[6]

However, it is in Galatians 5:22-23 that Paul gives to us his systematic catalog of *the fruit of the Spirit.* "But the fruit of the Spirit is love, joy, peace, patience, kindness, goodness, faithfulness, gentleness, self-control; against such there is no law." It was with the purpose of fruitbearing that Jesus commissioned His disciples (John 15:16; Matt. 28:18-20; Acts 1:8). Likewise Christ's disciples recognized that fruitbearing was His purpose for the believers' spirit-filled lives (II Peter 1:8).

Paul sets the *fruit of the Spirit* against the background of the evil works of the flesh (see Gal. 5:15-21). The *fruit of the Spirit* is singular in number here, as elsewhere in the New Testament, and is thus designed to emphasize the one source from which the fruit can issue, even the Spirit Himself, and the unity which His indwelling presence produces. The *works of the flesh* are given in the plural and indicate the disunity and destruction which sin effects in the life.

Many analogies and analyses have been used to express the fruit of the Spirit. Paul is fond of the use of triads to express great truths. He writes of *faith, hope* and *love* (I Cor. 13:13); of the *work of faith, labor of love,* and *steadfastness of hope* (I Thess. 1:3); and in many other instances he uses the triadic combination of truth, though they are not always as obvious as in the foregoing instances. His treatment of the *fruit of the Spirit* in Galatians is not an exception to this practice. In fact this treatment naturally falls into three sets of triads,

---

5. *Notes, op. cit.,* p. 575.
6. *Op. cit.,* p. 250.

or a triad of triads.[7] Each of these three triads of *the fruit of the Spirit* will be examined in the order in which Paul presents them.

B. The First Triad of the Fruit of the Spirit (Gal. 5:22a)

The first triad of the fruit of the Spirit is concerned, primarily, with the state of the believer's relationship to the Spirit.

First, Paul's order here is logical. God is love, the Spirit is divine, and therefore the indwelling Spirit is the love of God implanted in the heart of the believer. Wesley says that "love is the root of all the rest."[8] Paul uses the Greek word *agape* to express love as the fruit of the Spirit. This *agape* is basic to all else. This is the word generally used in the New Testament to express divine love in distinction from human love, or friendship (Greek, *philia*). In fact all other *fruit of the Spirit* springs from this one Spirit-implanted source of the love of God. This is the love that expresses the heart of the *Great Commandment*—love for God with all the heart, soul, strength, and mind; and for one's neighbor as one's self (Luke 10:27). Jesus made the possession and exercise of this love the one necessary condition for eternal life (Luke 10:28). Paul canceled out every other "great thing" in life as absolutely worthless in the absence of love's motivation (I Cor. 13:1-3).

Second, joy belongs to *love* as fruit belongs to the living plant. The two are inextricable. They are, so to speak, *Siamese twins.* Paul writes to his Thessalonian converts reminding them that they "received the word in much tribulation *with joy of the Holy Spirit.*" Paul and Silas received one of their most violent treatments at Philippi, but at midnight, incarcerated in the city jail with backs sore and bleeding from the day's flogging, but with hearts filled with the Spirit, they "were praying and singing hymns of praise to God," with the prisoners listening, when God sent an earthquake that freed them and resulted in the conversion of the jailer and his entire household (Acts 16:25-34).

Little wonder that Paul could write later to his converts at Philippi saying: "I rejoice and share my joy with you all. And you too, I urge you, rejoice in the same way and share your joy with me"

7. The Author is indebted to J. Oswald Sanders for this most excellent insight into the *triadic* nature of this passage which is found in his book, *The Spirit and His Gifts* (Grand Rapids: Zondervan Publishing House, rev. ed., 1970), p. 147.

8. Wesley, *Notes, op. cit.,* p. 697.

(Phil. 2:17, 18). These words were written from Paul's prison cell at Rome where he eventually suffered martyrdom at the hands of the cruel emperor Nero. Again in the same letter Paul's exuberance seemed to know no bounds as he exhorted: "Rejoice in the Lord always; again I will say, *rejoice!*" (4:4). It is the function of the Spirit to administer to believers the joy that Christ made possible for them.

Third, peace is a member of this trilogy of the *fruit of the Spirit*. Christ had assured His disciples, "Peace I leave with you; my peace I give to you" (John 14:27). As the Prince of Peace, Christ qualified to bequeath His peace to His followers. And the Spirit freely administers this provision through His personal indwelling presence. This fruit of the Spirit is not dependent upon or altered by the circumstances of life since it is the "peace of God" administered by the Spirit, and not the believer's peace. His presence insures the peace. His absence robs the soul of its peace. Clarke calls this peace, "The calm, quiet, and order which take place in the justified soul. . . ."[9]

C. The Second Triad of the Fruit of the Spirit (Gal. 5:22)

In this second triad Paul sets forth the Spirit's outworking activities through the believer's *patience, kindness,* and *goodness.* Here the fruit of the Spirit looks outward to the believer's fellow men.

First, this is the fruit of *forebearance.* The *KJV* renders it *long-suffering,* which simply means "to suffer long." Clarke calls it *long-mindedness,* and then remarks:

> bearing with the frailties of and provocations of others, from the consideration that God had borne long with ours and that, if He had not, we should have been speedily consumed; bearing up also through all the troubles and difficulties of life without murmuring or repining; submitting cheerfully to every dispensation of God's providence, and thus deriving benefit from every occurrence."[10]

Patience as a fruit of the Spirit implies nonretaliation, a forgiving spirit, and a willingness to pass over, or even forget, wrongs inflicted by inconsiderate or vicious persons. Christ left His own example in this respect, and the Spirit makes His grace available to the followers of Christ.

Second, this is the fruit of *kindness.* Love has no greater virtue than kindness. Drummond says:

---

9. Clarke, *op. cit.,* p. 1166.
10. *Loc. cit.*

Kindness is love active. He [Christ] spent a great proportion of His time simply in making people happy, in doing good turns to people. . . . The greatest thing a man can do for his Heavenly Father is to be kind to some of His other children. . . . I shall pass through this world but once. Any good thing therefore that I can show to any human being, let me do it now. Let me not defer it or neglect it, for I shall not pass this way again."[11]

Clarke says of kindness ["gentleness," *KJV*] that it is "benignity, affability; a very rare grace, often wanting in many who have a considerable share of Christian excellence."[12] Wesley says: "*Gentleness*—Toward all men; ignorant and wicked men in particular."

Third, it is the fruit of *goodness.* In Ephesians 5:9, Paul speaks of *all goodness* as a *fruit of the light (Spirit). Goodness* is not a passive, pietistic withdrawal from fear of social contamination. Rather it is love active in benevolent deeds to others. Clarke says it is "The perpetual desire and sincere study, not only to abstain from every appearance of evil, but to do good to the bodies and souls of man to the utmost of our ability."[13]

Peter has a remarkable word concerning Christ in relation to the Spirit and His goodness. He says: "You know of Jesus of Nazareth, how God anointed Him with the Holy Spirit and with power, and how He *went about doing good,* and healing all who were oppressed by the devil; for God was with Him" (Acts 10:38). Likewise it is said of Barnabas that "he was *a good man,* and full of the Holy Spirit and faith, and a considerable number [lit., "multitudes"] were brought to the Lord" (Acts 11:24). Were more Christians characterized by this *fruit of the Spirit,* there would be more non-Christians converted and added to Christ's church. Wesley says of *goodness:* "The Greek word means all that is benign, soft, winning, tender, either in temper or behaviour."

D. The Third Triad of the Fruit of the Spirit (Gal. 5:22b-23)

The fruit of the Spirit's influence upon the character of the believer is *faithfulness, gentleness, and self-control.* Christian conduct is the reflection of Christian character, and Christian character is made possible only by the indwelling presence of God's Spirit in the

---

11. Henry Drummond, *Wesleyan Bible Commentary,* Chas. W. Carter, ed. (Grand Rapids: Wm. B. Eerdmans, 1965), V. 211. *NOTE* for treatment of "divine love" by Drummond the interested reader is referred to the foregoing volume, pp. 204-213.

12. Clarke, *op. cit.,* 1166.

13. *Loc. cit.*

believer's life. No amount of culture, education, or effort on man's part that is not motivated by God's Spirit can produce the fruit of Christian character. Character is what one is. Conduct is what one does. And one cannot enact a true Christian life without the motivation of the Spirit within.

First, in this third trilogy of *the fruit* of the Spirit is *faithfulness*. While "faithfulness" seems the best translation here, though the *KJV* has "faith," it is not possible to separate *faithfulness* from *faith*. Whether in relation to God or man, where there is no faith there can be no sincere faithfulness. *Faithfulness* is a Christian characteristic because it was characteristic of Christ. The author of the Epistle to the Hebrews gives us an exhortation to, and an example of faithfulness when he says: "Therefore, holy brethren, partakers of a heavenly calling, consider Jesus, the Apostle and High Priest of our confession. *He [Christ] was faithful* to Him who appointed Him, as Moses also was in all His house" (3:1-2).

Faithfulness means fidelity, or loyalty, to a person, cause, or trust committed to one. Joseph exemplified this virtue as a servant in Potiphar's house, even when it cost him a prison term. Hebrews 11 is literally a "Hall of Fame" of those who were faithful to God, even at the cost of their lives. Stephen became the first Christian martyr as a result of his faithfulness to the truth of God. At the end of a long and fruitful career of service for and devoted to Christ, Paul could witness: "I have fought the good fight, I have finished the course, I have kept the faith" (II Tim. 4:7). Clarke offers a very *practical* definition of *faithfulness*.

> "fidelity"—punctuality in performing promises, conscientious carefulness in preserving what is committed to our trust, in restoring it to its proper owner, in transacting the business confided to us, neither betraying the secret of our friend nor disappointing the confidence of our employer.[14]

Second, *gentleness* is listed in this third trilogy of the *fruits of the Spirit*. Christ exemplified this virtue of gentleness, and Paul writes to the Corinthians: "Now I Paul myself urge you by the *meekness* and *gentleness of Christ* . . ." (II Cor. 10:1a). *Gentleness is meekness*, but it is *not weakness*. It has at its command the energy of the Spirit, and it is only by the Spirit's enabling that it becomes a genuine Christian characteristic. The Spirit-possessed Christian cannot be uncivil, ruthless, rude, or unmannerly to his fellows. Drummond says that good manners, or courtesy, are

---

14. *Loc. cit.*

"Love in relation to etiquette." Politeness has been defined as love in trifles. Courtesy is said to be love in little things. And the one secret of politeness is love. Love *cannot* behave itself unseemly. You can put the most untutored persons into the highest society, and if they have a reservoir of love in their heart, they will not behave themselves unseemly.... You know the meaning of the word "gentleman." It means a *gentle man*—a man who does things gently with love.[15]

It was said of Amanda Smith, the converted slave washer-woman who became a world-renowned evangelist, that though she knew nothing of the culture of the schools, she behaved with perfect grace when entertained by European royalty. Wesley says of *meekness:* "Holding all the affections and passions in even balance."[16]

The third, and final *fruit of the Spirit* in this last trilogy is *self-control.*

This virtue is well expressed in modern parlance as "built-in control." Without the power of the indwelling Spirit any man is a potential devil. Moody is reported to have said once when he observed a staggering drunk on the street: "There goes D. L. Moody, *but for the grace of God."* The author of the Proverbs said: "He who is slow to anger is better than the mighty, and he who rules his spirit, than he who captures a city" (16:32). There is no greater power in the universe, with God or man, than that of self-control. Paul saw the importance of this virtue and said: "everyone who competes in the games exercises self-control in all things. They then *do it* to receive a perishable wreath, but we an imperishable" (I Cor. 9:25, see also vv. 26-27). To disregard this admonition is to disqualify oneself for the Christian race, and may in the end lose the crown of life (II Tim. 4:7; cf. I Cor. 9:25, 27; Heb. 12:1-13; Gal. 5:16-18). Self-control in the Christian life is not a *negative, ascetic, repressive* attitude. It is a *positive, active Spirit-enabled, directed,* and *disciplined life.* It is what Paul calls a "walk by [or, "in"] the Spirit" (Gal. 5:16; cf. John 12:35; I Cor. 7:17; Eph. 5:2, 8; Phil. 3:16; Col. 2:6; 4:5).

But self-control, by the enabling of the Spirit, presupposes crucifixion of the old sinful-self, or death to the sinful nature on the cross, in order to be resurrected with Christ into the new life. Paul expresses this great truth so excellently when he says: "I have been crucified with Christ; and it is no longer I who live, but Christ lives in me: and the life which I now live in the flesh I live by faith in the Son of God, who loved me, and delivered Himself up for me" (Gal. 2:20; cf. 5:24-25).

---

15. Drummond, *op. cit.,* p. 209.
16. *Notes, op. cit.,* p. 697.

Thus, *the fruit of the Spirit* is *the harvest of the cross*! Christ's own emphatic words substantiate this great truth. "Truly, truly, I say to you, unless a grain of wheat falls into the earth and dies, it remains by itself alone; but if it dies, it bears much fruit" (John 12:24). And, again, Christ said to His disciples: "By this is My Father glorified, that you bear much fruit, and so prove to be My disciples" (John 15:8). The *Spirit-filled life* will ever be a *fruitful (fruit-filled)* life!

IV. THE GUARANTEE OF THE SPIRIT (II COR. 1:22)

The word *guarantee* is used here to express a great truth concerning the Spirit's relationship to believers, as set forth in the New Testament, though it is not the term used in the *KJV, ASV,* or the *NASB.* The *RSV,* however, does use the term *guarantee* instead of *earnest* or *pledge.* This truth is expressed in two exceptionally vivid figures conveying certain phases of the work of the Spirit in the lives of believers, namely, "the *seal of the Spirit,*" and "the *earnest of the Spirit.*" However, these two figures and the ideas they represent are very closely related and, in some occurrences at least, they are inseparable.

Further, while Paul only of the New Testament writers uses the word *earnest,* the word *seal* is a favorite term of both Paul and John, and is used exclusively by them in the New Testament. However, John uses the term only two times in relation to the Spirit. The first is in John 3:33-34 where it is used in relation to believers, and the second in John 6:27 where it is used in relation to Christ, evidently in reference to the descent of the Spirit upon Him at His baptism by John the Baptist. In the Revelation John makes frequent use of this word, but in other associations than with the Spirit. It is Paul who gives the term special significance in relation to the work of the Spirit, though he uses the word several times in other, sometimes indirectly related, connections (see Rom. 4:11; 15:28; I Cor. 9:2; II Tim. 2:19).

It is to the use of the term *earnest,* or "pledge," in relation to the Spirit that we shall give first consideration.

A. The Pledge of the Spirit

The Greek word from which our word *pledge (NASB)* derives is *arrabōn.* Souter notes that this is a word of Semitic origin, and that it means "an earnest, earnest—money, a large part of the payment, given in advance as a security that the whole will be paid afterwards."[17] However, Arndt and Gingrich, while also giving the word a Semetic origin, say that it means a

> *first installment, deposit, down payment, pledge,* that pays a part of the purchase price in advance, and so secures a legal claim to the article in question, or makes a contract valid . . . in any case, *arrabōn* is a payment which obligates the contracting party to make further payments . . . [God] *has deposited the first installment of the Spirit in our hearts*—2 Cor. 1:22. The Spirit is the *first installment* . . . Eph. 1:14.[18]

Since the word *earnest* may be little understood by many today, and "guarantee" seems to cover both ideas of the *pledge* and the *seal* of the Spirit, the word *pledge* seems best suited to our use here.

In Paul's use of the term *pledge* (*arrabōn*) in II Corinthians 1:22, when taken with the preceding verse 21, he combines three other acts of God with the pledge. Thus He says: "Now He who *establishes us* with you in Christ and *anointed us* is God, who also *sealed us and gave us the Spirit in our hearts as a pledge* [or, "down payment"]." Thus this act of God in relation to the believer is fourfold. Clarence Zahniser remarks on this passage:

> Here is a continuous confirming, an act of anointing, an act of sealing, and a pledge of the Spirit. These are not necessarily different experiences but several ways of emphasizing the varying aspects of the abiding work of the Holy Spirit. The confirming signifies a strengthening in Christ which is a constant process; the second point refers to a past anointing (*chrisas*, aorist tense) which makes us like Christ who is God's anointed (*Christos*); the third is a definite sealing (aorist) which confirms either Christian experience (Eph. 1:13), or ministerial appointment (I Cor. 9:2), though in this [later] instance the sealing is not of the Spirit; the fourth is *the earnest of the Spirit* (arrabōn), a pledge or down payment that ratifies the sale, and that gives a foretaste of the full expectation (Gen. 38:17, 18; 43:9; Prov. 6:1).[19]

Paul's second use of pledge (*arrabōn*) is in II Corinthians 5:5: "Now He who prepares us for this very purpose is God, who gave to us the Spirit as a pledge [or, "down payment"]." It will be noted from the context of this passage that what Paul is talking about is death, the resurrection of the body, and the future life of the believer with God. In short, he speaks of the assurance of the

---

17. Souter, *op. cit.*, p. 38.

18. William F. Arndt and F. Wilbur Gingrich, *A Greek-English Lexicon of the New Testament* (Chicago: Chicago University Press, 1957), p. 109.

19. Clarence Zahniser, *Wesleyan Bible Commentary*, V, 270. (Grand Rapids: Wm. B. Eerdmans Publishing Company, 1965), V. 270.

believer's immortality, and says that God has prepared us for this eventuality, and assured it to us, by giving us a *down payment* on our redemption purchased for us by Christ, in the person of the divine Spirit deposited in our hearts. Thus the guarantee of the believer's acceptance by God at the close of the present life will be the presence of the Spirit in his heart at that hour. Little wonder that among Wesley's last words on his death-bed was the exclamation: "The best of all is that God is with us."

Paul's third use of *arrabōn* ("pledge") is found in Ephesians 1:14, but in conjunction with the sealing of the Spirit in verse 13. Here is one of the most beautiful and meaningful passages that comes from the pen of the apostle Paul. However, since both the *seal* and the *pledge* of the Spirit are included in this passage we shall note only the meaning of the *pledge* here and return to the seal subsequently. Paul says that "the Holy Spirit of promise . . . is given as a pledge [or, "down payment"] of *our* inheritance [Jew and gentile Christians alike], with a view to the redemption of God's own possession, to the praise of His glory" (Eph. 1:13b-14).

Paul means that the believer's present possession of the Holy Spirit is God's *pledge* or *guarantee* that he is accepted and approved of God, and that eventually he will come into the full possession of his inheritance in Christ (cf. I Cor. 2:9; I Peter 1:3-5). The time of the final redemption of God's own possession evidently refers to the resurrection of the righteous, as the body too is redeemed.

B. The Seal of the Spirit

In three instances Paul uses the figure of a "seal" to express the work of the Spirit in the lives of believers (II Cor. 1:22; Eph. 1:13; 4:30). However, before examining these uses he makes of the *seal* as a symbol of the Spirit, let us note the meaning of this symbol.

Arndt and Gingrich note that this English word *seal* derives from the Greek *sphragizo* and it may mean "the sealing of a closed building so that it cannot be opened"; "to seal up something in order to keep it secret"; "to mark with a seal for identification"; "to mark an animal so that the mark denotes ownership and carries with it the protection of the owner." Its use in II Corinthians 1:22 signifies, in addition to a mark of identification, the enduement of power from heaven. It may mean "to attest," "certify," "acknowledge," as a seal does on a document.[20] Thus Paul is using here a very rich and

20. Arndt and Gingrich, *op. cit.*, p. 804.

meaningful word with a variety of implications.

As Paul uses the term in II Corinthians 1:22 he is thinking primarily of the divine *seal* of his apostleship which was under severe attack at Corinth and called forth this severe letter from the apostle. He makes clear that it is God who has placed upon him this mark of identification, anointed him for his apostolic office, and empowered him with His Spirit for his ministry. But Paul goes beyond the attestation of his apostleship to assure them that he belongs to God in a personal, saving relationship, the evidence of which is the *arrabōn*, or *pledge* of the Spirit in his heart.

In Ephesians 1:13 Paul's use of the term *seal* has a somewhat different meaning. As he reviews the experience of these believers he states that they "were sealed *in* Him with the Holy Spirit of promise." Thus, this was a sealing of their saving faith in Jesus Christ, the token or evidence of which was the *arrabōn* or pledge, the very Spirit Himself—*"the Holy Spirit of promise."*

Later in this Epistle Paul warns them against grieving "the Holy Spirit of God, in whom . . . [they] were sealed unto the day of redemption" (Eph. 4:30; cf. John 3:33; Rev. 22:10; Rom. 8:16; II Cor. 1:22; II Tim. 2:19). Paul likely had several things in mind in this utterance. For one thing, a seal is a token of ownership. Paul must have had this in mind when he wrote to the Galatians: "I carry on my scarred body the mark of my owner, the Lord Jesus" (6:17),[21] or as another translates the passage, "I carry on my body the scars that mark me as Jesus' slave."[22]

Western cattlemen brand the seal of ownership upon their cattle and they are thus protected by law against theft or molestation. An owner in Roman times customarily sealed his property with his signet to indicate his ownership, which guaranteed his right of claim at a later time. Likewise the Christian's seal by the Holy Spirit was God's attestation of ownership. Likely the twelve disciples who had been thus sealed at Ephesus (Acts 19:1-7) were among the readers of the Epistle and would understand well the meaning of these words.

But again, a seal suggests *authorization,* as the official seal stamped upon a document. The validity of a passport rests upon the seal of the government that issues it. In this respect Christians bear the seal

---

21. J. B. Phillips, *The New Testament in Modern English* (New York: Macmillan Company, 1958), p. 410.

22. Charles B. Williams, *The New Testament: A Private Translation in the Language of the People* (Chicago: Moody Press, 1950), p. 423.

of divine authority upon their lives that authorizes them to live in a world that is unfriendly to grace and protects them while they do so.

But a seal may also suggest *preservation.* By the operation of the Holy Spirit Christian believers are insulated against the deteriorating contamination of the world's sinfulness. However, moral purification is essential to moral preservation, just as the destruction of bacteria is essential to the preservation of fruit or vegetables under seal. This is suggested in Christ's high-priestly prayer for His disciples (see John 17:15, *RSV*). Peter is clear on this point when he reports to the first general council of the church at Jerusalem that God witnessed to the gentiles, "giving them the Holy Spirit just as he did to us" [the Jewish disciples at Pentecost, Acts 2:1-4, *RSV*]; "and he made no distinction between us and them, but *cleansed their hearts by faith*" (Acts 15:9, *RSV*).

Thus these gentile believers had heard the gospel preached, they had believed it as the Word of truth, and they were made the sons of God, in consequence of which God purified their hearts through the baptism with the Holy Spirit, sealed them as His own possession, and authorized them to become living witnesses to him in the present evil world.

But why is the Spirit here called *the Holy Spirit of promise?* He was in fact the fulfillment of the divine promise. He had been promised by God through the ancient prophets (Joel 2:28), by Jesus Himself to His disciples (John 16:7-15), and again just before His ascension (Acts 1:4), and Peter declared that the Spirit's coming on the day of Pentecost was the fulfillment of the Father's promise (Acts 2:16-18, 38-39). The Ephesian readers were among those to whom the Father's promise extended. However, the Father's promise of the Spirit also extends to every Christian believer today (Acts 2:39).

F. F. Bruce notes that we are reminded by the title "the Holy Spirit of promise" that beyond the fact of our living in the fulfillment age of God's ancient promise, our possession of the Holy Spirit is itself a promise of God's purpose to consummate the redemptive work He has begun in us as believers.[23]

Paul's third use of the expression is found in Ephesians 4:30. Here it is used in the form of a warning against *grieving* the Spirit by which they were sealed.

23. *The Epistle to the Ephesians: A Verse by Verse Exposition* (New York: Fleming H. Revell Company, 1961) p. 37.

Here Paul means that the life in Christ calls for respect and reverence for the person of the Holy Spirit (v. 30). It would appear that Paul's admonition *to grieve not the Holy Spirit of God* has a twofold implication. First, He is the Holy Spirit of God, and such a person is capable of being grieved. The believers are sealed in Him until the resurrection day of the redemption (cf. Eph. 1:13-14). To grieve Him is to break the seal and thus lose the hope and promised benefits of ultimate redemption.

Second, this admonition seems to hark back to the preceding verse, and thus it indicates that the Holy Spirit is grieved by *corrupt speech*. Therefore, right thinking and right speaking are essential to the Christian life if God's Holy Spirit is to be reverenced and honored, and the body of Christ that consists in Him is to be kept intact. To grieve a fellow Christian or cause him to stumble is to grieve the Holy Spirit and endanger His seal in the believer's life.

Chapter 13

The Holy Spirit
in the General Epistles
and the Revelation

While direct references to the Spirit in the General Epistles and Revelation are not as numerous as are found in the writings of John's Gospel, the Book of Acts, and Paul's Epistles, they are not in any sense less significant. In fact some of the richest teachings in the Bible concerning the Spirit are found in these books of the New Testament. Where the Spirit is introduced in such a way as to duplicate the treatment in previous portions of the Bible the reader will be, for the most part, referred to those earlier treatments rather than unnecessarily duplicating what has been said earlier.

I. THE HOLY SPIRIT IN THE BOOK OF HEBREWS

A. The Spirit's Warning Against Neglect of Salvation

The first mention of the Spirit in Hebrews is in 2:4. It should be noted that this mention of the Holy Spirit is found in the first of seven "Exhortations and Warnings" delivered to these Hebrew-Christian readers.[1]

---

1. The "Interludes" of combined "Exhortations and Warnings" are found in the Book of Hebrews as follows: (1) "Beware of Drifting" (2:1-4); (2) "Beware

It is indeed interesting and significant that the first direct mention of the Spirit in this great book should be by way of warning to Christian believers against drifting from their moorings in Christ. This warning is somewhat reminiscent of God's early warnings to the human race when He solemnly cautioned: "My Spirit shall not strive with man forever . . ." (Gen. 6:3a). This first "Exhortation and Warning" is placed against the background of the history of God's dealings with His people throughout the course of His redemptive plan and work.

God's witness to the world of men, but especially Israel, has been accompanied by divinely given "signs," "wonders," "miracles, or works of power," and "gifts, or *distributions* of the Holy Spirit" (Heb. 2:4). What becomes evident in these words is that all of the foregoing divine manifestations, both in the Old and the New Testament eras, have been *distributed,* or ministered by the agency of the Holy Spirit.

Thus the warning against the "neglect [of] so great a salvation" (2:3) as God has provided in Christ is made the more serious by the fact that the readers have been the recipients of these great divine manifestations ministered to them directly by the Holy Spirit. This leaves them without excuse. Clarke says: "He did not leave the confirmation of these great truths to the testimony of men; He bore His own testimony to them [through the Spirit] by *signs, wonders,* various *miracles,* and *distributions* of the Holy Ghost."[2]

B. The Spirit's Warning Against Doubting God

Likewise the next direct appearance of the Spirit is found in the second "Exhortation and Warning" which is against "doubting God" (3:7, 12). Here the Holy Spirit is represented as urging upon man the importance of immediate action in response to the revelation of God: "as the Holy Spirit says, Today if you hear His voice do not harden your hearts . . ." (3:7, 8).

God's time is always "now" for the person to whom the Spirit speaks. Thus as the word *today* is here used, it places a present

of Doubting" (3:7-19); (3) "Beware of Delaying," or "Procrastinating" (4:11-16); (4) "Beware of Spiritual Deadness" (5:11-6:12); (5) "Beware of Denying Christ" (10:19-39); (6) "Beware of Denying God's Message" (12:25-29); (7) "Beware of Departing from God" (13:9-16). See Chas. W. Carter, *The Wesleyan Bible Commentary* (Grand Rapids: Wm. B. Eerdmans Publishing Company, 1966), Vol. VI, Hebrews.

2. *Commentary on the Holy Bible,* p. 1250.

responsibility upon the readers to act in accordance with God's will. When God speaks, He releases Himself in His Word, and thus man finds himself immediately and at once confronted with all eternity. Such a confrontation cannot be ignored or denied without its hardening and deadening effect upon the spiritual sensibilities of the one so confronted. Nor does such a divine encounter allow of the chronological future. Today is always God's time, and with Him there is no tomorrow. When God speaks through His Holy Spirit, it is man's time to respond. To disregard the voice of the Spirit *today* means certain disaster tomorrow.

Clarke's perceptive insight is valuable where he says, concerning verses 7 and 8, that since these words are quoted from Psalm 95:7-8, and "were written by David, and attributed here to the Holy Ghost, it proves that David wrote by inspiration of God's Holy Spirit."[3]

C. The Spirit's Warning Against Spiritual Deadness

In the fourth "Exhortation and Warning" the author of the letter to the Hebrews reminds these Hebrew Christians that they had once been enlightened and have tasted of the heavenly gift and have been made partakers of the Holy Spirit" (6:4). The words are in the context of the author's warnings against "spiritual deadness" and the necessity of overcoming this state through obedience to God and diligent effort toward Christian maturation. The key to understanding this passage (6:1-12) is found in the exhortation, "let us press on to maturity ["perfection," ASV].

That it is actually possible, though never necessary, to have become renewed unto salvation in Christ and to have been the recipient of the Holy Spirit, but by careless or willful neglect to go on to perfection in love, and then fall away to final reprobation is the plain teaching of this passage (Heb. 6:1-8). D. D. Whedon's translation of this passage is both graphic and consistent with the context and the purpose of the epistle.

> For those that were once enlightened (Greek aorist participle) and tasted of the heavenly gift and that became partakers of the Holy Spirit, and tasted both the good word of God and powers of the incoming dispensation, and that fall away, it is impossible again to renew unto repentance, recrucifying (as they are now doing, present participle here instead of aorist) unto themselves the Son of God, and setting him forth as a public exhibition.[4]

3. *Ibid.*, p. 1253.
4. "The Epistle to the Hebrews": *Commentary on the New Testa...* York: Phillips and Hunt, 1880), V, 78.

The Cambridge Bible correctly observes on this passage, "nothing can be clearer than the fact that, but for dogmatic presuppositions, no one would have dreamed of explaining them to mean anything less than full conversion."[5] That the Holy Spirit may be grieved to the point of leaving the apostate to his lost fate while he persists in his apostasy is certainly the clear teaching of this Scripture. Again to quote the *Cambridge Bible:*

> The plain meaning of this passage is, that so long as wilful apostasy continues there is no visible hope for it. The writer is pointing out to the Hebrew Christians with awful faithfulness the fatal end of deliberate and insolent apostasy.[6]

On the other hand, there is nothing in this passage, or any other in the Bible, that teaches the impossibility of the apostate's return to God if he ceases to persist in his apostasy and by the Spirit's help pleads the mercy and restoring grace of God. The Spirit may be grieved to the point of departure, but He may also return when genuine repentance and faith are exercised toward God.

D. The Spirit Points the Way into God's Holy Presence

The obvious meaning of Hebrews 9:8 is that the Holy Spirit spoke through the divinely appointed services of the tabernacle, and perhaps the Temple later, perhaps showing the limitations of those shadowy appointments under the old Mosaic system. However, just as the Spirit revealed the limitations of the tabernacle with its appointments, so He also revealed the reality of the salvation provided in the person and work of Christ, in the new Christian system of grace.

As the Spirit signified to the ancient Israelites that the way into ̃ ̃sence of God was not open in the material, shadow-taber-
̃ ̃ pointed beyond that closed curtain barring the way into
̃ ̃ies to another way that was to be opened into the
̃ ̃d's holiness for all men, by the Great High Priest,
̃ ̃ered that presence to remain forever (9:9-14).
̃ ̃d," or pointed the worshipers to the reality,
̃ ̃rnacle was but the shadow, they could by
̃ ̃ reality and thus be saved, even under the

̃estament Commentary, comment on Hebrews

̃ws 6:7.

E. Christ Offered Himself Through the Eternal Spirit

It may be noted in passing that the absence of the article before the word *spirit* in Hebrews 9:14 has led many interpreters to the conclusion that spirit here is not in reference to the Holy Spirit.

However, Clarke's explanation of this somewhat difficult passage is commanding of respect.

> This expression is understood two ways: (1) Of the Holy Ghost himself. As Christ's miraculous conception was by the Holy Spirit, and He wrought all His miracles by the Spirit of God so His death or final offering was made through or by the eternal Spirit; and by that Spirit He was raised from the dead, I Pet. iii. 18. (2) Of the eternal Logos or Deity which dwelt in the Man Christ Jesus, through the energy of which the offering of His humanity became an infinitely meritorious victim; therefore the deity of Christ is here intended. But we cannot well consider one of those distinct from the other. It is probable that the Holy Ghost, not the Logos, is what the apostle had more immediately in view. But still we must say that the Holy Spirit, with the eternal Logos and the almighty Father, equally concurred in offering up the sacrifice of the human nature of Christ in order to make atonement for the sin of the world.[7]

On the words "Who through the eternal Spirit" Wesley remarks: "The work of redemption . . . [is] the work of the holy Trinity. Neither is the Second Person alone concerned even in the amazing condescension that was needful to complete it."[8]

F. The Spirit's Witness to the Inspiration of Scripture

In Hebrews 10:15 we have another most interesting and meaningful reference to the Holy Spirit. The *witness* of the Spirit here is twofold, namely, to the inspiration of Old Testament Scripture, and to Christ's redemptive work in the experience of the believer.

First, these words give assurance that the quotation from Jeremiah, here used to describe and confirm the finished redemptive work of Christ, was the very message that God moved the prophet to write; or in other words, that Jeremiah wrote under the inspiration of the Holy Spirit of God. Thus Christ's finished redemptive work perfectly corresponded with God's Word. In this sense Christ fulfilled prophecy (Isa. 53), as well as the law. He was thus the fulfillment of the "law and the prophets" upon which Judaism was founded.

However, these words evidently have a second and more far-reaching significance in relation to the believer's appropriation of the

---

7. *Op. cit.*, p. 1269.
8. *Op. cit.*

benefits of Christ's finished work, in the practical application or inauguration of the provisions of Christ's atonement in the experience and life of the believer. As Christ offered Himself to be the final and perfect sacrifice on the cross to open the way back to the immediate presence and fellowship of God for sinfully divorced man "through the eternal Spirit" (Heb. 9:14), so the "eternal" *Holy Spirit* now offers the benefits (*the good things*), procured by Christ's offering, to the believer. As He was the divine aid in Christ's offering, so He is now the divine administrator of the benefits of that offering to the believer.

Christ makes this truth very clear to His disciples in His closing discourses with them. In John 16 He promises that when He has returned to the Father, He will send the Holy Spirit to the believers (v. 7), and that in His relations to them, He (the Holy Spirit) will direct them into an understanding of all truth concerning Christ Himself, truth both actualized and potential (v. 14). Also He will glorify Christ in their lives by revealing to them the fruits of Christ's finished work for their spiritual benefit (vv. 14-15).

This relationship between Christ's atonement and the Holy Spirit is made explicit by Peter in his Pentecostal Day sermon recorded in Acts 2. Especially is the Pentecostal Day effusion of the Holy Spirit interpreted by Peter as the Spirit's administration of the fruits of Christ's atonement in the infant church (Acts 2:32-36, 39; cf. 1:8; 5:32; I John 5:6-10). Paul further makes this great truth explicit in its application to the individual believer in Romans 8:9-17. The apostle declares that it is the specific function of the Holy Spirit to bear "witness with our spirit that we are the children of God" (v. 16, *KJV*). J. Phillips translates these words of Paul in most vivid language thus:

> All who follow the leading of God's Spirit are God's own sons. Nor are you meant to relapse into the old slavish attitude of fear—you have been adopted into the very family circle of God and you can say with a full heart, "Father, my Father." The Spirit himself endorses our inward conviction that we really are the children of God. Think what that means. If we are his children we share his treasures, and all that Christ claims as his will belong to all of us as well! Yes, if we share in his sufferings we shall certainly share in his glory.[9]

Specifically, then, the Holy Spirit convicts the sinner of the divine condemnation of his sin and of his need of a Savior (John 16:7-11).

---

9. *The New Testament in Modern English* (New York: Macmillan Company, 1958).

He applies the regenerative efficacy of Christ's atonement to the believing penitent's inner nature (John 3:5-6). He extricates him from the power of sin (Rom. 8:11; cf. Acts 26:18), and witnesses to his acceptance by the Father (Rom. 8:16). He cleanses his inner nature from its original and acquired corruption (Rom. 15:16; Matt. 3:11; Acts 2:3; 15:8, 9). He aids him in his communion with the Father (Rom. 8:26-27). And He inwardly fortifies him against the pressures of evil from without (Acts 1:8; Eph. 3:16-17; cf. I John 4:4). All of this, and infinitely more, belongs to the executive office and work of the Holy Spirit as He dispenses to men the *good things* of Christ's atonement.

G. The Spirit's Warning Against Discounting Christ's Atonement

The final specific reference to the Spirit in Hebrews appears in the fifth "Exhortation and Warning" (10:19-39) in verses 28 and 29. Here the readers are given an exceedingly serious and solemn warning against a twofold sin, namely, the accounting of Christ's blood as a common or unholy thing, and despising and insulting the Spirit of God. The latter comes close to, if it is not identical with, the unpardonable sin against the Spirit of which Christ spoke in Matthew 12:31-32. To "insult the Spirit of grace" (v. 29b) is to cut off the soul's only avenue of access to God's saving mercy.

To be convicted, by the testimonies of two or three witnesses, of rejecting and despising the Mosaic law, resulted in the merciless execution of the offender. However, under the new covenant the sin is incomparably greater, and the judgment will be likewise incomparably greater. There he despised and rejected the *shadow*, the law. Under Christ he rejects the *real* by downgrading and depreciating the sacrifice of Christ by which he was saved, and by despising the Spirit (Holy Spirit) who administered the benefits of the atonement to his soul. Under the Mosaic law the offender suffered the punishment of physical death. Under the new covenant the offender suffers everlasting spiritual death, or separation from God.

On the author's words, "has insulted the Spirit of grace," Clarke's comment is significant.

> The apostle means the Holy Spirit, whose gifts were bestowed in the first age on believers for the confirmation of the gospel. See chap. vi. 4-6. Wherefore if one apostatized in the first age, after having been witness to these miraculous gifts, much more after having possessed them himself, he must, like the scribes and Pharisees, have ascribed

them to evil spirits, than which a greater indignity could not be done to the Spirit of God.[10]

The apostle James appears to make no specific, or explicit, reference to the Holy Spirit in his Epistle, though undoubtedly the person and work of the Spirit underlies much of his thought.

II. THE HOLY SPIRIT IN I AND II PETER

These two epistles are rich in their references to the Spirit. This is quite natural, and to be expected, when it is remembered that the author was present and witnessed the mighty effusion of the Holy Spirit on the Day of Pentecost. Also, it was Peter himself who served as the chief spokesman in explaining the meaning of the outpouring of the Spirit on that occasion. Peter, probably better than any other apostle understood the fuller significance of the person and work of the Holy Spirit. He had been with Christ and had heard His great teachings concerning the Spirit, and he had been the personal recipient of the Spirit at Pentecost, as also a witness to the Spirit's work in the lives of others at and following Pentecost.

A. The Sanctifying Work of the Holy Spirit

The apostle Peter lays the foundation for his entire epistolary writing in the person and work of the Spirit. In his very opening benediction he says that it is by *"the sanctifying work of the Spirit, that you may obey Jesus Christ and be sprinkled with His blood: May grace and peace be yours* [lit., "be multiplied for you"] *in fullest measure"* (I Peter 1:2b).

In the opinion of Bengel, I Peter 1:2 is a summary of not only this Epistle of Peter, but also of the entire plan of redemption. Bengel remarks: "The mystery of the Trinity and the economy of our salvation are intimated in this verse."[11]

Charles S. Ball says:

> It does present a significant digest of Peter's theology in which he assigns to each member of the Trinity some aspect of man's redemption. . . . The Father is regarded in the Scriptures as the Author of the plan of salvation. He has chosen us and this choice is based on what He knew to be best and was in His plan from the beginning, even "before the foundation of the world.[12]

10. *Op. cit.*, 1273.
11. As quoted by Marvin R. Vincent, *Word Studies in the New Testament* (Grand Rapids: Wm. B. Eerdmans Publishing Company, reprint, n.d.), I, 629.
12. *The Wesleyan Bible Commentary*, VI, 250.

It was in fact Peter's contention in his defense of the gospel for the gentiles before the Jewish Christian church at Jerusalem, that their acceptance by God was through their sanctification by the Spirit. He says: "the Holy Spirit fell upon them [Cornelius and his people at Caesarea, Acts 10:44-47] just as He did upon us at the beginning. . . . God therefore gave to them the same gift as He gave to us also after believing in the Lord Jesus Christ" (Acts 11:15-17). Then again Peter made the same assertion before the first general Christian Council at Jerusalem when he said: "And God, who knows the heart, bore witness to them, giving them the Holy Spirit, just as He also did to us; and He made no distinction between us and them, cleansing their hearts by faith" (Acts 15:8-9).

Ball grasps clearly the sanctifying significance of the Spirit's work in the Christian's experience when he says:

> Christians become in fact the *elect . . . in sanctification of the Spirit.* The Holy Spirit, as the agent of the Trinity, makes real in the hearts of believers what the Father has planned and the Son has provided. Here and in succeeding verses (1:15-16), Peter declares holiness of heart and life to be God's criterion for His people. Barnes aptly states that "all the evidence which any man *can* have that he is among the elect is that he *is* practically a holy man, and desires to become more so." He is one of the elect just so far as he has holiness of heart and life and no farther.[13] Paul also emphasized the same truth when he wrote: "God chose you from the beginning unto salvation in sanctification of the Spirit and belief of the truth" (II Thess. 2:13).[14]

On these words of Peter, "by the sanctifying work of the Spirit ["through sanctification of the Spirit," *KJV*]," Wesley remarks: "Through the renewing and *purifying* influences of His Spirit on their souls."[15] The moral results of the Spirit's sanctifying work in the experience of the believer become evident in Peter's words: "Since you have in obedience to the truth purified your souls ["through the Spirit," *KJV*] for a sincere [lit., "unhypocritical"] love of the brethren, fervently love one another from the heart [Some mss. read, "a clean heart"] (v. 22).

Ball notes that while the word *purified* does sometimes suggest ritual or ceremonial purification both in the Old Testament (Josh. 3:5; I Chron. 15:12; I Sam. 16:5), and in the New (John 11:55; Acts 21:24, 26; 24:18), it is not limited to this meaning. He thinks rightly that "in this context it seems more appropriate to interpret purifica-

---

13. John Albert Barnes, *Notes on the New Testament:* "James–Jude, ed. Robert Few (Grand Rapids: Baker Book House, reprint, 1962), p. 112.
14. *Op cit.*, p. 250.
15. *Op. cit.* (reprint), p. 873.

tion as a moral and spiritual [experience] rather than as a ceremonial or ritualistic exercise, for it issues in *"an unfeigned love of the brethren."* One recalls Peter's summary of the abiding results of the baptism with the Holy Spirit, whether upon Jews or gentiles (Acts 15:8, 9).[16] Wesley takes Peter's words in the same light when, understanding the word "Spirit" to be implied in the passage, he says,

> who bestows upon you freely, both obedience and purity of heart, and *unfeigned love of the brethren,* go on to still higher degrees of love. *Love one another fervently*—With the most strong and tender affection; and yet *with a pure heart*—Pure from any spot of unholy desire or inordinate passion.[17]

B. The Holy Spirit in Prophecy

The apostle Peter has no doubts about the Spirit's inspiration of Old Testament Scripture, and especially the prophecies of those Scriptures. On the Day of Pentecost it was Peter who quoted the prophecy of Joel concerning the Spirit (Acts 2:16-21), and he identified that prophecy with what had just happened in the mighty effusion of the Holy Spirit on that occasion. Thus we should not be surprised to hear him saying in this epistle:

> As to this salvation, the prophets who prophesied of the grace that *would come* to you made careful search and inquiry, seeking to know what person or time the Spirit of Christ within them was indicating as He predicted the sufferings of Christ and the glories to follow. It was revealed to them that they were not serving themselves but you in these things which now have been announced to you through those who preached the gospel to you by the Holy Spirit sent from heaven—things into which angels long to look (I Peter 1:10-12).

Four things concerning the Spirit stand out in bold relief in the foregoing passage. First, Peter identifies the Spirit in the prophets' utterances with Christ Himself when he refers to Him as "the Spirit of Christ" (v. 11a). Paul likewise identifies the Spirit with Christ (II Cor. 3:17); and Chadwick, as we have seen, refers to the Holy Spirit as the "Other Self of Christ."[18] Second, in contrast to the usual Old Testament expressions that the *Spirit came upon, rushed upon,* and other similar forms indicating an *external* rather than *internal* experi-

16. Ball, *op. cit.,* p. 256.
17. *Op. cit.* (reprint), p. 876.
18. *Op. cit.,* p. 21.

ence of the Spirit in the Old Testament, Peter understands the prophets' experiences of the Spirit as *internal.* He speaks of "the Spirit of Christ *within them.*" The Spirit was not simply an influence bearing upon the prophets from without and using them as instr·. ments to convey God's messages of future events, as though they were mere penmen in a mechanical dictation of Scripture. They were, as Peter understands them, men *in* whom the Spirit dwelt *internally.* Thus the Spirit inspired their minds and directed their thoughts to understand, at least in part, the future events of which they wrote. The Spirit *signified* the messages of God to their minds, while at the same time allowing them to express those revealed truths through their own personalities, cultures, thought-forms, and vocabularies.

The Spirit inspired, illuminated, and directed them *from within,* rather than arbitrarily using them as impersonal instruments through which to channel His revelations. Only such a view of the inspiration of Scripture can account for the rich variety of vocabulary, thought-forms, and literature as are found in both the Old and the New Testaments.

The third thing that strikes us in this passage is Peter's statement that the gospel, foretold by the prophets, had been announced to his readers "through those who preached the gospel to you by *the Holy Spirit sent from heaven*" (I Peter 1:12). This is at once suggestive of Christ's promise to His disciples in Acts 1:8, and of Luke's description of the Spirit's effusion on the Day of Pentecost where he says, "And . . . *there came from heaven* a noise like a violent rushing wind . . . and *they were all filled with the Holy Spirit . . .*" (Acts 2:2-4). Christ had promised that when He returned to the Father He would send the Holy Spirit to abide *in* and *with* them forever (John 14:16-17). Peter is highly sensitive to the supernatural origin and character of both the Holy Spirit and the gospel of Christ to which the Spirit witnesses.

But a *fourth* characteristic of the Spirit revealed in this passage reflects Peter's memory of Christ's own words concerning the Holy Spirit's mission in the world. Jesus said to His disciples that when the Holy Spirit comes He will *bear witness to Me*" (John 15:26b). And again, He said: "He will not speak on His own initiative . . . He shall glorify Me; for He will take of Mine, and will disclose it to you" (John 16:13, 14).

Likewise, Peter says that in the ministry of the Spirit through the

Old Testament prophets, "He predicted the sufferings of Christ and the glories to follow" (I Peter 1:11). Of these glories, Wesley notes: "the glory of His resurrection, ascension, exaltation, and the effusion of His Spirit; the glory of the last judgment, and of His eternal kingdom; and also the glories of His grace in the hearts and lives of Christians."[19] Christ and His redemptive work is always and ever the object of the Spirit's witness. Ball sums up this passage concerning Peter's treatment of the Spirit in the following admirable manner.

> For Peter the testimony of the prophets was authoritative and final. On the day of Pentecost he appealed to Joel and David (Acts 2:16-21, 25-28). Subsequently he cited Moses (Acts 3:22), and also said: "Yea and all the prophets from Samuel and them that followed after, as many as have spoken, they also told of these days" (Acts 3:24). Relative to Peter's references to the prophets, Professor Moorehead said: "He was at no loss to discover the Messiah in the words of the prophets. He saw in them unmistakable predictions of His advent, His sufferings, and His glories."[20] And this spiritual insight of the prophets was attributed to the Holy Spirit, called the *Spirit of Christ . . . in them.* Inspired by the Holy Spirit, Peter in referring to the prophets and their messages, "brings forward with deliberation and skill the thought of the unity of the two Testaments."[21]

> With notes of mystery and victory, Peter closes his exposition about the revelation of God's grace which portrays the ministry of the Father, the Son, and the Holy Spirit and commands the faith and perseverance of those who believe.[22]

Clarke adds a rich note to this passage of Peter when he says,

> the redemption procured by Him for mankind . . . [was] made known, in a general way, by the prophets; but they themselves did not know the time when these things were to take place, nor the people among and by whom He was to suffer. They therefore "inquired accurately or earnestly," and *searched diligently. The glory that should follow.* Not only the glory of His resurrection, ascension, exaltation, and the effusion of His Spirit; but that grand manifestation of God's infinite love to the world in causing the gospel of His Son to be everywhere preached, and the glorious moral changes which should take place in the world under that preaching, and the final glorification of all them who had here received the report and continued faithful unto death.[23]

---

19. *Op. cit.* (reprint), p. 875.
20. William G. Moorehead, *Outline Studies in the New Testament, Catholic Epistles and Revelation* (New York: Revell, 1910), p. 48.
21. B. W. Beare, *The First Epistle of Peter,* rev. ed. (Oxford: Basil, Blackwell, and Mott, 1958), p. 64.
22. *Op. cit.,* p. 253.
23. *Op. cit.,* pp. 1300, 1301.

C. The Holy Spirit in the Inspiration of the Scriptures

1. Peter's Conviction of the Spirit-Inspired Scriptures

Peter is ever certain of the God-givenness of the divine revelation—Holy Scripture. Just as the inspired prophecy of Joel formed the basis for Peter's moving message on the Day of Pentecost (Acts 2:16-21), so now in his second Epistle he expresses his firm confidence in Scripture as having come from God, since it was confirmed by God's own identification of Christ as its fulfillment, which divine identification he had personally heard on the Mount of Transfiguration (Matt. 17:1-8; Mark 9:2-8).

In this Transfiguration event Peter had seen the divine identification of the Old Testament prophecies with their New Testament fulfillment in Christ as Moses and Elijah appeared together with Christ, and God's voice out of heaven said, "This is My beloved Son, with whom I am well pleased; hear Him" (Matt. 17:5). Thus God was saying that Christ was the redemptive fulfillment of that which the Old Testament prophets, represented by the presence of Moses and Elijah on the Mount with Him, had predicted.

However, the continuity of the divine redemptive revelation becomes even clearer when we remember that Christ's "inner circle" of disciples, Peter, James, and John, were also present to hear and witness the events of this most significant occasion. They were to receive from Christ the commission to proclaim His redemptive work to the Jews first and then to the whole world of the nations after their enduement with the Spirit at Pentecost. It is of further interest that what Peter and the other disciples heard discussed between Moses, Elijah, and Christ on this mountain was Christ's redemptive work through His cross, resurrection, and ascension.

It is in Luke's account of the event that we learn the nature of the conversation that took place between Moses, Elijah, and Christ. Luke records: "And behold, two men were talking with Him; and they were Moses and Elijah, who, appearing in glory [or, "splendor"], were speaking of *His departure which He was about to accomplish* at Jerusalem" (9:30-31). Two most significant things emerge from Luke's account of this event in relation to our present consideration. First, they were discussing Christ's *departure*. Our English word *departure* comes from the Greek word *ĕxodos, which means* "going out," "departure from a place," or "death." The word is used here in Luke 9:31 of Christ's death, and it is used by Peter of his own anticipated death, or "departure" [*tēnèmēn ĕxodon tēn*] (II Peter 1:15).

Likewise, the same word is used of Christ's *departure,* or death, when Luke says Moses and Elijah spoke with Him of *His departure* [*ĕxodon—aŭtou*] (9:31). Now this is the same word used for the name of the second book of the Old Testament—*Exodus.* And it is the same word that is used to describe the redemptive deliverance of Israel from their more than 400 years of bondage in Egypt. So what Moses, Elijah, and Christ talked about on the Mount of Transfiguration was Christ's victorious *redemptive* death, or *Exodus.*

His "going out" through His cross, resurrection, and ascension in which He won not only His own deliverance over Satan's power ["death"], but, like Moses, He won the same deliverance for all His people. Consequently to Christ and Christian believers death is no longer the victor but rather the vanquished—no more than a *passageway* from the present life to the future. It is but a tunnel illumined by the light that radiates from God at the other end.

However, Luke uses another most significant expression concerning Christ's death, of which they spoke on the Mount. He says they "were speaking of His *departure* [*ĕxodos*] which He was about to *accomplish* at Jerusalem. Now this English word *accomplish* comes from the Greek *plērō* which means "to fill up to the full," or "fulfill," "completion," "to carry out." Thus Luke says that they were speaking of Christ's *plēroun* or fulfillment of the redemptive plan. This suggests to us that even in the darkest hour of His death on the cross, Christ was on the offensive and master of the situation.

At no time in His life was He ever driven to the defensive. Even in death itself we hear Christ saying with His last word on earth, Father "into Thy hands I commit My spirit. And having said this He breathed His last" (Luke 23:46). Likewise, in His great parable of the Good Shepherd Christ had declared His victory over death in advance of that event when He said, "I lay down My life that I may take it again. No one has taken [lit., "takes"] it away from me, but I lay it down on My own initiative. I have authority to lay it down, and I have authority to take it up again" (John 10: 17, 18a).

In fact the nature of Christ's death, or "going out" [*ĕxodon*] from this world can be summed up, as He presents it in this parable, in a threefold manner. *First,* His death is *voluntary:* "I lay down My life. . . . I lay it down of My own initiative" (John 10:17, 18). *Second,* His death is *vicarious* "the good shepherd lays down His life *for the sheep.* . . . I lay down My life for the sheep" (John 10:11,

15). *Third,* Christ's death is *victorious:* "I lay down My life *that I may take it again.* . . . I have authority to lay it down, and *I have authority to take it up again"* (John 10:17, 18b).

Thus Spirit-inspired Scripture ("the prophetic Word") is made *more sure* because Christ answered to, and fulfilled in His own person, those prophecies.

2. The Effect of Spirit-Inspired Scripture upon Believers

A *second* consideration that emerges from these words of Peter, concerning Spirit-inspired Scripture, is its effect upon those who believe them. He says to his reader: "to which you do well to pay attention as to a lamp shining in a dark place, until the day dawns and the morning star arises in your hearts" (II Peter 1:19b). There can be no greater final evidence of the inspiration of the Bible than the transforming influence which it has upon the believers, those who believingly "pay attention" to them. Somewhere Roy L. Smith, formerly editor of the *Methodist Advocate,* records Wesley's evidence for the inspiration of Scripture thus: "The proof of the inspiration of the Scriptures is their power to inspire." He then quotes Wesley as follows:

> I beg leave to give a short clear strong argument for the divine inspiration of the Holy Scriptures. The Bible must be the invention of good men or angels, bad men or devils, or of God.
> 1. It could not be the invention of good men or angels, for they neither would nor could make a book and tell lies all the time they were writing it, saying "Thus saith the Lord," when it was their own invention.
> 2. It could not be the invention of bad men or devils for they could not make a book which commands all duty, forbids all sins, and condemns their own souls to hell for all eternity.
> 3. Therefore I draw the conclusion that the Bible must be given by divine inspiration.

God's Spirit—inspired Word is always and everywhere "as a lamp shining in a dark place," and when it is mixed with faith on the part of the recipients a new "day dawns and the morning star arises in . . . [men's] hearts" (II Peter 1:19b; cf. John 1:4-5, 7-9; Acts 26:18; Eph. 5:13-14).

3. The Revelation of God's Mind in Spirit-Inspired Scripture

We come to the *third* consideration of the inspiration of Scripture. Peter says: "But know this *first of all,* that no prophecy of Scripture is [or, "can properly be"] a matter of one's own interpretation, for no prophecy was ever made by an act of human will" (II Peter 1:20-21a). The *KJV* would seem to make clearer the meaning of this utterance where it says "that no prophecy of the Scripture is of any *private* interpretation." The reason for Peter's assertion here is found in verse 21: "for no prophecy was ever made by an act of human will, but men moved by the Holy Spirit spoke from God," or as the *RSV* renders these words: "because no prophecy ever came by the impulse of man, but men moved by the Holy Spirit spoke from God."

Thus Peter lays down as the *first principle of hermeneutics* the recognition and conviction (*"knowing this"*) that in Scripture we are confronted with the mind and thought of God revealed to men. Since the author of any book is its best, and perhaps only reliable interpreter, the one who would understand aright the divine revelation given in the Bible is thrown back upon its author, the Holy Spirit, for enlightenment and instruction in righteousness. A second consideration is that since Scripture is of divine, and not human, origin it reflects the infinite, rational mind of its author. Therefore, when properly interpreted and understood, by the aid of the Holy Spirit, it may be rightly expected that the entire divine revelation given in Scripture will reflect the continuity and consistency of the infinite, rational mind of their divine author. This rules out once and for all the *private* or personal interpretation of any portion of the Bible that would bring that portion of Scripture interpreted into conflict with the overall divine revelation.

When critical scholars, under the guise of the so-called scientific approach to Scripture, interpret it in such a manner as to bring its essential saving truths into conflict and contradiction they become guilty of two serious errors. First, they set up *changing, factual, scientific knowledge* above the *ultimate truth* of God itself and thus insult the Holy Spirit who revealed God's rational mind in Scripture. This may be done in sincerity and honesty, or it may be an expression of intellectual pride. But in either event it fails to recognize that by its very nature scientific facts are always subject to error and change, since they are descriptive of changing phenomena, and therefore as such factual data will necessarily demand correction, alteration, or extension as new facts appear. To equate such factual data with the ultimate truth of God revealed in Scripture is to reduce God to a natural phenomenon and make Him subservient to the scientific knowledge of man. This is plainly another occurrence of the age-old disposition of proud man to supplant God by himself. It is also, of course, a form of human prejudice, since it prejudges the divine revelation on the basis of inadequate factual knowledge, rather than humbly, prayerfully, and patiently searching Scripture, with the aid of the Spirit, to discover the ultimate truth of God.

However, such an approach to the Bible commits a yet more serious error—the age-old error of the Roman Catholic Church. Long before the scientific era the Roman Catholic Church exalted the conciliar decisions and papal utterances to a position above the judgment of God as revealed in His Word, and thus made God and His revelation subservient to the wishes and will of men who sit in judgment. In its practical outworking there is really nothing new or *essentially* different about the foregoing type of so-called, scientific approach to the Bible from that of the age-old Roman Catholic position. Man simply judges God rather than submitting to God's judgment.

On the other hand, Peter's words "that no prophecy of the Scripture is of any private interpretation," or a matter of one's own [or, "private"] interpretation, are a warning against careless, unscholarly, or fanatical interpretation or use of Scripture out of context.

Again it is necessary to distinguish between the Spirit-inspired record, and what is sometimes said in that divinely inspired record. Here is where the dictation theory of inspiration sometimes runs into serious problems. Certainly no one would wish to assign the words of Satan in Job to God. Yet the inclusion of those words in a divinely inspired record is necessary to understand the entire picture of satanic subtlety against which man finds himself pitted.

Ball takes note of several different views of Peter's words that "no prophecy of Scriptures is a matter of one's own interpretation." However, he concludes that "the simplest view, in the light of the grammar and context, is that prophecy is not the product of human origin, and that the following verse (v. 21) is an amplification of the principle stated in verse 20."[24] However, since the word *private* comes from the Greek *idios,* meaning "one's own," while *interpretation* is from the Greek *epilusis* meaning "loosening" or "untying, as a hard knot,"[25] it seems reasonable that Peter's idea may very well be

---

24. *Op. cit.,* p. 291.
25. Vincent, *op. cit.,* IV, 688.

that a correct understanding of any Scripture requires a contextual consideration. This conclusion would require consideration not only of the immediate context, but a harmonization with the entire Biblical revelation. In any event, since all Scripture is of divine origin, the aid of the divine author, the Holy Spirit, is essential to a correct, interpretation of what He revealed.

Ball has a perceptive insight on Peter's statement that "men moved by the Holy Spirit spoke from God" (v. 21). He says:

> This reference to the Holy Spirit is the only one in Second Peter, but it contains one of the greatest teachings about His work to be found in the Bible. The passage supplements the teaching about the Holy Spirit given in I Peter 1:11-12.
>
> Thus, in the first section of his epistle, Peter has laid the ground work for his condemnation of heresy by a strong presentation about true knowledge. This he did by showing that knowledge is the gift of God (vv. 1-4); it must become fruitful and practical (vv. 5-11); and finally, this knowledge is grounded in apostolic teaching and prophecy inspired by the Holy Spirit (vv. 12-21).

III. THE HOLY SPIRIT IN JOHN'S FIRST EPISTLE

The first of John's three epistles *only* contains explicit references to the Spirit. In this epistle there are six direct references to the Spirit, some of which appear to reflect John's earlier teaching on the Spirit in his Gospel.

A. The Spirit As God's Gift of Assurance

John's first direct reference to the Spirit in this epistle is found in 3:24: "And we know by this that He abides in us, by the Spirit which He has given us."

Certain great truths concerning the Spirit emerge from this passage. First, John speaks of the Spirit as the believer's assurance of salvation. In his Gospel John records Christ as saying that the Spirit will abide with His disciples forever (John 14:16). On the Day of Pentecost the believers were all *filled* with the Holy Spirit, a fact which speaks of an inner personal experience. John confirms this reality by saying that "He [the Spirit] abides in us." Again in his Gospel John records Jesus as saying to His disciples that "He [the Spirit] abides with you, and *will* be *in* you" (John 14:17b). That promise finds its fulfillment in the believer's experience of the inner *abiding presence* of the Spirit (cf. I Cor. 3:16, 17; 6:19). This is the believer's "witness of the Spirit" to his personal saving relationship. On this inner assurance of salvation by the "witness of the Spirit" Wesley is definite and explicit. He says: "by the witness of the Spirit, I mean, an inward impression on the soul, whereby the Spirit of God immediately and directly witnesses to my spirit, that I am a child of God . . . and I, even I, am reconciled to God."[26] On the question of the *evidences* for the *certainty* of the Spirit's witness to personal salvation, Wesley says further:

> "But how shall I know that my spiritual senses are rightly disposed?" This also is a question of vast importance; for if a man mistake in this, he may run on in endless error and delusion. "And how am I assured that this is not my case; and that I do not mistake the voice of the Spirit?" Even by the testimony of your own spirit: by "the answer of a good conscience toward God." By the fruits which He hath wrought in your spirit, you shall know the testimony of the Spirit of God. Hereby you shall know that you are in no delusion, that you have not deceived your own soul. The immediate fruits of the Spirit, ruling in the heart, are "love, joy, peace, bowels of mercies, humbleness of mind, meekness, gentleness, long-suffering." And the outward fruits are, the doing good to all men; the doing no evil to any; and the walking in the light—a zealous, uniform obedience to all the commandments of God.[27]

Many will readily agree with Wesley that the Spirit gives inner assurance of a *saving relationship* with Christ. However, the further question arises concerning the inner witness of the Spirit to a crisis experience of sanctification, or heart cleansing. Likewise Wesley is clear and definite on this issue. By a question and answer presentation he says:

> Q. But how do you know, that you are sanctified, saved from your inbred corruption?
> A. I can know it no otherwise than I know that I am justified. "Hereby know we that we are of God," in either sense, "by the Spirit that he hath given us."
> We know it by the witness and by the fruit of the Spirit. And, First, by the witness. As, when we were justified, the Spirit bore witness with our spirit, that our sins were forgiven; so, when we were sanctified he bore witness, that they were taken away. Indeed, the witness of sanctification is not always clear at first; (as neither is that of justification;) neither is it afterward always the same, but, like that of justification, sometimes stronger and sometimes fainter. Yea, and sometimes it is withdrawn. Yet, in general, the latter testimony of the Spirit is both as clear and as steady as the former.[28]

---

26. *Sermons:* "The Witness of tne Spirit": I, 2-4 (S., II, 344-45).
27. *Ibid.*, I, II, 9-14 (S, I, 216-18).
28. *Work*, "A Plain Account of Christian Perfection" 25 (X1, 420).

326   *THE PERSON AND MINISTRY OF THE HOLY SPIRIT*

In the second instance John speaks of the Spirit as a divine gift to believers: "the Spirit He has given us." This is not a new truth with John or other New Testament writers. In his Gospel he has recorded many of Christ's promises to give the Spirit. In the Book of Acts we find the fulfillment of those promises. And in the epistles of Paul the gift of the Spirit figures large. The Spirit is not something that belongs to man's natural constitution. He is something adventitious—something that comes directly from God into the life of the believer as a divine bestowal. In the gift of the Spirit God gives Himself to the believer. Leo G. Cox writes of this abiding relationship as follows:

> Union with Christ involves a mutual abiding. The Christian *abideth in him* and Christ abides in the Christian. "The Omnipotent dwells in the believer, and the believer dwells in the Gibraltar of God's strength."[29] Paul recognized this same union when he used the terms "in Christ" and "Christ in you" (Col. 1:27-28).
> Further evidence for this mutual abiding is *the Spirit which he gave* (see 4:13). The indwelling of God in the believer is in the person of the Holy Spirit (cf. Acts 2:4). The Spirit witnesses to this union (5:7; cf. Rom. 8:16) by making His presence known. Consequently the believer has confidence before God, because he possesses loving obedience, loving trust, and the voice of the Spirit.[30]

B. The Criteria for Certain Knowledge of the Spirit

1. The Believer's Certainty of Religious Knowledge Through the Spirit

In his first epistle John reflects his concern that Christian believers possess a *certain knowledge* of their relationship with God, as indeed he does in all his writings. A characteristic expression with this apostle is the word *know*. It runs like a golden thread throughout his Gospel and epistles.[31] In the passage under consideration John is concerned that his readers should not be mislead by *other spirits* professing to be divine. Thus he writes:

> By this you know the Spirit of God: every spirit that confesses that Jesus Christ is come in the flesh is from God; and every spirit that does not confess Jesus is not from God; and this is the spirit of

29. Daniel Steel, *Half-hours with St. John's Epistles* (Chicago: Christian Witness Company, 1901), p. 92.
30. *The Wesleyan Bible Commentary* VI, 346, 47.
31. See James Strong, *Strong's Exhaustive Concordance* (Marshallton, Del.).

antichrist, of which you have heard that it is coming, and how it is already in the world" (I John 4:2-3).

Certain special emphases emerge from this statement of John, namely, certain *knowledge, divine identification,* and *secular,* if not demonic, *differentiation.* We shall consider these emphases in the foregoing order.

John's special emphasis upon the certainty of religious knowledge obviously arises out of present opposing anti-Christian forces. According to tradition this apostle outlived all the other apostles and probably died about A.D. 100. His epistles were most likely written during his last years, near the close of the first century according to Westcott.[32] By this time there was a fairly well developed form of Gnosticism which was especially prevalent in western Asia Minor, the region of the location of the churches to which John wrote his three epistles. This religious error had invaded, if indeed it had not arisen within these churches, and it seriously threatened the very foundations of Christian faith.

Now the Greek expression which John uses here for "you know" is *ginōskete,* and his word *know* is from the Greek verb form *gnōskō,* meaning "I am taking in knowledge," "I come to know," "learn: *aorist* tense, I ascertain," "realize."[33] Thus John's use of this word has a special significance for his readers and for all Christians. What he seems to suggest is that genuine knowledge of Christian experience does not arise from within the believer, but that it invades his mind and spiritual consciousness from *without* and is thus impressed upon his mind and deepest spiritual consciousness. In other words, Christian knowledge has a supernatural origin and is God's gift to the believer in Christ, though he must open himself to the reception of this divine gift. This knowledge of which John writes is something quite different from scientific or philosophical knowledge which has its origin in the senses or the speculations of the mind. Right here is the crux of the problem with which John is dealing.

The *Gnostics*[34] (lit., "the knowing ones") were a class of professed Christians who laid claim to a superior, secret, mystical knowl-

---

32. Brooke Foss Westcott, *The Epistles of St. John* (Cambridge and London: Macmillan Company Publishers, 1886), xxxi-xxxii.
33. Souter, *op. cit.,* p. 56.
34. The interested reader will find an excellent brief treatment of Gnosticism in Lars P. Qualbens, *A History of the Christian Church* (New York: Thomas Nelson and Sons, 1942), pp. 74-79.

edge attained by the outreach of their own minds. Thus they taught a professed salvation by knowledge, rather than by faith in Christ and His mediatorial work. In fact since they claimed that by their superior intellectual acumen they were able to penetrate and acquire secrets of God, they needed no mediator. Through their professed occult knowledge some of these Gnostics actually professed identity with divinity, and thus these were pure pantheists.

2. The Problem of Religious Certainty in Relation to Gnosticism

But another failure of their professed knowledge was that all matter, and consequently the human body itself, is evil. Intellectual transcendence of matter and the physical body was for them man's highest attainment. Two, in reality three, quite different methods were employed by different schools of the Gnostics in an attempt to attain their goal of freedom from the limitations of this evil material body. One branch attempted to deny the reality of body and all physical matter entirely by relegating it to a phantom, or something existing in empirical evidence only, but without any substantial reality.

The modern successors of this branch of Gnosticism will be recognized as the so-called Christian Scientists. The other two schools of Gnosticism admitted the real existence of matter, but in both instances they considered body as something in which evil inhered and consequently salvation could be attained only through deliverance from the mind-inhibiting evil body. These two schools sought deliverance through two quite opposing methods.

One school concluded that by denying the physical senses their pleasurable satisfactions they would die a natural death by reason of starvation and the spirit, or mind, would be freed from the body to attain its occult knowledge. This quite naturally led to extreme forms of asceticism which in turn gave origin to monasticism, which eventually expressed itself within the church in the monastery, the nunnery, celibacy in the priesthood, and various other forms of unnatural self-denial within the Roman church.

Nor should it be overlooked that the influence of this movement has persisted in some forms of Protestantism to the present. This is especially characteristic of certain extreme tendencies to legalism within certain branches of the so-called holiness movement. That this Gnostic influence first invaded early Christianity from its Alexandrian base and then spread to the north and west is well known.

However, that the Alexandrian school of thought was greatly influenced by Indian Hindu asceticism as well as Platonic thought long before the rise of Christianity, and Neo-Platonism at a later time, is not as well known, though equally real.

The other branch of Gnosticism also held that matter, and thus body, was evil and consequently a hindrance to the mind's occult knowledge. However, this branch pursued an opposite course for the destruction of the evil, material body. It held that by indulging the sense pleasures of the body they could be surfeited and thus destroyed. Consequently they taught and practiced sensual indulgence as a method of destroying the body and thus freeing the spiritual, or mental for its attainment of occult knowledge. The contemporary position of such relativistic ethicists as John A. T. Robinson approximates this teaching.[35]

Now by the time of John's writing of his epistles these various forms of Gnosticism had invaded certain sections of the Christian church and threatened to destroy its very existence. Whether these so-called Christian Gnostics were still working within the churches to which John wrote his epistle, as some suppose, or threatening it from without, as in the views of other scholars, it was against this background that the apostle wrote with a view to saving and securing the faith of his followers. Thus *genuine Christian knowledge* as the *gift of God's revelation through the Spirit,* in opposition to the occult, humanistic knowledge of these Gnostics was the object of John's writing.

But it should be noted further that the Gnostic teaching, of whatever branch, struck directly at the heart of the Christian faith, namely, the incarnation of Jesus Christ. If matter was unreal then Christ's body was a mere phantom, and thus God did not appear in the flesh, or bodily form. If, on the other hand, matter was allowed, but regarded as evil *per se,* then it would have been beneath the dignity of God to assume a sinful, material body. So in either case they denied the incarnation.

But, incidentally, it should be noted that this error struck at another great essential of the Christian faith, namely, the resurrection of Jesus Christ. If matter and body were unreal then the idea of a physical resurrection would be utterly absurd. If matter and body were real, but evil *per se,* then it would be quite as absurd that an evil

---

35. *Christian Freedom in A Permissive Society* (Philadelphia: Westminster Press, 1970).

body should be resurrected to hinder the salvation of the soul through humanistic, intellectual, occult wisdom. Thus in either event both the incarnation and the resurrection were ruled out of their pseudo-Christian philosophy. It was likely against this background that Paul wrote his great defense of the doctrine of the resurrection in I Corinthians 15.

In the light of the foregoing situation, John declares that a true Christian believer's knowledge and experience of the Spirit's witness to personal salvation may be tested against faith in the incarnation of Jesus Christ. He says: "By this we know [or, "distinguish"] the Spirit of God" from false spirits because that "every spirit that confesses that Jesus Christ has come in the flesh is from God; and every spirit that does not confess Jesus [in the flesh] is not from God; and this is the *spirit* of the antichrist, of which you have heard that it is coming, and now it is already in the world" (I John 4:2-3).

The problem with which John is dealing is one of "spirits." The Gnostics who deny the reality or value of bodily matter are vying for the faith of the Christian believers for their position that salvation is via occult spiritual knowledge without the necessity of the *God-man* mediator. Thus in effect these Gnostics are claiming to be divine spirits and threatening to supplant the Holy Spirit who represent Christ the mediator in their lives. The question in the minds of the belivers, which John is answering, is how can they be sure that they are following the true Spirit of God. John answers that question by saying that the spirit that represents the incarnate Christ is the Spirit of God, any spirit that denies the incarnate Christ is the enemy of Christ and Christianity—in fact such a spirit is the spirit of antichrist.

In verses 12-13 the same argument applies to the same problem, though amplified somewhat. In verse 12 John seems to deny the claim of the Gnostics that through their occult knowledge they know God apart from Christ's mediation.

In I John 5:6, 7 John further amplifies his argument against the Gnostic heresy by emphasizing the fact that Christ was more than a temporary human-divine representative by reason of His baptism and divine approval under John the Baptist's ministry, as some of the Gnostics taught. Thus he emphasizes the truth of Christ's incarnation by saying, "This is the one who came by water *and blood,* Jesus Christ; not with the water ["water baptism"] only, but with the water and with [lit., "in"] the blood." Here John means to say that Christ was the true incarnation of God by reason of the fact that He was conceived and born of human generation by the virgin Mary who conceived by the supernatural intervention of the Holy Spirit. Then he adds that the foregoing fact is attested by the divine Spirit Himself: "And it is the Spirit who bears witness, because the Spirit is the truth" (v. 7).

There seems to be a threefold witness of the Spirit involved in John's words. He was a witness to the incarnation of God in Christ by reason that Christ was begotten in the womb of Mary by the Holy Spirit. He bore witness to Christ's divine Sonship at His baptism by John the Baptist when the Spirit descended upon Him in the form of a dove, and the Spirit bore witness to the incarnation of God in Christ in the hearts of the believers. Thus the Spirit's threefold witness met the requirements of the Mosaic law and established the truth of Christ's incarnation and Saviorship in the hearts of the believers.

John climaxes his argument with a summary statement in verse 8 that "there are three that bear witness, the Spirit and the water and the blood; and the three are in agreement." It may be added that John may have in mind, in addition to Christ's birth by a human mother, the further evidence that His body was a true human body by reason of His blood shed on the cross. It is highly significant that John only of the four Gospel narrators says that when the soldiers broke the legs of the crucified thieves on their crosses, they intended to do likewise to Jesus,

> but coming to Jesus, when they saw that He was already dead, they did not break His legs; but one of the soldiers pierced His side with a spear, and immediately *there came out blood and water* (19:33-34).

Thus the shed blood of Christ on the cross bore witness to His humanity, as the empty tomb bore witness three days later to His divinity through His victory over death. Then this apostle, wishing to leave no doubt in the minds of his readers concerning the evidence for Christ's incarnation which he has presented, adds his personal testimony. "And he who has seen has borne witness, and his witness is true; and he knows that he is telling the truth, so that you also may believe" (19:35).

IV. THE SPIRIT IN THE EPISTLE OF JUDE

Jude makes two references only to the Spirit in his brief epistle— one negative and the other positive. In his negative reference he obviously refers to the same class of Gnostics against whom John argued. He declares that "these are the ones who cause divisions, worldly [or, "natural"] minded devoid of the Spirit" (v. 19). Positively he exhorts the believers: "But you, beloved, building yourselves up on your most holy faith; praying in the Holy Spirit." This exhortation of Jude concerning prayer in the Spirit is quite fully developed by Paul in Romans 8:23-27, to which the reader is referred in the chapter on "The Spirit in Paul's Epistles."

V. THE SPIRIT IN THE BOOK OF REVELATION

Let it be observed from the very outset of this brief treatment of the Spirit in the last book of the Bible that the author's purpose is in no way an attempt to interpret the message of this great book, or any part of it beyond the place and meaning of the Spirit as He appears in the several instances.

A. The Apostle John in the Spirit: "I was in the Spirit on the Lord's day" (Rev. 1:10a)

It was indeed fitting that preparatory to the great vision, or succession of visions, which the apostle John was about to receive he should have been *in the Spirit*. In fact any servant of God who has a special message to receive from God or mission to perform for God can only succeed as he is *in* the Spirit of God. There are two very important features of this initial experience of John on the Isle of Patmos. The first is suggested by his relation to the Spirit of God. We have noted that from Pentecost onward, especially, the usual New Testament expression indicates the Spirit's *indwelling* presence. However, John's declaration is that *he was in the Spirit*. This is indeed reminiscent of the Old Testament prophets' preparation for and during their special prophetic experiences.

Clarke thinks this expression, "I was in the Spirit," means that John "received the Spirit of prophecy, and was under its influence when the first vision was exhibited."[36] Wesley likewise regards John as "in a trance, a prophetic vision; so overwhelmed with the power, and filled with the light, of the Holy Spirit, as to be insensible of outward things, and wholly taken up with spiritual and divine."[37]

---

36. *Clarke's Commentary:* "The New Testament of Our Lord and Saviour Jesus Christ," II, Romans to Revelation, p. 972.
37. *Notes, op. cit.* (reprint), p. 938.

Harvey J. S. Blaney says that "John became overpowered by the Spirit of God, much like Ezekiel by the River Chebar in Babylon, and . . . saw and heard wonderful things . . . He 'fell' into the Spirit, or as we might say, he fell into a trance, as Peter had on the housetop in Joppa (Acts 10:10).[38]

All great accomplishments for God, as also notable secular accomplishments, may be said to have begun with visions which have given foresight and form, as well as inspiration for the accomplishment of the undertaking. Peter suggests this fact in his Pentecostal Day sermon when he quotes Joel's prophecy saying: "I will pour forth of My Spirit upon all mankind; and your sons and your daughters shall prophesy, and your young men shall see visions" (Acts 2:17a). Thus as the church was inaugurated at Pentecost with a Spirit-inspired vision, so John's great revelation is inaugurated by a God-sent, Spirit-inspired vision.

In the second instance, it is noteworthy that John's experience took place on "the Lord's day." This was of course a Sunday, the first day of the week, which was observed as the Christians' Sabbath, by reason of Christ's resurrection on that day. Wesley says of John's vision "on the Lord's day" that "On this [day] the ancients believed He will come to judgment. It was, therefore, with the utmost propriety that John both saw and described His Coming."[39]

B. The Spirit's Messages to the Seven Churches

"John to the seven churches that are in Asia [Asia Minor]: Grace to you and peace, from Him who is and who was and who is to come; and from the seven Spirits who are before His throne . . . " (Rev. 1:4).

We have here John's introductory greetings to the seven churches of western Asia Minor with which he was most intimately associated, though there were several other churches in this region. Evidently these seven churches are intended by John to represent the church universal. The number seven here, as also applied to the Spirit, and used in several other connections in Revelation, seems meant to represent completion or perfection.

Following the salutation of *grace* (God's special favor), and *peace* (the state of the believer's soul as a result of God's grace), John

---

38. Blaney, *The Wesleyan Bible Commentary*, VI, 424.
39. *Notes, op. cit.*, p. 939.

announces the origin of these benedictions. They come from the eternal God, the Jehovah of the Old Testament, the Father in the Trinity (Rev. 1:4); from Jesus Christ, the second member of the Trinity (Rev. 1:5a); and from the seven spirits which are before His throne (Rev. 1:4b), presumably representative of the third member of the Trinity. Thus on the basis of this interpretation John introduces his great Revelation with the triune God.

It will be noted, however, that among scholars there is a difference of opinion concerning the identification of the "seven Spirits." Clarke prefers to regard them as angelic messengers of God. On the other hand, Wesley, with apparent better reasons, considers them to be a sevenfold manifestation of the Holy Spirit. He argues:

> By these *seven spirits,* not seven created angels, but the Holy Spirit is to be understood. The angels are never termed *spirits* in this book ... *the seven spirits* neither stand up nor worship [as do the angels, Rev. 7:11]. To these "seven spirits of God," the seven churches, to whom the Spirit speaks so many things, are subordinate; as are also their angels. ... He [the Holy Spirit] is called *the seven spirits,* not with regard to His essence, which is one, but with regard to His manifold operations.[40]

The seven churches to which the Spirit bears His messages are located in Ephesus, Smyrna, Pergamum, Thyatira, Sardis, Philadelphia, and Laodicea. A message especially fitted to the needs of each of these churches is delivered by the Spirit (Rev. 2-4). Severe as are some of these messages, each of them concludes with a message of hope. The sevenfold refrain of the apostle reads: "He who has an ear, let him hear what the Spirit says to the churches" (Rev. 2:7, 11, 17, 29; 3:6, 13, 22). The message of hope is delivered by the Spirit to each of the seven churches. It is a promise especially suited to each of the *overcomers.* Whatever the condition or need may be, there is always *hope* through the ministry of the Spirit for the *overcomer.*

C. The Spirit and the Righteous Dead (Rev. 14:13)

The announcement of the voice from heaven saying, "Blessed are the dead who die in the Lord from now on!" is confirmed by the Spirit, who defines their blessedness as "that they may rest from their labors, for their deeds follow with them."

---

40. *Ibid.,* p. 964. Wesley's position seems to have support from Rev. 4:5.

Wesley's comment on this passage is interesting and helpful when he says:

> (1) because they escape the approaching calamities; (2) because they already enjoy so near an approach to glory. *Who die in the Lord*—In the faith of the Lord Jesus. *For they rest*—No pain, no purgatory follows; but pure, unmixed happiness. *From their labours*—And the more laborious their life was, the sweeter is their rest. How different this state from that of those (verse 11) who "have no rest day or night"! Reader, which wilt thou choose? *Their works*—Each one's peculiar works. *Follow*—Or accompany them; that is, the fruit of their works. Their works do not go before to procure them admittance into the mansions of joy; but they follow them when admitted.[41]

D. John's Transport in the Spirit

In two different passages John asserts that he was transported "*in* the Spirit" (Rev. 17:3; 21:10). In the first instance John was transported "*in* the *Spirit* into a wilderness" where he beheld the corruption and wickedness of the secular realm, however this may be interpreted or to whomsoever it may be applied, the city in the wilderness which stands in opposition to all that is righteous. In the second instance John was transported "*in* the Spirit to a great and high mountain" where he was privileged to see the sacred city with all of its goodness and glory, in contrast with the degradations of the secular city which he beheld in the wilderness.

It is the function of the Spirit to illumine and inform the servants of God on the wickedness of the secular world, as well as the righteousness of the sacred realm. Man presently lives in relation to two worlds—the secular and the sacred—the city of Satan and the city of God. The one is from below, the other from above. The Spirit illumines both to the mind of the believer that the glory of the one may appear in bold relief against the dark and desolate background of the other.

E. The Spirit's Invitation: "And the Spirit and the bride [the Church of Christ] say 'Come' " (Rev. 22:17)

As the Bible opens with the *creative work of the Spirit,* so it closes with the *call of the Spirit.* In Genesis 1:2 the Spirit broods over the

---

41. *Ibid.,* p. 1015.

336 THE PERSON AND MINISTRY OF THE HOLY SPIRIT

face of the great deep, bringing order out of chaos. In these closing words of John's Revelation, He broods over the chaos of human alienation and depravity to bring about the restoration and salvation of all men to the God of mercy and order who waits for man's return in response to the Spirit's last call.

As the Spirit of God first appears in the Bible in universal creation, so He last appears in a universal call to lost men to salvation in Jesus Christ. He first appears in the Bible in universal diffusion in creation. He last appears in universal diffusion in His call to salvation, "And the Spirit and the bride ["the church"] say, COME!"

Bibliography

Allen, Ronald. *Pentecost and the World:* "The Revelation of the Holy Spirit in the Acts of the Apostles." London: Oxford University Press, 1917.

Arndt, William F. and F. W. Gingirch. *A Greek-English Lexicon of the New Testament.* Chicago: University of Chicago Press, 1957.

Asbury, Francis. *The Journal of the Rev. Francis Asbury.* 3 vols. New York: Bangs and Mason, 1821.

Baer, F. W. *The First Epistle of Peter* (rev. ed.). Oxford: Basil, Blackwell, and Mott, 1958.

Ballenger, A. F. *Power for Witnessing.* Minneapolis, Minn.: Bethany Fellowship, Inc., 1963.

Barclay, William. *The Promise of the Spirit.* London: Epworth Press, 1960.

Barnes, Albert. *Notes on the New Testament James, Peter, John, Jude.* Grand Rapids: Baker Book House, 1962 (reprint).

Barnes, Charles Randall (ed.). *The People's Bible Encyclopedia.* Chicago: People's Publication Society, 1913.

Barrett, C. K. *The Holy Spirit and the Gospel Tradition.* New York: Macmillan Company, 1947.

Barth, Karl. *The Holy Ghost and the Christian Life.* London: 1938.

Berkhof, H. *The Doctrine of the Holy Spirit.* Richmond, Va.: Knox Press, 1964.

Blackwelder, Boyce W. "The Glossolalia at Pentecost," *Vital Christianity.* Anderson, Ind.: Warner Press, Mar. 10, 1963.

Blaikie, William G. *A Manual of Bible History.* New York: Ronald Press Company, 1940.

Blauw, Johannes. *The Missionary Nature of the Church,* New York: McGraw-Hill Book Company, Inc., 1962.

Boer, Harry R. *Pentecost and Missions.* Grand Rapids: Wm. B. Eerdmans Publishing Company, 1961.

Boettner, Loraine. *The Inspiration of the Scriptures.* Grand Rapids: Wm. B. Eerdmans Publishing Company, 1937.

Brengle, Colonel S. L. *When the Holy Spirit is Come.* New York: Salvation Army Printing and Publishing Company, 1914.

Brown, Charles C. *The Meaning of Sanctification.* Anderson, Ind.: Warner Press, 1945.

Brownville, C. C. *Symbols of the Holy Spirit.* New York: Fleming H. Revell, 1940.

Bruce, F. F. *The Acts of the Apostles. Greek Text with Introduction and Commentary* (2nd ed.). London: Tyndale Press, 1952.

_____. *Commentary on the Book of Acts: English Text with Introduction, Exposition and Notes.* Grand Rapids: Wm. B. Eerdmans Publishing Company, 1954.

_____. *The Epistle to the Hebrews.* New York: Fleming H. Revell, 1961.

_____. *The Letters of Paul: An Expanded Paraphrase.* Grand Rapids: Wm. B. Eerdmans Publishing Company, 1970.

Bruner, Frederick. *A Theology of the Holy Spirit: The Pentecostal Experience and the New Testament Witness.* Grand Rapids: Wm. B. Eerdmans Publishing Company, 1970.

Buchanan, James. *The Office and Work of the Holy Spirit.* London: Banner of Truth Trust, 1843.

Butner, Robert W. and Robert E. Chiles. *A Compendium of Wesley's Theology.* Nashville: Abingdon Press, 1954.

Buttrick, George Arthur (ed.). *The Interpreter's Bible.* 12 vols. Nashville: Abingdon Press, 1954.

Cadbury, Henry J. *The Book of Acts in History.* London: Adam and Charles Black, 1955.

Cannon, Wm. R. *The Theology of John Wesley.* Nashville: Abingdon Press, 1946.

Carroll, B. H. *The Holy Spirit.* Grand Rapids: Zondervan Publishing House, 1939.

Carter, Charles W. *The Bible Gift of Tongues.* Syracuse, N.Y.: Wesleyan Methodist Publishing Company, 1954.

––––––. *Road to Revival.* Butler, Ind.: Higley Press, 1959.

––––––. (Gen. ed.) *The Wesleyan Bible Commentary.* 7 vols. Grand Rapids: Wm. B. Eerdmans Publishing Company, 1964-1969.

––––––. (Gen. ed.) *Wesleyan Theological Journal.* 7 vols., 1966-1972. Published by Wesleyan Theological Society.

––––––. "A Wesleyan View of the Spirit's Gift of Tongues in the Book of Acts." *The Wesleyan Theological Journal* (Spring 1969), Published by the Wesleyan Theological Society, pp. 39–68.

––––––, and Ralph Earle. *The Acts of the Apostles* (rev. ed.), Grand Rapids: Zondervan Publishing House, 1973.

––––––, and Ralph Earle. *The Acts of the Apostles* (rev. ed.). Grand Rapids: Zondervan Publishing House, 1959.

Cattell, Everett Lewis. *The Spirit of Holiness.* Grand Rapids: Wm. B. Eerdmans Publishing Company, 1963.

Cell, G. C. *The Rediscovery of John Wesley.* New York: Henry Holt & Company, 1935.

Chadwick, Samuel. *The Way to Pentecost.* Berne, Ind.: Light and Hope Publications, 1937 (reprint).

Chapman, J. B. *The Terminology of Holiness.* Kansas City, Mo.: Beacon Hill Press, 1947.

Chapman, J. Wilbur. *Receive Ye the Holy Spirit.* New York: Fleming H. Revell, 1894.

Clarke, Adam. *Adam Clarke's Commentary:* "One-Volume Edition." Abridged from the original six-volume work by Ralph Earle. Grand Rapids: Baker Book House, 1967.

––––––. *Clarke's Commentary.* 6 vols. Nashville: Abingdon Press, n.d.

––––––. *Entire Sanctification: The Twelfth Chapter of Clarke's Christian Theology.* Louisville, Kentucky: Pentecostal Publishing Co., n.d.

––––––. *Memoirs of the Wesley Family, Collected from Original Documents.* 2 vols. London: J. Haddon, 1834.

Coke, Thomas, and Henry Moore. *Life of the Rev. John Wesley, Including an Account of the Great Revival of Religion in Europe and America of Which He Was the First and Chief Instrument.* London: G. Paramore, 1972.

Coleman, Robert E. *The Spirit and the Word.* Wilmore, Ky.: Asbury Theological Seminary, 1965.

Collier, F. W. *John Wesley Among the Scientists*. New York: Abingdon Press, 1928.

Conn, Charles W. *Like a Mighty Army, Moves the Church of God. 1866-1955*. Cleveland, Tenn.: Church of God Publishing House, 1955.

Conner, Walter Thomas. *The Work of the Holy Spirit*. Nashville: Broadman Press, 1949.

Conybeare, W., and J. S. Howson. *The Life and Epistles of St. Paul*. Hartford, Conn.: S. S. Scranton and Company, 1899.

Cook, Thomas. *New Testament Holiness*. London: The Epworth Press. U. S. Distributors, Christian Literature Crusade, Fort Washington, Pa., n.d.

Corlett, D. Shelby. *The Baptism with the Holy Spirit*. Kansas City, Mo.: Nazarene Publishing House, n.d.

Cox, Leo G. *John Wesley's Concept of Perfection*. Kansas City, Mo.: Beacon Hill Press, 1964.

Cumming, J. Elder. *Through the Eternal Spirit*. London: S. W. Partridge & Company, n.d.

Davidson, W. T. *The Indwelling Spirit*. New York and London: Hodder and Stoughton, 1911.

Dillistone, F. W. *Holy Spirit in the Life Today*. Philadelphia: Westminster Press, 1947.

Dollar, Geo. W. "Church History and the Tongues Movement," *Bibliotheca Sacra*. Dallas: Pub. Dallas Theo. Seminary, Oct.-Dec., 1963, p. 316ff.

Douglas, J. D. (ed.) *The New Bible Dictionary*. Grand Rapids: Wm. B. Eerdmans Publishing Company, 1962.

Downer, A. C. *The Mission and Ministration of the Holy Spirit*. Edinburgh, 1909.

Dummelow, J. R. (ed.) *A Commentary on the Holy Bible*. New York: Macmillan Company, 1936 (reprint, 1951).

Dunn, James D. G. *The Baptism in the Holy Spirit*. Naperville, Ill.: Alec R. Allenson, Inc., Copyright S.C.M. Press Ltd., 1970.

Earle, Ralph. *The Gospel According to Mark*. Grand Rapids: Zondervan Publishing House, 1957.

Edersheim, Alfred. *The Life and Times of Jesus the Messiah*. New York: Longmans, Green, and Company, 1904.

Erdman, C. R. *Spirit of Christ*. New York: George H. Doran Company, 1926.

Fieck, Lerome L. "The Doctrine of the Holy Spirit in Contemporary

Thought." *Bulletin of the Evangelical Theological Society,* Vol. 3, No. 3, Summer 1960.

Finegan, Jack. *Handbook of Biblical Chronology.* Princeton, N. J.: Princeton University Press, 1964.

Finlayson, R. A. "Trinity," *The New Bible Dictionary.* J. D. Douglas (ed.). Grand Rapids: Wm. B. Eerdmans Publishing Company, 1962.

Fisher, George Park. *History of the Christian Church.* New York: Charles Scribner's Sons, 1951 (reprint).

Fletcher, John. *The Works of the Reverend John Fletcher,* 4 vols. New York: Lane and Scott, 1851.

Flew, R. Newton. *The Idea of Perfection in Christian Theology.* London: Oxford University Press, 1934.

Forell, George W. *The Protestant Faith.* Englewood Cliffs, N. J.: Prentice-Hall, Inc., 1960.

Forrell, Frank. Art. "Outburst of Tongues: The New Penetration." *Christianity Today.* Washington, D.C. Sept. 13, 1963.

Freeman, D. "Feast of Pentecost." *The New Bible Dictionary.* Grand Rapids: Wm. B. Eerdmans Publishing Company, 1962.

Gabelein, A. C. *The Holy Spirit in the New Testament.* New York: Our Hope, n.d.

Gamertsfelder, S. J. *Systematic Theology.* Harrisburg, Pa.: Evangelical Publishing House, 1952 (reprint).

Geiger, Kenneth, et al. *The Word and the Doctrine:* "Studies i. Contemporary Wesleyan-Arminian Theology." Kansas City, Mo.: Beacon Hill Press, 1965.

Girdlestone, Robert Baker. *Synonyms of the Old Testament:* "Their Bearing on Christian Doctrine." Grand Rapids: Wm. B. Eerdmans Publishing Company, 2nd ed., 1897, (reprint) n.d.

Godbey, W. B. *Commentary on the New Testament.* 7 vols. Cincinnati: M. W. Knapp, 1896.

Godet, F. *Commentary on the Gospel of Luke.* Grand Rapids: Zondervan Publishing House, (reprint) n.d.

Gordon, A. J. *The Ministry of the Spirit.* Philadelphia: Judson Press, 1950 (reprint).

Greathouse, William. "Who Is The Holy Spirit?" *Herald of Holiness.* Kansas City, Mo.: Nazarene Publishing House, May 10, 1972, pp. 8-12.

Green, James B. *Studies in the Holy Spirit.* New York: Fleming H. Revell Company, 1936.

Green, Richard. *The Works of John and Charles Wesley*. A Bibliography: Containing an exact account of all the publications issued by the brothers Wesley arranged in chronological order, with a list of the early editions, and descriptive and illustrative notes. London: C. H. Kelly, 1896.

Harnack, Adolph von. *The Mission and Expansion of Christianity in the First Three Centuries*. 3 vols. New York: G. P. Putnam's Sons, 1908.

Harrison, A. W. *John Wesley, the Last Phase*. London: Epworth Press, 1934.

Harrison, Everett F. (ed.) *Baker's Dictionary of Theology*. Grand Rapids: Baker Book House, 1960.

_____. *Introduction to the New Testament*. Grand Rapids: Wm. B. Eerdmans Publishing Co., 1964.

Hendry, G. S. *The Holy Spirit in Christian Theology*. London, 1957.

Henry, Carl F. H. (ed.) *Revelation and the Bible: Contemporary Evangelical Thought*. Grand Rapids: Baker Book House, 1958.

Henry, Matthew, and Thomas Scott. *Commentary on the Holy Bible. Matthew—Acts*. Grand Rapids: Baker Book House, 1960 (reprint).

Henry, Matthew. *Commentary on the Whole Bible*. New York: Fleming H. Revell Company, n.d.

Hills, A. M. *Holiness in the Book of Romans* (Formerly, *The Establishing Grace*). Kansas City, Mo.: Beacon Hill Press, 1937.

Hodge, Charles. *Systematic Theology*. 3 vols. New York: Scribner, Armstrong and Co., 1877.

Huffman, Jasper Abraham. *A Comprehensive System of Christian Doctrine*. Butler, Ind.: Higley Press, 1959.

_____. *Golden Treasures from the Greek New Testament*. 2nd ed. Marion, Ind.: Wesley Press, 1951.

_____. *The Meaning of Pentecost and the Spirit Filled Life*. Winona Lake, Ind.: Standard Press, n.d.

_____. *The Unique Person of Christ*. Winona Lake, Ind.: Standard Press, 1955.

Hull, J. H. E. *The Holy Spirit in the Acts of the Apostles*. London, 1967.

Hume, Robert Ernest. *The World's Living Religions*. New York: Charles Scribner's Sons, 1924.

Hurst, John Fletcher. *Short History of the Christian Church*. New York: Harper and Brothers Publishers, 1892.

Jackson, F. J. Foakes. *The Acts of the Apostles: The Moffatt New Testament Commentary*. London: Hodder and Stoughton, 1931.

Jackson, F. J. Foakes, and Kirsopp Lake (eds). *The Beginnings of Christianity*, Part I. London: Macmillan Company, 1945 (reprint).

_____. *"The Development of Thought on the Spirit, the Church and Baptism"*. BC 1 (1920) pp. 321-44.

Jackson, Thomas (ed.). *The Works of John Wesley*. 14 vols. Grand Rapids: Zondervan Publishing House, 1959.

Jacob, Edward. *Theology of the Old Testament*. London: Hodder and Stoughton, 1958.

James, William. *The Varieties of Religious Experience*. New York: Longmans, Green & Company, 1902.

Jessop, Harry E. *Entire Sanctification:* "What Is It; For Whom Is It; And How To Receive It." Fort Wayne, Ind.: The Old Time Religion Tabernacle, n.d.

Jones, E. Stanley. "The Holy Spirit and the Gift of Tongues." *The Nazarene Preacher*. Kansas City, Mo.: Nazarene Publishing House, November, 1963, pp. 6-9.

Keen, S. A. *Pentecostal Papers or the Gift of the Holy Ghost*. Cincinnati: M. W. Knapp, 1896.

_____. *Pentecostal Sanctification*. Apollo, Pa.: West Publishing Company, (reprint) n.d.

Kennedy, A. R. S. "The Book of Samuel," *The New Century Bible*. London: Coxton, n.d.

Kenyon, John B. *The Bible Revelation of the Holy Spirit*. Grand Rapids: Zondervan Publishing House, 1939.

Kildahl, John P. *The Psychology of Speaking in Tongues*. New York: Harper and Row, 1972.

Kinlaw, Dennis F., William C. Cessna, Gilbert M. James. *The Sanctified Life*. Wilmore, Ky.: Asbury Seminary Press, 1968.

Kittle, Gerhard, et al. *Theological Dictionary of the New Testament*. Trans. Geoffrey W. Bromiley. 8 vols. Grand Rapids: Wm. B. Eerdmans Publishing Company, 1964-1972.

Kluepfer, P. *The Holy Spirit in the Life and Teachings of Jesus and the Early Christian Church*. Columbus, Ohio: Lutheran Book Concern, 1929.

Kuyper, Abraham. *The Work of the Holy Spirit*. New York: Funk & Wagnalls Co., 1900, Grand Rapids: Wm. B. Eerdmans Publishing Company, 1964.

Lake, Kirsopp. "Note 9. The Holy Spirit," BC, 5 (1933), pp. 96-111.

Lange, John Peter (ed.). *Commentary on the Holy Scriptures*. New York: Charles Scribner's Sons, 1866.

La Rue, Wm. Earle. *The Foundations of Mormonism.* New York: Fleming H. Revell Company, 1919.

Law, William. *A Serious Call to a Devout and Holy Life.* New York: E. P. Dutton & Company, 1955.

_____. *Power of the Spirit.* 2nd ed. London: James Nisbet & Company, 1896.

MacGregor, Geddes. *Readings in Religious Philosophy.* Boston: Houghton Mifflin Company, 1962.

Mahan, Asa. *The Baptism of the Holy Ghost.* Noblesville, Ind.: J. Edwin Newby Book Room, 1966 (reprint).

Marsh, F. E. *Emblems of the Holy Spirit.* New York: Alliance Press Company, 1911.

Marston, Leslie R. "The Crisis Process Issue in Wesleyan Thought," *Wesleyan Theological Journal.* Published by Wesleyan Theological Society, 1969.

Martin, Paul. *The Holy Spirit Today.* Kansas City, Mo.: Beacon Hill Press, 1970.

Mattheson, George. *Voices of the Spirit.* London: James Nisbet & Company, 1888.

Matthews, John. *Speaking in Tongues.* John Matthews, Publisher, 1925.

Mattke, Robert A. "The Baptism of the Holy Spirit as Related to the Work of Entire Sanctification." *Wesleyan Theological Journal,* Spring 1970, pp. 22-32.

McCone, R. Clyde. In "Other Tongues: What Meaneth This?" Department of Anthropology, California State College, Long Beach Calif.: An unpublished manuscript.

McConnell, F. J. *John Wesley.* New York and Nashville: Abingdon-Cokesbury Press, 1939.

Mink, Nelson Geo. "Estatic Utterances." *The Preacher's Magazine.* Kansas City, Mo.: Nazarene Publishing House, July, 1963, pp. 9-13.

Moffatt, James. *An Introduction to the Literature of the New Testament.* New York: Charles Scribner's Sons, 1911.

Moore, Henry. *The Life of the Rev. John Wesley,* A.M., in which are included the Life of the Reverend Charles Wesley and Memories of this family. 2 vols. New York: N. Bangs and J. Emory. 1826.

Moorehead, William G. *Outline Studies in the New Testament. Catholic Epistles and Revelation.* New York: Fleming H. Revell Company, 1910.

Morgan, G. Campbell. *Spirit of God.* London: Hodder and Stoughton, 1900.

Morris, Leon. *The First Epistle of Paul to the Corinthians.* Grand Rapids: Wm. B. Eerdmans Publishing Company, 1958.

———. *Spirit of the Living God.* London: Inter-Varsity Fellowship, 1960.

Mould, Elmer W. K. *Essentials of Bible History.* New York: Ronald Press Company, 1957.

Moule, H. C. G. "Ephesian Studies." *Cambridge Bible.* Cambridge: Cambridge University Press, 1907.

———. "The Epistle of Paul the Apostle to the Romans," *Cambridge Bible.* Cambridge: Cambridge University Press, 1891.

———. *Veni Creator.* (London, 1890).

Murray, Andrew. *Back to Pentecost.* London: Oliphants, n.d.

———. "The One Thing Needful," *The Full Blessing of Pentecost.* London: Oliphants, 1944 (rev. ed.).

———. *Spirit of Christ.* London: James Nisbet & Company, 1888.

Nicholson, Roy S. *The Arminian Emphasis.* A Series of eight Lectures given at Owosso College, Owosso, Michigan. No date or Publisher Listed.

———. Art. "The Holiness Emphasis in the Wesleys' Hymns." *The Wesleyan Theological Journal* (Spring 1970), Published by Wesleyan Theological Society.

Nichol, John T. "*The Role of the Pentecostal Movement in American Church History. Gordon Review.* Boston: Published by the Gordon Faculties, December, 1956, pp. 127-135.

Nottingham, Elizabeth K. *Methodism and the Frontier: Indiana Proving Grounds.* New York: Columbia University Press, 1941.

Onerton, John H. *The Evangelical Revival in the Eighteenth Century.* Epochs of Church History. London: Longmans, Green, & Company, 1900.

———. *John Wesley.* London: Methuen & Company, 1891.

Owen, J. *The Holy Spirit.* (Grand Rapids, 1954).

Pache, René. *The Person and Work of the Holy Spirit.* Chicago: Moody Press, 1954.

Palmer, Edwin H. *The Holy Spirit.* (rev. ed.). Philadelphia: Presbyterian and Reformed Publishing Company, 1971, Copyright Baker Book House, 1950.

Peter, John Leland. *Christian Perfection and American Methodism.* New York: Abingdon Press, 1956.

Philip, Robert. *The Life and Times of the Reverend George Whitfield.* New York: D. Appleton & Company, 1838.

Phillips, J. B. *The New Testament in Modern English.* New York: Macmillan Company, 1958.

Piette, Maximin. *John Wesley in the Evolution of Protestantism.* New York: Sheed & Ward, 1937.

Plumptre, E. H. "The Gospel According to Luke," *Commentary on the Whole Bible,* ed. by C. J. Ellicott. Grand Rapids: Zondervan Publishing House, (reprint) n.d.

Purkiser, W. T. (ed.). *Exploring the Old Testament.* Kansas City, Mo.: Beacon Hill Press, 1964.

Rall, Harris Franklin. *New Testament History: A Study of the Beginning of Christianity.* New York and Nashville: Abingdon-Cokesbury Press, 1914.

Ramsay, W. M. *The Church in the Roman Empire Before A.D. 70.* Grand Rapids: Baker Book House, 1954 (reprint).

Rattenburg, J. Ernest. *The Conversion of the Wesleys, A Critical Study.* London: Epworth Press, 1938.

Reece, T., *The Holy Spirit.* (London, 1914).

Ridout, Samuel. *Person and Work of the Holy Spirit.* New York: Loizeaux Brothers, n.d.

Robertson, A. T. "Languages of the New Testament," *The International Standard Bible Encyclopedia.* Grand Rapids: Wm. B. Eerdmans Publishing Company, 1957 (reprint).

_____. *Word Pictures in the New Testament.* New York: Harper & Brothers, 1931.

Robinson, Benjamin Willard. *The Life of Paul.* Chicago: University of Chicago Press, 1928.

Robinson, H. W. *The Christian Experience of the Holy Spirit.* London, 1928.

Robinson, Wayne A. *I Once Spoke in Tongues.* Wheaton, Illinois: Tyndale House, 1973.

Rose, Delbert R., *A Theology of Christian Experience.* Minneapolis: Bethany Fellowship, Inc., 1965.

Samarin, William J. *Tongues of Men and Angels.* New York: Macmillan Company, 1972.

Sanders, J. Oswald. *The Holy Spirit and His Gifts.* Grand Rapids: Zondervan Publishing House, 1970 (rev. ed.).

Sangster, W. E. *The Path of Perfection.* Nashville: Abingdon-Cokesbury Press, 1943.

Schaff, Philip. *The Creeds of Christiandom.* New York: Harper & Brothers, 1879.

Schweizer, E. *Spirit of God.* (London, 1960).

Simon, John S. *John Wesley and the Methodist Societies.* London: Epworth Press, 1923.

Simpson, A. B. *Emblems of the Holy Spirit.* Nyack, N.Y.: Christian Alliance Publishing Company, 1901.

_____. *The Holy Spirit, or Power From On High.* 2 vols. Harrisburg, Pa.: Christian Publications, Inc., n.d.

Smith, Joseph H. *Things of the Spirit.* Chicago: Chicago Evangelistic Institute, 1940.

Smith, Timothy L. *Called Unto Holiness.* Kansas City: Nazarene Publishing House, 1962.

_____. *Revivalism and Social Reform.* Nashville: Abingdon Press, 1957.

Soltau, George. *Person and Mission of the Holy Spirit.* Philadelphia: Philadelphia School of the Bible, n.d.

Souter, Alexander. *A Pocket Lexicon to the Greek New Testament.* Oxford: Clarendon Press, 1966 (reprint).

Southey, Robert. *The Life of John Wesley; and the Rise and Progress of Methodism.* 3rd ed. London: Longman, Brown, Green, 1846.

Steele, Daniel. *A Defense of Christian Perfection.* New York: Hunt and Eaton, 1896.

_____. *Half-hours With St. John's Epistles.* Chicago: Christian Witness Company, 1901.

_____. *Love Enthroned, Essays on Evangelical Perfection.* New York: Nelson and Phillips, 1877.

Stolee, Haakon J. *Speaking in Tongues.* Rev. Ed. Minneapolis: Augsburg Publishing House, 1963.

Strachan, R. H. *The Fourth Gospel.* 3rd ed. London: SCM Press, Ltd., 1960 (reprint).

Sugden, E. A. (ed.). *Wesley's Standard Sermons.* 2 vols. Nashville: Lamar and Barton, 1920.

Swete, Henry Barclay. *The Holy Spirit in the New Testament: A Study of Primitive Christian Teaching.* London: Macmillan Company, 1910.

Synan, Vinson. *The Holiness Pentecostal Movement in the United States.* Grand Rapids: Wm. B. Eerdmans Publishing Company, 1971.

Taylor, Jeremy. *Works.* Reginal Heber (ed.). 3rd ed. 15 vols. London: Longman, 1839.

Telford, John (ed.). *The Letters of the Rev. John Wesley.* 8 vols. London: Epworth Press, 1931.

_____. *The Life of John Wesley.* 8 vols. London: Epworth Press, 1931.

Thayer, Joseph Henry. *Greek-English Lexicon of the New Testament.*

New York: American Book Company, Harper & Brothers, 1886.

Thomas, W. H. Griffith. *The Holy Spirit of God.* Chicago: Chicago Bible Institute Colportage Association, 1913.

Torrey, R. A. *Baptism of the Holy Spirit.* New York: Revell, 1897.

Tozer, A. W. *How to Be Filled With the Holy Spirit.* Harrisburg, Pa.: Christian Publications Inc., n.d.

Turner, George Allen. *The More Excellent Ways. The Scriptural Basis of the Wesleyan Message.* Winona Lake, Ind.: Light and Life Press, 1951.

Tyerman, Luke. *The Life and Times of the Reverend John Wesley, M. A.* 3 vols., New York: Harper & Bros., 1872.

_____. *The Life of John Wesley.* 8 vols. London: Epworth Press, 1931.

Van Dusen, Henry P. *Spirit, Son and Father: Christian Faith in the Light of the Holy Spirit.* New York: Scribner's, 1958.

Vaughan, C. R. *The Gifts of the Spirit.* Richmond, Va.: Presbyterian Committee of Publication, 1894.

Vincent, Marvin R. *Word Studies in the New Testament.* 4 vols., Grand Rapids: Wm. E. Eerdmans Publishing Company, 1957 (reprint).

Vos, Geerhardus. *Biblical Theology Old and New Testaments.* Grand Rapids: Wm. B. Eerdmans Publishing Company, 1948.

Walker, James B. *God's Wisdom in the Plan of Salvation,* ed. by Charles W. Carter (Formerly, *Philosophy of the Plan of Salvation*). Butler, Ind.: Higley Press, 1958.

Walvoord, John F. *The Holy Spirit: A Comprehensive Study of the Person and Work of the Holy Spirit.* Wheaton, Ill.: Van Kampen Press, 1954.

Watkin-Jones, Howard. *The Holy Spirit from Arminius to Wesley.* London: Epworth Press, 1928.

Watson, G. D. *Types of the Holy Spirit.* Cincinnati, Ohio: Revivalist Office, n.d.

Watson, Richard. *Life of Reverend John Wesley.* New York: Carlton & Porter, 1831.

_____. *Works.* 2nd ed., 12 vols., London: John Mason, 1834.

Wesley, Charles. *Journal.* London: R. Culley, 1910.

_____. *Sermons.* London: Baldwin, Cradock & Joy, 1816.

Wesley, John. *A Compendium of Natural Philosophy.* II, 447-49.

_____. *Explanatory Notes Upon the New Testament. London: Epworth Press,* 1954 (rep.).

_____. *Explanatory Notes Upon the Old Testament.* 3 vols. Bristol:

Printed by William Pine in Wine—Street, 1765. Note: These volumes are little known and extremely rare with only three known sets or parts of sets in the U.S.A., one full set of which is in Asbury Theological Seminary at Wilmore, Ky.

———. *The Journal of John Wesley.* Chicago: Mooay Press, n.d.

———. *A Plain Account of Christian Perfection.* Louisville, Ky.: Pentecostal Publishing Company, n.d.

———. *Wesley's Sermons: "Five Select Sermons."* 2nd ed. Kansas City, Mo.: Beacon Hill Press, n.d.

Westcott, Brooke Foss. *The Epistle to the Hebrews.* 3rd ed. London: Macmillan Company, 1906.

———. *The Epistles of St. John.* Cambridge & London: Macmillan Company, 1886.

Whedon, D. D. "The Epistle to the Hebrews," *Commentary on the New Testament.* New York: Phillip and Hunt, 1880.

Whitehead, John. *The Life of the Reverend John Wesley, M.A., With the Life of the Reverend Charles Wesley, M.A.* 2 vols., London: Stephen Conchman, 1793.

Wilcox, Leslie D. *Be Ye Holy: A Study of the Teachings of Scripture Relative to Entire Sanctification with a Sketch of the History and the Literature of the Holiness Movement.* Cincinnati: The Revivalist Press, 1965.

Wiley, H. Orton. *Christian Theology.* 3 vols. Kansas City, Mo.: Beacon Hill Press, 1941.

Williams, Charles B. *The New Testament: A Private Translation in the Language of the People.* Chicago: Moody Press, 1950.

Windsch, Hans. *The Spirit-Paraclete in the Fourth Gospel.* Trans. James W. Cox, "Facet Books," Biblical Series, 20, Philadelphia: Fortress Press, 1968.

Winslow, O. *The Work of the Holy Spirit.* London, 1843 (reprint 1961).

Wood, J. A. *Auto-Biography of Rev. J. A. Wood.* Chicago: The Christian Witness Company, 1904.

———. *Perfect Love; or . . . Christian Holiness,* rev. ed. Chicago: The Christian Witness Company, 1910.

Wood, Skevington. *The Burning Heart: John Wesley, Evangelist.* Grand Rapids: Wm. B. Eerdmans Publishing Company, 1967.

———. *The Inextinguishable Blaze.* Grand Rapids: Wm. B. Eerdmans Publishing Company, 1968.

Wynkoop, Mildred Bangs. *Foundations of Wesleyan-Arminian Theology.* Kansas City, Mo.: Beacon Hill Press, 1967.

_____. *John Wesley: Christian Revolutionary.* Kansas City, Mo.: Beacon Hill Press, 1970.

_____. *The Religion of Love.* Kansas City, Mo.: Beacon Hill Press, 1972.

_____. "The Communion of the Holy Spirit" (An unpublished mimeographed essay).

Yates, J. E. *The Spirit and the Kingdom.* London, 1963.

Zimmerman, Thomas F. "Plea for the Pentecostals." *Christianity Today:* Washington, D.C., Jan. 4, 1963.

Index

American Methodism, 181-84
Annual feasts, 196-97
Anointing with oil, 65-66
Arndt, William F., 127 fn., 301, 302
Asbury, Francis, 181-82

Ball, Charles S., 314, 315-16, 318, 324
Baptism in the Spirit, 176-259
  neglected emphasis, 176-78
  misrepresentation of Wesleyan teaching, 181-84
  related to sanctification, 184-89
  reluctance to use term, 178-81
Baptism, Jesus', 100-03, 219, 300, 331
Baptism, water, 176-77, 227
Baptismal formula, 113-14
Barclay, William, 21, 43, 100, 104
  105-06, 107, 108, 109-10, 111-
  12, 115, 119-20, 125, 126, 130,
  131, 139, 141, 269, 285
Barth, Karl, 44
Believer's need for advocate, 128-29
Bengel, Johann A., 195-96, 314
Blackwelder, Boyce W., 200-01, 209-
  15, 217

Blaikie, William G., 196
Blaney, Harvey J. S., 193, 209, 333
Blasphemy against, 23, 110-12
Blauw, Johannes, 90, 93
Boer, Harry R., 90
Bonar, Horatius, 29-30
Bonhoeffer, Dietrich, 140
Bonner, Norman N., 123 fn.
Brightman, Edgar S., 164
Brown, Charles C., 178-79
Bruce, F. F., 177, 194-95, 254-55,
  256, 276, 304
Buber, Martin, 28-29
Burnet, Thomas, 27

Calvin, John, 276
Cane Ridge Revival, 183
Cannon, William Ragsdale, 27-28
Carter, Charles W., 123 fn.
Cartright, Peter, 182
Centrifugal method, 93
Centripetal method, 93
Chadwick, Samuel, 15, 165, 174-75, 316
Characteristics of O. T. prophetic
  ministry, 56-57

351

Christian Holiness Association, 182
Christ's ascension, 126-43
Christ's teaching, 21, 23-24, 25, 116-43, 219
Christ's temptation, 102-03
Church's conquest, 256-59
Church extension, 247-59
Church Growth Movement, 229
Clarke, Adam, 31, 33-34, 38, 48, 51-52, 53, 54-55, 57, 65, 67, 75, 81-82, 86-87, 101, 102, 104, 108, 110, 113, 114, 119, 124, 126, 127, 133, 135, 139, 155, 171, 195, 196, 203, 204, 208-09, 228, 233-34, 236, 293, 296, 297, 298, 308, 309, 311, 313-14, 318-19, 332
Communion of saints, 229-245
  in fellowship, 234-35
  in giving, 244-45
  in instruction, 232-34
  in prayer, 237-41
  in sacraments, 235-37
  in thanksgiving, 241-44
  in their faith, 229-32
Contemporary emphasis, 15-17
Cox, Leo G., 326
Creeds, 15-16, 26, 27
Crisis-Process issue, 186-87

Dayton, Donald W., 188-89 fn., 293
Demons, 108-12. *See also* Evil spirits; Familiar spirits
Diaspora, 197-99, 201
Divine attributes, 24-25
Divine control, 174-76
Drummond, Henry, 118, 292, 296-97, 298-99
Dummelow, J. B., 150-51, 171, 276
Dunning, H. Ray, 188 fn.

Eadie, John, 281, 282
Earle, Ralph, 101, 177, 200
Edwards, Jonathan, 183
Ethical qualities of O.T. prophetic ministry, 57-58
Etymology of *Spirit* and *Holy Spirit* in Bible, 17-18
Evil spirits of Satan contrasted with Holy Spirit in O.T., 48-49

Familiar spirits contrasted with Holy Spirit in O.T., 49-50

Finegan, Jack, 171, 256
Finney, Charles G., 183
Finlayson, R. A., 26, 32-33
Fletcher, John, 180, 184-85
Forell, George W., 29
Freely offered, 118-26
Freeman, D., 146-47
Freud, Sigmund, 122-23
Fruit of Spirit, 291-305
  distinguished from gifts, 291-92
  faithfulness, 297-98
  gentleness, 298-99
  goodness, 297
  joy, 295-96
  kindness, 296-97
  love, 292-93, 295, 316
  patience, 296
  peace, 296
  self-control, 299-300
  triads, 293-300

Gamertsfelder, S. J., 26-27
General Epistles, 307-32
Gifts of Spirit, 274-89
  activates natural abilities, 274-75
  administration of, 270-72
  artistry and craftsmanship, 50-52
  distinguished from fruit, 291-92
  apostles, 288, 481
  divine healing, 276-77, 288
  evangelists, 282
  government, 288
  impartially distributed, 274
  interpretation of tongues, 279-288
  issue from Spirit's personality, 279
  languages, 278-79, 288
  manner of bestowal, 272-73
  ministers, 280-81
  miracles, 288-89
  pastors and teachers, 282-83, 288
  prophecy/prophets, 277-78, 281, 288
  related to faith, 275-76
  spiritual discernment, 278
  superhuman physical powers, 52-55
  unification
    adds meaning to variety, 285
    complementary, 287-89
    constitutes Christ's body, 285-86
    develops mutual concern, 287
    variety essential to unity, 286-87
  variety of, 273-80
Gingrich, F. Wilbur, 127 fn., 301, 302

Girdlestone, Robert Baker, 17, 18, 32
Godet, Frederic L., 105
Great Awakening, 183
Great Commission, 164, 174, 202, 256
Greathouse, William M., 158-60
Grieving the Spirit, 266-67
Gnostics, 327-30, 331-32
Guarantee of Spirit, 300-05

Harnack, Adolph, 227, 251, 293
Hebrews, Book of, 307-14
Henry and Scott, 203-04
Henry, Matthew, 196, 207, 254
Huffman, Jasper A., 128, 138-39, 140, 142
Hymnody, 29-30, 242-44, 263. *See also* Wesley, Charles

Incarnation, 97-99. *See also* Work, in Christ's conception; O. T. references; O. T. prophets
O. T. references to, 66-67
Influence of Spirit-filled life, 124

John (apostle), 235, 237, 242, 248, 249, 250, 300. *See also* John's Gospel; John, Epistles of; Revelation, Book of
John, Epistle of, 324-31
John's Gospel, 115-43, 219, 268, 325
John the Baptist, 93-97, 100, 102, 168-69, 176-77, 219
Jude, Epistle of, 331-32

Kennedy, A. R. S., 66 fn.

Lactantius, 257
Law and O. T. Pentecost, 151-53
Leitzman, Hans, 227
Lordship of Christ, 112-13
Luther, Martin, 21, 142, 179

Mahan, Asa, 188 fn.
Martyr, Justin, 257
Mattke, Robert A., 177, 184, 187
McGonigle, Herbert, 179, 185
Meaning of *Spirit* and *Holy Spirit* in Bible, 17-18
Messiah, ministry of, 63-65, 103-14
Morgan, G. Campbell, 155
Morris, Leon, 21, 286
Mould, Elmer W. K., 198 fn., 208
Moule, Hadley C. G., 281, 283-84, 294

National Holiness Association, 182
Nevius Method, 229
New birth, 116-18
N. T. references, 18-25, 28, 63-336
Nicholson, Roy S., 30, 78-79
Nicodemus, 116-18, 122, 124, 132, 173, 263

Ockenga, Harold, 218
Other spirits in O. T., 47-50
O. T. prophets, 55-61. *See also* Incarnation
O. T. references, 18, 19-20, 28, 31-35, 37-87, 268. *See also* Incarnation

Palmer, Edwin C., 24
Paraklētos, 126-27, 160-61
Paul, 22-23, 113, 118, 122, 123, 132-33, 136, 142, 148, 151-52, 163, 165-66, 172, 176, 185-86, 193, 199, 204, 206-15, 218, 224, 225, 226, 227, 230-31, 234, 236, 238-39, 240-42, 250, 251-56, 312, 330, 332. *See also*, Pauline Epistles.
Pauline Epistles, 261-305. *See also* Paul
Pentecost, Day of, 20, 89, 97, 107, 120, 125-26, 134, 145-46, 154-56, 247-48, 312, 314, 316, 317, 319. *See also* Tongues speaking at Pentecost
linguistic composition of audience, 199-203
promise in O. T., 153-54
Pentecost in Wesleyan theology, 158-60
Personal characteristics, 22-24
Personification of truth, 131-33
Personality, 18-25
evidences of in Scripture, 22-25
Peter, 25, 171, 194, 205, 218, 222, 224-25, 226, 229, 232, 237, 239-40, 242-43, 247, 248, 249, 251, 262, 297, 312, 333. *See also* Peter, Epistles of
Peter, Epistles of, 314-24. *See also* Peter
Pledge of Spirit, 300-02
Power of Spirit
adequacy of, 165-66
availability of, 163
for demon explusion, 167

for enduring persecution, 166-67
for healing, 167-68
for sanctification, 166
for witnessing, 166
necessity of, 163-64
personality and, 164-65
practicality of, 166-68
priority of, 162-63
symbol of, 160-61
Prayer, 106, 107
Problems of Wesleyan view, 176-84
Promise fulfilled, 157-58

Rall, Harris, F., 192
Ramsey, William, 224
Religious awakening, 64-65
Revelation, Book of, 332-36
Robertson, Archibald, T., 272 fn., 276
Robinson, Benjamin W., 197-98, 200
Robinson, John A. T., 329
Rose, Delbert R., 182

Sabellianism, 29
Seal of Spirit, 300, 302-05
Seven churches, Messages to, 333-34
Smith, Joseph H., 182
Smith, Timothy, 188 fn.
Souter, Alexander, 18 fn., 127, 300-
    01, 327
Spinoza, 30
Spirit as gift, 267-70
Spirit of materialistic militarism in O.
    T., 46-48
Spirits of mighty men contrasted with
    Holy Spirit in O. T., 48-49
Strachan, R. H., 21
Synan, Vincent, 189 fn.
Synoptic Gospels, 21, 89-114

Taylor, Richard S., 116
Tertullian, 26, 257
Test of faith, 108
Thayer, J. H., 141, 160, 192, 193
Thompson, Francis, 70-71, 73
Tillotson, John, 27
Tongues of fire, 170-72
Tongues speaking, 181-84, 191-219
    at Caesarea, 203-04, 205, 239-40,
        251
    at Corinth, 205-15
    aspects of, 206-08
    perversions of, 207-09, 219
    problems of, 205-06, 216, 289

at Ephesus, 204-05, 241
on Pentecost, 191-203, 205, 215-19
    221-22
    meaning, 192-96
    necessity, 191-92, 196
    prediction of prophets, 202-03
    practicalized, 194-96
    rationale, 196-205
    reaction to, 221-22
    results of, 222-29
    testimony of Church Fathers,
        202-03
Trinity, 24, 25-35, 102, 113-14, 134-
35
    Doctrine in history, 25-31
    Doctrine of O. T., 31-35, 37

Van Baalen, Jan Karl, 178
Vincent, Marvin R., 195, 276, 281,
    282

Walker, James B., 162-63
Wesley, Charles, 30, 180, 242
Wesley, John, 8, 10, 20-21, 27-28, 32,
    33, 39, 40, 45-56, 77, 82, 85,
    96-97, 101, 102, 103, 105, 106,
    107, 117, 120, 123, 136-37,
    141, 143, 178, 179-81, 184,
    185-89, 195, 245, 264, 282,
    291-92, 293-94, 295, 297, 299,
    302, 311, 315, 316, 318, 321,
    325-26, 332, 334, 335
Wesleyan terminology, 187-89
Westcott, Brooke, F., 327
Whedon, D. D., 309
Wiley, H. Orton, 165
Wilson, Charles R., 66
Work of the Holy Spirit
    advanced gospel in Gentile world,
        251-56
    applies God's Word, 100, 321
    assures of salvation, 324-26
    bears witness, 135-38, 317-18, 331
    calls, 335-36
    comforts, 334-35
    convicts, 139-40, 223, 226
    creation, priority in, 38-41
    essential, 262-66
        for Christian living, 263-64
        for Christian service, 264-65
        for fruitbearing, 266
        for salvation, 262-63
        for worship, 265

executes redemptive plan, 42-44
gives victory, 248-51
illumines, 72-75, 223-26, 317, 335
in Christ's conception, 311, 330-31
in Christ's human nature, 311
in prophecy, 316-19, 332-36
in unconverted world, 138-43
inculcates prophetic relationship to
  God, 67-70
indwells believer, 332-33
inspired Scripture, 311-13, 319-24
inspires to human achievement,
  50-55
leads to repentance, 73, 223
motivates penitent petition, 75-80
  for effacement of sin, 75-76
  for mercy, 75
  for restoration of joy, 78-79
  for soul's preservation, 77-78
  to renew covenant, 79
  to serve God, 80
points way to God's presence, 310
predicted coming Messiah, 63-67
prepared work of redemption, 89-94
produced visions, 335
produces personal religious experiences, 70-80, 226-28
produces sense of responsibility
  toward God, 73
  promised future age, 80-87

internal, 83
  New Covenant, 83-87
  universal, 81-83
purifies, 122-23, 168-72
  symbol of, 169-170, 171-72
re-creates, 41-46
  man, 45-46
regenerates, 134, 173-74
restores, 172-173
  confidence, 80
  divine image, 44-45
reveals
  God's mind, 322-24
  man's depravity, 74
  redemptive plan, 41-42
sanctifies, 134, 186-87, 314-16
stimulates
  church growth, 247-48
  identification with other believers,
    228-29
warns
  against discounting Christ's atone-
    ment, 313-14
  against doubting God, 308-09
  against neglecting salvation, 307-
    08
  against spiritual deadness, 309-10
Wynkoop, Mildred, 178

Zahniser, Clarence, 301